Julia

Also by James Spada

Julia

HER LIFE

James Spada

St. Martin's Press ⚯ New York

www.stmartins.com

ISBN 0-312-28565-5

First Edition: February 2004

10 9 8 7 6 5 4 3 2 1

This book is dedicated,
with deep and abiding love,
to my partner, Terry Brown, who
literally helped save my life.

CONTENTS

Prologue

MARCH 25, 2001

"Thank you. . . . I'm so happy, thank you. . . . I love the world!"

—Julia Roberts, accepting her Academy Award
as Best Actress for *Erin Brockovich*

The weather cooperated on what would be the biggest day of Julia Roberts's professional life. It was cool for Los Angeles, with a high of just sixty-two degrees, and there was no rain in sight. That was very good news for a woman who wanted to look better than she ever had, just in case her name was called as Best Actress of 2000. If it was, she would accept the Oscar in front of 250 million viewers worldwide.

Her appearance—particularly her dress—was of paramount importance, the only thing over which she still had control. She had given the best performance of her career in *Erin Brockovich;* the film had won rave reviews upon its release a year earlier; and it had made over $125 million at the U.S. box office, her third such success in under a year.

Like a colossus, Julia Roberts by 2001 stood astride every other actress in Hollywood. Her films since she became a star had earned $1.5 *billion* in the United States alone (and about three times that much internationally). As a result she had become the highest paid actress in history, with a paycheck of $20 million for *Brockovich.*

As the big day approached, every designer in the world sought frantically to get the nominees and other celebrities attending the awards ceremony to choose one of their dresses. When Joan Rivers inquired, "And who are you wearing?" during the pre-Oscar show, it provided priceless publicity when the actresses replied, "Valentino" or "Dior" or "Vera Wang."

The designers desperately wanted to dress Julia Roberts, not only because she would be the biggest star there but because she was the odds-on favorite to win the prize, having won seven Best Actress awards in the previous few months, including the Golden Globe, the British Academy Film Award, and the Screen Actors Guild Award, strong harbingers of success at the Oscars. "Nothing's for sure this year," *The New York Times* said, "except maybe Julia Roberts winning best actress."

Speculation about which designer would be anointed by La Roberts ran rampant. London's *Sunday Express* ran a full-page article on The Day, headlined THE FIGHT TO WIN JULIA'S DRESS OSCAR. "At the moment," Gary Morgan wrote for the paper, "America's Calvin Klein and Italy's Giorgio Armani are leading the race. But which of them—or indeed any of their many rivals—gets the job remains as much of a mystery as who will win Best Picture."

Design houses such as Versace, Armani, Calvin Klein, and Prada, which hoped to send representatives to Julia's home along with jewelers and hairdressers to court her with the promise of a complete—and free—decking out, knew disappointment. Julia was on holiday in Mexico and didn't return to Los Angeles until the Friday before the ceremony. On Saturday she tried on "a bunch" of dresses (about two dozen), few of which rang her chimes.

"Finally," Julia told a reporter, "Sunday morning I had narrowed it down to a couple of dresses, one of which—the one that I wore—my girlfriend Debbie Mason, who's a stylist, had just said, 'Oh, darling, I thought you might like this frock,' and she brought it over."

Julia did indeed like the "frock," a vintage (1982) Valentino gown of black velvet with white satin trim forming shoulder straps that came together just below the bust and continued as one stripe down the front of the dress. But it was the gown's backside that truly impressed: seven strips of white satin that began at the shoulders and cinched at the waist; and ten stripes that flared out down the back of the dress into a train.

As far as jewelry was concerned, Carol Brodie, a coordinator for the jeweler Harry Winston, agreed that Julia's best bet was to keep things simple. "A lot of jewelry would detract from her beautiful bone structure. For less than a hundred and fifty thousand, Julia would look absolutely fantastic, with a classic old-style look which would be in keeping with her 'less is more' appeal."

That is precisely what Julia did—she wore only diamond-drop earrings and one diamond bracelet from Van Cleef & Arpels. Her shoes, black-strapped sandals by Sergio Rossi, with tiny diamanté details, couldn't really be seen because of the length of her dress, but they completed the elegant, simple look.

Julia was nervous about the outcome of the race, despite—or perhaps because of—the nearly unanimous predictions that called her a shoo-in. She had been nominated twice before and lost, for Best Supporting Actress in *Steel Magnolias* in 1990 and for Best Actress in *Pretty Woman* in 1991. Oscar history is replete with stunning upsets, and Julia later said she was certain that Ellen Burstyn would win. The only vote she could be sure of was her own. "Honey, you'd vote for yourself!" she told Oprah Winfrey. "You see your name on that ballot; it's an easy check."

A year earlier, Julia had been nominated for a Golden Globe as Best Actress in a Musical or Comedy for her turn as a troubled movie superstar in *Notting Hill*. She didn't win, but her lover, Benjamin Bratt, had wired her before the ceremony, "You've already won." It's safe to assume he told her something similar as she prepared for Oscar night. She and Bratt had taken that "restful holiday" in Mexico with her sister, Lisa, and Lisa's husband, Tony Gillan; the couple would accompany Julia and Ben to the awards.

As departure time neared, a team of stylists put the finishing touches on Julia's look. Serge Normant of Jed Root Salon did her hair, a tight do with a hairpiece and grips creating a large bun at the back that extended down to her shoulders. "I've learned to wear tight hairdos [at awards shows]," Julia has said. "If your hair is loose, they can see you trembling." Her makeup was done by Genevieve of Sally Harlor Salon, highlighting her eyes with smoky-gray eye shadow and black eyeliner. Her blush was kept light, and she decided, as usual, on a neutral lip shade.

At about five, Julia, Ben, Lisa, and Tony climbed into a black stretch limousine and headed for the Shrine Civic Auditorium near downtown Los Angeles. "The four of us just went into the night with such a sense of fun," Julia recalled. "It was just so exciting, and I felt like I had to ride the wave, go with the flow. If you let it overwhelm you, and if you don't relax, a night like that will be over and you'll be saying, 'Wow, what happened? Was it fun? Did I enjoy myself?'"

When Julia arrived at the Shrine, the first person to greet her was Hilary Swank, the previous year's Best Actress for *Boys Don't Cry*. Hilary wished her luck, and Julia replied, "I'm freaking out." Out of earshot, Hilary whispered to her husband, Chad Lowe, "Oh, wow, I tried on the dress Julia is wearing!" Other women who greeted Julia took one look at her dress and offered some advice. "I got some tips from a few gals who were tight-dress-clad like myself," Julia said. "Every time she passed, Hilary would say, 'Breathe. Just try to breathe.' Believe me, it isn't so easy in this dress."

Julia practically held her breath through most of the evening, since the Best Actor, Best Actress, and Best Picture awards weren't announced until the very end. *Erin Brockovich* had been nominated for five awards but hadn't won any by the time the Best Actress announcement came; that can sometimes be a bad omen. Julia had not written an acceptance speech, feeling that "there's nothing more annoying than hearing someone say, 'Oh God, I can't believe it!'—and then pull out a big script they wrote a week ago."

When 1999's Best Actor, Kevin Spacey, announced the Best Actress winner, all the prognosticators were proven right. Julia, after a fourteen-year career in films and two prior nominations, had finally won her industry's highest honor.

As she bounded up the stairs to accept the statuette, she tripped over her train, and her chivalrous, handsome consort leaped out of his chair to lend her a steadying hand. Julia was giddy with joy. "I was out of my mind," she said about a year afterward. "To this day, Benjamin or my sister or my friends . . . they just laugh at me when they remember how I was that night. It was such an out-of-body experience. Just the adrenaline alone—I have a newfound respect for anybody who gets up on that stage and shows any kind of poise, because to me it was a physiological impossibility. My heart was pounding like a rabbit's."

The Oscar show's producer, in an effort to avoid the four-hour-plus telecast of the year before, had limited every winner to a forty-five-second acceptance speech. In an attempt to ensure that, he had offered a state-of-the-art wide-screen television to the winner with the shortest speech.

Julia very quickly made it clear that her joy and gratitude were not to be constrained by time limits. After saying, "Thank you, thank you ever so much. I'm so happy, thank you," she went on, "I have a television, so I'm going to spend some time here to tell you some things." Then, addressing Bill Conti, the conductor whose baton prompts reminded speechmakers their time was up, she said, "And sir, you're doing a great job, but you're so quick with that stick, so why don't you sit, because I may never be here again."

She acknowledged the other nominees and thanked twenty-three people by name (and "my mom"). Her speech exceeded the limit by three minutes, and Conti brought the music cue in several times. Julia ignored the reminders. "Stick man, I see you," she said at one point. She ended her speech by declaring, "I love the world!"

One person she forgot to mention in her thanks was Erin Brockovich herself—the woman without whom there would have been no part for Julia to play. "I was having an existential moment," Julia said months later. "I forgot people, and I feel bad. But I don't wish I had written anything down. You can't go back in time, you can't fix it, you can't change it."

Julia and Ben partied until two-thirty A.M. after the ceremony, which ended before nine P.M. West Coast time. Their first stop was the de rigueur Academy Governor's Ball, at which Julia could barely sit still. She jumped up every few minutes to greet well-wishers; she hugged and kissed Ben, and credited him for giving her the confidence to ratchet up her career from mere superstardom to the stuff of Hollywood immortality. (Bratt had advised her to make both *Notting Hill* and *Erin Brockovich*.)

Next they made an appearance at the other must-attend affair, the Vanity Fair gala. "Julia drank lots of champagne but was too excited to eat," said an observer at the party. A reporter asked Bratt whether he and Julia planned to continue celebrating once they got home. "I can't tell you," he replied with a sly grin, "because it's X-rated."

Julia Roberts, who has been called "Pretty Woman" for more than a decade after her enormous success in that film, is now just as often called "America's Sweetheart." Millions clearly adored her and had plunked down more money to see her films than they had for any actress since Barbra Streisand.

She seemed to be the all-American girl, a Georgia native who considered herself gawky and unattractive in high school and had developed into one of the most elegantly beautiful women in the world. Her smile lit up movie screens like "a thousand-watt lightbulb," one of her costars said. Her vivacity and joie de vivre, coupled with a deep vulnerability that centered in her brown eyes, endeared her to millions. Men wanted to make love to her and protect her; women sensed she'd make a hell of a girlfriend.

But it is her personal life and the press and public's almost inordinate fascination with it that has elevated Julia Roberts from movie star to one of the cultural phenomena of the last twenty-five years. Her childhood could be an afternoon TV special on the tragedy of broken homes, childhood emotional abuse, or the early loss of a beloved parent. Her love life—a long string of high-profile boyfriends, two broken engagements (one called off three days before a sumptuous wedding on the 20th Century–Fox lot), a short-lived marriage to a very unlikely groom, and a second marriage to a man who was already married when she met him—provides enough juice for a Jackie Collins miniseries. Her years-long feud with her famous brother, Eric Roberts, could be a plotline on *The Sopranos*.

Julia Roberts is, considering all these aspects of her life and career, a Pretty Fascinating Woman.

Part One

THE ROBERTSES OF ATLANTA

*"I come from a real touchy family.
A lotta hugging, a lotta kissing, a lotta love."*

—Julia Roberts

"Julia is in denial."

—Eric Roberts

CHAPTER ONE

W*ell, if that don't beat a goose a-gobblin'!"* exclaimed Jimmie Glen Roberts on Christmas Day 1933 when she heard the news that her twenty-eight-year-old son, Walter Thomas Roberts and his wife, the former Beatrice Beal, had had their first child, a boy they named Walter Grady. Walter would grow up to be the father of Julia Roberts.

The fifty-five-year-old Jimmie Glen, Née Corbitt, was herself no stranger to childbirth. Between her marriage to the strapping six-foot-tall Florala, Alabama–born farmer John Pendleton (J. P.) Roberts on December 13, 1899, and her second stillbirth in a row in 1923 (when she was forty-five), the feisty four-foot-eleven redheaded Irish-Scottish woman had borne nine children.

Baby Walter, of Irish, Scottish, and Welsh extraction on his father's side and English-Scottish extraction on his mother's, was J.P. and Jimmie Glen's fourteenth grandchild, and they would have seven more. Walter's cousin Glenda Beard recalled that the Robertses were a big but "very close-knit family, and they were a very honorable and Christian kind of family." Another cousin, Gloria Jones, recalled that "by the time my great-grandmother died, there were ninety-six of us [in and around Atlanta]."

All the Robertses, with the exception of Walter's parents and two aunts, lived within walking distance of one another in downtown Atlanta. Walter's father, whom everyone called Tom, lived with his family on Belleview Avenue in the rural West Fulton area of Atlanta. In 1933 America was in the grip of the Great Depression, and while Tom was never unemployed, there wasn't a lot of extra money to go around. "Their home was very small," Gloria recalled. "It had only three rooms. A huge kitchen—I guess what you'd call a keeping room—with a fireplace and a stove. That room was nice, but the living room and the bedroom were just tiny. The children [Walter was joined by a sister, Shirley, in 1942] slept in the kitchen." They did not have a telephone. "If you wanted to talk to somebody, you went to their house."

Tom Roberts loved horses and kept several on his property. After his retirement in the 1960s, he bought land across the street from his house and opened a riding academy that boasted more than a dozen horses. (It was there that his granddaughter Julia learned to ride.)

According to Gloria, Tom, his son, Walter, and his grandson Eric Roberts all look very much alike. "I saw Eric on TV the other night, and it was Walter made over. Julia can do it, too. When she acts like she's mad or upset, she can get that look that her dad and her granddad could get."

Walter's mother, Beatrice, Gloria felt, was not a particularly warm woman, "but she was sweet as she could be if you came to her house. She'd bake chocolate, she'd cook, whatever, but she didn't come to *your* house. She never bothered anybody. She was just a very quiet homebody. She was good with her children. They worshiped her."

Tom Roberts supported his family by working at the same job for forty-six years—first as a truck driver and then as a supervisor for the Driveway Company, Inc., a paving concern. "He supervised construction crews that did custom cement work on some of the biggest and finest homes in Atlanta," Gloria recalled. "They did driveways that looked like they were made of pine straw, but they were cement."

Glenda Beard remembered Tom Roberts as "a very hard worker. Kind of a macho-type person. He had rigid opinions about what a man should be." Gloria agreed: "I never saw Uncle Tom in anything but work shirt and jeans. He was *very* conservative. He believed that you went to work, you stayed with the same company, you didn't complain. And if you didn't do that, something was wrong with you."

As far as Tom Roberts was concerned, there was something wrong with his son, Walter. As the boy grew up, it became clear that he was nothing like his father; rather, he displayed the sensitivity and artistic temperament of the creative soul. Tom Roberts didn't think there was any future in that sort of thing for a young man.

"Walter had a brilliant mind and a delightful personality," Glenda recalled. "He was *different*—that was kind of the family name for him. Walter liked everything. He liked art, he liked music, he liked clothes. There wasn't enough that he could get into. Like most brilliant people, Walter got bored easily. I think that's why he was always into something different."

Another relative, Lucille Roberts, felt that Walter was effeminate, and recalled that he "played with dolls as a boy and was a little bit of a 'sissy boy.' " But Glenda disagreed: "I don't think he had a feminine quality. [When he got older] he did dress differently. He liked to wear black turtlenecks. Maybe a little bit tighter clothes, a European cut on his jackets, that kind of thing. Kind of artsy."

It was clear to his family by the time he was a teenager that "artsy" described Walter Roberts exactly. "He was the first person I ever saw wear an ascot!" Gloria said. At West Fulton High School, "he was a real avant-garde type," who loved writing and theater. "I remember going to family reunions, and we'd have to act out little plays that Walter made up. He wouldn't write anything down, he'd just tell you what he wanted you to do. He was always the star, always the main character. Walter could sing and play the piano. His daddy did let him take piano lessons."

By the time Walter and Gloria were teenagers in the late 1940s, the Robertses had been settled in Atlanta for four generations. "We had uncles on the police force and a cousin in the fire department," Gloria said. "We couldn't go anywhere that someone wasn't calling my parents and saying, 'I saw so-and-so at so-and-so.' " Unlike most of their relatives, the Tom Robertses were not a particularly religious family. "I don't remember them ever going to church except a couple of times when we were at our grandparents' and we'd go with them," Gloria said.

By the time he was eighteen, Walter Roberts had grown to five foot ten. He cut an arresting figure, and not just because of his ascots and European-cut clothes. His wavy jet-black hair crowned a chiseled, high-cheekboned face set with blazing dark eyes. (Roberts family lore has it that somewhere in the past, a Cherokee entered their gene pool.) Although he hadn't been particularly athletic as a boy, his frame was lean and solid. "The girls *loved* Walter," Gloria recalled. "Every girl I knew in my high school who didn't have a steady boyfriend wanted to go out with him. And I got them dates with him."

In December 1951, just before his eighteenth birthday, Walter was graduated from West Fulton High School. He found himself at a crossroads. Tom wanted him to join the paving business, or at least get a similar good, steady job that would help him support a family and live the kind of rock-solid life his parents had enjoyed for twenty years. Walter longed to go to college; his mind roiled with the prospect of immersion in everything from theater to psychology to English. His father would have none of it.

"Tom thought Walter was too intellectual!" Gloria recounted incredulously. "He didn't want him to go to college, and he definitely didn't want him to get involved in theater. That was just not what a man did." Tom refused to pay any of the costs of sending Walter to college, and father and son frequently battled over the issue. Since both had hot tempers, the fights often turned nasty. "They crossed swords often," said Gloria. "Tom could cuss like hell, and he didn't mind doing it."

Finally Tom relented, but he still refused to help his son out financially. Secret funding from Beatrice and a scholarship allowed Walter, in March 1952, to enroll at Emory University's Emory College of Arts and Sciences. The Methodist school, founded in 1836 and racially segregated until 1963, was situated on more than one hundred acres in Druid Hills, a suburb fifteen minutes from Atlanta. Walter lived in one of the makeshift plywood-and-tar-paper barracks that had been built to temporarily accommodate the influx of GI Bill students after World War II, when the school's enrollment nearly tripled in three years.

Walter proved to be something of a Renaissance man in college. Despite his overarching interest in the arts, his major area of study was psychology, and he joined the Omega Psi Phi fraternity. He also studied drama and joined the Emory Players and the Atlanta Theater Guild. He appeared in a number of plays, including *Desire Under the Elms, Life with Father,* and *Ah, Wilderness!* He joined the nearby Agnes Scott College's BlackFriars theater troupe, the oldest in Atlanta. (Emory's almost all-male student body supplied men for the all-women Scott College's productions.)

Walter met most of the girls he dated through the BlackFriars. On a number of occasions he went out for a night on the town with his cousin Gloria and his college roommate. "Walter *loved* girlie shows!" Gloria recalled. "He and his roommate—who was more fun than a barrel of monkeys and looked like Buddy Hackett—would egg the girls on and get the biggest kick out of it. They'd clap their hands and yell 'Go!' and things like that. I thought it was *awful.* They laughed at me and thought I was so naive."

Walter left Emory after eleven months. Gloria felt he did so because of poor grades. "He was just having too much fun and not concentrating on his studies. It was his first time away from home, and he was sowing his wild oats."

On March 12, 1953, Walter joined the air force, mainly to take advantage of the GI Bill. He still wanted an education, despite his apparent lack of attention to his studies at Emory. After ten weeks of basic training at Lackland Air Force Base in San Antonio, Texas, Walter was transferred to Keesler AFB in the hot and humid Gulf Coast city of

Biloxi, Mississippi. He served in the medical corps, first as a student, then as a helper, and finally as a medical administration specialist.

Walter Roberts chafed at military life; he was not a man who enjoyed being told what to do, and he had already developed a well-honed sense of intellectual superiority. Still, he won a Good Conduct Medal and a National Defense Service Medal. Mainly he stuck it out for the sake of his education, and there were compensations. He won a short-story-writing contest the base held, and he decided to audition for a part in the Keesler production of the George S. Kaufman and Moss Hart play *George Washington Slept Here*. He not only won the role, he also won the heart—and the hand in marriage—of the play's vivacious blond ingenue, Betty Lou Bredemus.

By 1954, Betty Lou had spent most of her twenty years longing to be a performer. Born in Minneapolis on Monday, August 13, 1934, she was the second child of thirty-year-old Wendell John Bredemus—a native of Minneapolis and a former football star and coach at the University of Minnesota—and the former Elizabeth Ellen Billingsley, thirty-six, born in Indianapolis. A brother, John, had been born in May 1927. Her paternal grandmother was born Eleanor Johnson in Sweden on April 30, 1882, and emigrated to the United States in 1900. She settled in Minneapolis, married a butcher, John Bredemus, in 1903, and a year later gave birth to Betty Lou's father, Wendell John.

In the midst of the Great Depression, Wendell Bredemus's career as a salesman forced him to relocate his family twelve times in search of work. Betty Lou attended ninth grade at Austin High School in Austin, Minnesota, a "one-horse town" a hundred miles south of Minneapolis whose main claim to fame, the Hormel meat company, brought it the nickname "SPAMtown." In 1950 Betty Lou transferred to another school in Excelsior, fifteen miles southwest of Minneapolis, for tenth and eleventh grade. She returned to Austin High for her senior year and graduation.

One of her classmates, Barbara Gaddis, remembered Betty Lou Bredemus as a pretty, blue-eyed, blond-haired girl, "a little on the short side and a little on the chunky side. She was attractive, with beautiful eyes. Her eyes and her smile are so much like Julia's."

Despite her two-year absence from Austin, Betty quickly resumed her place and took part in school and social activities. She joined the chorus and the school's drama group, Dirk & Bobble, appearing in their productions *You Can't Take It with You* by Kaufman and Hart and *A Murder Has Been Arranged* by Emlyn Williams. Betty Lou also wrote for the school newspaper, *The Sentinel,* reporting on the club activities of her classmates. Barbara was the paper's editor and recalled that Betty was "very reliable. She was a quiet person, but she could be a bit dramatic. I guess that was the theatrical part of her."

Betty Lou was graduated from Austin High in the spring of 1952. That summer she joined a stock company in northern Minnesota and appeared in a number of plays, including *A Date with Judy, The Hasty Heart,* and *Deep Are the Roots.* In September she returned to Austin and went to junior college, majoring in dramatic arts, her sights set firmly on a professional career as an actress. But later that year, her father became ill and could no longer work. "The money for college sort of disappeared," Betty recalled. Her father passed away three years later.

Her brother, John, seven years older, had served as a navy pilot and got his college education with the help of the GI Bill. It was he who suggested that Betty do the same. She chose the air force, signed up for two years, and arrived at Lackland AFB in San Antonio, Texas, for her basic training on August 27, 1953. In less than three months, she was transferred to Chanute Air Force Base in Rantoul, Illinois. (She and Walter Roberts missed serving together at Lackland by about a month.) On April 1, 1954, she received her final assignment, to Keesler AFB, where her background in theater brought her to special services, a division of personnel that oversaw entertainment for the servicemen, produced everything from variety shows to sports events, and ran the Service Club and the library, where Betty worked.

Betty earned a National Defense Service Medal during her hitch, but she never considered making the military a career. What she enjoyed most were the base's theatrical productions, most of which she tried out for. "This was a great experience, and I enjoyed every minute of it," she recalled. "I probably learned the most about acting when I worked with Rance Howard."

In March 1955 she auditioned for a part in Keesler's production of *George Washington Slept Here.* Howard, the show's director, had met Betty a year before at Chanute's Service Club, and he was delighted to learn that she had also been transferred. In her first year at Keesler, she and Howard worked together on such plays as *Command Decision, The Voice of the Turtle,* and *My Three Angels.*

"She was an attractive, sweet young WAF," Rance Howard recalled. "Very pleasant, a nice young woman. She seemed very lively and outgo-

ing, always upbeat, with a big smile." In the Keesler production of
Command Decision, Betty was cast in a role originally written for a
man in the all-male World War II army air force drama. In *George
Washington Slept Here,* she played Rina Leslie, half of a young dating
couple in the play.

To play her boyfriend, Howard chose Walter Roberts, whom he had not
met before. "He was handsome and clean-cut, very personable and very
talented. He gave a terrific reading, a cold reading. He had enthusiasm and
obviously was experienced, so I cast him. I really enjoyed working with
him." Howard found Betty just as enthusiastic. "I called a rehearsal once
for early Sunday morning, and Walter and Betty were the first to arrive.
That was pretty impressive."

They may have gotten up together, because shortly into rehearsals,
Howard had noticed they were a twosome in real life, not just onstage.
"They made a very attractive couple," he recalled. By the time Betty finished basic training, she had a lovely buxom figure. It was one of the first
things Walter Roberts noticed about her.

As they rehearsed their roles, their mutual passion for theater became
evident. But while Betty's dream was to be an actress, Walter wanted to
be a writer. He had won that writing contest at Keesler, and, he told
Betty, he was working on several plays. Although Rance Howard found
him a good actor, Walter was dismissive of the breed. "Actors are mind-
less," he reportedly told Betty, which couldn't have pleased her. What
undoubtedly did please her was to look at Walter Roberts's handsome
face, to stare into his hypnotic dark eyes, and hear him wax eloquent
about the joys of the artistic life in his basso-profundo voice.

For over a year, Walter (whom Betty Lou called Rob), Betty Lou,
Rance, and his wife of seven years, Jean, also an actor, worked in plays
together at USO facilities around the Southeast. "We toured with a couple of shows," Howard recalled. "I know we went to Pensacola, Florida,
and did *Voice of the Turtle,* which was only a three-character play and
thus easy to move around—there wasn't much scenery. Jean and Betty
and I were in that."

Only a matter of months after they met, Walter and Betty Lou
decided to get married. At the home of another librarian on the base,
the Reverend Victor Augsburger of Biloxi's First Presbyterian Church
united the not yet twenty-one-year-old Betty Lou Bredemus and the
twenty-one-year-old Walter Grady Roberts as husband and wife on July
1, 1955. Looking at their wedding picture years later, their daughter
Julia exclaimed, "They look like babies! My dad, he's so skinny, my mom

just looks so beautiful, but they both look *terrified!*" Rance and Jean Howard didn't attend the wedding because he had taken advantage of a lengthy leave to appear in the film *Frontier Woman*, along with Jean and their eighteen-month-old son, Ron.*

Less than a month after the wedding, Betty received her discharge from the air force. She continued to live on base with Walter, who still had two years to serve. Six weeks after the marriage, the couple learned that Betty was pregnant. On April 18, 1956, she gave birth to a small but healthy boy she and Walter named Eric Anthony.

On January 21, 1957, Walter's active military service came to an end. He received his discharge papers, collected his mustering-out pay, packed up his car, and headed with his wife and son to Louisiana. It was time for him to again pursue his dream of a college education and a career as a writer. He chose New Orleans's Tulane University, one of the South's preeminent schools. With credit for his year at Emory, he entered Tulane's College of Arts and Sciences as a sophomore for the spring term of 1957, with English literature and psychology as his major areas of concentration. The Roberts family lived on campus, in the Stadium Place apartments/dormitories. Rob attended classes for four straight terms—spring, summer, fall of 1957, and spring of 1958— then took a summer off and returned for the fall 1958 and spring 1959 terms.

To help support the family, Betty worked as an office clerk for an insurance company, then as a salesclerk in a chess and game shop in the French Quarter. In the spring of 1958, she began taking evening courses at Tulane's University College as a "special student," concentrating on English literature. Walter studied writing at Tulane, wrote short stories and poetry, and in 1959 created a Saturday-morning television series for children, *Creole Capers,* that aired on New Orleans's WDSU-TV.

The Robertses' life in New Orleans ended abruptly when Rob angrily

---

* Rance, Jean, and Ron Howard went to Hollywood; Rance and Jean had another son, Clint, in 1959. Since then, Rance has enjoyed a forty-seven-year career in television programs such as *That '80s Show* and films such as *The Music Man* and *Splash.* Jean Howard acted in dozens of movies and television shows; she died in 2000. Clint has appeared in several dozen movies, including all three of the *Austin Powers* films. Ron, of course, played Opie on *The Andy Griffith Show* and Richie Cunningham on *Happy Days,* produced and/or directed some of the biggest films of the '80s and '90s, and won an Oscar in 2002 for his direction of *A Beautiful Mind.*

withdrew from Tulane within two terms of earning a degree. "He had a great deal of animosity toward the professors," Betty recalled, "and was convinced there was nothing more they could teach him." His temper and his sense of superiority had gotten the better of him.

Pining for Georgia, Walter relocated his family in Decatur, an Atlanta suburb, where they moved into a small apartment complex on Scott Boulevard in 1960. Over the next five years, while Betty worked in the publicity department of Emory, Walter held a series of jobs that he invariably left after disputes with his bosses. He sold milk for the Atlanta Dairies Co-op, did publicity for Atlanta's Academy Theater, and built scenery for the Harrington Scenic and Lighting Studio.

"Walter Roberts was one of the most charming people I've ever met," Frank Wittow, the Academy Theater's director, told journalist Aileen Joyce. "He was very dynamic, very verbally adept, and, since he had some background in theater, he seemed well suited for the position." Wittow, however, came to feel that his new employee "had other interests" and did not devote enough time to his duties. Walter angered Wittow by staging an ill-advised publicity stunt involving a stolen painting and left the theater after less than a year. "He was very bright, and he was king, as far as his family was concerned," Wittow said. "But he was somewhat manipulative, and I felt he had some emotional problems."

Walter's stint at Harrington didn't last much longer. Charles Walker, who later became the studio's owner, recalled that "he was kind of like a butterfly. He seemed to want to dig in, but then he'd fly away. . . . He was all right unless you crossed him. He was a bit pompous, and I remember he got on Mr. Harrington's nerves."

Walter's cousin Gloria Jones recalled that he also worked as a maître d' and as a waiter in the early 1960s, but he never kept any job for very long. "Walter could be a jackass. He had a very hot temper, and if he didn't like you, he let you know it. He got along much better with children than he did with adults."

CHAPTER TWO

On the Saturday morning of September 12, 1964, the number-one single in America was Roy Orbison's "Oh, Pretty Woman." All across the greater Atlanta area, children sat in front of their flickering black-and-white television sets to watch the first episode of *Bum Bum and His Buddies,* a new kiddie show on WAII-TV, Channel 11. Betty Lou Roberts, in costume as Bum Bum the Clown, introduced the show's first story, "The Day the Children Tried to Be Good," written by Walter Roberts. Thirteen-year-old Evan Lee was one of the cast members. "It was about these little kids who discover a witch's house," Evan recalled. "I played the oldest kid, and Eric Roberts was one of the kids. Rob [Walter] was supposed to have played Bum Bum, but Betty had to do it because he was too busy writing, directing, and producing the shows. Betty would set it up every week with a very brief introduction explaining what that week's show was about."

The shows were videotaped on Thursday nights. The first show, shot with three cameras, took eight hours to finish. "It should have taken an hour and a half at most," Lee recalled. That night's stress level rarely lessened through the ensuing episodes. Another cast member, Blaise Dismer, a handsome eighth-grader, recalled that "Mr. Roberts had this explosive, intermittent anger, and it was scary. I remember we were rehearsing a script, and I had one of the main parts. I forgot my lines, and Mr. Roberts screamed at me. He was just livid. I was only twelve years old, and I was mortified. I started crying, and Mrs. Roberts came over to me and said, 'Honey, he wasn't mad at you. He was just upset about the situation'—she was real sweet and comforting. But I remember being so terrified by this one flash of anger from Mr. Roberts."

During the introductions, Betty urged the show's young viewers to write to Bum Bum, and she would read some of their letters on the air. This came to present a problem. "She complained to her husband that some of the letters were obscene," Blaise said. "Walter just said, 'Well, go ahead and read 'em—embarrass the little assholes!' But Betty wasn't interested in doing that."

In all, Walter produced fifteen episodes of *Bum Bum and His Buddies,* including a tongue-in-cheek version of *Jack and the Beanstalk* and *The Little Pioneers,* a script he wrote based on a nineteenth-century newspaper article he found in one of Eric's schoolbooks. It was about a family of children home alone on America's western frontier who were attacked by Indians. Eric played a crippled child in that one.

Part of the stress on Walter Roberts was financial. As Evan Lee recalled, "Rob and Betty financed this thing on their own nickel, because there wasn't any advertising except for public-service announcements." After the first fifteen episodes, Walter found a potential sponsor, but when he asked the station for the tapes to show the man, he was informed that they had all been erased to save money. "Rob was devastated," Evan Lee said. "But then he went right out and started the theater."

Walter's interest in writing and producing plays for children stretched back to his creation of *Creole Capers.* During his job as a set painter at Harrington Scenic and Lighting, he met Mr. Harrington's wife, the former Edith Russell, known as the doyenne of children's theater in Atlanta. His conversations with Edith refueled his interest and led to *Bum Bum and His Buddies.* They also led to his decision to found the Actors and Writers Workshop, which was incorporated as a nonprofit educational organization in late 1964 and provided classes and performing opportunities for children from five to eighteen.

Edith Russell wasn't pleased when Walter Roberts set up a rival children's theater. "That renegade so-and-so tried to take our kids!" she thundered. The attempted thefts proved successful in many cases. "I left Edith Russell to join Rob's theater because Rob was so much damn fun," said Evan Lee. "We were what was happening. We were doing original stuff, all written by Rob, and also things like Shakespeare—I got to play Malvolio in *Twelfth Night* when I was fifteen! I'm sure I would cringe now if I could see it, but the fact was that for a kid it was a terrific experience."

At first Walter and Betty taught classes in the living room of their Scott Boulevard apartment. Parents paid five dollars a month for their children (as many as four from one family) to learn acting, diction, and movement. The children then appeared in plays written or adapted by Walter, in roles for both children and adults, and learned stagecrafts such as lighting, sound techniques, and costume and scenic design. During the summer, the city of Atlanta commissioned the workshop to present plays as part of the city's free Summer Theater Festival in Piedmont Park. The first summer, 1965, Walter and Betty put on five plays and a new ballet, despite the fact that Betty was expecting their second child, a daughter born on August 7 whom they named Lelisa Billingsley and nicknamed Lisa.

The children involved in the workshops and productions found them a magical experience. "Rob was a great director as far as teaching kids what it meant to be in the theater," Evan said. "After a year in the workshop, you knew what it meant to be a professional actor. He expected that out of people. We worked hard—there were some days during the summer when we would rehearse eight hours a day—but we just had a ball doing it."

"When we did the summer theater, it was like we were doing summer stock," recalled Lyn Deadmore, who joined the workshop at fifteen. "I helped with the costumes and watched a woman make big beautiful butterfly wings out of wire and a gossamer material. It was the first time in my life that I felt I was good at something, and I had mentors. Walter Roberts was like an adult child. That's why he was so good with the children's stuff and so good with the children—he was like a big kid. He would say something and look at you for a reaction, and his eyes would be twinkling."

By the end of 1965, the workshop had burgeoned to over three dozen students, more during the summer, and had outgrown the apartment on Scott Boulevard—as had the Roberts family after Lisa's birth. After a brief search, Walter found the perfect place for home and workshop: a rambling three-story Victorian house at 849 Juniper Street in midtown Atlanta. The Robertses turned the first floor into workshop/rehearsal rooms and the second into their living space.

The imposing house stood fifteen steps above the street. To the left of the staircase on the first floor was a library, to the right a large living room and a sunroom. In the back of the house, the kitchen featured a large pantry, which became the costume storage room. The upper floor's four rooms became an office for Walter, a bedroom for him and Betty, a bedroom for nine-year-old Eric, and a nursery for baby Lisa.

Walter worked eighteen hours a day to keep the workshop running smoothly, teaching, writing, directing, and producing nearly every show—more than fifty between 1965 and 1970. In the summer the students arrived at the Roberts home at nine in the morning, six days a week, and didn't leave until nine at night. Betty—in addition to a full-time day job as an office clerk—handled the workshop's publicity and mailings, taught classes, and directed some of the shows. "While Rob was rehearsing a play upstairs," Evan Lee recalled, "Betty would be directing a play downstairs."

In December 1965 the workshop put on a production of *The Emperor's Nightingale*, Walter's adaptation of a Hans Christian Andersen tale, at the Community Playhouse in Atlanta. It was an enormous undertaking. Fifty-five young people were involved in the production (twenty-one had speaking parts), including Blaise Dismer as the emperor. The play featured a narrator, a parade, seventy different costumes, thirty children in yellow makeup to signify Chinese ancestry, and twenty-five in orange makeup as Japanese.

Walter Roberts clearly had faith that his young actors could do anything he asked of them: *The Emperor's Nightingale* opened with three pages of unbroken narration, a challenge for an actor of any age.

The show proved the workshop's most successful production. It played to sellout audiences of six hundred for eight performances. Attendance was bolstered by a full-page article about the production in *The Atlanta Journal* five days before the opening.

How Walter found the time is hard to fathom, but he also wrote poetry. In 1966 William Masters, a gynecologist, and Virginia Johnson, a psychology researcher, published the book *Human Sexual Response*, which created a sensation and prompted Walter to write a poem, published in *Poetry Parade*, in which he avowed that he gave no credence to sex surveys because as the poem's final line said, "good girls lie about it."

In 1966 the Actors and Writers Workshop was the only children's theater troupe in Atlanta, Edith Russell's having disbanded. It was also the first integrated theater in Georgia. At the time Atlanta's motto was "the city too busy to hate," but segregation was still widespread. Lester Maddox achieved national notoriety in 1964 when he drove African-Americans from his restaurant at gunpoint in defiance of federal civil rights legislation and then closed the establishment rather than desegregate it. In 1966 he ran for governor of Georgia as an avowed segregationist with the support of the Ku Klux Klan. After an inconclusive election, he was chosen governor by the state legislature.

"Rob was a southern liberal who walked the walk," Evan Lee said. "Betty and Rob's mission was not civil rights, but they quietly advanced the cause of integration. I was a kid in my mid-teens, a white southerner, who interacted with black kids for the first time in the workshop. That affected children in a very positive way in Atlanta."

(The integration of the workshop had occurred gradually. In May 1964, before he established the workshop, Walter produced his first play in Atlanta, Shakespeare's *Othello*. Betty played the Venetian noblewoman, Desdemona, and Walter played the black Moor, Othello. Later, he certainly would have cast the play differently.)

Among the workshop's students were the four children of the civil rights leader Dr. Martin Luther King, Jr., and his wife, Coretta: Yolanda, eleven in 1966; Martin, nine; Dexter, five; and later, Bernice, who turned five in 1968. "We called Yolanda 'Yokie,' " Evan recalled. "She was a fairly quiet, very nice girl who could be very funny at times. Yokie was the most involved of the King children, and being the oldest, she kind of shepherded her brothers around. Dr. King came to class one night. I didn't get to meet him, but he shook hands with a lot of the kids."

To Yolanda, "Mr. Roberts was so imposing. I love him, but I was also a little intimidated by him. He taught me so much—he and Mrs. Roberts—about the work, and just about living and being really open, grabbing life and making the best of it."

On April 4, 1968, came the shocking news that Dr. King had been assassinated in Memphis. "Everyone went into a panic," Betty recalled. "We were afraid to take Yokie home for fear of further attacks on the King family. When I did drive her home, I was met immediately by members of the Secret Service and ushered into the house. Coretta King asked that I stay and help her greet the many dignitaries arriving to pay their respects. I was the first to welcome [former] Vice President Richard Nixon when he arrived at the King home."

Coretta King, according to Betty, "was very supportive, both emotionally and financially." Yolanda recalled that "it was a constant struggle to get funds to keep [the workshop] going. My mother was very much committed to them. But it was always a case of just barely getting by, paying the rent, getting the costumes."

Indeed, one of Walter's most time-consuming tasks was fund-raising. A 1967 program lists twenty-seven financial backers of the workshop, including Dr. and Mrs. King and King's parents. An Educational Opportunity Act grant supported part of the 1968 summer program, but Walter's application for a fellowship from the Guggenheim Foundation proved unsuccessful.

Still, Betty and Walter soldiered on, nourished creatively, even spiritually, by doing what they loved. He took every opportunity to get his productions seen by as many people as possible, and in the process make a little money. One of his enterprising efforts was the Showmobile, a truck with a stage built on its flatbed, which carried young actors and costumes and scenery from area to area, usually for audiences of inner-city kids or rural youngsters who had never seen live theater. "We were going into housing projects with integrated casts in the late sixties," Evan Lee recalled, "and busing kids in from places called Buttermilk Bottom. Rob would tell the city, 'For a quarter a head, we'll bus 'em in to see my show.' So we would go out onstage, and there would be five hundred little black kids in the audience who were having their first theater experience."

Not everyone in the black community appreciated Walter Roberts's pioneering efforts. Eric would recall that on occasion, when the Showmobile rolled into ghetto areas, some people threw rocks at the troupe.

In the spring of 1967, Betty discovered that she was pregnant again. After a nine-year gap between Eric and Lisa, only two years would separate this baby from the last. It was probably not the best time for the family to have two small children to mind and to pay for—the Robertses were madly busy with the duties of the workshop and living on about fifty dollars a week of disposable income—but Walter and Betty were happy with the news, and the members of the workshop were ecstatic. "I remember everyone anticipated the birth of the baby," said Lyn Deadmore. "I felt like a member of their family. Betty was huge at the end—it was a very visible pregnancy—and she worked right up until the time of the birth. I wish I could tell you that we waited and stars appeared in the sky as Julia's birth approached, but it wasn't that way."

CHAPTER THREE

In the Jessica Parker Williams Pavilion of Crawford Long Hospital in Atlanta on Saturday, October 28, 1967, at sixteen minutes after midnight, thirty-three-year-old Betty Lou Roberts gave birth to a healthy baby girl named Julia Fiona. The weather was typical for fall; the day before, the Dow Industrials average had fallen 1.10 points to close at 889.79. The headline in *The Atlanta Constitution* announced U.S. LOSES 14 JETS IN WEEK OF BOMBING in Hanoi. The year's big Oscar films, *Bonnie and Clyde* and *In the Heat of the Night,* had already opened, while *Gone With the Wind,* which had premiered in Atlanta twenty-eight years earlier, drew crowds to the Loews Grand Theater to see a new seventy-millimeter print of the classic.

Betty brought the new baby home to the oohs and aahs of her large extended family. (*Atlanta* magazine later reported that since Walter was unable to pay the hospital bills for Julia's birth, Coretta Scott King did so.) "I remember holding this swaddled infant in my arms," Blaise Dismer said. "Nowadays, I always say that my claim to fame is I once held Julia Roberts in my arms."

The family nicknamed the baby Julie, and Eric soon began to call her "Hoolie," pronouncing it as though it was Spanish. Unlike Eric and Lisa, who had inherited their mother's Scandinavian blue eyes, baby Julie had brown eyes like her father. The bubbly baby charmed everyone. "She was just so adorable," Yolanda King recalled. "So bright and perky and into everything and just all over the place."

From June to September of the following year, Julie accompanied her parents and siblings on their second annual Showmobile tour. She would watch with fascination all the frantic, colorful activity buzzing around her. "I still have traces of memory from when I was little," Julia has said, "of watching this magical world unfold in front of me."

Betty recalled, "I would put Julie in her stroller while I set up the sound system. In the ghetto areas the kids would come up and ask, 'Can I take her for a walk?' And I'd say, 'Sure.' Then one time someone said, 'Are you sure she's coming back?' But the black kids were fascinated with her, because a lot of them had never seen any white children."

By all accounts, Walter Roberts delighted in his little girls. He called Lisa "Lisa-Mouse" because she seemed always to be scurrying around (and when she made her stage debut at five, she wore a mouse costume). After Julia became a star, she spoke glowingly of her father to a reporter: "I had a great relationship with my dad. Nothing intellectual, just really caring and fun, singing the Oompa Loompas song or drawing and painting."

But Walter Roberts was nothing if not a complex man. As the struggle to keep the workshop financially viable wore him down, his marriage—and his son, Eric—suffered. "It was the best of all times," Blaise Dismer recalled, referring to the joy the students got out of learning every aspect of the theater. "And the worst of all times. Walter had an incredible temper that would show itself at certain times. The most frequent target for that anger was Eric. Walter had a tolerance level for all of his actors except Eric. With him, there could be no mistakes. He was unquestionably emotionally abusive to Eric, and although I don't know it for a fact, I suspect in other ways as well."

Twelve years old in 1968, beautiful, waiflike, and small for his age, Eric had not uttered a word until he was five, then suffered from a nearly crippling stutter. "When I knew Eric," Blaise recalled, "he was so eager to please, he was a delight—he was this really cute little kid who stuttered and who tried so hard." Although it was difficult to have a conversation with Eric because of his hesitant speech, none of the children in the workshop ridiculed him. At school, however, things were different. Eric was so afraid of taunts from his classmates that when his teachers went in order from student to student to read aloud, he would try to figure out which paragraph he'd be asked to read so he could memorize it first. (If he memorized something, he wouldn't stutter.) Too often, though, his calculation would somehow go amiss, and the stutter would return. "I used to get in fights over it," Eric said. "I'd fight until I was dead."

The school wanted to put Eric in special-education classes, but Walter vetoed the idea. Instead—after seeing Eric speak without a stutter in front of a mirror, reciting lines he had memorized—his father decided that the stage was where Eric belonged. The boy took to acting with remarkable ease, never once stuttering onstage, and before long became, in the words of Evan Lee, "the backbone of the company."

Blaise Dismer agreed: "Eric had a tremendous seriousness about acting. He knew his lines inside and out—God forbid that he should forget a line!"

The boy seemed to lead a lonely life, worried about pleasing his father. "Eric didn't seem to be close to anyone," Lyn Deadmore recalled. "He was a wonderful kid, very talented, but scared and sad. He seemed terribly unsure of himself. It seemed like he was trying to compete with his father. I had trouble integrating the fact that Mr. and Mrs. Roberts were role models for me, and yet he seemed to be abusive to Eric. It was verbal abuse—belittling him. He did that a lot with people—he would make fun of some of the students behind their backs. We would laugh, but it did occur to me that it was kind of cruel."

For years after Eric became a movie star, he told interviewers that his father was "a great man" who had taught him everything he knew about acting. "I worshiped my dad," he said. "I remember he always spoke with such wisdom, but in a way that was never condescending. I was only eight years old when I read *The Glass Menagerie*, and when I got older, I realized I had become educated peripherally because of books. My father was my book pal."

Members of the workshop recall Walter telling them that his most wonderful memory was running hand in hand with Eric down a hillside to go to a fair. One of Eric's earliest memories is of his sixth Christmas, when he and his father were in Rich's department store in Atlanta and Eric saw a Matchbox car he very much wanted. His father told him they couldn't afford it. "Then we got home, and he opens his hand—and there's that Matchbox car. I knew he stole it. But it was a love theft." In another interview, Eric said, "He was my best friend, my dad, and I loved him."

Today Eric's view of his father is quite different. "Through a lot of therapy," he said in an e-mail to this author, "I've come to realize my father was not the man I thought he was." Eric's wife, Eliza, also in an e-mail, elaborated: "Unfortunately, Eric has come to realize and has had to face the fact that his father, Walter, was a very sick man and Eric was a victim of Stockholm Syndrome,* with his father having damaged many

---

* In 1973 four Swedes held hostage in a bank vault for six days after a robbery became attached to their captors and defended them, a phenomenon dubbed the Stockholm Syndrome. Psychologists theorize that the abused in these cases bond to their abusers in order to avoid violence. Depending on the degree of his identification with the captor, the abused may deny that the captor is in fact at fault. In family situations, an abused child may feel tremendous love for the abusing parent and enter into denial about the parent's real personality and their relationship.

people's lives. Eric can in no way provide you with any positive thoughts about this man. He is sorry to have ever spoken lovingly of him."

Walter's flashes of temper became more frequent as the struggle to keep the family business afloat worsened. Although in 1969 Coretta Scott King established a scholarship fund in her late husband's memory for the workshop, calling it "one of Atlanta's most imaginative and exciting recent cultural efforts," the venture still did not allow the Robertses to live much above the national poverty line. "They were living hand to mouth," Lyn Deadmore recalled. The strain took a toll on Eric, on some of the young actors in the workshop, and on the Roberts marriage. Lyn recalled the day she saw Betty coming down the stairs from the family's quarters with a black eye. "What happened?" Lyn asked. "Oh, a black cat hit me," Betty replied. Lyn didn't think that made any sense, "but I just left it alone. I did wonder at the time if Walter had done it."

Greg Patin, a good-looking, well-built young man in his late teens, joined the workshop in the late 1960s and watched both its dissolution and that of the Roberts marriage at close hand for two years. Because he was older than many of the other students, he became a part of the inner sanctum of the Roberts family, spending time with them in their private quarters. "Walter would have big-time temper tantrums, where he would literally throw things," Patin recalled. "Betty would just leave the room, the kids would clear out, and he would sit and drink. He drank constantly. He'd carry this big jug of 'water' that was laced with bourbon just about everywhere he went. He said he needed the water for his kidneys, which he said were bad. I said, 'The alcohol can't be doing your kidneys a lot of good.' He'd just make these slurping noises, like the noise Anthony Hopkins made in *The Silence of the Lambs* when he was talking about the Chianti and fava beans."

In Patin's view, Walter was "a very pandering, manipulative sort of person. He was very evil, I think, perverted, devious. He was a brilliant man, very smart. But God, he was a really sick person."

According to Lyn, many of the boys in the workshop would joke about Walter's sexual advances toward them. He seemed to enjoy pinching their backsides. "I thought he had a thing for little boys," Lyn said, "and in fact I wondered if he had hurt Eric, to tell you the truth." Blaise recalled that Walter would tell the boys dirty jokes. "In retrospect, it was inappropriate," he said. "But at that time we eighth-graders were kind of brash, and we were a little bit of a fast crowd, being 'in the theater.'"

Walter was *too* fast for one of the boys, who spoke on the condition of anonymity. "We were eighth-graders, and we would make fun of homosexuals," he said. "That was something that Mr. Roberts would do, too. He would say, 'You know, there's some fags who live over on Eighteenth Street!' And one day he said to me, 'Hey, why don't we go over there? We can have a couple of laughs.' I took that to mean that we'd go there, and these guys would act effeminate, and we'd snicker and then go back to Juniper Street. So I said okay. But on the way over there, he said, 'After all, it's free sex!'

"I thought, *Oh my God—he's talking about us going over there and getting oral sex from those guys!* So I said, 'Hey, why don't you go, and I'll wait for you here.' He just said, 'No, forget it, no big deal, we'll go back.' So we went back. That incident kind of frightened me—I was totally caught unawares."

Greg had similarly disturbing experiences with Walter. "His sexual proclivities were very strange," Patin said. "He was very cunning and crafty about his sexual business. It went beyond advances. He had a very basso voice—he did seem effeminate in some of his gestures, but he was barrel-chested, and he had a very resonant voice. But he could do a female voice that didn't sound like a falsetto at all; it sounded like a woman talking. And he would call people, me included, with this female voice and start talking about sexual issues. I didn't realize it at the time, but he was getting off on the other end of the phone with this stuff. When I realized what he was doing, Eric wasn't the only one scarred; I was, too, because I believed in this man."

Another untoward factor among the "fast crowd" of workshop participants was drug use. In the relatively progressive Atlanta of the late 1960s, drugs would have been difficult to avoid. "Grass and acid were part of the company's lifestyle," wrote Fred Schruers in a *Premiere* profile of Eric in 1995. "It happened to all of us," Schruers quoted Philip DePoy, a workshop teenager, "but check out how much younger [Eric] was. So he got knocked in the head by some of these drugs when he was maybe eleven." (Eric has said he first used marijuana when he was thirteen.) Gloria Jones recalled (without having any firsthand knowledge) that "we heard through some of the other family members that Betty gave Eric marijuana." Even if Eric didn't get marijuana from his mother, he began to use the drug not for recreation but to alleviate his fears and confusion and depression. He would have many reasons to feel all three emotions over the ensuing years, and drugs would prove a serious, nearly fatal problem for him.

The breakdown of the Roberts marriage put a tremendous strain on Betty as well. She gained weight (as had Walter) and lost the effervescence people had loved in her before. "She was there, but then she wasn't," Greg recalled. "She would try to be a part of things, but she just seemed to be severely depressed all the time."

In 1970 Betty and Greg costarred in a production of Tennessee Williams's *Sweet Bird of Youth*, a drama about an aging movie star who gets involved with a handsome young drifter. One night after a rehearsal, according to Greg, Betty showed up at his apartment. "She was drunk and wanted to get it on with me. She promised that if we just got it on once, there would be no longing looks later on, and all that kind of stuff, nothing I would have had to worry about. I said no—she was not attractive to me. She spent part of the night weeping on my doorstep."

When Greg, fed up with both the Robertses, abruptly quit the workshop, Betty asked him, "How could you leave like this, after all that Walter has done for you?" He told her, "I cannot take this madness any longer. You don't know what I'm going through."

"I know what Walter does," Betty replied.

In 1970 a program for the workshop carried a dual biography of Betty and Walter, likely written by him: "Their work with the workshop is very much a dual effort, though Walter insists that Betty is the real teacher in the family, and she contends that he is the only director in the house. . . . They have recently begun work on a theater text book dealing with their own rather unique approaches to working with young people. It is tentatively titled *How to Talk to a Half-witted Child*."

The book never saw print, and its proposed title may have spoke volumes about how Walter actually felt working with child actors. "I know Walter had the ambition that the workshop would also become an adult theater," Evan Lee recalled. "He called those of us who made up the core group 'the junior company,' as though he expected there eventually to be a 'senior company.' I don't know why it never happened—except that he was caught up in the struggle of running things day to day."

That struggle sunk the workshop; an interracial version of the sex comedy *The Owl and the Pussycat*, starring sixteen-year-old Yolanda King as a New York prostitute, proved its most daring and final production. By the end of 1970, the Roberts marriage was nearly over as well, rent by all the struggles, including infidelity and more and more frequent battles. Julia retains a memory from the age of four, she told a reporter. She and Lisa were having a tea party when their parents began a loud, bitter argument. "So my sister and I [had] the tea party as a sort of 'Let's pretend none of this is happening.'"

Walter and Betty were still together in February 1971, when they moved from the rambling rooms on Juniper Street to a small but appealing house at 432 Eighth Street, across the street from Grady High School, where Eric was completing his sophomore year. Walter took out a $17,800 mortgage on the property, with a $136 monthly payment.

The alleviation of the stress and financial strain of keeping the workshop afloat—and Walter's getting a regular job as a vacuum-cleaner salesman at Rich's department store—was not enough to save the marriage. According to Walter's cousin Dorothy Whitmire, the coup de grâce occurred shortly after the move: "Eric came home early from school and found his mother in bed with Michael Motes [the man she would later marry]." Devastated by what he saw as Betty's betrayal of his father, Eric called Walter at Rich's and told him what he had seen. Glenda Beard, Gloria Jones, and Lucille Roberts confirmed the story.

"One of the glaring errors of Walter's history," Gloria said, clearly on the Roberts side of the issue, "was that he was blamed for the divorce from Betty, and that was not true. If Eric would be truthful with you, he could tell you exactly what happened—not a pretty picture. That wasn't the first time, either, but it was the first time [one of] the children caught her. Eric had suspicions of his mother having affairs with other men before Motes, and she did. Walter knew about them, but he tried to keep them secret. He knew how his dad would treat him if he divorced her. There had never been a divorce in our family. But there comes a time. You can just put up with so much and be embarrassed. Walter was affiliated with some of the most important people in Atlanta, and she was making a fool of him."

With more than enough blame to go around, Betty filed for divorce on June 14, 1971. She charged Walter with "cruel treatment," said that he was "gainfully employed and earns a substantial salary and is capable of supporting plaintiff [Betty] and their minor children," and asked for custody of Eric, Lisa, and Julie. Three weeks later, the Robertses entered into a seemingly amicable agreement that granted the divorce, gave Betty custody of all three children, and the right to remain in the Eighth Street house and assume its mortgage. Walter got the family's 1968 Volkswagen and was ordered to pay $195 per month in child support. He was also granted "reasonable" visitation rights. The divorce became final on January 28, 1972.

By then Betty had become more deeply involved with Motes, and she would marry him in September 1972. Their relationship laid the groundwork for an acrimonious split that divided the Roberts family irrevocably. "Obviously my mother wanted to have a relationship and wanted to take care of her children," Eric said in 1998. "But I don't think she knew what she was getting into by agreeing to marry Motes. It was common knowledge where we grew up that Motes was a freak. He would have stood out in a crowd of ten thousand. Whether he married my mother to get close to her children or not, I don't know. But clearly, marrying him was not a good decision or a healthy thing for her children. Our mother's husband terrorized and abused me, and I fear he terrorized my sisters, Julia and Lisa, as well." In 1997 Eric told the journalist and author J. Randy Taraborrelli, "The guy that raised us was fucked up. My mother marrying him was a mistake, but she did, so what can I say? That was her choice." Asked whether Julia and Lisa had had "a tough time with him," Eric replied, "I know they did. That's what I'm telling you. Who knows what they went through with this guy?"

A safe assumption that Julia's ten years with her stepfather were indeed unhappy can be made from the fact that she doesn't speak of him in interviews. "After my parents divorced, my mother, sister, and I moved to Smyrna," she once said, not mentioning her mother's remarriage. In another interview she explained why she will not speak of Motes. "I have very strong opinions about things, and I have a young [half] sister who is a product of my mother's second marriage, and out of respect for her and my mom, I don't think it's really fair."

CHAPTER FOUR

Born James Virlyn Michael Motes on January 10, 1945, in Atlanta, Michael Motes was the first of two children of Virlyn Moore Motes of Atlanta and Nelle Birmingham of Tallulah Falls, Georgia, who were married in Atlanta on September 15, 1942. As a teenager at Smyrna's Campbell High School, Motes bore the brunt of ridicule as "strange . . . a sissy type," a classmate told Julia biographer Aileen Joyce. Tall and heavyset, he wore horn-rimmed glasses and suffered from alopecia areata, a little-understood disease thought to be an autoimmune dysfunction that causes complete baldness. He wore hairpieces that a classmate told Joyce "weren't very attractive, and they were very obviously hairpieces, sort of reddish-colored."

Motes developed a fascination with his family's genealogy, tracing it back twelve generations, and joined dozens of organizations celebrating southern and American history, including Children of the Confederacy and the National Society of Sons of the American Colonists. He also claimed hereditary membership in Britain's Descendants of the Knights of the Most Noble Order of the Garter, established by King Edward III in 1348.

In 1971, at twenty-six, Motes worked as a drama critic for *The Atlanta Constitution,* and attended a Smyrna community-theater production of *Arsenic and Old Lace* featuring thirty-seven-year-old Betty Lou Roberts as Aunt Martha, one of the delightfully deranged elderly sisters who poison their boarders and conduct funeral services in the cellar.

After the show, Motes and Betty were introduced, and although no one who knew either of them could fathom why, they began an affair. Many people considered Motes weird-acting and weird-looking, and called him Mr. Clean because of his bald pate. Physically, he was the antithesis of Walter Roberts's "devilishly handsome," raven-haired figure. Others who knew him questioned his sexual preference. "I wasn't surprised when Betty married Michael Motes," Greg Patin said, "even though he was about as interested in women . . . I figured that was just a Betty thing."

Betty's marriage to Michael Motes on September 11, 1972, and Motes's ill treatment of Eric, led Walter in October to petition the court for a modified divorce agreement. He alleged that Betty had "neglected the minor children, specifically our daughters, by staying out very late at night without providing any adult care and supervision for the girls," and that "all during the winter months our daughters had colds, appeared extremely tired and listless, and on occasions when petitioner [Walter] saw them had fevers." Walter also said that Betty would leave the girls in his care for prolonged periods of time "while she would be absent . . . and could not be located."

Walter further claimed that Julie was "not being cared for well at all. She's an innocent child who needs tenderness, and she's definitely not getting it. I fear it will affect her in years to come. I do not want her to suffer as an adult for anything that happens to her as a child."

Walter also stated that before Motes's marriage to Betty, the man "on many occasions slept overnight with respondent [Betty] in the home with the knowledge and in the presence of all the minor children." On May 13, 1972, Walter said, Motes had struck and injured Eric "without cause," and two days later, Betty "ordered our son Eric from the home and refused thereafter to care for him. . . . Michael Motes has and continues to mistreat our minor children, specially our son Eric."

Eric has never said exactly what transpired between him and Michael Motes. He once said that someone in his family, whom he did not identify, had beaten him "until I could barely walk." Later, he told a reporter that his mother "beat the hell out of me for years. [It's] something that never goes away." More recently he said, "With my mother it was grab a stick and beat the shit out of somebody—me. I grew up scared of everything." He added that "Julia is in denial" about the family's history of abuse. "I tried talking to her about how I was abused by violence and she just started screaming at me. She didn't want to hear about the abuse. She says it was my father who was abusive. He could mentally run you into the ground [but there was no physical abuse]. All my childhood, [my mother's] beatings were an almost daily occurrence. But Julia doesn't want to hear about it, and that's affected our relationship for years."

The night Betty ordered Eric, then sixteen, out of the house after a physical altercation with Motes, he walked in a pouring rainstorm from Smyrna to Atlanta—a distance of more than ten miles—after failing to reach his father, who was out on a date with his new girlfriend, Eileen Sellars, a legal secretary twelve years his junior. Eric called Eileen's mother, Virginia, who picked him up in downtown Atlanta. "I felt so sorry for him," Virginia recalled. "He couldn't get in touch with his father, and he didn't have any money. He was just soaking wet, and he was so upset that he was stuttering something awful."

In response to Walter's complaints about Betty's behavior and her treatment of the children, Judge Ernest Tridwell ordered him, Betty, and Michael Motes to "separately arrange to meet with and be examined by" Dr. W. J. Clark, an Atlanta psychologist, who would advise the court on the custody matter. Walter was ordered to pay for the sessions and was allowed to retain custody of Eric until the court's decision. Betty was permitted to keep Lisa and Julie. Walter received visitation rights "of having all three children with him every other weekend from 6 P.M. on Friday until 6 P.M. on Sunday commencing the weekend beginning on the 24th day of November, 1972."

In a January 1973 answer to Walter's court petition, Betty denied all charges and countercharged that Walter had failed to turn over the title to the Eighth Street house and had, during the previous summer (while Betty and the girls vacationed at Cass Lake, Minnesota, at a camp owned by Betty's brother, John), removed "a large number of items from the house, including furniture, appliances, clothing, art objects, et al., many of which he has refused to restore to the Plaintiff [Betty]."

Betty further alleged that Walter had been delinquent in his child-support payments and had "grossly abused his visitation rights by telling malicious lies to the minor children concerning Plaintiff's behavior, in order to prejudice the children against Plaintiff and induce them to leave her custody and live with Defendant [Walter]. Further, Plaintiff shows that the Defendant has influenced the parties' oldest child, Eric, to join in his attempts to alienate the younger children from their mother."

Betty asked the court to order Walter to comply with all provisions of the original divorce settlement, revoke his visitation rights to Lisa and Julie, and order that "the Final Judgment and Decree be amended to place custody of Eric Roberts [with] the Defendant."

In May 1973 the court's final decision came down: Walter would have temporary custody of Eric and would not have to pay child support for him. Betty would get permanent custody of Lisa and Julie. Walter could have both daughters "with him for a single two-week period during each summer while schools are on vacation. . . . In addition, [Walter] shall be entitled to have the daughters visit him for Christmas Day in odd-numbered years, and for Christmas Eve in even-numbered years."

(Betty was granted the right to have Eric visit her during summer vacations, but he wanted nothing more to do with his mother. He did not see or speak to her for another fifteen years, and then only because Julia was close to death in a Los Angeles hospital. At the beginning of his career, journalists reported that his mother was dead.)

The court at last ordered that both Betty and Walter "avoid harassment of the other, either at their homes or places of employment. Further, each party is directed to avoid attempting to employ the son as a means to cause distress to the other party or create emotional disturbance in the daughters."

Neither Walter nor Betty abided by the order's no-harassment provision. Late one night in 1974, police officers pounded on the door of the small Motes bungalow on Privette Road in Smyrna, rousting Michael, Betty, Lisa, and Julie from their beds. The local narcotics squad had received a telephone tip that drugs could be found in a hollowed-out Bible on the living room coffee table. Armed with a search warrant, the officers looked in the Bible and did indeed find drugs. "The husband started crying," one of the officers, Troy Ballinger, told Aileen Joyce. "He got really upset and began wringing his hands, saying he had young children in the house and how he would never have drugs around them."

Betty told the officers that Walter had stashed the drugs in the Bible and phoned the police in order to strengthen his claim on custody of Lisa and Julia. While it's possible he called in the tip ("That sounds like something he might do," said Gloria Jones), it is unlikely he planted the drugs, since he was not allowed in the Motes home—all visitations with Lisa and Julie were in his home. But Betty's insistence that Walter had engineered the episode led the officers to decide that "things didn't fit," according to Ballinger. "So we never charged them, and the whole thing was dropped."

(Nine years later, the Moteses divorced, and a custody agreement stipulated that Motes would have visitation rights to their daughter, Nancy, born in 1976, providing the "Husband does not carry his child to any Narcotics Anonymous meetings, and the Wife does not carry the child to any Nar-Anon meetings.")

According to Gloria, Betty soon retaliated against Walter. "She had him arrested on a tip from her, claiming that he had stolen photographs from the Atlanta public library. He didn't steal the pictures."

"I grew up in a very dysfunctional home," Eric has said. "Everybody hated each other and made it clear."

. . .

The effect all this turmoil had on the tender psyche of Julie Roberts, who turned seven in October 1974, can easily be surmised. Those who have observed, interviewed, and written about her over the years agree that she has a dread of confrontation. A Hollywood writer close to her has said, "Julia avoids conflict at all cost, even with people she's close to. The moment you hear her arguing with someone—even a lover—you can start ticking the moments until it's over."

Her parents had argued furiously toward the end of their marriage, and so did Betty and Michael Motes, almost from the start of theirs. One of the main areas of contention, as before, was money. If Betty had hoped her marriage to Motes would provide financial security, she rapidly was disabused of that notion. During her second marriage, she or Motes would be sued for delinquent back rent, charge accounts, and other bills no fewer than six times. On March 24, 1974, Rich's department store—where Walter worked—sued Motes for passing a bad check of $23.33. Apparently, neither Motes nor Betty tried to make good on the debt, and on June 18, Betty's wages were garnisheed.

As a child, hearing her mother and stepfather argue late into the night, Julie turned for solace to her sister, with whom she shared a bed in their small, ramshackle house next to a water tower in Smyrna. "Lisa has this celestial thing," Julia told GQ in 1989. "I would wait until she was asleep and touch her, to tap into that safe place so I wouldn't be scared at night."

As an adult, Julia developed a protective veneer that filters out the bad memories. "When I look back on my childhood, my mind focuses first on the best bits," she said in Parade in 1998. "I'm a person for whom time softens all rough edges." This is why few of her fans know how tumultuous and rife with unhappiness Julia's first fourteen years were. She distilled her youth with the comment "I come from a real touchy family," she said in Rolling Stone in 1990. "A lotta hugging, a lotta kissing, a lotta love."

Eric has spoken far more frankly about the Roberts family past. "Children who grow up in a troubled environment usually blame themselves for their pain," he told the journalist Leon Wagener in 1998. "You figure you've done something bad to have suffered so. You come to think you deserve the pain. That kind of guilt leads to self-destructive behavior."

Eric, who had often baby-sat for both Lisa and Julie, hated that he would no longer be around to protect them from the danger he feared

Michael Motes presented. "I was horrified when I thought about what my poor sisters were going to have to endure living with Motes."

Wagener, in his profile of Eric in the British magazine *Here!*, wrote that "when Julia was ten and living with her mum and stepfather in Smyrna, Georgia, Motes began sexually molesting a teenage boy, often in the family home. He preyed on Shawn Melton, 13, for four years. . . . Eric claims Motes's behavior was not only directed toward strangers' children—he says he was terrified of his stepfather—and believes that living in Motes's household during their formative years has had a profound effect on Julia and himself."*

In one of her moments of candor with a journalist, Julia admitted that in her family, "We've all had to grow up fast."

---

* In a telephone conversation with this author, Shawn Melton confirmed that he had been sexually molested by Michael Motes. He declined to provide any further details.

CHAPTER FIVE

By 1973, Walter Roberts, although disappointed by the loss of the workshop, had achieved a level of serenity he had not felt in years. He had reconciled himself to his new life. He earned more money as a sales representative for Eureka vacuums at Rich's than he ever had before, and he was now engaged to Eileen Sellars, whom both Eric and the girls liked very much.

If Michael Motes was the antithesis of Walter Roberts, Eileen in many ways contrasted with Betty Lou. A kindhearted, studious brunette who held a master's degree from Florida State University, she was described by her aunt Vivien McKinley as "a very shy person, a very conservative person, in both her manner and her dress. Walter brought her out. She was like a flower that bloomed. He liked her to wear her hair down. He even bought some of her dresses, things she never would have bought herself. She had a calming effect on him . . . he was so upset about the girls, you know. That he saw them so seldom. But he seemed crazy about her, and they seemed happy together."

Neighbors in the Ansley Forest apartment complex in Atlanta, Walter and Eileen met one summer day in 1973 as Walter walked around the grounds with Lisa holding one of his hands and Julie the other. When they stopped to chat, five-year-old Julie did the introductions. "This is my father," she chirped to Eileen. "His name is Walter. But you can call him Daddy!" The following week Eileen and Walter went out on a date, and a year later, on April 4, 1974, they were married in a small civil ceremony in Atlanta.

Michael Motes's fascination with Confederate history brought Betty and her girls into the world of those who mourn for a South that will never be again: The Motes family were photographed with Michael wearing a Confederate Army uniform. The October 10, 1974, issue of the Atlanta Catholic archdiocese's newspaper, *The Georgia Bulletin* (for which both Betty and Motes later worked), carried a photograph of Julie and Lisa cleaning headstones. The accompanying story began, "Julia and Lisa Roberts, parishioners at St. Thomas the Apostle in Smyrna, were among the members of the Alfred Hold Colquitt Jr. Chapter of the Children of the Confederacy who met at the Confederate Cemetery in Marietta to whitewash the tombstones of unknown Confederate soldiers as part of the youngsters' scheduled activities."

Several years later, the Moteses threw a "holiday tea." Julie and Lisa wore ribbons across their blouses proclaiming them "junior hostesses." Betty and Michael apparently had very high hopes for an A-list party; among the sixty-five people they invited were the incumbent Georgia governor, Jimmy Carter, and his wife, Rosalyn; the former Georgia governor George Busby; the future Georgia governor and the state's present-day senator Zell Miller; Jack Spaulding, the editor of *The Atlanta Journal*; and U. H. Howell, a rear admiral in the U.S. naval reserve. All of these invitees sent their regrets.

At the sixty-third Convention of the Georgia Division of Children of the Confederacy, held at the Pacemaker Inn in Kennesaw, Georgia, Julie and Lisa were listed in the program as "special pages to convention chairmen, Children of the Confederacy and United Daughters of the Confederacy."

Many African-Americans and others are offended by commemorations of the Confederacy, since the War Between the States was fought partly over the issue of slavery. Considering Julia's strong attacks as an adult against bigotry and racial prejudice, it's little wonder that she has never mentioned this chapter of her upbringing.

Like his father, Eric in 1974 seemed happier than he'd ever been. The pressures of Walter's perfectionist approach to the workshop and its stage productions no longer weighed on him. Walter seemed to have transferred his theatrical ambitions to his son. He had told Greg Patin that although Eric was a good actor, "he'll never make it because he's too much of a clown." Still, in the summer of 1973 he was prepared to put every resource he had behind his seventeen-year-old son's dream of attending England's Royal Academy of Dramatic Art, the most prestigious acting school in the world. "It seems poignant to me," workshop member Philip DePoy told Fred Schruers. "Rob just said, 'Theater is incredibly hard. . . . My son wants to act, so I'm gonna stay in a dinky little apartment and not spend any money, 'cause I'm gonna send Eric to the Royal Academy.' It was kind of vicarious: 'I couldn't do the big dream, but Eric can.' "

"Eric may have borne the brunt of Walter's anger," Evan Lee said, "but there's no doubt in my mind that he taught Eric how to act, and he was a great facilitator of Eric's success. The parents paid the dues for the kids, and the kids benefited from it. Professionally, at least. Personally, I don't know."

What began as a summer-school stint in London turned into a two-year course of study for Eric. With his son thousands of miles away, Walter missed his daughters all the more, and in June 1974, on the assumption that his marriage to Eileen might buttress his case, he asked the court for increased visitation rights. "Walter and his father and mother did not like the fact that Betty had the girls," Gloria Jones said. "None of the Roberts side of the family ever saw them after that. All we knew was things people would tell us. His parents were upset, because here they had these two beautiful granddaughters and never had a chance to see them."

The court's decision granted Walter just one fifteen-minute telephone conversation with the girls every Wednesday night. It restrained him from going anywhere near the Motes home, perhaps a result of Betty's allegation that he had planted the drugs in that hollowed-out Bible.

Walter took to sneaking visits with Lisa and Julie, sometimes with his mother in tow. Somehow, Betty never caught wind of this. "It tore him up," Eileen's aunt Vivien said. "It tormented him that he didn't get to see the little girls. And that upset Eileen. I remember her saying, 'It's just not fair. He's a good father. He needs them, and they need him.' "

Betty apparently tried to limit Walter's contact with his daughters as much as possible. "For instance," Eric said, "Betty once intercepted a gold bracelet that Walter had sent Julie for Christmas. She then told Julie that her father had forgotten to send a gift. There were many episodes like that over the years. At a formative age, Julia felt unloved by our natural father. She also thought that if she was a different kind of girl, he would want her. She would have changed anything about herself if she thought it would make Dad want her."

Both Walter and Eric anticipated the summer and Christmas visits the court allowed with Julie and Lisa. In July 1974, Walter took his three children to Washington, D.C., where Julie was most impressed with the

Lincoln Memorial. "Washington had a profound effect in me," she recalled to Kevin Sessums in *Vanity Fair.* "I had an enormous crush on President Lincoln. I can actually remember my father explaining to me about the Lincoln Memorial and that he was buried there and how they had dug him up to check to see that he was still there before they put him in the ground with the cement and the whole thing. I asked why they had looked to see if he was in there, and he said to see if someone had taken him. And I said, 'What kind of kooky freak would do that?' It was my father who first explained to me how *people were strange.*"

Like Atlanta twenty years earlier, Smyrna was a city in transition—as was, indeed, most of the South in the early 1970s. There were still large pockets of racial hatred, ignorance, and misplaced machismo throughout the region, especially in rural areas, but acceptance of racial and sexual differences was increasing. The 1980s were a boom period for Smyrna: New housing, new businesses, the Galleria and the Cumberland Mall all served to give the area a multicultural quality closer to that of Atlanta. Although *National Geographic* had referred to Smyrna in 1968 as "a redneck city," enlightened Smyrneans preferred to be characterized by the blazing spring yellow of their abundant hillside jonquils. What was unquestionably red about Smyrna was the area's clay soil. "Whenever it rained," Julia recalled, "all the kids would traipse through the red mucky clay and track it into their houses. Our mothers *hated* it!"

The rare time Julie spent with her father appears to have been the most serene and happy of her young life: vacations, holidays, excursions, and undemanding love from a man who adored her and a stepmother she liked. "We would paint with watercolors," Julia remembered, "and he would draw these great pictures. He drew this one picture of the cast of *The Wizard of Oz*—there is the Scarecrow, the Tin Man, Dorothy, the Lion . . . and Frosty the Snowman! At the bottom he wrote, 'We are going to the Land of Oz, Frosty, would you like to come along?' Hello? *Frosty?* Everything [he did] had its own bend on it."

For six months hiatus the 1975 holidays, Walter—with help from Eric, when he was on hiatus from the Royal Academy—assembled a large elaborate dollhouse as a surprise for Lisa and Julie. When Walter couldn't see his daughters, he wrote them letters. Julia lost most of them over the years and spoke later of having just one left, written on July 6, 1977. "If anyone ever took that away from me, I would just be destroyed. It doesn't mean anything to anybody else, but I can read that letter ten times a day, and it moves me in a different way every time." In 1996 she said that she had found other letters from her father. "I think I have four now, and they are funny. I read his letters and reflect back on conversations that we had. . . . He was always interesting and interested in what you were saying."

Although Walter had cajoled and browbeaten Eric into being an actor, he did not do the same with Julie—most likely because his world no longer revolved around the performing arts. "The only thing my father ever directly said to me about acting," Julia said, "was 'Don't ever say anything unless it means something, unless you're telling people something they don't already know. There's no reason to speak unless you're doing that.'"

Walter dreamed of a day when all three of the Roberts children would be reunited full-time with their father. "Eric and Walter spent hours talking about when the girls were old enough to choose, maybe they'd want to live with Walter," recalled Vivien McKinley. "Eileen told me that Eric used to say, 'When I'm famous, I'm going to buy a big home in Hollywood, and we can all live out there.' They were the dreams of a kid, of course. But it really saddens me to think about how much Walter put into those dreams with Eric."

For Eric, many of those reveries were beginning to come true. After two years at the Royal Academy, he moved to New York City and, while living at the YMCA, studied at the American Academy of Dramatic Arts, which had trained actors like Spencer Tracy, Grace Kelly, and Robert Redford.

Although Eric had immersed himself in the theatrical world and loved it, his childhood traumas led him to bouts of depression. "I submerged myself in an environment that was black, that was homosexual, that was runaway, that was unhappy," he told *The Advocate* in 1996, "people looking for something they couldn't find."

While he studied at AADA, he took odd jobs. "It was an adventure. It was also very depressing at times. But it didn't matter. I could be a delivery boy and not feel bad about it. My first regular job was at a bookstore. I loved it . . . [but] I got caught stealing books, so I was fired."

After a year of study in New York, Eric won a few roles in off-Broadway productions, and in 1977 he joined the cast of the daytime television drama *Another World,* playing the part of Ted Bancroft, a character who was one of the staples of soap operas—a well-built hunk.

At twenty, Eric was most often described as "beautiful" and "intense." His track running and other athletics in high school had given him a lean but muscular physique, which the directors of *Another World* were eager for him to reveal at every opportunity. His character, a spoiled rich kid, had a drug problem.

Julia has said that watching Eric on television made him "hugely famous to me, I used to have this big fantasy that Farrah Fawcett would be his girlfriend and they would come to my school to pick me up, and that all my friends would see Farrah Fawcett and my brother and me with my schoolbooks."

Walter was thrilled that his son had regular work as an actor. On the day Eric made his TV debut, he tuned every set on display in Rich's appliance department to the soap opera and told everyone within earshot, "That's my boy."

In August 1977, Walter used his two-week visitation period with Lisa and Julie to take them to New York City. The girls loved seeing Eric, who served as tour guide to the city's attractions. He was on hiatus from *Another World,* so they couldn't watch him filming, but he did take them to see the set. Lisa, who already had dreams of being an actress, was enthralled—and so was Julie, not yet ten, who until then had aspirations to be a veterinarian. It was her trip to New York, she said, that first stirred in her fantasies about becoming Grace Kelly or Audrey Hepburn.

Despondent about having to return the girls to Betty, Walter at least could look forward to a weekend he and Eileen had planned with Eric for the third week of September at the scenic Lake Lanier resort, about fifty miles north of Atlanta.

On Friday, September 16, Walter and Eric strapped a canoe to the top of Eileen's green Ford Maverick and headed up to the lake, where Walter had rented a houseboat in the Six Mile Creek area. The next morning at about nine-thirty, Eileen and Eric decided to take the canoe out. Although Eileen couldn't swim and had promised her aunt Vivien that she would wear a life jacket, she didn't, because of the heat. As Eric paddled away from the houseboat, according to Glenda Beard, Walter began taking pictures. Eileen smiled and waved to the camera. No one took much notice of a passing speedboat, but within seconds a series of strong waves rocked the canoe.

Eileen jumped up in panic and fell overboard. She screamed for help and thrashed violently in the water. Eric called for his father, and both men dived into the lake. They made repeated attempts to save her, but, a distraught Eric told police, "She just slipped away."

By early October, Walter had fallen into a depression and was not feeling well; a cough he'd had for several months had worsened, and swallowing was difficult. His doctors at first thought the symptoms might be a psychosomatic reaction to Eileen's death and sent him to a psychiatrist, who determined that the problems were indeed physical. Walter was admitted to Emory University hospital for tests in mid-November.

He never came out. The tests revealed that Walter, not yet forty-four and a nonsmoker, had throat cancer. "Walter was so depressed over Eileen's death," his cousin Dorothy Whitmire said, "and he got sick very shortly thereafter. I think there definitely was a connection."

Eric, who had been fired from *Another World* after disagreements with the producers, was involved in a series of auditions in New York for the title role in the feature film *King of the Gypsies.* His father called him to say, "I have terminal cancer, and they tell me I have ninety days to live." Eric flew to be with him the next day. Walter told him to go back, to make sure he didn't lose the rare opportunity for a starring role in his first movie. Eric did so, won the part, and returned to his father's bedside. "I just watched him dry up and blow away," he said.

Although Walter's relatives, friends, and colleagues provided a steady stream of visitors, his daughters were not among them. Betty would not allow Lisa and Julie to see him—she didn't even tell them he was ill. "I was pretty annoyed about that," Julia said years later.

Walter's cousin Lucille Roberts recalled visiting him several days before his death. "He told me that he felt contented because Eric 'had a picture in the can.' I didn't know what he meant." (The expression means that a film has completed production, but what Walter apparently meant was that Eric had won the role in *King of the Gypsies.* He had returned to New York to begin preparations.)

On Thursday, December 1, the hospital notified Eric that Walter's death was imminent. He flew out of New York that night, and a high school friend, George Pefanis, picked him up at the airport. Two days later, Walter succumbed to the illness. "I was with Eric the night that Walter passed away," Pefanis recalled. "Walter did not want Eric to see him die in such pain—and he knew when—so he said to me, 'Take Eric out and get him drunk.'"

Julia recalled being taken to the home of her grandparents Tom and Beatrice, and it was there that she was told her father was dead. "Not a good day," she said. She remembered feeling confused and said, "I don't understand why this has happened, and no one seems to be able to explain it to my satisfaction. How can your life be different in one afternoon? One minute you're with your mom, hanging out, the next minute you put on a nice pair of pants, you go to your grandparents', and your entire life is different."

Eric took over the arrangements for his father's funeral. "He was very matter-of-fact," Dorothy Whitmire said. "He didn't show much emotion, but I know he was feeling it." Dorothy was taken aback when she saw Walter in his coffin at the H. M. Patterson & Son funeral home in Spring Hill on December 7. "He was laid out in an off-white turtleneck shirt. I had never seen a deceased person who wasn't formally attired." Apparently Eric either sensed or was told by Walter that he would prefer to appear in death as he had most often in life—dressed casually in a turtleneck. "He wanted to be cremated," Eric said years later, "and I still have his ashes in my safe."

Betty did not attend the funeral, but she did allow Lisa and Julie to go. Eric hired a limousine to take him to the service, which included friends who told anecdotes about Walter and a tape that played his favorite piece of music, the love theme from Franco Zeffirelli's film *Romeo and Juliet*. Glenda Beard recalled that many of Eric's relatives found his use of the limousine pretentious. "It seemed he wanted to impress the family, to show them that he had succeeded."

"When he died," Eric said, "I lost my everything, because he was everything to me."

CHAPTER SIX

Walter had not written a will prior to his illness, likely because he thought he had very little to leave his heirs. As it turned out, he stood to inherit over $100,000 from Eileen's estate, primarily from an inheritance she had received from her mother, who died eighteen months before Eileen. That bequest included a one-quarter interest Eileen held in a downtown Atlanta office building that was about to be sold to the Georgia Department of Transportation. Thus, just days before he died, Walter signed a will, witnessed by two nurses in his hospital room, that left all his money and personal effects to his three children and named Eric as executor of the estate.

Three weeks after Walter's funeral, Eric asked the court to probate the will and name him guardian of Lisa and Julie. Betty filed an objection. She asked that Walter's will be overturned and that she be named trustee and guardian of Walter's property. Barring that, she asked that a bank be appointed to the position. Finally she asked that, if the court decided in Eric's favor, he be required to post bond amounting to twice the value of the estate. "Eric Anthony Roberts is not a fit and proper person to serve as guardian and trustee," Betty claimed in her challenge, then added, "He is a New York City actor with no regular income and caveators [Lisa and Julie] fear the waste of their inheritance."

Complicated by a lawsuit filed by one of the other holders of interest in the office building, Walter's and Eileen's estates were not settled until December 12, 1979, when the Georgia Supreme Court ruled in favor of a lower court's decision that Eric, Lisa, and Julie were the rightful heirs of Eileen and Walter Roberts. After Betty and Eric compromised on the guardianship issue by agreeing that a Cobb County attorney, C. R. Vaughn, would oversee the girls' trusts, Eric, Lisa, and Julie each received a payment of approximately $28,000 after costs and attorneys' fees. Eric was given the money outright, since he was over eighteen;

Lisa's and Julie's shares were put into trust funds until they reached legal maturity.

"My childhood was real weird to me," Julia has said. "I feel like I grew up twice. Once till I was about ten. After that it was completely different. My father died around then, which probably changed me a lot more than I realized. It was a rough time."

"For many weeks after the funeral," a friend of the family reportedly said, "Julia walked around in a daze." She felt, she said, that a "boundless injustice" had been done to her, "and that's not a fun bag to carry. I think you are forever changed" by losing a parent at a young age. "I did feel a whole confusion, which was just really being pissed off."

Now her father could no longer provide periods of respite, however brief, from the home life with her stepfather that Eric has called "abusive." Friends of the family say that Julie "feared and despised" Michael Motes, and that he, at least, alternately ignored, pushed around, and denigrated his two stepdaughters. Not surprisingly, Julie blamed her mother for the situation. "I didn't always love my mom as much as I do now," she said years later. "And I don't think she loved me as much, either. I admit there was a time when I wasn't exactly a joy to be around."

Some of the financial pressures had been relieved when Motes received an inheritance upon the death of his father on September 6, 1977. He and Betty purchased a three-bedroom ranch-style home on a heavily wooded one-acre plot on Maner Road in a secluded area on the outskirts of Smyrna. Julie had her own bedroom, and the house was big enough for her and Lisa to avoid their stepfather much more than in the cramped Privette Road house. This provided a degree of protection from family turmoil—and so did the veneer that Julie had begun to wrap around her psyche to deal with the pain of her situation.

Betty now worked at *The Georgia Bulletin.* On September 21, 1978, the publication ran a biographical sketch of Betty that did not mention her son, Eric, or that she had ever been married to Walter Roberts. It also didn't name her current husband. "With a husband, three children, a full-time job, and a semi-invalid mother to care for, Betty hasn't had much time for theater in the last few years. . . . These days, all of Betty's spare time goes to work with children and the several historical groups to which she belongs. Last year she served as President of the PTA at Fitzhugh Lee Elementary School, where middle daughter Julie was a student. . . . From secretary to Father Noel Burtenshaw at the *Bulletin* office, to 'Mommy' to Lisa, Julie and Nancy at home, this member of Sacred Heart parish—this week's Catholic—certainly stays on the go!"

Theresa Gernazian, who worked with Betty at the *Bulletin*, recalled that after Michael Motes "stopped working for the paper, it was hard for him to get a job, so that was one cause of some of the problems Betty had with him later."

The ten-year-old who would go on to become America's Pretty Woman considered herself an ugly duckling at Griffin Middle School in Smyrna. She wore thick eyeglasses and had braces to correct a gap between her front teeth, as she put it, wide enough "you could shove a Popsicle stick between them." (The braces, put on by orthodontist Dr. Ted Aspes when Julie was eight, also helped correct protruding upper teeth caused by her thumb-sucking. While Eric called Julie "Hoolie," his friend George Pefanis called her "Bucktooth Hoolie.") Classmates mocked her large mouth. "I had an unusual mouth," she has said, "unlike the girls who had perfect mouths with little heart-top lips." Taller than many of the boys, she usually felt awkward and ungainly. She wasn't particularly popular, and she recalled an ugly incident in sixth grade when "the kids called me names and painted names on my locker because I entered a dance contest with a black classmate."

Children who were in Julie's pod (a grouping of students within a class) recalled her, in the words of one classmate, as "shy, modest, and down-to-earth. She was a good kid—she never got into trouble." Indeed: Julia belonged to the Girl Scouts of America and later proudly told a costar that she had "won every merit badge."

Up till the New York trip, Julie's ambition had been to be a veterinarian. "I thought I was Dr. Dolittle," she has said. "I was convinced I could talk to the animals. But then I went to school and discovered science, which I hated, so that went out the window."

By the spring of 1978, her vision of a future as an actress, which she has said "was just kind of there in my mind all the time," started to coalesce. Eric's film, *King of the Gypsies,* was about to open, and Paramount Pictures was giving him a multimillion-dollar publicity buildup as a sex symbol. A photograph of his handsome face and bare-chested well-muscled torso glared out from the movie's posters and advertisements, and the buzz in Hollywood was that Eric Roberts was the heir to the young-rebel throne held before him by Montgomery Clift, James Dean, and Marlon Brando.

When the film premiered in Atlanta, Eric offered to have limousines pick up his grandparents and sisters. "Uncle Tom and Aunt Beatrice weren't keen on going, but they did," Glenda Beard recalled. "Eric has been more showy, more pretentious, in some of his actions than the family would have liked."

Eric, though, had a right to be proud: His film debut remains one of the splashiest in Hollywood history. The film's story revolves around and is narrated by his character, a young man born into New York City's Gypsy subculture. Played by a younger actor at first, Eric's character makes his first appearance about forty-five minutes into the story, when he is about eighteen. Eric looks achingly beautiful—and very much like his father—with sad, moist dark blue eyes that could tug at the hardest heartstrings. One of his first lines must have had particular resonance for him, and for his sisters: "Who gets to pick where they're born—or pick their mother or father? Nobody even gets to say anything about it. But all your life you live with it—or fight against it."

Watching her brother on-screen, and all the excitement that the premiere created within her family (Tom and Beatrice's resistance notwithstanding), made a tremendous impression on Julie. *If he can do it,* she thought, *why can't I?* At the beginning of the following school term, when she was asked by one of her teachers about her career goals, she replied, "I want to be in movies, just like my brother." She began to participate in the school's drama club plays, and her classmates saw a marked change in her. "She was an average student who blended into the crowd," a classmate recalled, "except when she was participating in the drama productions in the auditorium. Then she beamed. She was like a different person when she was in the spotlight."

A few years later, Julie experimented with makeup for the first time. "I snuck into my mom's bathroom before school," she told Billy Crystal in *Harper's Bazaar.* "My mom has really beautiful eyes, and she would wear this liquid eyeliner, kind of like Audrey Hepburn, for a party or something. I took it and I put it here [pointing to the rim of her lower eyelid], and then I closed my eyes. My eyeballs went black—I thought I was going blind. Not that I didn't wear makeup anymore. It's the twelve-year-old girl in you wanting to be fabulous, stylish, graceful—all those things that [movie stars] are. Like Grace Kelly—you want your hair, once in life, to look that soft and that shiny. But you know it never will, so you just kind of aspire to have that whispery, breathy voice. . . . I talk like Olive Oyl. I'm Shelley Duvall. After a double espresso."

Betty would later call her marriage to Michael Motes "the biggest mistake I ever made." Whether she knew about his molestation of the thirteen-year-old Shawn Melton is unknown, but by 1982 Betty had had it with Motes's surly attitude toward her and the girls, his sporadic employment record, and the flurry of lawsuits filed against him for unpaid bills. They separated in October of that year, and in her divorce action Betty accused him of "cruel treatment" and called the marriage "irretrievably broken." The divorce was granted a year later, in October 1983.

The court allowed Betty to continue living in the Maner Road house and granted her custody of seven-year-old Nancy. Motes won visitation rights every other weekend, with that provision that he not take Nancy to Narcotics Anonymous meetings. (One of the witnesses on Betty's behalf at the custody hearing was Bobby Spann, a member of the Marietta, Georgia, police narcotics squad.) Betty also won custody of the family's 1977 Ford Pinto, while Motes had to settle for their 1975 Plymouth. Motes was ordered to pay $75 per week for Nancy's child support. (In 1990, Betty sued Motes for $1,950 in unpaid child support.) No mention was made of Lisa or Julie in the court papers.

Among the household items Motes asked to keep were "2 government upright headstones, the UDC and DAR magazines which are the husband's, 1 set of salmon-colored bed sheets and pillowcases, and 1 family portrait of Ashley Spencer," a Motes ancestor.

When Michael Motes left the family home, it likely felt as though a giant weight had been lifted from Julie's shoulders, and it also vastly improved her relationship with her mother. "Things were bumpy in my early teens," she has admitted, "but when I reached about sixteen [the time of the Motes divorce], we came to some great meeting place and have been great friends since. She listens to all my dramas, big or small, and has a way that moms do to sum them all up in one sentence. It's great."

Motes's absence left the family more financially strapped than ever. With money so tight, Julie got her first job at thirteen. After classes, the school bus would drop her off in front of a pizza restaurant, where she cashiered and occasionally donned a bear suit to bring out the cake for a child's birthday party. "It was the plight of my youth. [My mother] was single, broke, and had three children. When I was a kid, I didn't get tons of presents at Christmas because my family couldn't afford it. But I got that one perfect thing that made me realize that not only was Mom putting money in the coffee can all year, but she had listened to everything I'd said. She had paid attention."

In 1982, Julie's seventy-seven-year-old grandfather Tom Roberts was living with his daughter, Shirley, and her family in Smyrna. Ernestine McElhaney, a local nurse, cared for the white-haired man one week while Shirley was out of town. "He was alert and dressed and shaved himself," Ernestine recalled. "He wasn't on any medication; he slept well and ate well. He loved biscuits and gravy and grits. His eyesight was good. He didn't even take a nap during the day."

Tom's mind, apparently, remained sharp as well. Gloria Jones recalled visiting him at Shirley's home not long before his death in 1983. "He had this huge portrait of Eric, Lisa, and Julie on the wall—it must have been forty by sixty inches. I said to him, 'That's a good-looking bunch you've got up there.'"

"They're as crazy as hell," Tom Roberts replied.

In September 1982, Julie enrolled in ninth grade at Campbell High School on Atlanta Road in Smyrna, a sprawling one-story brick complex in a residential area with huge pine trees to one side. She already knew through her sister—a junior there—that unlike Griffin Middle School, Campbell had no drama club.* That presented no problem for the budding actress: Julie would just have to display her thespian skills in the classroom rather than on a stage.

---

*It has one now, and offers the Julia Roberts Award to its best student actors.

CHAPTER SEVEN

Julie's tenth-grade English teacher, David Boyd, couldn't figure out what she was dressed for. She came into his class wearing a toga over her usual outfit of boys' Levi's and a button-down shirt. The toga wasn't hard for Boyd to understand, since that day she and another student were scheduled to read a scene from *Julius Caesar*. But over the toga Julie wore an old T-shirt. "I could not figure out for the life of me what *that* was for," Boyd recalled.

Boyd assigned all of his students a recitation from one of Shakespeare's plays. "These presentations were usually pretty good, but most of the students didn't really get into their parts, they would just do what they had to do. I gave them a couple of days to practice. They didn't have to memorize the lines; it wasn't an acting class, but when they read the lines, I expected them to try to get across the emotion of the words they were reading, to bring the play to life."

Julie and her classmate were assigned Act 4, Scene 3, in which Cassius (played by Julie) confronts Brutus, his coconspirator against Caesar, and accuses him of wronging Cassius in a number of ways, not least of which is a failure to honor him with affection. The two students read the passage with such emotion that Boyd recalled thinking, *Boy, they're really getting into it.* "And the class was getting into it, too," Boyd said. "You could have heard a pin drop."

Julie intoned the following monologue:

> Come, Antony, and young Octavius, come,
> Revenge yourselves alone on Cassius,
> For Cassius is aweary of the world;
> Hated by one he loves, braved by his brother,
> Checked like a bondman, all his faults observed,
> Set in a notebook, learned, and conned by rote,

To cast into my teeth. O, I could weep
My spirit from mine eyes! There is my dagger;
   [*He offers his unsheathed dagger*]
And here my naked breast; within, a heart
Dearer than Pluto's mine, richer in gold . . .

When Julie read the line, "And here my naked breast," she ripped open the front of her T-shirt. Boyd and his students were agog. "The class is like, 'Whoa, what is *this?*'" Boyd recalled. "We were just blown away by that. It was just excellent, and her group got an almost perfect score. I didn't think much about it afterwards, until she got into acting, and I thought, you know, there was something there, early on, that was a little bit special."

Paula Monteith, a classmate, recalled another unscripted instance of Julie's emotive abilities. "She was—I wouldn't say spastic, but a little hyper. She was rambunctious, she was enthusiastic, always laughing, having fun." Her big booming laugh—one fellow student likened it to a hyena's—frequently got her into hot water with the teachers.

"One day she got in trouble for talking," Paula recalled. "The teacher called her in front of the whole class and told her that she would have to stay after class and pick up all the staples that had fallen on the carpet. Well, Julie reacted very dramatically. She got down on her hands and knees and was banging her fists on the floor and crying, 'Oh, please, Miss Partridge, don't make me do that!' We all thought this was hilarious, and the more we laughed, the more it egged her on. Finally the teacher said, 'Oh, just go back to your chair and forget the whole thing!'"

David Boyd—known as Coach Boyd to his students, because he coached the boys' basketball team—recalled that Julie frequently had a trick up her sleeve whenever he got ready to give the class homework. "All of a sudden she would raise her hand and ask a question that had nothing to do with the subject we'd been on. I would be kind of charmed by her and would start talking about something else, and then the bell would ring and it would be too late to give the students the assignment. That was her way of getting the class out of the assignment. I wouldn't realize she had set me up until the bell rang."

Other teachers weren't as entranced by Julie. Her algebra teacher disliked her intensely, Julie felt, and she was flunking the class. She got up the nerve to confront the instructor. "I said, 'Look, let's just be honest, there's no way I'm going to pass this class,'" she recalled on *Inside the*

Actors Studio in 1998. " 'I don't think you'd miss me if I wasn't here, so if I vow to go to the library every day—I won't leave school or go home or anything—can I please not come to this class anymore?' "

Surprisingly, the teacher agreed, and during her first few periods in the library, Julie discovered Walt Whitman's volume of poetry *Leaves of Grass*. "I spent the rest of that whole quarter reading this book every day in the library." It remains one of her favorites, and she later recited a favorite line from the first poem in the anthology, entitled "To You": "Stranger, if I pass you and wish to speak with you, why should I not speak with you and why should you not speak to me?" She explained the reason the lines resonated with her: "I enjoy talking to people."

Another teacher Julie liked was Mrs. Gutterman. "She had me do an oral report on *The Canterbury Tales*, and I was drawn into it. Next [in class] was the film *Becket*, with Peter O'Toole. I was so captivated by it. It just grabbed me by the throat. . . . It was the first time I was aware of really good acting." (Apparently Eric's performances hadn't impressed her *that* much.) Once again, acting ambitions stirred within her. "I thought about being an actress," she recalled, "but not out loud."

Keith Gossett, Julie's junior-year American literature teacher, remembered her as "delightful, intriguing, very interested in what was going on around her. She had a really captivating personality and was an excellent student. She has said that she loved to read Thoreau and Whitman, but she also writes. I don't remember how well she wrote, but she was enthusiastic about writing."

She didn't share her compositions with anyone; they were reserved for her diary-cum-journal, which she titled "All the Makings of Insanity." She once said, half jokingly, that its contents ("moments in my life that have had an effect on me") "could crucify me . . . actually, it's mostly fucking hearts-and-flowers poetry."

"Most of us really thought she was going to be a writer," her classmate Joan Raley recalled. "She wrote wonderful poetry. I still have a poem she wrote for me about a boy I was going out with."

By the time she reached junior year, Julie was no longer a bespectacled, buck-toothed little girl. She now wore contact lenses, and her teeth had been beautifully fixed by Dr. Aspes's braces. She had a luxuriant mane of reddish-brown hair—worn shoulder-length, sometimes streaked with blond, and feathered—and the smile that would captivate millions of moviegoers in less than four years. Her height, which still made her ungainly at times, on other occasions gave her an air of elegance and the coltish quality observers would later note in her.

"There was a time when I just thought everything was fabulous," Julia has said. "I was one happening girl—at least I thought I was. But I must have been either way ahead of my time or behind my time, because no one really dug me for a long time." This left a residue of hurt inside her. The school's great beauty and most popular girl, Julia recalled, was the homecoming queen, Kelly Jones. "She was the end-all at our school. I spent many an hour struggling to emulate this woman. I wasn't a cheerleader, I wasn't a homecoming queen. I have no idea what became of Kelly Jones."

Kelly said that Julia "always said my hair was perfect, and she'd run her hands through it, saying, 'Oh, I feel much better now.' She was always joking." According to Paula Monteith, Julie "was popular with the boys, but she wasn't in the very central little inner group. A friend said to me that Julie always wanted to be in the 'in' group, but I never got that impression. She didn't strike me as someone who needed to be in that popular crowd to have validation."

Joe Thompson didn't do much to improve Julie's self-confidence in her looks and sex appeal. She carried a torch for the handsome, six-foot-five basketball star, and Coach Boyd noticed that she had started to come to practices and games. "She had a sort of crush on him," Boyd recalled. "He was an independent thinker, intelligent, but just a little different. He was sort of aloof." *Cold* might be the word Julia would use. Apparently, after one date, Joe told her he just wanted to be friends, but Julie wasn't able to turn off her feelings for him. "The more he rejected her," Boyd recalled, "the more of a challenge he became." One of Julie's best friends in high school, Holly Aguirre, said that Joe "gave her the brush-off big time. She is totally obsessed with men because she is so dependent on them. . . . She was given the brush-off by a lot of men."

Julia's later penchant for turning to a long series of men for validation might be blamed on her experience with Joe Thompson. Still, a number of boys, including her classmate Jeff Hardigree, were attracted to Julie. "I tried to seduce her a number of times and failed," Hardigree said. Another classmate, Keith Leeper, a senior at Campbell, had better luck after dating Julie for about six months. He told a reporter in 1990 that during a 1983 Christmas party at his home in Smyrna, he and Julie stole off to the family den. "We were alone and kissing," he said. "It wasn't anything we had planned. The timing was right. I took her by the hand and led her upstairs to my bedroom. We stayed there for about an hour before joining the party again. She didn't tell me until later that it was her first time."

Julie and Keith had met at a teen club in Atlanta six months earlier. "I was standing at the bar, and she came over to me and said I looked like Sting," Leeper recalled. "I asked her to dance, and we exchanged phone numbers." Julie was thrilled to have consummated the romance, Holly Aguirre recalled. "She called me five minutes later. She lost it with Keith on Christmas Day. She compared it to qualifying for the Olympics."

The sexual relationship continued, often in the back of Keith's pickup truck on the remote back roads around Smyrna. "We were always naked," he said. "I saw her differently after we had sex. I started to fall in love with her. I was physically attracted to her at first, but then we also became best friends."

Julie's affair with Keith Leeper didn't last, but her infatuation with Joe Thompson did. After she began her career, she traced his movements when he left Georgia to work as a private detective and then a real-estate agent in various cities before settling into a carpentry career in Vermont. She invited him to previews of her films; for one, she sent a limousine to pick him up, and when he arrived, she excitedly ran up to him with a big hug. But it was clear that even after she became a movie star, she couldn't win Joe over. She introduced him to friends as "the guy who dumped me in high school."

Thompson prefers to think of himself as a link to the real world for Julia Roberts, rather than as an unrequited love. "I suppose Julie calls me when she may feel the people around her have ulterior motives. I suppose I'm a soul friend, someone in the real world she can count on. She knows she will get the truth from me." One of those truths, which may have pained Julia to hear, was that Joe Thompson considers her choice of career "a silly way to lead your life."

In most of the ways that matter, Julie Roberts was a typical southern American teenager. Except for her parents' localized fame as theatrical pioneers and her brother's success in New York and Hollywood, there was little reason to expect that she would not go on, as she has said she was expected to do, to a college career, then marriage, motherhood, and a settled life in or around Smyrna. "In high school," Julia recalled, "I was like everybody else. I had my girlfriends, I did sports. I wasn't really great at anything, just middle-of-the-road, a basic kid. I enjoyed school, but somehow I never really fit." Still, Julia has also said that her "fondest memories are of high school, when I'd hang around with my best friend, Paige Amsler. We'd have tuna fish sandwiches and Diet Coke, watch soap operas [*Days of Our Lives* was their favorite], and talk about what we wanted to do with our lives when school was over." They would also listen to records. Elvis Costello was Julie's favorite; she liked Styx, ABBA, Billy Idol, Rick Springfield, and the Rolling Stones as well. She remembered going home to visit her mother one Easter years later, dragging out her old records, and being amazed that "I still knew *every* word to *every* song."

Although she was nowhere near a star athlete, Julie played tennis for three of the four years she attended Campbell. "She wouldn't give up [on tennis] when they said her left eye wasn't good enough," her mother recalled. "She has too much determination."

Life in Smyrna for teenagers largely revolved around the Galleria Mall. "It was our hangout," Paula Monteith recalled. "It was a specialty mall, so it wasn't someplace where kids would spend money. But it had a theater and an arcade and a food-court area. Julie worked there. The kids would stand around the mall, to be seen—the girls would hope the boys would see them." During her teens, Julie worked in the mall's movie theater, a snack shop, and an ice-cream store.

Julie did stand out from her classmates in one major way, thanks to her brother. Beginning in 1981, when Julie was thirteen, Betty allowed her to visit Eric in New York during her school vacations. Most of her classmates would go to Fort Lauderdale for spring break, Julia recalled, and come back with a deep suntan. "I'd come back pale, having been in New York, where it was freezing. So I was always a little different from everybody else. It was also funny because I would come back from New York and I would have met somebody, and nobody would believe me. I felt kinda stupid talking about it, because they're all talking about these great parties, talking about people we all knew, and I would sit there and say, 'Well, Robin Williams said to me that, uh . . . '"

As Christmas break of her senior year approached, Julie was aflutter with the news that Eric was going to fly her down to Australia to be with him while he filmed the movie *The Coca-Cola Kid*. "She was so excited and couldn't wait," Paula Monteith recalled. "Eric paid her way because they hadn't seen each other in a long time. When she came back, all she could talk about was her trip. She had pictures of herself with Eric. But her greatest prize was that she had met Billy Idol on the plane down there, and she was ecstatic about that. They were both in the first-class section, and she got his autograph. Billy Idol was very popular when we were in high school. I wonder if he remembers meeting her."

When Julie got home, a surprise awaited her: a brand-new Volkswagen Bug. It was a gift from Eric.

CHAPTER EIGHT

Since his flashy screen debut in *King of the Gypsies*, Eric Roberts's life and career had become a roller coaster, the lows as much a result of his personal demons as the highs were a result of his enormous talent. His impact in *Gypsies* was so strong that despite its failure at the box office, the producer Dino De Laurentiis offered him a three-picture deal, and Paramount Pictures dangled a $900,000 contract in front of him with a promise of a role in *The Godfather, Part III*.

Eric turned down both offers; the first because, as he recalled it, the movies De Laurentiis proposed he star in "were something like *Bora Bora: The Shark Boy*," and the second because Paramount balked at granting him the artistic control he sought. And so, instead of "going Hollywood," Eric made a series of small but classy films that showcased him as an actor: PBS-TV versions of Willa Cather's *Paul's Case* and Nathanael West's *Miss Lonelyhearts;* and a relatively small but moving role as Sissy Spacek's tender sailor lover in the feature film *Raggedy Man*. He also won an off-Broadway role as a questioning Roman Catholic seminarian in *Mass Appeal*. It promised him a Broadway debut with its planned move uptown in the fall of 1981.

All this time Eric battled depression and drugs, mostly cocaine and marijuana. At twenty-one he began an affair with the actress Sandy Dennis, twenty years his senior, who had won a Best Supporting Actress Oscar for *Who's Afraid of Virginia Woolf?* in 1967 and was also well known for her roles in *Up the Down Staircase* and *The Out-of-Towners*. Sandy had seen Eric on television in *Paul's Case*, was attracted to him, and called their mutual manager, Bill Treusch, to invite Eric to her house to "talk about acting." Recalling the meeting, Eric spoke with mock horror: "I *hate* to talk about acting, about choices, all that kind of stuff!"

But, as Dennis had no doubt hoped, the subject soon changed, and

Eric found himself equally attracted to the kind and gentle blonde, who provided him the mothering he felt he never got from Betty. He bought a house near hers in Connecticut and spent a good deal of his time at her home, along with her dozens of cats (as many as sixty at one point).

"We're attracted to each other because we're opposites," he said. "She's very social and pulls me into being with people. And I like aloneness and pull her into a room for five days and close the door and close the windows."

In 1996 Eric told *The Advocate* that he had never had any interest in gay sex, and that he had lost his virginity at a "very young" age with two women. "And it's the last threesome I ever had . . . and here is where I expose myself as being a really redneck square: I look back to that encounter . . . and it didn't occur to me to see the two women together. It occurred to me, *How can I keep them both busy at the same time?*"

Eric said that Sandy Dennis was honest with him about her prior lesbian affairs. "She'd tell me everything. At twenty-one it was risqué for me to hear these stories: 'Wow! Really!' Sandy appreciated the beauty of women. But Sandy also liked and appreciated what a very, very young man could do to a woman. I suppose."

On the evening of June 4, 1981, Eric drove his Jeep away from Sandy's house with her German shepherd beside him. As he rounded a corner, the dog began sliding across the upholstery toward the doorless passenger side. Eric took his eyes off the road to reach for the animal and woke up in a hospital three days later. "When I came to, there was a very large black nurse next to the bed. I said, 'What happened?' And she said, 'Honey, you tried to climb a tree in a CJ5.'"

He learned that the first emergency workers on the scene had laid him on the ground, thinking him beyond help until he moaned, then they rushed him to the hospital. He had suffered brain trauma, broken facial bones, a broken nose, collarbone, and hand, and two broken ankles. Julie and Lisa came up to visit him in the hospital, but he did not want to see Betty.

"When I limped out of the hospital a month after the accident," Eric said, "I was basically a cripple with an impaired memory. Without my memory, I thought I might never be able to act again. It was devastating to me, and I did contemplate ending my life. Fortunately, I was able to heal and get on my feet again."

Through extensive physical and occupational therapy, and sheer willpower, Eric had recovered enough by autumn to begin tryouts in

Boston for the Broadway-bound *Mass Appeal*. His looks had changed; like Montgomery Clift after his auto accident, Eric was still handsome but not perfectly so: His broken nose would always be apparent, as well as scars above his left eye and on his forehead.

Eric never got to Broadway with *Mass Appeal*. He quit the show in Boston after a disagreement with the director, Geraldine Fitzgerald, over his interpretation of his role. Rather than cite artistic differences, the producers, Eric said, blamed his departure on the accident, saying he was not recovered enough to undertake the rigors of the play.

This proved a blow to his career. "The phone calls stopped overnight," he said. The acclaimed director Bob Fosse proved Eric's salvation in 1982 when he chose him over Richard Gere to play the lead in *Star 80*, the story of Paul Snider's relationship with and murder of his wife, the *Playboy* model and would-be actress Dorothy Stratten. Eric played Snider—a sleazy hustler and one of the most unsympathetic major characters in movie history—with squirm-inducing realism. His portrayal was so on the mark that for years afterward it colored the opinions of many about Eric himself: He never could have played Paul Snider so convincingly, the reasoning went, if he wasn't very much like the man.

Star 80 was Eric's fifth movie. "I didn't learn till about my sixth movie how to leave characters behind," he said. "Sometimes they'd linger for months after. I was a pain in everybody's ass, including my own." Sandy Dennis, to whom Eric was now engaged, came out to California to be with him during filming; it was then that he told her he couldn't go through with their marriage plans. When he began an affair with the actress Ellen Barkin, Sandy ended their relationship. Eric asked her to give the engagement ring back, and she threw her jewelry box on the floor in front of him. He fished through the scattered baubles, recovered the ring, and left.

"I never went back there," he said. "To show you the kind of pain that I was in without even knowing it, I had that ring on another girl's hand in two months." Eric never married (or identified) the girl he gave the ring to; Sandy Dennis died of ovarian cancer in 1992 at the age of fifty-five. Eric continued to give acclaimed performances of unsympathetic characters in *The Pope of Greenwich Village* and *Runaway Train* (for which he received an Oscar nomination as the Best Supporting Actor of 1985). But his drug use and neuroses would keep him from the superstardom his talent seemed destined to win him, and before long his problems resulted in both his arrest and his estrangement from everyone in his family, including Julia.

When she left Smyrna in June 1985 to pursue her acting dreams in New York, Julia has said, being Eric Roberts's sister proved a mixed blessing. His show business contacts unquestionably eased her way into the movie business. But she found that "for as many people I met that love Eric Roberts, I met just as many that think he's a jerk. It doesn't help, it doesn't hurt."

Julie's senior year at Campbell High School was a busy one. In addition to her matches with the girls' tennis team and duties on the student council, she was elected class treasurer for the second year in a row. In her campaign, she described herself as "a person who can communicate ideas from students to the administration."

She also came to the forefront in the senior history class's annual mock political convention, designed to give students a fuller understanding of America's political process. "A certain few of us were the candidates who ran for president," Julia recalled. She took on the role of Elizabeth Dole, who was President Ronald Reagan's secretary of transportation and the wife of Senator Bob Dole of Kansas. While Elizabeth Dole would run for president in 2000, in 1985 most saw her husband as the most likely future candidate. (He did win the Republican nomination in 1996.) "This was how crazy my high school was," Julia said with a laugh. "When all was said and done, my friend Kevin Hester, who was [vice president] George Bush, was elected as president, and I, as Elizabeth Dole, was vice president." When Kevin Sessums of *Vanity Fair* asked her what the key to playing Elizabeth Dole proved to be, Julia replied, "Well, wearing a dress was key. Wearing [the proper] shoes was also key. That really impresses a group."

By the time Julie was a senior, she had gained enough confidence in herself to enter Campbell High's Miss Panthera contest. (The mascot for Campbell's football team, the Panthers, was a black panther, and the yearbook was called *The Panthera*.) One of several dozen entrants, Julie modeled casual and formal wear and gave a short speech about her activities and her reasons for wanting to be chosen. The pageant was judged by local radio and television personalities and former Miss Pantheras, and sometimes local housewives. The winner of the 1985 contest was Julie Sams, but Julie Roberts was one of the twelve finalists. A yearbook photograph of her accepting the honor at the Cobb County Civic Center shows a lovely young woman in a flouncy taffeta gown who looks a tad bewildered by the whole affair. "Oh my God!" she reportedly cried when she heard that she was a finalist. "I can't believe they picked me!"

In May 1985, Julie attended her senior prom with Bill Knight, a beefy, good-looking junior at Atlanta's Lovett School. She and Knight had met the previous summer while working at the ice-cream parlor and had dated for about four months. "It was an infatuation," Knight recalled, "and lasted as long as infatuations last. . . . It didn't get real serious. Mostly we went out to eat and to the movies." They remained friends after they stopped dating, and Julie asked him to escort her to her big night.

Knight arrived at the Maner Road house in his Oldsmobile, wearing a white dinner jacket and carrying a pink corsage. Julie wore a simple black taffeta dress with a sweetheart neckline. "She looked charming," Knight said. "She had her hair all done up nicely." The evening ended relatively early because Knight had to take a college entrance examination the next day; he kissed Julia good night around eleven P.M. "It's turned out to be a little amusing," Knight has said of his prom date's international movie success. "You don't think of your friends being in the movies."

Julie Roberts, of course, had a *brother* in the movies. "I remember her saying the last week of school that she was going to New York City the week after classes ended," Paula Monteith said. "She said she was going to be an actress—not a Broadway actress but a movie actress. I think she thought she could use her brother's influence to help her. Eric and her sister, Lisa, were both in New York, and she could use their support system."*

Julia said, "[I had] a restlessness without focus, an urgency, an anxiety, like something's going to break. I still feel that sometimes, but for different reasons than I did when I was seventeen and wanted to leave Georgia." She later professed a lack of confidence that her dreams of movie stardom would come true. "I figured I would give this a go, [but] I knew I'd end up back at my mother's house in Smyrna and become a dental hygienist."

Luckily for her fans the world over, things worked out a little better than that. "If I did nothing else for my sister," Eric has said, "I got her out of Smyrna."

---

*Lisa had moved to New York two years earlier to establish an acting career of her own.

Part Two

FITS AND STARTS

"[Julia] flirted with everybody. She would have one boyfriend who was a grip, and then she'd have another boyfriend and they'd disappear for the whole night."

—Lexi Masterson, a costar of Julia's
in *Blood Red*

CHAPTER NINE

"Where are you *from*, girl?"

Julie had grown weary of the reaction. At auditions in New York, the minute she answered the question "Hi. How are you?" with "Hah! Ahm fahn. How're *yew*?," her molasses-thick Southern accent raised eyebrows. Mary Sames, a talent agent Julie met with shortly after arriving in Manhattan, recalled to Aileen Joyce that "she had the thickest southern accent I've ever heard—and I'm from Texas myself!"

Apart from the accent, Sames was impressed with the teenager who sat across the desk from her, "with her legs crossed, her arms folded. . . . [S]he seemed so innocent, so completely without guile, and yet at the same time so guarded, so wary, that I was fascinated by what I perceived to be a unique personality. I mean, here was this free spirit, this breathtakingly beautiful young girl, who was nevertheless shy and awkward and gave off vibes of a fragile, wounded bird."

While intrigued, Sames felt Julie needed more personal attention than the agent was able to give at the time. "I realized instantly that this demure, shy, waiflike girl sitting across from me needed somebody special and kindhearted to take care of her, that she was going to need twenty-four-hour-a-day nurturing, and frankly, I didn't have it in me at the time." Sames suggested that Julie see Bob McGowan, an up-and-coming personal manager who specialized in developing young performers. Sames called McGowan, who replied, "Great, have her call me."

Early in June 1985, Julie had packed clothes, toiletries, and some of her favorite books and records into her VW, kissed her mother and half sister, Nancy, good-bye and driven away down Maner Road. She picked up Route 75 near the Cumberland Mall and took first Route 85 and then Route 95 north seven hundred miles to the New Jersey Turnpike, driving for nearly fourteen straight hours before she arrived at Eric's opulent apartment on West Seventy-third Street, close to Central Park. She stayed with her brother a few days, then moved into Lisa's apartment at 306 West Eighteenth Street in the Chelsea neighborhood, not far from Greenwich Village.

Julie preferred to live with her sister, with whom she was much closer. "Lisa really cushioned a lot of things for me," she later said. "I always considered her fearless. When we were kids, I always thought she would protect me if I was scared. And at seventeen, in New York, it was the same thing."

After she settled in, Julie wasted little time finding work, even though she was due to receive the bulk of her inheritance from Eileen—$28,000—when she turned eighteen in October. "I had a couple of different jobs," she recalled. "I worked at this Italian-ice place down in the Village, and it was horrible, because I can't make egg creams, and that was all anybody ever wanted. Egg creams! Eggs and cream. Even the thought of those two words together makes me want to vomit. Seltzer water and chocolate? It's like, *Ugh. I can't even believe I have to do this!*"

The job Julie kept the longest was at the Athlete's Foot on Seventy-second Street and Broadway. "That was a fun job . . . We were right next to Popeye's Chicken—and I gotta tell you, doing inventory in the basement, side by side with Popeye's Chicken . . . it was purgatory, that's what it was."

Lisa, nineteen and pretty, though in a different way than Julie, studied acting at the Neighborhood Playhouse in Greenwich Village. She suggested that Julie try modeling as a way into acting. Absent much enthusiasm, Julie went along with the suggestion, using $850 her mother sent from her trust fund to have a modeling book of photographs taken. Above "Julie Roberts," the photo she sent out to agencies showed a pretty girl in a high-collared white shirt, grinning widely, her hair upswept on the left side and cascading over her forehead and shoulders on the right.

The photograph—and her contemporary style and youthful zest— won her a slot with the mega-modeling agency Click. Frances Grill of the agency recalled that Julie's height and weight "were fine for a model, and she has an incredibly photogenic face." But Julie didn't stay in the field very long. "I don't think she really gave it her best shot," Grill said. "Her focus was to become an actress."

Horrible is the word Julia has used to describe her modeling experience. Just as she had felt herself unattractive and unpopular in high school despite evidence to the contrary, she felt her failure as a model could be traced to the same factor: "I wasn't attractive." When interviewer James Lipton of *Inside the Actors Studio* responded incredulously, "Pardon me?," Julia said, "No, I've sort of grown into my cuteness."

Much closer to the real reason for her lack of success: "I was not terribly interested." Still, when Eric introduced her in 1986 to a reporter who had come to interview him about *The Coca-Cola Kid,* he said, "This is my sister Julie. She's a model."

"We always said I was a model. *I* always said I was a model. But I was never a model. I was always just pretty and didn't have a job, so everybody said I was a model: 'Yeah, she's cute, she's unemployed, she's a model.'"

Julie impressed Bob McGowan when they met. "As soon as she walked in, she lit up the room," he recalled to Aileen Joyce. "There were a bunch of adults in there, and she came in and kind of took over the conversation. She was only seventeen, but she had a presence even then. She was seventeen going on forty. She looked like a kid, but mentally she was much older."

Although McGowan was skeptical about her gawkiness and her southern accent, he decided to accept her as a client "because I felt sorry for her. She didn't have a dime." He managed Julia for four years and was apparently never aware of her inheritance, which came her way a few months after she met him. He says that while he never became involved in her personal affairs, "I can tell you that she was broke when she was around nineteen or twenty, because she was always borrowing money from me, always a couple of hundred there, a couple of hundred here. . . . I remember one day she called me up and said she needed three thousand dollars right away. I said, 'Okay, I'll give you a check.' And she said, 'No, it has to be in cash.'"

Acquaintances have described Julia Roberts as a "penny-pincher," and it seems that she did anything but squander her stepmother's money. In 1992 her friend Daniel Ramos said that "back then [in the late eighties], she was able to make twenty-eight thousand dollars go a long, long way. In fact, she still has some money left over from the inheritance from her stepmother. . . . She's that cheap, she really and truly is."

McGowan stressed that Julie always paid him back. "She was very good that way." He also occasionally helped her with her rent payments, although he rarely knew exactly where she lived. "She was always moving around . . . with her sister, then not with her sister, then back with her sister . . . who could keep track?"

The first demand McGowan made of his new client was that she see a vocal coach to get rid of her accent. She readily agreed. "I thought, *Either I play Ellie May Clampett parts for the rest of my life, or I fix it.*" Julie went to Sam Chwat, a newcomer to the field, who has since gone on to correct—or change for a particular role—the speech of numerous celebrated performers. Chwat taught Julie not to drop the final *g* on *ing* words, to soften her *r* sounds, and to avoid dropping *t* sounds and putting unnecessary stress on certain words in a sentence, as in "Wha' are you *up* to, honey?"

"I couldn't hear my accent," Julia later said. "It was maddening. So I went to [the] speech class and said, 'Cat. Dog. I'm go*inggg* to the restaurant.'" She proved a quick study, and before long, all traces of where she was from had disappeared from her speech. Still, she had the same problem with rejections as everyone who has ever attempted to begin a career in show business. There are always excuses: You don't have enough experience; you don't have the right look; you're too different; you're too special.

With Julie, casting directors' biggest complaints were her awkwardness and her lack of experience. When she auditioned for a role on *All My Children,* the show's casting director, Joan D'Incecco, turned her down because she felt Julie had little screen presence: "She was still unfinished as an actress." Julie had no more success auditioning for other soap operas.

The rejections didn't help bolster what little self-esteem she had fostered since her early high school days. "I went in for a lot of TV shows and never got them. I thought, *What is it about me that I'm losing jobs? Is it the way I look or talk?* But I kept glued to the pursuit."

Bob McGowan told Julie that it was very important for her to study acting. She did, but not for long. "I always quit the classes. Halfway through, I thought, *This guy's full of shit* . . . I felt the things that were being discussed were pointless. You know, things to do with your eyes, things not to do with your eyes. Not only did it make you way too hyperaware of what the hell you're doing with your eyes, it just seemed hokey. It made you self-obsessed."

Julie decided to ask for Eric's help with an upcoming audition. It didn't turn out well. "The one time Eric directly helped me with an audition, he nearly drove me crazy. He'd take me out to dinner, and we'd talk about this audition I had for *Spencer: For Hire*, and then we'd read this scene over and over. He wouldn't give up. And I'd get bored, because I just wanted to have dinner. I'm not much on just rehearsing and rehearsing, anyway."

Julie didn't get the part, or any other for nearly eighteen months, despite flying to Los Angeles to test for the role of Hayley Benson on *Santa Barbara*. The repeated rejections might have daunted a lesser ambition, but Bob McGowan remembered Julie being hell-bent on an acting career. "She would even go on calls and auditions that were [my] other clients' callbacks. She would bug me or my secretary to find out where the auditions were, and then she would just show up. She's a pip, that one."

Finally, in the fall of 1986, Julie got a part. The good news was that it was in a feature film. The bad news was that the role consisted of a fifteen-second walk-on with no dialogue. The worse news was that the film, *Firehouse*, proved to be a Grade Z sexploitation comedy with labored situations and hammy acting that, to quote the critic Pauline Kael about *Hello, Dolly!*, "makes one's teeth ache, and the smirky dialogue might pass for wit among not too bright children."

Directed by J. Christian Ingvordsen (who sometimes went by the alias John Christian), the film centers around three young women who begin their firefighting careers in Hose One, the firehouse with New Jersey's worst reputation. The dimwitted firemen and their equally dull supervisors spend more time quenching feminine fires of lust than the real kind. The film also contains several scenes of women dancing topless in a bar.

Peter Onorati played Ron J. Sleek, the sleaziest womanizer in the brigade. Onorati, an ad-space salesman for *McCall's* with acting ambitions, heard about a casting call for the film, got the part (his first), and took his sick days to make the movie across the Hudson River in Jersey City, New Jersey. (He has gone on to a steady career in films.)

Julie's brief appearance comes twenty-seven minutes into the picture. She is holding on to Onorati's right arm, and another beautiful young woman is on his left. Onorati wears a leisure suit, a red-and-white diagonally striped shirt open to his midchest, and several gold chains. Julie wears skintight red vinyl pants, a black-and-white patterned blouse, a cinched black vinyl belt, and dangling earrings and bracelets. The other girl, who looks to be of Spanish descent, wears a black vinyl miniskirt and a blouse similar to Julie's.

As Sleek walks into the station house, the captain is telling the three new female recruits, "We do things by the book in here!" He turns to see Sleek and his two questionable companions. "I know I'm on duty," Sleek says, "but I have something important to take care of." Then he and the girls ascend a staircase as Julie smiles broadly and chomps on gum. "What was that you were just saying?" one of the recruits asks the captain. (The hilarity never ceases in this film.)

Onorati found himself attracted to Julie. "I was lucky to have such a beautiful girl on my arm for this walk-on. She had a great deal of presence. It was a male-female thing. It wasn't anything about talent, it was just like 'Wow!' " He decided to make a move on her in the best way he knew how: He offered her a job. "How do you feel about selling ad space?" he said to her as they waited to start their scene. "It's a great career."

"Oh, be quiet!" Julie replied.

It took less than a day to film Julia Roberts's film debut.* She received no screen credit, and if one's attention understandably wanders during the movie, one can easily miss her. *Firehouse* was never released in theaters but went straight to video in July 1987. "I don't think I've ever seen the film," Onorati said. "My parents have a copy of it, and it's not something you want your parents to see—your first tits-and-ass movie." It's unlikely Julie told her mother to run out to the video store to rent it, either.

Shortly after *Pretty Woman* made Julia Roberts a superstar in 1990, *The National Enquirer* ran a story entitled PRETTY WOMAN'S SEX SECRETS. The article, purportedly based on interviews with Julie's high school classmates, alleged that she "liked to steal other girls' boyfriends, and went alone to the senior prom so she could chase other gals' dates"; "She had regular 'hunting seasons' for boys—stalking halfbacks during football season, hoop stars during basketball season, etc."; and "her classmates called her 'Hot Pants.' " The piece quoted an unnamed classmate describing a Saturday-night party: "We were all having a great time and drinking vodka and Coke. Then Julie maneuvered my boyfriend off into a dark corner and started kissing him. The next thing I knew, they'd

---

*Some of Julia's filmographies list a 1983 movie made for British television, *Forever Young*, as her first film. While there is a girl in the background of a classroom scene who somewhat resembles Julia, it is very unlikely that she would have made a film in the U.K. while still a sophomore in high school, and Eric recalled nothing about her doing such a film.

disappeared and I was left to find my way home alone. Julie sent out vibes that she was available. All the other girls were disgusted by her behavior."

The story, which strongly implies that Julie "went all the way" with any number of boys, strains credulity. One of the problems with it is that Julie did attend her senior prom with a date, Bill Knight. And none of Julie's classmates interviewed for this book painted such a picture. "I don't recall that about her," a classmate, Bill Nazarowski, said. "I think a lot of that is a fabrication."

Whatever the extent of the story's truth, Julie Roberts did appear to have had an aggressive interest in attractive young men—at the very least from the time she arrived in New York. "I guess you could say she was boy-crazy," said Bob McGowan. He recalled that Julie called him from the Empire Diner one day and said, "Bob, the cutest guy is waiting on me. His name is Charlie Walsh. I'm going to tell him you're interested in meeting him, because you were in here eating one night and saw him. And that you sent me down here to have him call you, because you didn't know how to reach him. Okay? And when he calls you, you make an appointment, and I'll just happen to be in your office."

The meeting turned out successfully for all concerned. McGowan signed up Walsh, who changed his name from Charlie to Dylan and became one of McGowan's top clients, with dozens of movie and television roles. And Dylan and Julie dated, McGowan said, "for a while, on and off, and I believe they're still friends."

In her 1993 biography *Julia*, Aileen Joyce quoted an unnamed former acquaintance who said, "In those days Julia was very outgoing, very much a party girl, and had a lot of friends, especially boyfriends. She was very flirtatious, even with guys who didn't really interest her. She had a lot of flings, at least four that I personally know of in New York. From what I've heard, she didn't change her lifestyle on movie sets, either. She operated the same way."

Her next film assignment—which provided her with her first speaking part in a feature film with the opening line "*Sì, Papa*"—provides a case in point. Eric had signed to appear in director Peter Masterson's film *Blood Red* not long after his Academy Award nomination as Best Supporting Actor of 1985 in *Runaway Train*. Masterson, who had been an actor (*The Stepford Wives*) and is the father of Mary Stuart Masterson, had guided Geraldine Page to a Best Actress Oscar that same year in his first directorial effort, *The Trip to Bountiful*. Hemdale Films asked him to take over *Blood Red*, a project that had been bouncing around

Hollywood since 1977. Masterson agreed, even though the project was budgeted at $6.5 million ("Tight," he said ruefully). He went to New York to see Eric, who was the only cast member signed at that point. "I had met Eric briefly, and I'd seen him do readings at the Actors Studio, and I thought he was a very good actor. We got along fine and decided to do this thing together." Eric's salary was set at $500,000; Masterson doesn't recall what Julia was paid but thinks it was probably Screen Actors Guild minimum.

Her casting in *Blood Red* meant that Julie would have to join SAG. When she applied, she was told they already had a Julie Roberts registered, and their rules prohibit two actors from sharing a name. Julie called her mother for advice—she couldn't decide between her birth name, Julia, or her middle name, Fiona. Betty urged her toward the former. Thus was Julia Roberts reborn.

Blood Red cast Eric as Marco Collogero, the hotheaded scion of a grape-farming family in California's Napa Valley, circa 1890, headed by their Sicilian-born patriarch, Sebastian (Giancarlo Giannini). The family is thrown into crisis when Sebastian refuses to sell his land to a railroad magnate, William Berrigan (Dennis Hopper), who plans to lay new train tracks through the acreage. (In a subplot, Marco falls in love with the daughter of a rival grape-growing family.) Berrigan hires thugs to force Sebastian to sell and sets off what becomes a bloody range war. Sebastian is killed and strung up next to his barn in the presence of his daughters; Marco avenges his death by shooting the killers and dynamiting a railroad tunnel. The film ends happily for the Collogeros when Berrigan gives up his fight.

Masterson had cast Giannini; Hopper; Francesca De Sapio as Sebastian's wife; Lara Harris as Marco's love interest; Susan Anspach as a madam we see bathing Marco in a claw-foot tub in his opening scene; his own wife, Carlin Glynn, as Miss Jeffrey, the local schoolteacher; and his daughter Alexandra in the small role of Anna, one of Sebastian's daughters. The slightly larger role of Sebastian's other daughter, Maria, was still not cast.

"Eric asked me if Julia could be in the movie," Masterson recalled. "I knew nothing about her. But they had grown up in an acting family, so I didn't have any concerns about casting her. I took her on Eric's recommendation. I figured who could be better to play Eric's sister?" (Julia's resemblance to Eric couldn't have hurt her chances much either.)

On August 17 the "People" column of the New York *Daily News* ran a small item about Julia's casting, headlined, JULIE ROBERTS IS PLAYING

SISTER OF ERIC. Oddly—perhaps because she didn't want to be seen as the beneficiary of nepotism—Julia told the reporter that Eric had no knowledge of her casting until he returned from that year's Cannes Film Festival. "He didn't even know I tried out for the part and that I got it. . . . I told him and he really flipped. It's my first role and I'm only eighteen, and I'm planning to go to college, but that's off for now. I want to ride this lucky break to the fullest."

Ten weeks later, in November 1986, Julia and Eric flew together from New York to the location shooting, at a vineyard outside San Jose. Julia and Alexandra (Lexi) Masterson were roommates for most of the shoot, and Julia made a lasting impression on Lexi. "She was someone who would walk into a room or onto the set, where the crew was, and she was friends with *everybody*. The room would just light up, and everyone would turn her way when she entered. She was very magnetic, very charismatic. I wouldn't say that she was networking back then, but that's what it turned out to be. I don't know if she does it consciously, but if so, I've never seen anyone so good at it. I think it's just her natural way of doing things."

Lexi was taken by Julia's acting technique—or rather, her lack of it. "I was trying to do my work—my *acting*—and she just kind of *did* it. I never saw her rehearse, or even prepare for the camera to turn on. She'd be yakking, and they'd say, 'Ready,' and she would do whatever she had to do. She was very natural. I've never seen someone be so self-confident in their own body, even when she wasn't a big star."

It was clear to Lexi early on that Eric and Julia shared a strong bond. "I thought they were very loving, very affectionate, and very private—very intimate. I felt there was definitely some family history with them—I had no idea what it was, but I felt he was very protective of her and very much a great older brother. I felt there was a lot of family drama there—like they came from Dysfunctionville."

Julia's one big scene in the film showcased her horrified reaction to seeing her father murdered and strung up. "I was very pleased with what she did," Peter Masterson recalled. "I thought she was very good in the movie. We did some scenes under very difficult conditions. It was cold at night, and she was out there doing a big emotional scene. She worked hard on that scene—she was very dedicated to getting it right. I didn't have to tell her what to do to summon up the emotion; she found it somewhere within herself."

Lexi credits Eric with that. "When she had to do a scene that required emotion or crying, he would come and talk to her and whisper in her ear. I had no idea what he said to her, but she would burst into tears, and

I'd be like, 'Hold on!'—because that's not how I learned to get emotional. But obviously there was something very private and intense between them."

Although Lexi said Julia rejected her friendship midway through the shoot, she at first found Julia fun to room with. "She was entertaining. It was like a slumber party with us—we'd yak and yak and yak, and finally one of us would say, 'C'mon, we gotta go to sleep!' Julia would order big burgers and fries, and I'd say, 'Wait a minute, I should only be eating lettuce!' She never worried about her figure—she was a tall girl."

A few days into the shoot, Lexi discovered that she couldn't always count on Julia to spend the night in their room. "She flirted with everybody. She would have one boyfriend who was a grip, and then she'd have another boyfriend and they'd disappear for the whole night, and then she'd have another boyfriend who was a grip. You never knew *who* she was dating! She'd move from one boy to the other, and it was very quick and intense. She would just lock on to someone, and that was it. Some of them didn't last more than one night."

Filming wrapped just before Christmas. "It was a difficult shoot," Peter Masterson said. "We didn't have time to do many retakes. [But] I thought it turned out okay—quite an epic." Most journalists who have written about Eric or Julia have dismissed the film. One profiler called it "a straight-to-video embarrassment," but that's neither accurate nor fair. The film did have a limited theatrical release in 1989 and was marketed on MGM video in 1997. The storytelling is a bit jerky, but it's visually sumptuous, the acting (and star power) is impressive, and as with the best westerns, viewers root for the good guys and hoot the bad ones. To Masterson's great credit, every dime of the film's small budget and then some is visible in the finished product.

Julia doesn't receive billing in the opening credits and is billed nineteenth at the end. She looks lovely in her opening scene, dressed in a pretty white long-sleeved, ankle-length Victorian cotton dress with lace at the collar, her hair up in a Gibson-girl do. She had to wear a corset for the entire film, and "she hated that," Lexi recalled. "But she didn't seem to pay much attention to the way she looked. She'd just wait until the clothes and hair people had her ready, and she'd say, 'Okay.' It surprised me, because she seemed not to take things seriously. But maybe she just wasn't vain."

A reviewer wrote of the film after Julia became a star: "Eric Roberts is more subdued than usual. [But] his scenes with real-life sister Julia Roberts are intriguing because of the visual match. She doesn't get much chance to emote, but that nascent star quality already is evident."

Eric said in 1989 that *Blood Red* "was the most fun I've had doing a movie. I've always wanted to play a cowboy, so I get to ride horses, kill the bad guys, and I even get the girl! What could be more perfect?" As for Julia, "She's great in it. She's very beautiful and very smart—but then I'm very biased." He loved both his sisters, he said, "like I love my life."

Julia hasn't much discussed the experience, but she did have a revealing comment for *Rolling Stone* in 1989: "*Blood Red* was an interesting thing for Eric and I, because we realized that even though we're related, even though we may look alike and be in the same profession, we don't go about the process of acting the same way at all. We're really different. He went to the Royal Academy of Dramatic Art in London. I'm a kamikaze actress."

Almost immediately after she completed her role in *Blood Red*, Julia won a small but juicy part in an episode of the NBC television drama *Crime Story*. She flew to Las Vegas for the shoot shortly after Christmas. Her episode, entitled "The Survivor," aired on February 13, 1987, and featured her as the abused stepdaughter of Steve Altman, a new colleague of the series' main character, Lieutenant Torello (Dennis Farina). In several emotionally wrenching scenes that total about eight minutes, Julia's character gradually reveals to Lieutenant Torello what she has been subjected to by Altman. Torello and Altman then have a bitter confrontation.

Julia handled the challenging role well, and she made such a strong impression on viewers that when she returned to Smyrna for the holidays ten months after the episode aired, she noticed people staring at her in the mall as she and her friend Paige Amsler shopped. "At first I thought it was just my imagination. But Paige noticed it, too. 'Why are people looking at you?' she said. Then a couple of people came up because they'd recognized me from that small role in *Crime Story*." Or people *thought* they recognized her. "They didn't *really* know who I was," Julia said with a laugh. "They'd just kinda go, 'Are you . . . ' And I'd say, 'Nah, you're in the *Cumberland Mall!*' "

Before long it would be impossible for Julia to use that ruse to ward off overzealous admirers.

CHAPTER TEN

Bob McGowan worked hard to get Julia acting jobs. He sent her out on calls for any part she was suitable for, and several that she wasn't. (Many managers feel that actors are helped by the experience of an audition even if the role is unlikely to come their way.) McGowan learned that Joanna Ray, a Los Angeles–based casting agent, was looking for four girls to play the lead roles in *Sweet Little Rock 'n' Rollers,* a low-budget romantic comedy about a girl band called Jennie Lee and the Mystery.

He telephoned Ray, who asked if Julia played an instrument. McGowan said he wasn't sure. He knew Julia had no musical talent, but he asked her if she knew anyone who played the drums and might be able to teach her. "I picked the drums because I figured it was the easiest instrument to learn," he said. By the time Julia met with Joanna Ray, she had immersed herself in a crash course in the drums, but Ray had already cast Trini Alvarado in that role. Julia persuaded Ray that she could learn the bass guitar well enough to pantomime playing it. Ray hired her for the smallish role of Daryle Shane, a young lady who, Jennie Lee's brother says in the film, "on a good day is a slut."

Sweet Little Rock 'n' Rollers, which was happily renamed *Satisfaction,* had its genesis in the fervid imagination of the screenwriter Charles Purpura, whose first script, *Heaven Help Us,* had recently been greenlighted for production and who was, in Hollywood parlance, "hot." "Everyone wanted to be in business with me," Purpura recalled. "One of the people I met with was Alan Greisman, Sally Field's husband. He wanted to do a film that involved a bunch of young women over a summer vacation."

Purpura, busy doing rewrites for *Heaven Help Us,* didn't give the matter much thought until Greisman called again to pressure him for an idea. Finally, Purpura called Greisman and said, "Rock-and-roll band." Greisman liked the idea, fledgling though it was, and he and Purpura pitched it to Alan Stewart at Warner Bros. who gave them the go-ahead to develop the screenplay. "Originally the story was very dark," Purpura said. "One of the girls died, and there was some lesbian stuff going on—I think the drummer was in love with Jennie. There was some comedy, but it had a bit of melodrama, too."

Warner Bros., unhappy with the downbeat script, put the project in "turnaround," effectively killing it at that studio. Greisman and Purpura then faced a long line of rejections from the other studios. "The [turn-downs] kept coming back...they wanted to push it toward a lighter comedy, more of a fun music thing."

Aaron Spelling, who had a development deal at NBC television, saved the project when he got the network to finance the film with the promise that the script would be leavened. "[NBC's involvement] auto-matically dropped the budget to about two million," Purpura recalled, "which is pretty low. The main thing was the casting. *Family Ties* was still on the air, and Alan got Justine Bateman interested—the movie was supposed to break her out into pictures. [Her costar Michael J. Fox had already made the move.] I heard that what NBC was thinking with the project was a feature film, pilot TV movie, and then a series."

As the screenplay evolved, Purpura decided to make one of the four band members a guy. The producers, Robert Alden and Armyan Bern-stein, hired Scott Coffey to play Nickie Longo. They also signed Britta Phillips to play Billy Swan. "Then they told me they had 'Eric Roberts's sister,' as she was known at the time," Purpura said. "So then they had the group." Liam Neeson, the Irish actor who would go on to great fame playing Oskar Schindler in Steven Spielberg's *Schindler's List,* signed on to play Bateman's love interest.

Once Julia had secured the role, which was big enough to require a contract, she needed to find an agent, since Bob McGowan, as her man-ager, could find her jobs but did not negotiate contracts. McGowan called his friend Risa Shapiro at the famed William Morris Agency; he had frequently called her to ask for help with landing Julia film roles. "But she'd always tell me the same thing, which was 'Bob, I just can't do that.' Every now and then, though, they'd send her on something idiotic like an industrial film, or some bullshit like that. This time I told her, 'Look, Julia's probably going to get something like fifty thousand [for *Satisfaction*], and you guys can do the deal.'" Risa remained skeptical, but the agency agreed to take Julia on after McGowan told them about Aaron Spelling's involvement and the film's potential as a TV series.

None of the established agents wanted to take on a neophyte, so Julia was assigned first to Risa, who was relatively new at the company, and later to Elaine Goldsmith, who has been with Julia ever since, first as her agent, then as a partner in her production company. "Elaine Goldsmith didn't want her. Neither of them wanted her," McGowan said. "Funny, huh?"

Julia spent four weeks learning to play the bass guitar, with private lessons each morning and a group rehearsal with her fellow cast members every afternoon. She found the process difficult. "There's nothing more frustrating than having this great instrument and a great song and not being able to put the two together." She plugged away and finally became proficient enough to mime playing the instrument, which was all she was expected to do. "We all knew the quicker we learned, the quicker it would be fun," Julia said. "We got it up fast, and we had a good time."

Charles Purpura attended some of the cast readings in New York with the director, Joan Freeman, and the actors. He came away from the readings most impressed by Julia. "I was very happy when she came on. The role she had was of an oversexed airhead, but she brought something extra to it. She gave me the impression that there was more than met the eye with that character. And she had this exuberance that was infectious for the rest of the cast. The first time I met them, they were rehearsing as a band, and you could tell right away that Julia was happy to be there. She was very attractive and very bubbly, not in a ditzy way, but she was just *up*. We all went out to dinner after the rehearsal, and she said to me, 'Thanks to you, we all have jobs.'"

On May 12, 1987, Julia flew to Charleston, South Carolina, for the start of a shoot that would be even shorter than *Blood Red*'s—thirty-five days. The script gave her less to do than the other players in a story that revolved around Bateman's character; the ragtag band manages to wrangle a summer gig out of burnt-out-songwriter-turned-bar-owner Martin Falcon (Neeson), and later, he and Jennie fall in love. Boy troubles, drug troubles, and a difficult decision for Jennie between college and a chance to go on tour in Europe complicate matters.

As brief as the filming was, problems still arose. According to Purpura, "I heard from Alan Greisman that the cast wasn't getting along with the director. I think there was a problem between Joan Freeman and Justine having to do with Liam. I don't think he liked Justine. He liked Julia."

Neeson liked Julia a *lot*, and the two began an affair that would result in their living together for the better part of the next year. "The relationship between Liam and Julia created some problems for Justine," Purpura said. "If you're playing a romantic lead opposite an actor, and he's in love with one of the actors playing a secondary character, that could screw up your head. Also, actors are a weird bunch. If Justine had immersed herself in the role so much that she believed Liam was really in love with her, who knows?"

Neeson knew he was making a turkey, while Julia, happy just to be working, tried to learn as much from the experience as she could. "Doing the film wasn't a pleasant experience for Liam," Joan Freeman said. "He felt it was creatively stifling. . . . There were people, too, who were not happy with him. . . . But there was one bonus—he met Julia through it."

A friend of Neeson's told his biographer, Ingrid Millar, "They were absolutely nuts about each other. They couldn't keep their hands off each other. It was incredible to watch. Liam is so cool, but he was very, very responsive with Julia. In complete contrast, she's a very tactile person. She seemed to spark him off, and they would be crawling all over each other."

Charles Purpura wasn't surprised by the relationship developing between the nineteen-year-old Julia and the thirty-five-year-old Neeson. "Affairs on movie sets are very common, because it's like being at war, where everybody bonds to an extreme extent, and they form a mentality of 'It's us versus them.' Everyone else is a civilian. It's very intense and overwhelmingly seductive to be part of a movie family."

Psychologists might infer that Julia, by falling in love with a man sixteen years older than she, sought the affections of a substitute father. Although she would have numerous on- and off-set relationships over the next decade, none was with a man more than a few years older than she. Several years later, she was asked by a reporter whether it was fair to say that her prodigious string of relationships "has something to do with the need to find a father figure." Her response was particularly frank: "I always thought that I bypassed that little-girl-looking-for-a-father thing because I really didn't have enough to draw on. I was so young when he died, I didn't have enough information to look for someone like that. But maybe my version of it was going with people like my brother rather than my father."

Neeson, like Eric, was a good-looking, intense, well-built actor (although much taller than Eric, at six-foot-four); like Eric, he'd had a broken nose that gave his face character. Also like Eric, he had been raised with sisters, a situation that left him, he said, with a deep appreciation of the opposite sex. "I love women! Every shape, size, and color created. They are the better sex." Like both Eric and Julia, he had come from a working-class background (in Ballymena, a small Northern Ireland town), swore a blue streak, and proudly considered himself salt of the earth. As Eric had said, "If I weren't an actor, I'd be a cowboy. I love to smoke and drink and not to bathe."

Liam and Julia liked to smoke as well (Julia confessed to a two-pack-a-day habit), and both could swear to shame a sailor. Once they began living together early in 1988, they apparently quarreled quite a bit. "When you live in a very small [place], like we did," Neeson said, "space is the reason you fight—if anybody comes into your sphere, you'll do anything to protect it." It is amusing to picture them at home having an argument, puffin' and cussin' up a storm. Despite its volatility, "it was a serious relationship," Neeson told *Hello!* magazine in 1993. "We met before she became Queen of the Box Office. . . . Julia and I will remain friends on some spiritual level for life. She's very special."

Perhaps because of the parallels between her boyfriend and her brother, Eric wasn't far from Julia's mind while she filmed *Satisfaction*, a situation that disturbed her when she found herself emoting as her brother might have. "There was a moment in *Satisfaction* that was absolutely frightening," she said, "because for one split second in time, I *was* Eric Roberts."

Julia faced her first sex scene in this film, and that made her nervous—doubly so because it turns into a near-rape. In the scene Daryle's handsome blond rich-boy summer fling brings her into the den of his family's home during a party. He pushes her down on the sofa and begins to kiss and grind against her. When she protests, he says, "Will you just shut up for two minutes," and continues his assault.

"What do you want—you want me to lay here and be quiet while you ball me?" she asks. When he replies, "Yes," she grabs a wooden duck from the table behind the sofa and hits him over the head with it. He falls off the couch, and she tells him, "You're an asshole," before she stomps out. "I was so scared and nervous" as the filming of the scene approached, Julia told *Playboy* in 1991, "I felt like I was twelve years old and had never been kissed. I was pacing in my trailer. I thought I was going to throw up. Then I called my mom, and then I *did* throw up. But it went very smoothly."

. . .

"Naming a movie *Satisfaction* is asking for it," the critic Michael Healy wrote in the Los Angeles *Daily News*, "especially if it happens to deliver none. Too bad Hollywood didn't learn a lesson when Michael J. Fox bombed in *Light of Day*, last year's attempt at using a [*Family*] *Ties* member in a teen movie about a struggling music group. This one's just as dumb but way more unsatisfying."

Most other critical reactions when the film opened quietly in February 1988 were equally negative. Few critics mentioned Julia by name, but Caryn James in *The New York Times* complimented the ensemble's acting in a backhanded way: "There's nothing wrong with the acting that better material—preferably nonmusical—wouldn't solve."

Julia took Eric to see the film in Westwood. "[He] laughed," she recalled, "but we talked, and he made it seem not so bad. But the film taught me a lot about what I hope never to do again in a movie." Still, she added, only one thing in the film actually embarrassed her, and she hadn't even been around for its filming. "There's a scene where I'm supposedly in the van with my boyfriend, and the van is rocking, and a grand amount of time passes, as if we've been going at it for quite long. Well, actually, it was an empty van, and there were a couple of grips behind it pushing it back and forth. I was at the beach all day."

The movie provides *some* satisfaction for Julia's fans. One charming scene shows the band members riding in their van singing "Hey, Now" while Julia blows on a bottle top and the drummer plays up a storm on a suitcase. In a scene at a marshmallow roast, a girl asks Julia's character what she does with her spare time. "A variety of things," Daryle replies. "I like to spend quiet times holed up with a good book." Asked what she had read lately, she replies, "*Thin Thighs in Thirty Days*."

Satisfaction brought in $8.3 million at the box office, a few million in profit for NBC and the releasing studio, 20th Century–Fox. When NBC aired the movie in April 1991, they changed the title to *Girls of Summer* and advertised Julia Roberts as its main attraction.

Elvis Costello saw the film on television years later. "It was kind of like the Brady Bunch meet the Bangles and do acid," he told an audience before performing "Mystery Dance," a song Jennie Lee and the Mystery perform in the movie. "They sing one of my songs. . . . It used to be one of my dreams to have [four] eighteen-year-old girls do one of my songs. It wasn't until I *saw* it . . ." He left it at that.

. . .

At around 2:45 in the morning on December 3, 1987, a woman flagged down two patrolmen near an apartment building on West Eighty-first Street in Manhattan. When Officers Brian O'Neill and Theresa Merrigan stepped off the elevator onto the building's second floor, they found Eric Roberts "very drunk" and pounding on the door of a woman who lived there. The frightened woman had telephoned her neighbor, who went downstairs to summon the police. The woman, who was never identified, opened the door to the officers and told them that although she had once met Eric at a party, she "didn't know him from a hole in the wall."

According to press accounts of the court papers, Eric told the police that the woman was "my mother's lesbian lover and I just wanted to talk to her." He also reportedly said, "My father died ten years ago today and he was cremated." Sergeant Ronald Betterle told reporters that the officers were attempting to escort Eric out of the building when "he began taking swings at them." He missed one of the officers, made contact with the other, and screamed, "It'll take a whole army of you to get me out of here. I'll knock your fucking heads off!"

The officers subdued him. On the way to the West Eighty-second Street station, Eric said to the officers, "I was drinking. I'm not a bad guy . . . I didn't mean to cause any problems. I'll send you a bottle of Dom Perignon." Despite the offer, he was charged with felony assault of a police officer, misdemeanor trespassing, and resisting arrest. When police found a quantity of marijuana and two glass vials of cocaine in the pocket of his down jacket, he was also hit with drug-possession charges.

Eric spent thirty-six hours in a holding cell, after which he was met by what the writer Fred Schruers described as "a frenzied covey of paparazzi." The New York City newspapers had a field day with the story; the *Post* headline cried MOVE STAR BUSTED—"BOOZY" ERIC ROBERTS ON DRUG RAP AFTER COP BATTLE. His attorney, Roanne Mann, told the *Daily News* that Eric had suffered a broken nose in the melee with the officers: "I hear he's not in very good shape." Police officials denied that Eric had been injured.

On April 30, Eric appeared before Judge Bruce Allen in Manhattan criminal court, dressed nattily in a gray pin-striped suit, blue shirt, and black cowboy boots. In a bargain with the prosecutor's office, he pleaded guilty to the minor offense of harassment, and the other charges were dropped. Years later, Eric indignantly denied that he had been using drugs the night of the incident. "I've done my weight in drugs," he said, "but not that night." What had precipitated the incident, he explained, was that he had been upset by "all these adolescent thoughts of 'I wish my daddy was here.'"

By the time *Satisfaction* opened, Julia had moved into Liam Neeson's apartment in a three-story stucco building three blocks from the Pacific Ocean in Venice Beach, California. (She has been bicoastal ever since.) Liam refused to see the movie. "I have no intention of ever seeing it," he said. He added that he had accepted the role only because, at the time he was sent the script, he was playing a deaf-mute skid-row bum in *Suspect*, with Cher and Dennis Quaid. "I was feeling a wee bit depressed and really ugly and awkward, and the script [of *Satisfaction*] had a lot of pretty girls running around, and I thought, *This sounds great!*"

In February, HBO aired Julia's next film—and a far better one—*Baja Oklahoma*, which she had filmed in Texas in the summer of 1987. Based on the 1983 novel by Dan (*Semi-Tough*) Jenkins, it is the story of Juanita Hutchens (Lesley Ann Warren), a barmaid at the grandiosely named Herb's Dining and Dancing in Fort Worth, Texas, whose dream is to be a country-western songwriter. Her life is complicated by the return of Slick Henderson, a lover who abandoned her nineteen years earlier (Peter Coyote), and by her nineteen-year-old daughter, Candy (Julia), who is involved with a handsome, smoothly charming drug dealer named Dove (Bruce Abbott). Juanita's best friend, Doris (Swoosie Kurtz), is a boozin', cheatin', cussin' bleached blonde whom Juanita constantly has to bail out of trouble with a suspicious husband.

Julia has five scenes in the movie and makes the most of them. She demonstrates her acting range as Candy goes from loving daughter to contemptuous rebel to battered woman at the hands of her boyfriend.

Baja Oklahoma offers a number of pleasures. There are several country-western tunes, including the title song by Willie Nelson and Dan Jenkins. Lesley Ann Warren's performance is touching. (She is one of the best actresses of her generation and has been criminally underused by Hollywood.) It is Swoosie Kurtz, though, who steals the movie; her rollicking performance earned a Golden Globe nomination. And the script, cowritten by Jenkins and the film's director, Bobby Roth, has hilarious moments. At one point Doris tells Juanita that she has realized pink is *her*. Not only will she wear nothing but pink from now on, she has also dyed her pubic hair to match. "How did you do it?" Juanita asks, appalled. "I used [her husband] Lee's toothbrush." Juanita's jaw drops. "You did what?!"

"Well, you don't think I'd use my own, do you? What do you think I am, some kind of pervert?"

In another scene, a music promoter who wants to manage Juanita's singing career tells her, "Don't worry about your voice. We got equipment down there that can make a fart sound like the Mormon Tabernacle Choir."

Two weeks after she completed work on *Baja Oklahoma,* Julia began to prepare for her most important audition to date, as one of the three female leads in a feature film set in a Mystic, Connecticut, pizza parlor. Her performance in that film would make Hollywood sit up and take notice, and would set her fledgling career off in the direction of the stratosphere.

CHAPTER ELEVEN

When she read the script of *Mystic Pizza*, a low-budget ($3.5 million) coming-of-age comedy/drama, Julia figured that only one of the three pizza-parlor waitresses fit her. Kat Araujo, pretty and serious, was a high school senior on her way to Yale, and Julia thought the character "too young" for her. Daisy, Kat's sexpot older sister, was described on page two of the script as "the kind of girl men would kill for." Julia didn't think she filled *that* bill. So she was left with Jojo, described as cute and down-to-earth and unable to commit to marriage with her fisherman boyfriend. *That I can play*, Julia thought.

When she arrived for the audition, however, she learned she would be reading for the part of Daisy. She was taken aback to see dozens of other would-be Daisies, all of whom, she felt, were at least as attractive as she. "I remember thinking, *What's going to give me the edge over these girls?* I had my Walkman on. I was listening to Jimi Hendrix live at Monterey, singing 'Wild Thing.' I played it over and over again, and the more I played it, the more cocky I got—and the more attention I got from the women in the room." She started singing along—loudly—and then began to throw pencils into the ceiling soundproofing tiles as though they were darts. "All the girls started getting very nervous, like I had the inside track or something. So I went in having manifested this bold attitude, and read for the part, which I thought went fine, and then was told I was good but physically wrong for the role." Her hearers thanked her with the kind of finality that chills every auditioner's soul. Never easily dissuaded ("I was desperate for a job"), Julia cornered Jane Jenkins, the lead casting woman, and asked what exactly was wrong with her physically. "Well," Jenkins replied, "you're a blonde,* and we're looking for someone darker and sort of ethnic-looking—she's supposed to be Portuguese." Julia pleaded for a callback, and Jenkins agreed.

*The summer sun always lightened Julia's hair.

"So I went to a Lamston's—I was working at the Ann Taylor's down by the seaport in New York, and the Lamston's was right next door—and bought some Color Me Happy mousse that was, you know, *way* black." She stayed up half the night painstakingly applying the gook to her voluminous tresses. She also decided to borrow one of Bob McGowan's suits. "That's when she started wearing men's suits," McGowan recalled. "I thought it was quite sexy, to tell you the truth. She'd wear the trousers and the jacket but nothing else. I thought it looked hot."

Looking decidedly more ethnic in the second go-round, Julia read again, this time for the film's director, Donald Petrie. He asked her back again a few days later to read with a young actor (Adam Storke) whom they were considering to play Daisy's boyfriend. She reapplied the mousse. "So we read together, and after reading, we sorta cuddled up, two strangers, cuddled up, and he kept, like, touching my hair. He's stroking my hair, and I'm trying to be in the moment and be organic and all these great actor things, and all I can think is *He's touching my hair and it's painted!* His hands wound up all black and my hands were black and it looked like massive mascara run. It just ran everywhere!"

Despite the mess, Donald Petrie felt that "Julia was real smart [to put] a rinse in her hair to make it jet black. . . . It made her look exotic and perfect for the part. She was exactly what I needed . . . unpredictable and willing to take chances, fiery, spirited, and yet very real." Later, when Petrie saw Julia's natural hair color, he did a double take. (Her hair, of course, was professionally colored for the movie, which prevented any further goop problems.)

One of the film's producers, Mark Levinson, recalled that the creative team behind *Mystic Pizza* did not have a strong handle on the Daisy character until they saw Julia's audition. "She was very much like a light at the end of the tunnel," Levinson said. "There was no doubt that she would be Daisy the minute she walked into the room. She made it a lot clearer for us on how to get to that character."

Signing a contract that paid her $50,000, Julia joined a cast of other young, largely untried actors: Annabeth Gish (a mere sixteen, and not related to the silent-screen legend Lillian Gish, although her grandmother shared that star's name) as Kat; Lili Taylor, twenty, as Jojo; Vincent D'Onofrio, twenty-nine, as Jojo's on-again-off-again fiancé; Adam Storke, twenty-five, as Daisy's wealthy blond Adonis beau; and William R. Moses, twenty-nine, the married man with whom Kat falls in love. The marvelously earthy actress Conchata Ferrell would play Leona, the proprietor of Mystic Pizza and keeper of its singular secret recipe.

As filming approached, Julia found herself insecure about her ability

to play Daisy. "I was so unlike her, and in a way I aspired to be extro-
verted like she was. I really worked the hair and wore the skirt, and in a
way that served a purpose—it was a nice flexing of that outward muscle." In 2001 she said, "I'm sure I said in the press clipping that I gained
twenty pounds to play the role. But no, it was adolescence. I was nineteen. I had an Oreo fetish. I was big, and I felt very uncomfortable with
myself, had very low self-esteem. I was not that girl."

To make sure audiences got the point that Daisy was voluptuous,
Donald Petrie kept his camera low and trained on her wriggling der-
riere for the first few moments of her appearance in the film, which
made her look—well, voluptuous.

As she had done and would continue to do for most of her career, Julia
ingratiated herself with the cast and crew of *Mystic Pizza* from the first
day of location shooting in Mystic. Adam Storke recalled his script
study being interrupted by "all this raucous laughter. I got up to see
what was going on, and there was Julia sitting on the steps of this house
with about fifteen of the crew around her. She had them eating out of
the palm of her hand. They were just cracking up."

Julia has admitted that in many ways, a film crew is a substitute for
the kind of warm, happy family she never had. "It's nice to complete
each other for a while and be this big, extended Waltons family. I've
always thought of location as an island, and all you have is one another.
A lot of bonding goes on." The crew teased Julia unmercifully about the
script's description of Daisy Araujo. "I would walk around the set and
the crew would kid me. They'd say, 'There's the girl men are going to kill
for today.'" Julia wasn't as amused as they thought she'd be. "How the
fuck can you live up to *that*?" she later asked plaintively.

Her friendliness was returned by many of the cast and crew. "There
was this particular excitement in the ensemble of actors, because most
of us hadn't done any movies," Julia recalled. "Bob Field was our gaffer.
Some people will just come up, move you over, and say, 'Stand here.' But
Bob would always take just that extra half-minute to *explain* to us. He'd
say, 'It's easier if you stand here. See that big shadow? If you move just
this much, it's not there.' So now I don't have to be told; I can find my
own light. I'm real grateful for things like that."

At the helm of his first film, Donald Petrie, the son of the director
Daniel Petrie and brother of the screenwriter Daniel Petrie, Jr., quickly

realized he had made a good decision to hire Julia as he watched rushes of the first few days' filming. "She has a wonderful spontaneity on-screen that really makes her light up. Most actors have that in their eyes. But Julia has it in her eyes and her face and everywhere. She's the kind of actress you want to shoot without rehearsal because she's so quirky that you never know what you'll get."

Julia was quite content to skip rehearsing. "I'm bad at rehearsal," she said on *Inside the Actors Studio*. "I only have so many chances of having it come out of me exactly the way I want it, and I don't want those to happen in the seven takes that we rehearse it and the camera's not rolling. I'm always afraid that there's only so many good ones in there, so better go get 'em."

During the filming, Julia discovered a book called *Nantucket Solitaire*, an amalgam of prose and poems by Roy Flanders, a Cape Cod real estate broker. "I just loved this book," Julia said. "It was all about this man who was living by himself in Nantucket, and he writes all these poems about being a frustrated writer and women and drugs and drink and all this stuff, and at nineteen, I was most impressionable. I thought this was the coolest guy in the world, and [in her mind's eye] he looked like Sam Shepard, and he was just perfect and he said, 'The women in my life they come and they go. I'm glad they come and I'm glad I come and I'm glad they go.'" (Considering Julia's later reputation as a "love-'em-and-leave-'em" gal, Flanders's lessons must have made a deep impression.)

Julia turned twenty on October 28, 1987. She missed Liam and her friends and family, and might understandably have succumbed to a little melancholy. She hadn't told any of her coworkers that her birthday was imminent, but during the afternoon she was surprised by a huge cake from the cast and crew in the shape of a pizza, festooned with twenty candles. So embarrassed that she blushed beet red and ran off the set, Julia returned a few minutes later and apologized. "I'm shy and I'm an extrovert," she later said. "So everyone seems to get a kick out of the fact that I blush very easily. Certain things kind of make me go, 'Well, I've got to run, see you later.'"

Mystic Pizza wrapped filming in November, after six weeks of locations in Mystic, Stonington, Groton, and Noank, Connecticut. Julia felt some sadness at leaving her new "family," but she looked forward to reuniting with Liam Neeson in Venice, California; within a month she would move from New York to live with him there full-time. "As different as Liam and I are, we are kind of becoming unsimple together," Julia told *Vogue* in 1988. "I think we will keep each other humble, and that we will be complex and happy—and together."

On May 6, 1988, the complex couple stayed home to watch the popular Friday night NBC drama *Miami Vice* with a few friends. The previous summer, between filming of *Satisfaction* and *Baja Oklahoma,* Julia had taped the episode aired that night, entitled "Mirror Image." In keeping with the stylized show's feral story lines, this one has Sonny Crockett (Don Johnson) grieving for his slain wife and accepting a dangerous undercover case to keep his mind off his sorrow. He searches for clues on a mobster's boat, which explodes in an attempt to kill the mobster, injuring Crockett instead and causing amnesia that convinces him he is a gangster. On behalf of the mobster, Manolo, Crockett kills several people. When he regains his memory, he must fight for his life. Julia plays Manolo's seductively dressed "secretary," Holly Wheeler, who is dispatched to seduce Crockett. When she learns he's a policeman, she still wants to hit the sack with him, but he demurs. Holly's disappointed.

Julia appears in five short scenes, none of them vital to the progression of the plot, and doesn't have much emoting to do. But she looks great, whether dressed in tight-fitting clothes or her boss's white bathrobe. The highly rated show probably exposed her to a larger audience than anything she'd done before.

Not long after "Mirror Image" aired, Julia began to feel ill. She thought she had the flu, perhaps because she was run down from her busy work schedule, but, she has said, "the exact source of [the illness] remains shrouded in mystery." She lay low for a stretch while Liam ministered to her. Over the next two weeks she grew progressively sicker, and finally her mother and Liam insisted she go to an emergency room.

The doctors at St. John's Hospital in Santa Monica determined that Julia had contracted viral meningitis and admitted her immediately. Within hours her fever had spiked to 104, and she was slipping into a coma. Since there is no cure for viral meningitis (as opposed to the bacterial variety, which can be treated with antibiotics), the only treatment is hydration, fever control, antibiotics to keep down any secondary infections, and careful monitoring. The fact that Julia had waited so long to seek help made her situation all the more precarious. The doctors told Liam, and later her mother, who flew in from Atlanta, that her chances of survival were only fifty-fifty. "I was incredibly ill," Julia recalled, "and I spent a number of weeks in the hospital. . . . I thought, *God, I'm never going to leave this room [alive]*. . . . I was just lying in bed, growing paler by the day."

Liam left an interview he was doing to publicize *Satisfaction* and rushed over to the hospital to bring Julia some broiled chicken, the only food she could keep down. "Just call me the Irish Florence Nightingale," Neeson said with a laugh when he was reminded of his ministrations.

Eric came to visit her—and came face-to-face with Betty for the first time in seventeen years. "It was all very civil," he said. "I restrained myself from being the asshole I love to be whenever I hear my mother's voice or her name or see her presence. I was quite fine. But it doesn't change the fact of what she is."

After her release from the hospital, Julia continued to recover at home, helped by Liam, Betty, and Lisa, who had flown in from New York to stay with her. "It really changed my life," Julia said of her illness. "I promised myself that if I did get out, I'd have a greater appreciation for the grass and the sky and the flowers and the people."

As she gained strength, Julia received a script, and Betty asked if she'd like her to read it to her. "No, I'll be feeling better, and I'll be able to read it myself," she replied. Written by Robert Harling and based on his off-Broadway hit *Steel Magnolias,* the script revolved around six sassy, wise-cracking southern women who gather at the local beauty salon to exchange gossip and give one another moral support. Truvy Jones (Dolly Parton) owns the salon, and her friends and employees are a mixed bag—the earnest M'Lynn Eatenton (Sally Field), whose daughter, Shelby (Julia), is a diabetic bride-to-be who is warned by her doctors that a pregnancy could jeopardize her life; the curmudgeonly Ouiser Boudreaux (Shirley MacLaine); the town's sardonic former first lady, Clairee Belcher (Olympia Dukakis); and a newcomer to town, the geeky, enigmatic Annelle Dupuy Desoto (Daryl Hannah).

Harling had left Tulane University shortly before he would have taken his bar exam, and moved to New York to pursue an acting career. Soon thereafter, in 1985, his sister Susan died of diabetic complications after giving birth to a baby her doctors cautioned her against conceiving. As a mournful tribute, he wrote *Steel Magnolias* in ten days, basing Shelby, of course, on Susan, and Shelby's mother on his own, Margaret.

The other characters, he has said, are amalgams of southern townsfolk with whom he grew up.

It was Susan, Harling recalled, who opened his eyes to the beauty-parlor phenomenon in their Louisiana hometown of Natchitoches (pronounced, confoundingly, NACK-uh-tush). "She pointed out to me that at around eight A.M. every Saturday, all the ladies in the neighborhood disappeared mysteriously into the beauty shop. They all returned a couple of hours later with the same hairdo, in the shape of a lacquered football helmet. Spooky. We considered it a tonsorial version of *Invasion of the Body Snatchers*."

Julia later said, "I grew up with those kinds of women. I know those kinds of women, but I never wanted to be one of [them]."

For Julia to play a dying woman so soon after her own brush with death, she later joked, would be "my first attempt at Method acting." She was both excited and intimidated by the project, her first big-budget Hollywood movie ($35 million), a paycheck of $90,000, and a cast of superstars. She and Sally Field had become friends through Sally's husband, Alan Greisman. Sally recommended her for the part, a pivotal one in the ensemble. Julia would be acting in the company of three Academy Award winners: Field (twice), MacLaine, and Dukakis. Dolly Parton had earned an Oscar nomination in 1980 for writing the title song for her film *9 to 5*. Rounding out the core cast was the gorgeous Daryl Hannah, who had made a big splash in Ron Howard's recent mermaid movie.

Sam Shepard (the actor Julia had imagined the writer of *Nantucket Solitaire* looked like) would play Dolly Parton's husband; Tom Skerritt was cast as Sally's hubby; and Dylan McDermott, a dark and handsome young actor, would play Shelby's fiancé (later husband), Jackson Latcherie. The film would be produced by the legendary (not always for positive reasons) Ray Stark, best known for producing the Streisand films *Funny Girl* and *The Way We Were;* and directed by a former choreographer, sixty-two-year-old Herbert Ross, who had directed Streisand in *The Owl and the Pussycat* and *Funny Lady,* guided Richard Dreyfuss to an Oscar in *The Goodbye Girl,* and directed MacLaine and Anne Bancroft in the brilliant ballet drama *The Turning Point.*

As overwhelmed as she was by the dimensions of her role and the blinding star power of her costars and director, Julia also knew that *Steel Magnolias* offered her a rare opportunity to jump into the Hollywood big time. She didn't think she'd win the part. "When I got the call to audition for the movie, I asked who was in it. When they told me, I said, 'Yeah, right.' I went to the audition with the intention of not getting it. I would go to the reading and do the best I could to try to impress somebody for a future role."

She grew further discouraged when she heard from Bob McGowan and Risa Shapiro that Herbert Ross didn't seem interested in her. According to McGowan, "Ross did not even want to look at the tape of *Mystic Pizza*," which was scheduled for release in the fall of 1988. Ross finally did watch the movie, but only to check out one of its other actresses, who was one of seventy-five he had lined up to audition for him personally. In a generous collegial gesture, Sally Field read with all the prospective Shelbys who were called back after they passed first muster with Ross.

Paul Hirsch, the film's editor, recalled that "I was present when Herb Ross was casting the part of Shelby, and saw him read every young actress in Hollywood at that time. I remember Laura Dern was remarkable, but she looked hopelessly unlike Sally, who was already cast as her mother."

In 1993, Ross told Stephen Rebello in *Movieline* magazine that Ray Stark, who had produced *Baja Oklahoma*, asked him to watch that movie in order to see Julia. Ross did and thought she "looked bad and gave a very bad performance. . . . I desperately wanted Meg Ryan [who instead decided to take the starring role in *When Harry Met Sally* . . .], and I was crazy about Winona Ryder, who was just too young." Ross continued to resist auditioning Julia until Sally Field stepped in and made a personal appeal, telling Ross that Julia was perfect to play her daughter. Sally recognized that Julia lived up to the sobriquet *steel magnolia* as much as any of the other actresses already cast.

Ross finally relented. "I had the great fortune of having my last audition be with Sally," Julia said. "She was great, and she, like, went into this little improv at the end, and I was like, 'Whew, here we go,' and we just did this whole thing and it was great. She was every reason why I got that part."

Paul Hirsch recalled that the director "was absolutely blown away" by Julia's audition. "To be honest, I didn't think Julia read particularly well, but Herbert recognized immediately the star quality she possesses. He couldn't stop talking about her after she left. He kept saying, 'Did you see that?' "

In his director's commentary on the DVD version of the film, Ross makes an odd claim: "Everybody was against my using her, because they didn't think she was pretty enough." It certainly wasn't everybody—at the very least, Ray Stark and Sally Field stood in Julia's corner, and few observers to date had expressed any reservations about Julia's attractiveness. Despite the apparently positive impression she had made, Ross put Julia through four more auditions. She recalled that she developed a mantra to get her through the uncertainty: "Don't forget who you are and *where you come from*."

At last Ross called her with the news that she had won the role. Julia recalled that she politely said, "Thank you," then she and a group of friends went to the Polo Lounge in Beverly Hills to celebrate. "We just got totally smashed and really whooped it up."

Her pleasure slipped a notch when Ross insisted a few days later that she lose weight (even though she was thinner than normal after her illness), dye her hair a lighter shade of brown, and change the shape of her eyebrows. She had to accomplish this in little more than a week, since rehearsals were set to begin in Natchitoches within two weeks of her casting.

CHAPTER TWELVE

The approximately eighteen thousand residents of that steamy, bucolic Louisiana hamlet on the Cane River (actually a lake, but a very narrow one) hadn't been swept up in such excitement since 1959, when John Wayne and William Holden set up camp to film the Civil War drama *The Horse Soldiers*. "It was staggering to the townsfolk that [so many big stars] would become residents in town," Robert Harling wrote in *Life* magazine. The town had only two restaurants, one of them Lasyone's, where the cast and crew tried the local culinary specialty, the Natchitoches meat pie—a spicy fried pie encased in a flaky outer crust—then polished it off with a piece of the local dessert specialty, Cane River pie.

The absence of hotel rooms left the production with "an important question," Harling recalled. "Where were the stars going to live? Moving out of your house and renting it to the 'movie people' became the civic thing to do." Tom Skerritt, who played the character modeled after Harling's father, lived in the house next to the writer's parents' home. Shirley MacLaine and Julia chose houses next door to each other (Julia shared hers with her basset hound puppy, Gatsby); Dolly Parton and Olympia Dukakis lived nearby. Only Daryl Hannah chose to avoid the hullabaloo; she rented a farm on the edge of town and rode horses when she wasn't needed on the set. "A staunch Republican living near Olympia tried to find a DUKAKIS FOR PRESIDENT sign to put in her yard," Harling recalled. (Dukakis's cousin Michael would accept the Democratic presidential nomination within weeks.) "[The woman] had no intention of voting for a Democrat, but she felt it was the neighborly thing to do."

Once the cast had assembled, they held a press conference, along with Ray Stark, Herb Ross, Mayor Joe Sampite, and Sheriff Norm Fletcher. The conference led off local news broadcasts and filled an entire page of the twice-weekly *Natchitoches Times*. "It's definitely a very big deal for us," said Eric Jenson, who covered the conference for the newspaper. "The stars said nice things about filming in this part of the country, and there were jokes about the hot weather and about learning to talk southern."

Julia, of course, had just learned how *not* to "talk southern," but she worked with a coach to master the Louisiana dialect. Even Dolly Parton, who grew up in the Tennessee Smoky Mountains, used a coach to make her accent more in tune with Louisiana. In the end, each of the six actresses had a different timbre to her twang, but few seemed to care.

Whatever trepidation Julia might have felt about working with such powerhouse costars—observers were already dubbing the project "Steel Divas"—she found each of the women to be supportive rather than competitive. "It was sort of like the environment dictated the necessity of keeping everyone's fearful side in check," Shirley MacLaine explained, "and that's what everybody did. So there was never an ounce or moment of fear—and that's what governs all those mechanisms of temperament."

Actually, Julia did have moments of trepidation, not least of which when she met MacLaine, a woman who had been a star for almost forty years, belonged to Frank Sinatra's Rat Pack, worked with Alfred Hitchcock and Billy Wilder, knew Jack Kennedy, costarred with Jack Nicholson, Jack Lemmon, Clint Eastwood, and Robert Mitchum, danced the cancan for Soviet premier Nikita Khrushchev, had a brother named Warren Beatty, and claimed to have lived any number of other lives through the ages. "The first time we met, I felt she was looking right through me, which is very funny to me now," Julia said several years later. "I went over to her house one day, and we got into this intense conversation in which I talked nonstop for an hour and a half about feelings and families and ideas and goals. And when I finished, this amazing woman dissected everything I'd said, starting from the beginning. I was absolutely blown away by her extraordinary gift of really *listening* to a person."

In her memoir *My Lucky Stars*, MacLaine was typically perspicacious when it came to her characterization of Julia. "Her cheekbones, her smile, her tall, thin, eye-catching body, and her raucous laughter were meant for stardom ... It wasn't so much her charisma, her carriage or command, that made her magnetic. It was the way she filled the spaces between her words and movement. Her facial expressions were immediately in sync with her feelings. The immediacy was so involving, it was hard to look at anyone else for fear of missing an electrifying moment of raw expression."

Julia's costars quickly established a team atmosphere. "I never really had time to stop and say, 'This is Sally Field, she's won two Academy Awards, she's made this many movies, okay, okay, oh my God.' I never had time to do that, because they so immediately took up the role of just being Sally and Shirley and being supportive friends, and they treated me like an equal before I ever began to deserve it." Sally Field became Julia's surrogate mother and "taught me how to give"; Olympia Dukakis "made me terribly political"; Daryl Hannah helped her realize "I am an okay girl and I have something to offer"; and Dolly Parton gave her a sense of gratitude to be in the singular position of movie star. "One day it was really hot," Julia recalled, "and we were all wearing winter clothes, and *everyone* was complaining except Dolly. I asked her why, and she said, 'A long time ago I said to myself, "I want to be a star. And if I ever get to be a big star, I will not complain, because I will have gotten what I asked for." Well, I am, therefore I don't.' "

Julia has said that because of her closeness to Sally Field, "the time I was with her was the longest period that I didn't call my mom. I wound up calling Sally instead. She has great maternal instincts as well as being a great actress." One day, while her mother visited the set, Julia called out, "Mom!" and both Betty and Sally turned around.

Julia bonded with Robert Harling and his family as well. "They are the nicest, dearest people," she said, "and they put me at ease immediately upon entering the house. It was, like, forget about handshakes—there was *hugging*. Mr. and Mrs. Harling and I didn't talk about Susan to a great extent until near the end of the show. Which was probably better, because the more I knew about her, the more I would just cry all the time. She was an unbelievable individual."

Julia needed all the emotional support she could get the very first day of filming, when Herbert Ross threw her feet-first into the fire by shooting, before anything else, "the dreaded scene," as he put it, "that we had rehearsed endlessly"—a harrowing one during which Shelby has a diabetic fit in the beauty parlor. It proved one of the toughest things Julia has to this day done on-screen. "I was concentrating so hard on what it would look like inside myself—the way my heart looked, the rate it was pumping, all the blood racing through my veins—I got so far down inside my body that as we were coming to the end of the scene, a panic went through me. I had gotten stuck down there and didn't want anybody to know. I thought, *I'm never going to get out of here!* I finally did, but I sobbed hysterically after it was over."

Shirley MacLaine recalled, "As I watched her work in front of the cameras, I realized she believed everything was truly happening to her. It wasn't acting, exactly. She went through real discomfort. . . . When an audience senses that an actor is dangerously real, they are riveted."

According to Harling, Julia "would take herself so far down, it was scary. She had this magnificent control. She came as close to death as you can while you're still alive. After every take, they'd have to pick her up and help her back to her trailer. I had been through this sort of thing with my sister, and I just wanted to go over and hug her and tell Herbert, 'Okay, stop it. Let's not do this anymore.'"

Sally Field did have to tell Herb Ross to "Stop it!" later in the filming. Unhappy with the performance she was giving, Ross gave Julia a very hard time, often upbraiding her in front of the ensemble. "There was a time when he was picking on me so bad that Sally, God bless her, said, 'If you don't let up, I'm just going to go wait, because I can't be around this. It's too pointless and it's too mean.'"

Paul Hirsch remembered, "Herbert often remarked that Julia hadn't yet learned technique, so he felt he needed to be her teacher, I imagine." At one point Ross asked Julia, "Are you going to go back to New York to study [acting]?"

"What for?" Julia replied.

Hirsch felt that Ross was equally hard on other actors. "He could be very demanding of his performers, and his style of directing grew out of his background in dance, where choreographers are notoriously blunt, even brutal, with their criticisms. Having said that, he was also the best director of actors I have ever worked with, and his pictures were often nominated for best performance in the acting categories. I don't know his record, but it must rank near the top in numbers of acting nominations. He was not above using tricks to elicit performances."

In 1993, Ross said his problem with Julia was that "she could only play the top of the scenes—bright and cheerful, in a general way, never understanding the subtext of her character's being desperately afraid. We shot and shot, and I somehow was able to get that subtext out of her falsely, by saying, 'That's not right, try this,' getting her very nervous."

Julia wasted little time firing back. "Let's just take a moment to talk about Herbert Ross," she told Christopher Connelly in the December 1993 issue of *Premiere*. "I just read an article in a magazine where Herbert gives me a tongue-lashing beyond comprehension. If there's any-one I've gone out of my way to be diplomatic about, it's Herbert Ross, because I don't play that game. . . . [If] someone asks me if he was hard on me, *yes* is the answer. But I have certainly never said anything bad about him to the press. He [says] that in my lack of technique, he found it very difficult—was hard on me—because I did not understand sub-text and could only play joyful and sunny. This I completely disagree with. Do I have no technique? I have my own technique. I don't know what it is. It's not anything you're going to read in a book. He made it sound like he was *forced* to hire me. He went out of his way to talk about the people he wanted over me, like I was shoved down his throat.

"I was very young and had just come from being very sick. He was mean, and he was out of line, in my opinion. Now he rationalizes it that he was trying to get a performance out of me that he felt I did not pos-sess. This is probably something we will always disagree about. Fine. I don't give a shit. But if he thinks he can talk about me in such a conde-scending way and not have me say something about it . . . then he's nuts."

Shirley MacLaine's take on Julia's problems with Ross came from her experience working with him on *The Turning Point*. "[He] regarded Julia as one of his 'baby ballerinas.' That is to say, he wished to have a ballet master's control over his new discoveries. He wanted [Julia] to never eat more than a thousand calories a day. He claimed he could detect the effects of an extra saltine cracker on an actress's face."

It's hard to imagine what more Ross could have wanted from Julia; her performance is well modulated and extremely touching. And while her technique may not have pleased him, she certainly had one, as evi-denced by her approach to both the diabetic-fit scene and her death scene, in which she lay in a hospital bed, hooked up to IV tubes. Julia remained still and comalike for hours, not even getting up between takes to have a Coke. "That created an eerie feeling," a crew member recalled. "You really felt there was a life hovering in the balance, even though we knew it was just a set built in a gymnasium. There was an incredible power in her stillness."

When she wasn't filming, Julia would write poetry, and some nights she would show up at the Bodacious nightclub on Highway 14, pick up the karaoke microphone, and, according to Shirley, "sing her heart out."

On the Fourth of July, Ross invited the cast to his house. As Julia recalled, "We went over and had dinner and fireworks, the whole thing, and we played a game called sardines—in which Herbert turned off all the lights in the house and hid [in a closet]. We were all supposed to independently try to find him, and when we did, we were supposed to get in the closet, and finally we would all be packed in the closet like sardines."

Kinky. But it never happened. "We were all too scared once the lights went out, we were all holding hands and running around and screaming like a bunch of . . . meemies."

The filming of the wedding scene of Shelby and Jackson created a reaction among the extras that Julia hadn't expected. "When we filmed the wedding, the more often we did it, the more untrue it was, the more we said, 'This is fiction, this isn't real,' the more the people loved it, and the more the people loved to see these two people in love. As the hours went by, I went up and down the aisle and up and down the aisle. And every time I went by, these people looked at me and were more joyous, more captivated . . . I got congratulated all over the place from people. People love to be in love, and they love to see it. I think when they become familiar with a couple, it's just that much more. They expect to see you together, and they know you'll always love each other."

What Julia failed to mention in this philosophical riff is that she was repeating the cliché of the on-set romance (and hardly for the last time). Julia had been drawn to the blue-eyed, rangy six-foot McDermott almost from the moment she saw him. A sturdily built twenty-five-year-old, he was born in Waterbury, Connecticut, and raised by his tavern-manager father in New York's Greenwich Village. His mother had died three years after divorcing his father, when Dylan was two.

"I was close by when it happened," McDermott said. "But I didn't see it happen. I was outside." Diane McDermott had shot herself in the head with her boyfriend's .32-caliber pistol. The Waterbury police judged the death an accident. "I don't talk about the specifics of how she died," McDermott said. "I was five. What happens is that you are no longer a kid. It made me who I am, good or bad . . . It was either going to kill me or make me stronger."

By his own account, he was "something of a delinquent" as a teenager until his stepmother, Eve Ensler (playwright of *The Vagina Monologues*), urged him toward acting. He had made his film debut in the

1987 Vietnam War drama *Hamburger Hill; Steel Magnolias* was only his second film assignment.

Friends of Liam Neeson have said he was shocked by the breakup call he got from Julia. "He was one of the nicest people you'll ever meet in your life," a friend said. "When Julia was in the hospital with viral meningitis, he called the hospital all the time. He was very worried about her, very concerned." Neeson's longtime colleague Tod Todoroff described him as "devastated" by Julia's rejection. "Liam got very sick over that. He was hurting big-time."

Neeson is loath to discuss his private life with reporters. When one asked him about his relationship with Julia and a later one with Barbra Streisand, he snappishly replied, "Is that what it's going to say on my tombstone? 'He dated Julia Roberts and Barbra Streisand'?"

Julia was later quoted by friends as having said, "I know I did a silly thing, letting my love affair with Liam slip away. I adored him as a person and admired him tremendously as an actor. I have only fond memories of Liam. I know I hurt him, and I'm sorry."

Shortly after *Steel Magnolias* wrapped, Julia took a major step: She got engaged to McDermott.

CHAPTER THIRTEEN

While Julia struggled to commit her characterization of Shelby Eatenton Latcherie to the screen, executives at Goldwyn—the studio that had signed on to distribute *Mystic Pizza*—got very excited by what they saw on-screen of Julia Roberts. Joe Roth, who would become Julia's producing partner and direct her in 2001 in *America's Sweethearts*, recalled his reaction when he first saw the film. "I didn't know who she was. I didn't know she was Eric Roberts's sister, and I couldn't take my eyes off her. I found myself sort of following her around on-screen, and afterwards, boy, I thought, *I'd better give this girl a call, because I think she's going to be a big star.*"

The executives at Goldwyn agreed, and encouraged by three successful advance screenings of *Mystic Pizza*, they committed $6.5 million to advertising and promotion (a record for a low-budget film, according to *Variety*). The movie was set to open on October 21, 1988, on 375 screens in the top-forty markets. Promotions included more than a hundred additional screenings, running from Labor Day to the second week of October, to start word of mouth; bridal-shop giveaways through local radio stations; and tie-ins with the pizza chains Domino's and Numero Uno, which planned to offer "Mystic Pizzas" and put the movie's advertising artwork on their boxes.

Not long after Julia completed filming *Steel Magnolias*, Goldwyn sent her out on a *Mystic Pizza* publicity junket with her female costars, the first time she'd been asked to do publicity for a film. The three women, who have remained friends, stressed what they felt made the film important. "There are so few films from women's perspectives," said Lili Taylor. Annabeth Gish added, "I think this movie is realistic. I have a lot of good friends who are women, and maintaining those friendships is important to me."

For Julia, the film's sense of reality was key. "I like to see movies that are real. Things with heart and soul, not ones that are just about sex or silly surface feelings. *Mystic Pizza* isn't *Apocalypse Now,* but we have a little heart and soul. All our characters are honest." All three actresses bemoaned the state of women in American films. "They're treated like pieces of dirt," Taylor said. "Or cheesecake," Gish interjected. "If women didn't play the kind of women that they wouldn't hang out with," Julia concluded, "there would be fewer of those roles. We wouldn't see so many surface cheese puffs."

When *Mystic Pizza* opened, its reviews, written mostly by men, were largely negative. Tom Matthews, writing in *Boxoffice* magazine, said, "It's funny that it took four writers to come up with 'Mystic Pizza,' seeing as how it is a virtual clearinghouse of every romantic cliché ever devised." Michael Wilmington, in the *Los Angeles Times,* agreed. "Ah, Daisy! Ah, Kat, ah, pretty little Jojo! Ah, you bouncing, beautiful bachelorettes on the loose! Where have we seen this trio before? A fiery sexpot, a shy intellectual, and a kooky kidder? Three girls dreaming their dreams, and breaking their hearts in the search for the best of everything . . . Even, as here, the perfect pizza."

It's true that there are few entirely original thoughts or situations in the film's 101-minute running time, but the screenwriters at least tried to put a modern spin on the scenes they stole. When Daisy's rich boyfriend, Charlie, gets a flat tire on the way to dinner, his outstretched thumb is unable to persuade any passing cars to stop. Then Daisy tries her hand at it. This is in homage to a famous scene from the Best Picture Oscar winner of 1934, *It Happened One Night,* starring Clark Gable and Claudette Colbert. When Clark's efforts to hitch them a ride fail, Claudette lifts her skirt, shows a little leg, and the next car down the highway screeches to a stop. In *Mystic Pizza,* after Daisy bends over to shake out her hair and adopts a come-hither posture, cars still zoom by. Finally, Charlie tries again (after mimicking the hair motion) and drops his pants. *That* brings a carful of young women to the rescue.

The film offers a number of other amusements. The scenes in the pizza parlor are frenetic and fun, helped along by Conchata Ferrell as Leona, the mother hen with the top-secret recipe. All three girls wear T-shirts with the words A LITTLE SLICE OF HEAVEN across their bosoms. Julia's first line in the film, after she nearly collides with her sister carrying a pizza tray, is: "Whoa—do you think I have eyes in my butt?" Kat replies, "That's where your brains are." When Charlie brings Daisy to his parents' winterized beach house, there isn't much time for sappy romanticism: Daisy is out of her clothes and upstairs before he even gets the fire going. She has left a trail of clothes up the stairs and calls out, "Chaaaarlieee—follow the bread crumbs!"

The tense scene in which Daisy meets Charlie's rich, prissy, prejudiced family is a gem, culminating in Charlie snapping the tablecloth to pull most of the dishes off the table. They are served lobster, which Daisy, as a Portuguese girl living in a fishing village, has pretty much had her fill of. Matt Damon, in his first speaking role in a movie, plays Steamer, Charlie's brother. His first line is "Mom, do you want my green stuff?" The father interjects, "That's called the tomalley, Steamer, and it's the best part." Then Charlie tells his brother, "It's the shit, Steamer. Don't eat it."

The movie's charm comes largely from the ingratiating personalities of its young stars, and their personal notices were better than the film's. "Gish and Roberts (a real working-class knockout) are especially attractive," Tom Matthews wrote. To Michael Wilmington, Julia was something of a revelation. "Best of them is Roberts, who suffered through *Satisfaction* but here has a minor triumph as Daisy. Roberts, the younger sister of actor Eric, shows a priceless movie quality: a real sense of danger and unpredictability. When she bemusedly lectures her sister or sizes up Adam Storke in the local bar, she begins generating her own smoky tension: the livid fire of a small-town belle, blazing up high against the possibility of inevitable small-town entropy or eclipse."

Julia does indeed smolder in her first extended scene, a pool-game-cum-seduction in which she looks stunning, fairly exhales sex, and sinks six cue balls in a row, once without taking her eyes off the blond hunk she has set her sights on. It's the kind of scene destined to make a performer a star, and it did just that. The buzz in Hollywood, even before *Mystic Pizza* opened, was that Julia Roberts, unknown a year earlier, had a career that was now on the fast track.

As part of the publicity blitz, Goldwyn sent Julia to Atlanta, where she was hailed as a hometown girl made good. JULIA ROBERTS ARRIVES, trumpeted *The Atlanta Constitution* article on October 29, the day after her twenty-first birthday. SMYRNA NATIVE'S NOT JUST ERIC'S LITTLE SISTER ANYMORE.

Wearing black bicycle pants, her hair "unruly," Julia held court with the *Constitution* staff writer Steve Dollar in her suite at the Ritz-Carlton in Buckhead, a fashionable area of Atlanta. "I think there's something to be said for the humility of coming from a small place," she said.

"Remembering where you came from and what it was like to have your feet stained with clay all summer long. I think coming back semi-frequently is a good, consistent grounding thing for me."

Dollar described Daisy Araujo as "a feisty part, in which Miss Roberts gets to swear a blue streak, trash her yuppie boyfriend's Porsche, and woo the camera with her radiant good looks." Julia added that "[Daisy] was somebody I might have been if I had been different, if that makes any sense. I could relate to her in a lot of ways, but at the same time she had a lot of gusto, a lot of chutzpah, that I never had. It was a little scary being Daisy, because she's kind of like ten feet tall, and I'm happy being five [foot] eight." Asked about the upcoming screening of the film at the Galleria, which her family planned to attend, Julia said, "I'm pleased with it. It's nice to be able to come back home with a triumph to lay at your mama's feet. That's a really neat feeling."

Julia said she'd been run ragged by the last two years of almost non-stop filmmaking and publicizing. "I could really use a hot bath and a nap to put it all back into perspective."

Perhaps because Daisy Araujo is a larger-than-life character, or because Julia was taller than her two costars, audiences came away from *Mystic Pizza* thinking her an imposingly big woman. "I think I disappointed a lot of people," Julia said. "They expected this dark-haired, stiletto-heeled thing, and then this willowy, washed-out blonde enters their office." In Rome, where she held a press conference to promote the film in the spring of 1989, she felt the disappointment quite strongly. "They expected this buxom chickadee to come walking in, and at that point I was really skinny. I sat down on the sofa, and they're all there, looking at the assistant of the girl they're waiting for, you know? When I finally said, 'So, anyone want to ask me anything?'—I mean, faces *dropped*. It was not good for the confidence level, I'll tell you that."

Mystic Pizza took in $14 million in domestic box-office receipts, hardly a blockbuster but not bad for a low-budget film. Enough people saw it that Julia found her privacy harder than ever to protect. Not long after the film opened, she recalled, "I was in the bathroom somewhere, and this girl followed me and said, 'Excuse me, girl in stall number one?' I said, 'Yeaaah?' She said, 'You were in *Mystic Pizza*.' I said, 'Yeaaah?' She said, 'Can I have your autograph?' I said, 'I'm a little tied up right now.' "

Matters got even more vexing for Julia when *Mystic Pizza* aired on national television in 1990, before *Pretty Woman* was released. "I was on Main Street in Venice, California," she recalled, "just kind of walking around—I looked like hell, I might add—and every store I went into, somebody mentioned *Mystic Pizza*. By the time I got home, I was a wreck. I mean, it was nice all these strangers had good things to say about the movie and my performance, because you work to entertain. But I was at home with my dog, Gatsby, and I was saying out loud, 'This is getting out of hand!' I remember calling my mom and having a mild breakdown."

Julia had also been wrung out by the rigors of playing Shelby Eatenton Latcherie under Herbert Ross's disgruntled direction. When *Steel Magnolias* was released in November 1989, however, the travails proved worth it. She had an idea something big was afoot when the September 4 fall-preview issue of *People* featured her and her five female costars on the cover of the magazine's "fab guide to the season's biggest and best movies, TV shows, music, books—and more." It was Julia's first national magazine cover, and it's interesting to note that, although her costars are baring their teeth in wide grins, Julia—who would soon become world-renowned for her "thousand-watt smile"—barely has an upturned mouth.

Steel Magnolias got mixed reviews; again, most of the bad ones were from men who couldn't relate to a "chick flick." Anthony Lane, the brilliant *New Yorker* critic who can skewer a film more thoroughly with wit than malice, later wrote of the movie, "The characters had names like Clairee, Truvy, and M'Lynn, the very sound of which, I recall, was enough to make me bring up m'lunch."

In a *Newsweek* review, David Denby wrote, "As directed by Herbert Ross, it is so intent on persuading the audience that it is having a heartwarming emotional experience you almost expect TelePrompTers to flash in the theater, instructing you to laugh and cry." He did, however, praise Julia, whom, he gushed, "lights up the screen with her liquid fire." Vincent Canby in *The New York Times* praised the performances of MacLaine, Dukakis, Parton, and Field but gave Julia less of a compliment: "Miss Roberts, the sister of Eric, plays a beautiful young woman who happens to be diabetic with the kind of mega-intensity the camera cannot always absorb."

It was just that "mega-intensity," combined with a fresh personality and breathtaking looks, that helped captivate audiences (about 70 percent of them women) who flocked to the film and helped it gross a whopping $90 million domestically ($130 million in 2002 dollars).

"You could definitely say the phone has been ringing," Julia's agent, Elaine Goldsmith, said in 1990. "The reaction we've gotten has been incredibly positive. People really feel she's one of a kind." *Parade,* in a profile of Julia on July 7, quoted Dan Polier, a veteran film buyer and producer's representative: "In my opinion, Julia Roberts generates the best qualities of Debra Winger, Audrey Hepburn, Meryl Streep, and Sigourney Weaver—range, intelligence, depth and a sense of humor. Add these to her own package of winning personality, likable presence and wholesome sex appeal, and you've got a winner. I keep telling people that she shows more potential for lasting stardom than any other young actress. Unless she succumbs to poor material—which I doubt, because she has a fine agent in Elaine Goldsmith at William Morris— I'd say that, in her, the industry has found a new rising star."

Julia found herself at a sometimes dizzying crossroads in her life. The local train to success she had hopped on three years earlier had suddenly turned into an express, and the ramifications left her at once exhilarated, exhausted, and confused. Her career decisions now had to be made with great care, and with an eye toward keeping her star on the rise. She would have to make major adjustments in the way she led her private life, if she hoped to retain a semblance of privacy. And she learned that relationships can be difficult to maintain for a busy actress, especially one involved with an equally busy actor.

For most of their first year affianced, Julia and Dylan had to be content to visit each other on movie locations, something Julia found difficult. In the summer of 1989, while she was in Los Angeles shooting her first starring role in a film then called *3000,* Dylan was in Morocco, nearly six thousand miles away, filming *Hardware,* a low-budget science-fiction film. The distance between them, exacerbated by his jealousy over her love scenes with her new costar, Richard Gere, would put an untenable strain on their relationship.

Julia's meteoric rise put a strain on her other relationships as well, both personal and professional. Shortly after *Mystic Pizza* opened, her management contract with Bob McGowan was set to expire. She visited his office, and he asked whether she would like to continue their partnership. "I'll never forget this," McGowan said. "She came over and hugged me and said, 'Bob, you started this. I want you in my life forever.'" Ten days later, McGowan got a phone call from Elaine Goldsmith. "Julia doesn't want you as her manager anymore," Goldsmith said. McGowan was stunned, and hurt that Julia hadn't told him herself about her change of heart (or perhaps had misled him). Julia's friends have often pointed out that she loathes confrontation, a legacy of the battles between her parents and between Betty and Michael Motes. It was far easier to let Elaine Goldsmith be the bearer of the bad news.

"That was the most difficult decision I had to make in my life," Julia said. "Bob had gone to bat for me, but I felt I had to be honest. We'd outgrown each other. There were too many people around me making decisions, and I wanted a clearer line between me and the work." McGowan professed to have no hard feelings toward Julia. "I think we *did* sort of outgrow each other. The only thing that bothered me was the way it was done."

Julia also had less time now to deal with the increasingly erratic behavior of her brother. She had moved back to Manhattan, into a sunny two-bedroom flat on the top floor of a brownstone in Greenwich Village, with a fireplace, a skylight, and wide-planked oak floors. In a *Rolling Stone* profile of Julia in 1989, James Kaplan described the place as "the kind of apartment an over-optimistic set designer might create for the Young Actress in a Neil Simon type of property . . . all that's missing is a cute, funny old cat named Mr. Raffles."

Living again in the same city as Eric brought his self-destructive behavior into sharp and painful focus for Julia. Press reports said that she had gone to Eric's apartment on West Seventy-third Street and found him "in a stupor." In tears, she begged him to let her help; she offered to fly him to California and pay for treatment at the Betty Ford Center. Eric refused the suggestion. "I don't have a problem," he said. "Everybody else does."

"I've tried to help him, but I can't get through," Julia reportedly told a friend. "I want to help, but I won't let him destroy me, too." At this point the family estrangement that began with Eric's refusal to see or speak to his mother (except when Julia was hospitalized with meningitis) extended to his sisters, both of whom drew away from him. Within two years, Julia would cease all communication with Eric. As of 2003 they have not spoken to each other—except testily, and through the media—in over ten years.

Eric blames childhood trauma for the chasm. "The abuse we suffered as children, and our inability to handle it, has caused a rift in the family." And while Eric accuses his mother as much as his father and Michael Motes for the abuse, Julia "is on my mom's side in every family squabble. My mom and I don't get along, so Julie and I don't get along. But I love her. I'll always love Julie. However, I think insecurities that maybe she's just now coming to terms with can be traced back to her tough childhood, where none of us got enough love."

Julia's behavior—entering into five serious romantic relationships within five years—would tend to support the notion that she had a deep-seated need for the validation of a man's love. While she has refused to discuss Michael Motes publicly, she has addressed Eric's decades-long addiction to marijuana and cocaine, which she blames for the rift between them. "Many moments of [her and Lisa's] youth were spent in trying to save Eric from the wreckage of his abuse," she told David Hochman of *Us* magazine in 1996. "You have to realize he's eleven years older than me. He's an adult. It's a very interesting scenario, seeing children trying to help the adult. It can be incredibly taxing and frustrating."

Appearing on television's *The View* in 2001, after he had been sober for several years, Eric acknowledged his fault in the matter. "I love both my sisters," he said, "but I was such a handful, see, I did [heavy] drugs for about ten years of my life, and I ruined every relationship I ever had. . . . I've tried to get in touch with them [Julia and Lisa] for about seven years now, but they won't call me back. And I've tried everything I can. I wrote letters, I sent telegrams. I sent gifts. I sent flowers. They really have had it with me. It's not their fault. If there's any kind of fault to take, it would have to be mine."

Part Three

THIS YEAR'S GIRL

"Pretty Woman *didn't come to the town I was working in while I was there. . . . [My agent] would call and give me reports on this movie's status. It was hard to believe what she was telling me.*"

—Julia, 1990

CHAPTER FOURTEEN

As often happens when a film grosses over $463 million worldwide, a legend has grown around the movie that made Julia Roberts a superstar and earned her the lasting nickname "America's Pretty Woman." Pop culture mavens can recite the story of how a dark script entitled *3000*—about Vivian Ward, a drug-addicted prostitute who is turned into Cinderella for a week by Edward Lewis, a wealthy business-man, then is sent back to the streets—was bought by Disney and trans-formed into a fairy tale with the requisite happy ending.

Julia herself has told the story vividly. On *Inside the Actors Studio*, she described the script of *3000*, written by J. F. Lawton, as "a really dark and depressing, horrible, terrible story about two horrible people . . . and [my] character was this drug addict, a bad-tempered, foulmouthed, ill-humored, poorly educated hooker who had this weeklong experi-ence with a foulmouthed, ill-tempered, bad-humored, very wealthy, handsome, but horrible man, and it was just a grisly, ugly story about these two people."

Julia has also said that she was eager to play the role, which lends cre-dence to Lawton's assertion that "the original story of *3000* was basi-cally like the movie *Pretty Woman* except for the ending—he didn't fall in love with her in the original script, and she does end up back on the street." Lawton admitted that in his original script, Vivian was "partially a crack smoker," and that her fellow hooker and friend Kit was very ill, "almost a *Midnight Cowboy* thing."

Lawton, twenty-eight at the time, had kicked around Hollywood for several years, editing film trailers and aspiring to write movies. After writing and directing *Cannibal Women in the Avocado Jungle of Death* under a pseudonym, he began to circulate the script of *3000*. "Everyone was interested in it," he recalled. He directed some scenes from the story at Robert Redford's Sundance Institute in Utah. Vestron Pictures bought the script and planned to make it as a low-budget ($3 million) feature "with the original ending and the original tone," Lawton said. "Hollywood has this strange dichotomy. They all want to make money, but deep down they all want to win Oscars. So they're always intrigued by things that seem uncommercial."

One of the Vestron producers, Gary Goldstein, had seen Julia in *Mystic Pizza* and thought she'd be perfect as Vivian. He sent the script to Elaine Goldsmith, who was now Julia's full-time agent. According to Lawton, "Julia really liked it." The soon-to-be Pretty Woman told Michael Reese of *Newsweek* that she "chased [the part] down like a dog. . . . I just loved [the character]. My reaction to her was a balance of intrigue and fear—the same balance I felt toward Daisy in *Mystic Pizza* and Shelby in *Steel Magnolias*."

Vestron, with its small budget, was all for hiring Julia Roberts, even though her ability to carry an entire feature film was untested. But the project collapsed, Lawton claimed, when the company went out of business. Lawton again had an unsold screenplay on his desk, and Julia, who had turned down dozens of scripts after *Steel Magnolias*, suddenly had nothing on her horizon.

Before long, according to Lawton, "a very shrewd producer named Steve Reuther got the rights to *3000* and teamed up with Arnon Milchan. They managed to secretly have a bidding war between Universal and Disney's Touchstone Films for the rights to the script." Touchstone won out, and *3000* had a green light, a $17 million budget, and a problem: With a budget that high, a downbeat ending "isn't necessarily a good idea," as Lawton put it. Still, he said, Touchstone executives weren't opposed to the original ending. "They had gotten some criticism for making 'fluff' movies like *Outrageous Fortune*, and they were very proud of another Bette Midler movie they had just done, *Beaches*, which Garry Marshall directed and which was a little darker." Touchstone wanted Marshall to direct *3000*, and neither they nor Marshall wanted an artificially upbeat ending, according to Lawton. "Garry was a little nervous about making the ending too upbeat, because the script was well respected in Hollywood and he didn't want to be accused of being the guy who turned it into fluff."

Touchstone asked Lawton to do another draft. He considered endings that would have Vivian starting a day-care center; going to work at the hotel where her trysts with Edward took place; or taking up with a different man. None seemed to work. "I did two drafts that made it more of a love story—they got together at the end. I took out the fact that he had a girlfriend he was cheating on with her and a few other things, and Disney's reaction was that I'd gone too far, lightened it up too much."

They asked Lawton to do another draft, but before he completed it, "they fired me and hired another writer, Stephen Metcalfe. Metcalfe made it even darker than my original script; he put in some bondage stuff, had her tie Edward up at one point, and they added this elaborate subplot about drug dealing and Vivian running away from drug dealers." (This may have been the script Julia described on *Inside the Actors Studio*.)

"Then they hired another writer, Robert Garland, and then Barbara Benedek. Garry Marshall had a bunch of writers punching up material, one-liner people. At that point I threw up my hands. I heard rumors they were thinking of hiring me back, but that never happened."

Marshall, a fifty-four-year-old Bronx-born mensch, had gotten his start as a television-comedy writer for Joey Bishop and Jack Paar. He wrote for *The Dick Van Dyke Show* and created classic sitcoms like *Happy Days, Mork & Mindy,* and *Laverne & Shirley* (which costarred his sister Penny). In 1982 he broke into feature films directing *Young Doctors in Love* (a spoof of soap operas). With successes like *Flamingo Kid, Overboard,* and *Beaches,* he had become one of the most sought-after directors in Hollywood.

Luckily for Julia, Marshall thought she'd be a terrific choice to play Vivian. He persuaded Touchstone executives to arrange a meeting. The uncertainty about the direction the story was to take, and whether Julia could handle a starring role in a big-budget movie, made the meeting a memorably muddled one. As Julia described it, "We were the most confused people talking to each other. [Marshall] was saying, 'I don't understand you. Some say you can't dress her up. Some say you can't dress her down. What do I do with you?' And I'd say, 'I don't understand *you*. You're *funny*, but this [script] is bad, and I don't understand what kind of job I'm trying to get.' So we both asked each other a lot of questions, and even until like the moment before we started to shoot the movie, I still was slightly bewildered and stayed in that state the whole filming of the movie."

Marshall and Julia came away liking each other. Julia told Marshall that when she was a little girl, she and Lisa used to pretend they were Laverne and Shirley, and she'd wear a big *L* on her sweater. But Disney continued to have doubts about Julia, so Marshall lobbied to have them test her. "I thought Julia was good" in the tests, Marshall said, "but I couldn't find out where her funny bone was. So I started testing her against men—Tom Conti, Sam Neill. Then I decided to test her against Charles Grodin. I told Julia, 'See this man—he's very funny—he's going to blow you off the screen.' So we did the scene, and of course Charles was ad-libbing and was hysterical. In the middle of the scene, I saw Julia suddenly take a stance, and she started holding her own against Grodin. I had found her funny bone.

"I remember calling the head of Disney after the test with Grodin and saying, 'Listen, we've got a picture even if we don't have a [big star to play the] guy.' I told them she could carry the picture alone, she's that great." Still Disney executives waffled. According to Elaine Goldsmith, "Julia had to wait until the eleventh hour before she got it. The studio was reticent about casting her until they'd cast the male lead. Finally we told them she would take another movie, so they finally agreed and signed her." Her fee, $300,000, was over three times what she had been paid for *Steel Magnolias*.

Now arose the pivotal question of who would play Edward. The producers considered Al Pacino, Sting, and Sean Connery, and Lawton felt that "If they'd hired Pacino, you can bet it would have been a darker movie." Marshall, however, felt he needed a leading man who matched Julia in beauty, freshness, and sex appeal. "I looked for two one-hundred-percent beautiful people," he said. "But there are lots of good-looking actors who can't act at all."

Then, according to Julia, "Somebody came up with the brilliant idea of Richard Gere!" The handsome thirty-nine-year-old had become a sex symbol after indelible performances in his breakthrough films, *Days of Heaven, An Officer and a Gentleman,* and *American Gigolo.* The only problem was that Gere had passed on *3000* months earlier. Julia and Garry Marshall traveled to New York to plead with him. Marshall recalled coming back from a trip to the bathroom in Gere's apartment and seeing Julia and Richard sitting next to each other on the living room sofa. "They were bathed in this eerie light, and they looked so good together that I thought, *We just have to get Richard.* I told Julia she had to persuade him to come on board."

Pressured from both sides by two extremely persuasive people, Gere agreed to join the cast—but only after Marshall promised to beef up the part of Edward. "[The character] was very underwritten," Gere said, "while Julia's character had all the energy. That was one of my problems." Later, he laughingly offered more insight into his original reticence: "In this film, the wild exotic flower was the girl. Usually *I'm* the wild exotic flower." Marshall credited Julia for Gere's change of heart: "I think Richard saw that she wasn't just some crazy girl, some starlet. She could act, and that impressed him."

The cast was completed with Jason Alexander hired to play Edward's sleazy lawyer Philip Stuckey; Laura San Giacomo as Vivian's fellow hooker Kit; Ralph Bellamy as Edward's business rival, James Morse; Alex Hyde-White as Morse's son, David; and Hector Elizondo as the manager of the hotel in which Edward ensconces Vivian.

Another problem had to be worked out before filming began: Julia balked at playing the nude scenes in the script. "There are certain people in this life who should know what you look like naked," she said, "and I just don't think my high school algebra teacher is a person who should be privy to what my butt looks like."

Julia recalled to Christopher Connelly in *Premiere* that she battled with the producers about the nudity issue for weeks. "This is a big movie for me and everything," she told them. "But I'm still not taking my clothes off, you know? I appreciate the job, but I'm not going to get naked for you." In the middle of a heated discussion between Julia and her agent in Elaine's office, the legendarily aggressive and corpulent über-agent Sue Mengers walked in. "I had never met her before," Julia recalled. "Didn't know who she was. She comes in, sits down, and she's got that voice: 'Hello, *dahling*, what's going on?' And Elaine's like, 'Uh, we're having this thing [about nudity],' and Sue goes, 'Oh, what's the big deal? We're not talking *beaver* here!'

"I looked at her. I thought, *Who is this woman?* Why is she saying these things to me? Why is she using that word? And then she's like, 'If I had your body, you'd see me in Gelson's going down the frozen-foods aisle naked!' I think I was breaking out into hives. This woman's talking about my naked body and . . . *Who are you?* Needless to say, I love Sue. Never at a loss for words. But boy, what a meeting. I'll never forget that for the rest of my life. 'Oh, we're not talking about beaver.' Does she know how old I am?"

Julia's body was well nigh perfect at this point in her life. She had lost the extra fifteen to twenty pounds that had helped make Daisy Araujo look voluptuous, and her willowy figure had just enough on top and down below to suggest the proverbial hourglass. The days of studio publicists touting an actress's measurements were long past, but Julia's then were 34-22-34, a nice "package" indeed. Still, she remained adamant in her refusal to show it off unclothed. At last the producers promised to keep any nudity chastely discreet, and Julia felt placated.

Filming on what was now called the "Untitled Garry Marshall Project" was set to begin in Hollywood and Beverly Hills on July 24, 1989. The elegant Regent Beverly Wilshire on the corner of Rodeo Drive and Wilshire Boulevard in Beverly Hills was the only hotel in the Los Angeles area that would grant Marshall permission to film its facade and re-create its lobby. "The Regent Beverly Wilshire," Marshall said, "was the only one that said, 'Well, maybe [we've had a prostitute in here] a couple of times.'" Sets were built in Burbank to replicate the hotel's interiors, as well as Edward's office.

Now all Julia had to do was figure out how to play a streetwalker.

CHAPTER FIFTEEN

Julia had decided that the streets were the best place to do research, so she approached working girls on Hollywood Boulevard. At first they were wary and uncommunicative—but, Julia said, when she offered to spring for a burrito lunch at Del Taco, they loosened up. Julia came away from the experience with a great deal of sympathy and admiration for these women. "These are girls, not unlike me, who look like your average girl, talk like your average girl," she told Myra Forsberg of *The New York Times*. "They have aspirations just like any girl does, except they're in this situation, and they don't really acknowledge it that much. . . . These girls cry a lot, but their common goal was a real focus on the future. One girl wanted to be a makeup artist for Jane Seymour. She was very specific. One girl wanted to be a psychologist. That was amazing to me."

A great deal of what Julia learned from these women wound up not only in her characterization but in the film's plot and dialogue. "A lot of it was improvisational," Julia said. "I would just say things that I knew, and Garry let me do that." One amusing line in the film was inspired by, of all people, Elaine Goldsmith. "Elaine is always saying, 'Let me give you a tip.' Well, Richard and I are doing the scene where he's doing the whole romance thing, and suddenly the absurdity of romancing a prostitute occurs to me. So I say, 'Let me give you a tip—I'm a sure thing.'"

It was at this point that Julia felt she had a handle on how to play Vivian. "That was sort of the beginning of thinking I was in control of this girl. That I had found her voice and what made her funny and silly. Even the first time I saw the movie, I couldn't believe I physically moved around that much. Even just walking to the door, I turned it into a symphony of movement with the boots, because I couldn't walk [in them], so I sort of cracked myself up. But I think it just found its own course."

On the first day of filming, Julia got a real taste of what it's like to peddle oneself on the streets of Hollywood. Dressed in a blond wig and an eight-inch leather skirt, Julia said she "took so much shit for that outfit" from passersby. "I know how to deal with any kind of attention that somebody's going to give Julia Roberts. But the attention that Julia got as Vivian, standing on Hollywood Boulevard in that outfit, was not the kind of attention that I am used to or prepared to deal with. At one point there were so many catcalls directed at me that I went back to my trailer and felt hideous. I just wanted to hide . . . Vivian would say, 'Fuck you! Blow it out your ass!' to anyone who barked at her. I turn red and get hives."

Garry Marshall sensed Julia's vulnerability early on (he nicknamed her "Bambi" a few days into filming) and took it as his mission to make her feel secure. "Julia needs a lot of holding and hugging," he said, "particularly in scenes where there's meanness. In the scenes where she got beat up by Richard's lawyer and when Richard screamed at her, she was playing the vulnerability off-camera, so she could play against it on-camera. So off-camera, I had a sobbing mess on my hands, but on-camera she fought against it, and I think that worked."

Marshall said he tried to accentuate Vivian's fish-out-of-water quality after she meets Edward by having her sit on the floor, on the edge of a desk or dining table. Rarely does she sit in a proper chair, and then she usually squats rather than sits. This kept the character—and Julia—a little off-kilter, which was right for the performance.

Julia appreciated Marshall's avuncular concern for her, especially during the scene in which Edward's attorney attacks her. "You know, some guy comes in and basically says, 'I'm gonna fuck you whether you like it or not,' and then throws you down on the floor and jumps on top of you, and you're screaming—I think you might feel a little fragile. Garry is a great hugger, a great supporter, he's really right on, but I got thrown on the floor a lot, and it didn't feel so good. I'm not going to pretend that I'm all brave and it's all really easy."

After one day's filming had extended into the early-morning hours, Julia passed out. "The crew was buzzed with this news that she might be sick or have appendicitis," Marshall wrote in his memoir, *Wake Me When It's Funny*. "But I had gotten to know Julia, and I suspected something else was up." Marshall asked her, "Sweetheart, when was the last time you ate anything?" She replied, "Yesterday I had an avocado."

"You probably should have eaten two avocados, and maybe you could have made it through tonight," Marshall concluded. Julia laughed, and Marshall gave her some of his tuna fish, which he ate in a sandwich every day like clockwork at four-fifteen in the afternoon.

Julia Roberts fairly bursts with joy after winning the 2000 Academy Award for Best Actress for her role as Erin Brockovich. In her speech, which went over the allotted three minutes, she exulted, "I'm so happy! Thank you!" (Kevork Djansezian/AP)

Julia's great-grandfather John Pendleton Roberts poses with his son Walter "Tom" Roberts, Julia's grandfather, on their Florala, Alabama, farm, circa 1913. (Courtesy Gloria Jones)

Julia's grandmother Jimmy Glenn Corbitt Roberts (left) with her mother, Jodi Gerke Corbitt, in a photograph taken circa 1938 in Georgia. (Courtesy Gloria Jones)

Julia's grandfather Tom Roberts at the age of twenty-five, in 1930. It was around this time that he married Julia's grandmother, the former Beatrice Beal. Tom spent his entire working life with the same company, and ran a horse farm/riding academy after he retired. (Courtesy Gloria Jones)

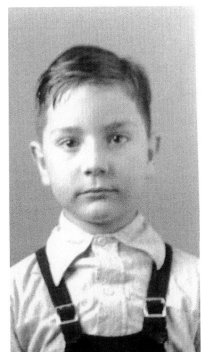

Julia's father, Walter Grady Roberts, in a school photo as a first-grade student in the rural West Fulton area of Atlanta in 1940. His family thought him "different." (Courtesy Gloria Jones)

Betty Lou Bredemus, Julia's mother, in a school photo as a ninth grader at Austin High in Austin, Minnesota, whose main claim to fame, the Hormel Meat Company, gave it the nickname "Spamtown." A classmate recalled, "She was a quiet person, but she could be a bit dramatic. I guess that was the theatrical part of her." (Photo by John Hockett/courtesy Barbara Gaddis Patrick)

An alternate photograph from the one used in Betty Lou's yearbook upon her graduation from Austin High in the spring of 1952. An aspiring actress, she joined a stock company in northern Minnesota and appeared in a number of plays, including *A Date with Judy* and *The Hasty Heart*. (Photo by John Hockett/courtesy Barbara Gaddis Patrick)

Walter Roberts's formal air force portrait. After ten weeks of basic training at Lackland Air Force Base in San Antonio, Texas, he was transferred to Keesler AFB in Biloxi, Mississippi, in 1953. He served in the force's medical corps, first as a student, then as a "helper," and finally as a medical administration specialist. It was at Keesler that Walter met, acted with, and married Betty Lou. (Courtesy Gloria Jones)

Julie, a second grader in 1974, in a school photo in the library of the Fitzhugh Lee School in Smyrna, Georgia. Her brother, Eric, called her "Hoolie," and a friend of his called her "Bucktooth Hoolie." (Archive photo/Guy D'Alema)

Julie, ten, and Lisa, twelve, hold their half-sister Nancy Motes, Christmas 1977. Betty's remarriage created a situation that Eric called "horrific": "The man terrorized and abused me. I was horrified [by] what my poor sisters were going to have to endure." (Author's collection)

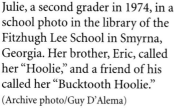

Julie is named one of twelve finalists in Campbell High School's 1985 "Miss Panthera" contest. She modeled, gave a speech, and was questioned by emcee Maddox Kilgore about her travels. "Oh my God!" she cried. "I can't believe they picked me!"
(Photo by Scott Wooley)

Kevin Hester as George Bush the elder and Julie as Elizabeth Dole were nominated for president and vice-president in Campbell's mock Republican convention. Hester was quoted in the school newspaper as saying that "our victory was a combination of good campaign." Julie told the voters, "Vote for us and vote for a better America." (Photo by Scott Wooley)

Julie's senior yearbook photo shows a lovely young woman with the smile that would captivate the world. Still, she thought herself unattractive. "No one really dug me for a long time." (Photo by Jimmy Riley Photography)

In New York in 1985, Julie sent this photo out to casting agents. Two years later she had to change her name back to Julia because SAG already had a Julie Roberts registered. (Archive photo/Guy D'Alema)

When Julie got to New York, she moved in with her sister, Lisa, in Greenwich Village. Here Lisa, Eric, his then-girlfriend Dana Wheeler-Nicholson, and Julie share a laugh in Lisa's apartment. "At least I got my sisters out of Smyrna," Eric has said. But his drug use and his hatred for their mother put a wedge between them that has not been repaired to this day. (Photo by Raeanne Rubinstein)

Julia landed a role on NBC's *Crime Story* in 1987. In the episode in which she appeared, Lieutenant Torello (Dennis Farina) discovers that the daughter (Julia) of the woman he's dating (Hanna Cox) has been sexually molested by one of his coworkers. (NBC/Globe Photos)

Julia's first appearance in a feature film, *Firehouse*, gave her a fifteen-second walk-on in a strained grade-Z sexploitation comedy. Peter Onorati, pictured here, was appearing in his first film as well, and tried to put the make on Julia by offering her a sales job. (Author's collection)

Julia's resemblance to Eric is clear in this scene from *Blood Red*, the 1986 film that gave her her first speaking role. Lexi Masterson, the director's daughter (also in this photo), said that Julia "flirted with everybody. She would have one boyfriend who was a grip, and then she'd have another boyfriend and they'd disappear for the whole night." (Author's collection)

Julia in *Baja Oklahoma*, a 1988 HBO movie. She had five scenes and demonstrated her acting range as her character goes from loving daughter to contemptuous rebel to battered woman at the hands of her boyfriend. Here, she shows her mother (played by Lesley Ann Warren) her bruises. (Author's collection)

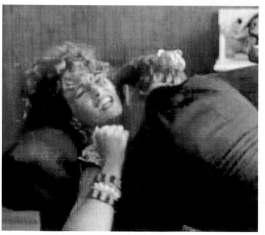

Satisfaction (1988) gave Julia a role as the bass player in a struggling band. She was nervous before shooting this scene, a near-rape, with Kevin Haley. The film brought her first on-set romance, with Liam Neeson, sixteen years her senior. A friend said, "It was incredible to watch...they would be crawling all over each other." (Author's collection)

Julia as Daisy, a waitress who beds a rich Adonis (Adam Storke) in *Mystic Pizza* (1988). She dyed her hair jet black for the audition after she was told that she didn't look Portuguese. She found the role difficult—Daisy's self-confidence and sexual allure were qualities that Julia felt she lacked at this age. (Author's collection)

The harrowing scene in 1989's *Steel Magnolias* in which Julia's character has an epileptic fit helped her win a Golden Globe Award and an Oscar nomination. Her director was less impressed with the performance. (Author's collection)

Julia had her second on-set romance in two years with Dylan McDermott, the handsome young actor playing her husband in *Steel Magnolias,* for whom she left Liam Neeson. Filming this scene, Julia felt that the extras treated her as though she were a real bride. She wanted to be— she and McDermott became engaged. (Author's collection)

Julia beams as she holds her Golden Globe as Best Supporting Actress for *Steel Magnolias,* January 1990. In her speech, she thanked "my beautiful blue-eyed, green-eyed boy, who does everything for me." She wasn't referring to McDermott, however. She had broken up with him in a fight over Richard Gere. (AP)

Julia's "beautiful" new beau, yet another costar, was Kiefer Sutherland, twenty-four. "Kiefer was unlike anyone else I'd ever met before," Julia said. "There's something about him that's so old and incredibly wise." The two began to live together almost immediately.
(Photo by Bob Scott)

Julia and Richard Gere in *Pretty Woman,* the 1990 film that made her a superstar. This moment, in which she lets loose the raucous laugh that would endear her to millions, came as a surprise to her. The director, in an attempt to "wake her up" after she spent a sleepless night breaking up with Dylan McDermott, told Gere to snap the jewelry box on her finger. (Author's collection)

Julia attempts to resuscitate Kiefer after he "dies" in their film *Flatliners* (1990). The director tried to leaven the dark shooting experience with humor. "I made Julia laugh so hard," he said, "that she'd be bending over the dying Kiefer and then suddenly start screaming with laughter." (Author's collection)

Julia and Kiefer attend the Oscars on March 25, 1991. Julia was nominated as Best Actress for *Pretty Woman*. A month later, the couple announced they would marry in June, even though papers had run photographs of Kiefer with a stripper. Julia believed his protestations of innocence, and they went ahead with plans for a lavish wedding. (Mark Terrill/AP)

Three days before the million-dollar nuptials, the engagement was called off. Julia and the twenty-five-year-old hunk Jason Patric then flew to Ireland. As they sat next to each other, the two beautiful young movie stars "were practically making love." They lived together for over a year in Patric's shabby apartment before breaking up.
(Globe Photos)

Julia vamps in front of a mirror to "Brown-Eyed Girl" in one of the few carefree scenes in *Sleeping with the Enemy* (1991), a tense woman-terrorized-by-her-husband thriller. The picture became her fourth smash hit in two years. (Author's collection)

Campbell Scott and Julia in a lighter moment from *Dying Young* (1991). Julia played a woman who falls in love with a cancer patient (Scott). In the original ending, she leaves him, but test audiences didn't like that. So a reshoot has her stay with Scott, who is still alive at the end. The film was a box-office dud, Julia's first since she became a star. (Author's collection)

Julia as Tinkerbell in *Hook* (1991). The film, and Julia, received poor reviews; one writer said Julia's wings made her resemble a horsefly. She was under such strain personally and professionally on this shoot that some members of the crew dubbed her "Tinkerhell." (Author's collection)

Julia's reaction to paparazzi early in her career was likened to "a deer in the headlights." Her grunge look off-screen earned her the top spot on Earl Blackwell's Worst-Dressed List in 1991. (Photo by Bob Scott)

Bruce Willis and Julia in the movie-within-the-movie in *The Player*. A pretentious scriptwriter insists that his movie have no stars and no happy ending. Naturally it ends with Bruce rescuing Julia from execution at the last minute. (Author's collection)

According to Marshall, "Very often the key to making a film is becoming best friends with the hair and makeup people. They tell you what mood the actors are in, so you can get a jump on what's going to happen that day. They tell you what happened, what didn't happen—'Julia broke up with her boyfriend, oh my goodness!' "

One day in particular, Marshall was warned that Julia would not be at her best—for that very reason. "Julia showed up for work exhausted, the result of a late-night quarrel with her boyfriend. Usually Julia was the consummate professional, but this was one of the few days when her personal life was out of whack with our production schedule. I told her to do the best she could and we'd try to help her out. But she was dragging and seemed quite willing to trade in her entire acting career for a one-hour nap."

The quarrel that made Julia lose a night's sleep—and her engagement to Dylan McDermott—arose from her barely disguised infatuation with Richard Gere. "She liked him a lot," said a girlfriend of Julia's who spoke on the condition of anonymity. "They dated when they did *Pretty Woman,* but he was so into Cindy Crawford that he couldn't see Julia in that way. So she was bummed about that, I remember. She cried over Gere. He was kind of a jerk to her. He led her on in the beginning, and they had a few romantic meals. But then, after the movie, he was done with her. She thought, *Wow, he was just interested in me for the film,* and she was right."

Rumors about a romance between Julia and Gere grew so rampant that two months into filming, the reports reached McDermott in Morocco, where he was still shooting *Hardware.* He called Julia to confront her about what he'd heard. While she denied having an affair with Gere, McDermott sensed something was up, especially since Julia had never come to Morocco to visit him as she had promised she would. An insider who requested anonymity said, "Dylan didn't believe a word she was saying. After all, he costarred in a film with her, and she started dating *him* when she already had a boyfriend. So he flew to Hollywood to find out the real deal."

McDermott made a secret visit to the set, and as lack of luck would have it, he caught a romantically charged scene between Vivian and Edward in which Gere seemed especially solicitous of Julia. "What he saw pissed him off," Julia's friend said. "Julia and Richard [were] getting along in a scene much more famously than Dylan would have liked. They seemed to have a special rapport. Richard treated her quite tenderly, purposely exploiting the fact that she was infatuated with him in order to make the scene work. Julia ate the whole thing up like chocolate ice cream. She was as giddy as a schoolgirl. She never dreamed that Dylan was lurking in the darkness, observing the whole thing. Later, they had a big fight over Gere. Julia screamed at Dylan, 'You don't own me, asshole!' "

With the relationship irretrievably broken, a deeply upset McDermott returned to Morocco to complete his film. Friends described him as "devastated," and he lost twelve pounds in the ensuing month. The syndicated columnist Liz Smith wrote of the breakup, "They started having a wild affair and seemed to be very, very much in love. Julia was very sweet to him, very into him. Then all of a sudden she dumped him. Her time limit seems to be twelve to eighteen months. As soon as the romance gets serious, she can't handle it. She can't seem to handle the reality of commitment."*

Once Julia broke up with McDermott, she reportedly tried to rekindle her romance with Liam Neeson. "She made a big thing of chasing Liam," said her friend, "phone calls, letters, the works. But he [had been too hurt and] just walked away."

Then there was Richard Gere, the man at hand. Julia almost never speaks ill of her coworkers; when she does, it's usually in reaction to someone speaking ill of her, as with Herb Ross. She has said nice things about Richard Gere, notably in *People:* "He stayed at the low end in performance terms, which is unique to talented people. He made Vivian an interesting character by making Edward show that he found her interesting—otherwise she would just seem like a wacko. He did it for me—even when it meant he himself was staying back. He is an incredibly generous actor."

In another interview, however, she uncharacteristically expressed resentment against Gere—perhaps created by his failure to return her romantic feelings. "He was complaining that I wasn't reacting the way he wanted me to. But I felt he was blaming me for *his* shortcomings. Unfortunately, I wasn't capable of protesting against such a sacred idol."

The day after her all-night battle with Dylan, Gary Marshall tried to come up with a way to help Julia "wake up." The first scene shot that morning was the one in which Edward gives Vivian, dressed in a stunning red gown, an equally stunning diamond-and-ruby necklace. "The scene wasn't all that special, and Julia was dragging anyway," Marshall

---

* McDermott, best known for his role as Bobby Donnell on ABC-TV's drama *The Practice*, has joked that for years, "That was on my résumé—it said I was engaged to Julia Roberts." But he added that he harbors no ill feeling. "I learned a lot from her. It happened so fast for her; she was just thrust into the spotlight. To see it up close was really helpful for me."

recalled, "so I told Richard that when Julia reaches into the jewel case to touch the necklace, he should snap it shut on her fingers. The box was velvet-lined, so I knew it wouldn't hurt her."

When Gere did this, a shocked Julia reacted with one of her patented guffaws. Not only did it help lift her spirits, but it provided Marshall with a charming moment that he decided to keep in the film. The scene would further endear Vivian to audiences. "A girl who looks like that, with a man like that, who can still laugh that bottomless laugh—well, that is a girl you can love," Marshall said.

Adding to Julia's stresses making this film were the several "dreaded" nude scenes: a bubble bath and a sexual encounter between Vivian and Edward. Marshall told her that although nothing would show in the bathtub scene, she would have to film it naked, because a visible bathing suit could ruin a take. "Sure, there were bubbles in the bath," Marshall said, "but bubbles aren't much comfort when there's a big guy with a tattoo on his arm holding a light above your head and saying, 'Honey, lean forward a little and push the bubbles up. We can see your boobs.' Short of putting Julia in a wet suit, I knew I had to think of something to calm her down."

Marshall had two female crew members hold up a towel to shield Julia from prying eyes as she climbed into the tub. She did the scene, a charming one in which Vivian, wearing headphones, sings along with Prince's "Kiss" while she negotiates her fee for a week with Richard. When they agree on $3,000,* she's so excited that she slides down and dunks her head under the bubbles.

When Julia came back up and opened her eyes, she saw that everyone had left, even the cameraman (who got the shot). "She was startled," Marshall recalled, "and then she laughed and got the idea that we were going to do this lightly."

For the lovemaking scene, Marshall had assured Julia that her breasts would not be revealed, but she still had to perform the scene naked. Marshall recalled that Julia appeared on the set covered in hives. When she got into bed next to Gere, Marshall also noticed that a large vein had popped out from her forehead. "It happens when I get nervous," Julia said sheepishly. "We had to stop the scene," Marshall said. "I got into bed with Richard and Julia. Together, he and I massaged her forehead, and even-

---

* This was the basis for the script's original title.

tually the vein disappeared. When the prop man came back with some calamine lotion for the rash, we were finally able to shoot the scene."

Marshall recalled another instance of Julia's emotional vulnerability, during a scene in which Edward tells Vivian, "I hadn't spoken to my dad for fourteen and a half years. I wasn't there when he died."

"It was clearly very painful for Julia," Marshall recalled. "I didn't pry, but held her tight between takes and had makeup standing close by to touch up her mascara. Sometimes a hug can be the best way to deal with a problem."

"Hug the schlumpy girl" was Julia's way of describing the situation, and she referred to herself in that self-deprecating way so often that Marshall took to calling her "my schlumpy girl."

But, Marshall added, even when she was schlumpy, Julia had elegance. "She moves around, Julia," he said. "She never quite stands still. You just kinda, sorta, see her, and that's the way we shot her. She's there, she's beautiful—bam, she's gone. We kidded about it: 'All right, we're doing Bambi in the penthouse today.' "

Julia took a lot more kidding after *Harper's Bazaar,* on the strength of *Mystic Pizza* and a preview of *Steel Magnolias,* named her one of America's ten most beautiful women. Her beauty, the magazine averred, was "contemporary." "Well," Marshall called out when she arrived on-set the next day, "I see we have a contemporary beauty in our midst."

The film's chief makeup artist, Bob Mills, spoke candidly of the effort that went into turning the "schlumpy, average" Julia into the Pretty Woman. "The hollows in Ms. Roberts's cheeks were filled in with highlights, as were the eye sockets. The jawline was also highlighted to broaden it. Shadows were added to slim the nose and contour the forehead. The cheekbone line was lowered to produce a fuller effect. Hidden liners to thicken the lashes were applied, [and] the lips were corrected to soften the very generous quality of her own."

On top of all that, rumor had it that a body double had been used in the film's first glimpse of Vivian, a pan up her legs and torso as she lies on a bed in her panties. Not so, according to Garry Marshall. "That was Julia's body. The reason people thought it was a double was that you don't see Julia's face, and that's usually a clue that a double was used. But the only reason we didn't show her face was that she wouldn't be waking up with her blond wig on, and we didn't want the audience to know that she wasn't really a blonde until later."*

---

*For unfathomable reasons, a body double for Julia *was* used for the print ads and posters of the film.

. . .

One of the key scenes in the film was one J. F. Lawton refused to write at Marshall's request: the polo-game scene in which Vivian embarrasses Edward by reverting to her street-talking ways in a moment of excitement. "I thought it was just too close to the Ascot scene in *My Fair Lady*," Lawton explains. "I had a similar scene—the same basic thing happens—but it had a different setting. It turned out to be a really cute scene, so you can give someone else credit for that."

One of the polo players, Alex Hyde-White, played David Morse, the son of Edward's business competitor (and a character Lawton considered pairing Vivian up with at the end). Hyde-White, the son of the esteemed British character actor Wilfrid Hyde-White (who had appeared opposite Rex Harrison and Audrey Hepburn in the 1964 movie version of *My Fair Lady*), found the shoot a joy. "Julia Roberts was fun to work with. She is a very natural, charming lady. In many ways I liken my experience working with Julia to my father's experience working with Marilyn Monroe on *Let's Make Love* [in 1960]. That was Dad's first Hollywood film. He found Marilyn to be one of the very few genuine eccentrics he ever met. Julia, like Marilyn, makes friends with everyone—[but] without ever causing production managers to tear their hair out, as Marilyn sometimes did. If those around Julia can keep their heads together—she certainly knows what *she* is doing—she'll do beautifully."

In some ways, the filming of *Pretty Woman* provided a tutorial for Julia in the acting styles required for different types of films. As J. F. Lawton recalled, "What I heard from Garry was that they were shooting three versions of each scene—a sad way, a funny way, and some third way, and they were basically going to put it all together in the editing room. At the time it seemed insane to me, and it certainly isn't my style of working. But since I've become more experienced, I've learned the power of flexibility when you're dealing with very heavy-handed development people. Garry Marshall is a very smart guy, and it's possible he let the development situation float around to kind of see what stuck to the wall."

"There were probably about seven movies in the footage that we shot," Julia said. "One good movie, and the rest bad, embarrassing, no-I-didn't-really-do-that-movie movies." The actual amount of film shot, Marshall said, was 326,300 feet. Approximately 54,000 wound up in the finished film. (So Julia's arithmetic was close to the mark.)

Spirits were high when filming ended on October 18, 1989. That weekend, a wrap-party band featured Marshall on drums, Gere on piano, Julia on bass, and two guitarists playing a repertoire the *Los Angeles Times* described as "easy-listening blues with some fusion, jazz, country and a little rock tossed in." Gere got the idea when he learned that Marshall had played drums in a Catskills dance band during his youth. "Then," Marshall said, "we heard that Julia played bass, and we thought, *Perfect!*"

Less than a week later, Julia flew to Chicago to rehearse and shoot her sixth movie, *Flatliners*. Her first day there, she met one of her costars, Kiefer Sutherland. Their highly publicized romance—and the bizarre manner in which it ended—would become the stuff of Hollywood legend.

CHAPTER SIXTEEN

Joel Schumacher lay sunbathing next to his pool, awaiting a visit from a young actress he was eager to meet. The fifty-year-old craggily handsome director, born and raised in New York City, had broken into films as a costume designer and made his directorial debut in 1980 with *The Incredible Shrinking Woman,* starring Lily Tomlin. Over the previous three years, he had cornered the youth market with the well-received films *D.C. Cab, St. Elmo's Fire,* and *The Lost Boys,* the last a stylish modern-day vampire story starring Kiefer Sutherland, Jason Patric, Corey Haim, and Corey Feldman. On this Sunday in late summer 1989, Schumacher had just returned from London, where he had met with Sutherland about the movie he was set to direct. *Flatliners,* with a script by Peter Filardi, was about a group of five medical students, four of whom flirt with death by stopping their hearts for a few minutes to experience what it means to die. The story turns from medical science fiction into horror when the four who have "flatlined" and been resuscitated realize that people from their guilty pasts have returned—literally, in some cases—to haunt or injure them.

Schumacher was in the process of casting the four male roles—which would go to Sutherland, William Baldwin, Kevin Bacon, and Oliver Platt—and he wanted Julia Roberts to play the female doctor in the group. The director had been impressed with what he saw of her in *Satisfaction.* "Even though she was just one of the girls, there was something about her that was so sexy and infectious. I decided to keep an eye on her. Then, when I saw her again in *Mystic Pizza,* well, that was it. That's all I had to see. When I decided to do *Flatliners,* she was my first choice."

Schumacher was disappointed when Julia, because of her commitment to *3000,* turned down the role of Rachel Mannus, who blames herself for her father's suicide when she was a girl. But during the summer of 1989, in the middle of making that movie, she read the script. "It provoked a lot of emotions in me," she said. "I was falling over myself to get to the phone to call my agent." She hoped it wouldn't be too late, and it wasn't—Schumacher still hadn't signed anyone for the part. But he told Elaine Goldsmith that Julia would have to begin shooting *Flatliners* very shortly after she completed *3000*. That worried Julia, though she was intrigued enough by the script—and her character's emotional ties to her dead father—to consider it. "We worked out a deal based on a creative meeting," Schumacher said, "which means that if either of us hated the other, the deal was off."

They needn't have worried. In the ensuing years, Schumacher has waxed loquacious about his initial in-person exposure to Julia Roberts. "I was sitting by my pool when Julia came bouncing over. She was wearing cutoff jeans, a little T-shirt, was barefoot, had no makeup, and all that gorgeous red hair* was piled in pins on top of her head. She was one of the most beautiful women I had ever seen, and she had absolutely no idea of just how beautiful and sexy she was."

"When I first arrived at Joel's house," Julia said, "I was polite and trying to act dignified. Once we started talking about the film, we both got very excited. I stood up on the sofa in wild analysis of the project." Julia was impressed by Schumacher's intense interest in the material. They talked about the deaths of their fathers (the director lost his at four); it was this aspect of the role that most affected Julia emotionally. Elaine Goldsmith might have argued against Julia taking the part, because she would be only one-fifth of an ensemble, and Rachel is the least developed of the four who flatline in the script. After starring in what was essentially a two-character film, Julia could have held out for roles of the same stature. But she liked the material and the character: "She seemed really dedicated to medicine and very determined. I liked that she was solid, because my character in *Pretty Woman* was all over the place. It's like nothing I've ever read before."

Julia agreed to make Schumacher's film, and Elaine Goldsmith, aware of how eager the director was to have her ("I would have killed myself if she hadn't agreed to do my film," he said), negotiated a fee of $550,000, nearly double what her client had been paid for the much larger role in *3000*.

---

*Julia had obviously had a henna rinse. Over the years her hair color would range from bright blond to deep red to dark brown.

. . .

Julia found the making of *Flatliners* a highly emotional experience on several levels. In addition to her identification with Rachel's sense of loss, there was the subject of death and its aftermath. Julia and her fellow actors watched medical movies in preparation and, she said, "We all played with syringes. We went through CPR training. . . . There is an autopsy scene in the movie that is very scary. It was a gross thing to film at seven in the morning. I wanted to pass out. I asked Joel to move the cadavers around because they were so real to me."

Also as part of her research, Julia read *The Tibetan Book of the Dead*, which sent her into a depression she alleviated by reading *The Tao of Pooh*. "When we started talking about the [Pooh] book on the set, we'd all get the giggles—Joel had it, too—and I saw him struggle; he wanted to give in to the hilarity, yet he was the director and had to maintain some kind of control."

Since the three men in the film who flatline are bare-chested when they're hooked up to the electrodes, they told Julia she should be as well. She said she would do it if they all stripped completely. Schumacher got Oliver Platt to pose for him au naturel, and blew one of the pictures up to life-size proportions, shocking Julia with it later in the filming. In spite of her dare, she did wear a bra during her flatlining scene.

It didn't take Julia long to feel she was in good hands with Schumacher. "Joel was just so intense and articulate. When we did small scenes, he would give us something [a piece of advice] back and then not say anything, but when he did say something, it was so succinct, so exactly right."

Schumacher returned Julia's admiration. "She does her emotional homework before she comes in," he said. "If she has to do a highly emotional scene, she's figured out what she's going to use from her own life and feelings to get there. And she would always let me know, either deliberately or in a more covert way, what the trigger would be from her life. For instance, my father's dead and her father's dead, and we'd have that to relate to between takes if she came over to me for help staying in the moment."

Like Garry Marshall, Schumacher adored Julia, and that was vital to her emotional health. "Some directors, they give you support," she said, "but they're essentially cool with their flattery because they don't want to give an actor a big head, which I think is poppycock. Half the time I'm thinking I'm delivering the biggest pile of garbage, and all I need is this one kind word that's going to save me from myself. On *Flatliners* we would do a scene, and when it was over, Joel would hoot, 'I can't wait for the dailies!' He would just start screaming and make you feel good."

The first scene Julia shot, immediately after she arrived at the Chicago location, was one from the movie's climax, in which she rushes to try to save Kiefer's character from flatlining himself to death. "We were shooting at night, and it was real cold," Julia said in *American Film*. "I had this easy thing to do, just run up these stairs, looking for the character played by Kiefer. I started talking to Joel, and I'm asking him, 'How did I get here, did I take the bus?' 'No,' he said, 'you ran.' I thought about how long it would have taken to run there, and all of a sudden I realized how panicked a situation this was. I'm running, and I have to get there for about ten reasons—the most of which is to save Kiefer's life, and the least is to tell him it's all right and he's my friend.

"So I get into this place in my mind where I'm breathing really hard, and I say to Joel, 'Is Kiefer here?' 'Yeah, he's in his trailer.' So I say, 'I really need to see him,' and Kiefer comes out there, he doesn't know what I'm doing, he doesn't even know who I am. He came out, and I just flailed my preparation at him, tugged at his shirt, and I didn't need him to say anything. I just needed him to be there, to be a person. I remember the three of us standing in the cold, and my feeling this support from Kiefer and Joel. That's why you make a movie, for the support, to be like a family. You can't ask for more than nights like that—amazing nights."

It didn't take long for either Julia or Kiefer to recognize their mutual attraction. According to Kiefer, he hadn't seen any of Julia's films. "I had no reason to like or dislike this person. There was no outside input except for my agent saying, 'Oh, I'm so glad Julia Roberts is doing this film.' And I was going, 'Julia who?' and thinking, *Okay, here's this novice.* Then she came into rehearsal, and she had a really incredible presence just as a person, which made me sit back and take a look."

Julia looked back just as intently, and their mouth-to-mouth resuscitation scene took on new meaning. Sutherland, the blond, insolently sexy twenty-three-year-old son of the actor Donald Sutherland (*M*A*S*H*, *Klute*), was already a veteran of sixteen films by 1989 and had something of a bad-boy image both on- and off-screen. At fifteen, he was expelled from school; he can't remember exactly why, but he thinks the reason was that he was asked to get his hair cut and responded by shaving it all off.

In 1987, at twenty, Kiefer had married the Puerto Rican actress Camelia Kath, fourteen years his senior. (One newspaper reported her to be fourteen years his *junior*, which would have made her a very young bride indeed.) A year later, the couple had a daughter, Sara. The marriage was in trouble before Kiefer met Julia, but his interest in her provided the fatal blow to the union. He and Camelia separated shortly after *Flatliners* filming began, and were divorced a year later.

"I fell for Kiefer the minute I laid eyes on him," Julia said. "We were filming . . . and he was up to his elbows in blood and gore. I fell in love with him during some of the most gruesome scenes." Julia and Kiefer soon found that their physical attraction was matched by a spiritual and intellectual one. They shared a love of books. Like Julia's, Kiefer's parents had divorced when he was young (four years old), after his father began an affair with his *Klute* costar, Jane Fonda. Further, Julia said, "Kiefer was unlike anyone else I'd ever met before. There's something about him that's so old and incredibly wise. It's staggering to think he's only a year older than I am. There was this scene we did together in *Flatliners* where he has flatlined and I'm watching him, and I was so fascinated by what he was saying that I'd forgotten I had to speak. I got really interested in what was actually happening—he has a profound effect on me."

On December 27, Julia learned she had been nominated for a Golden Globe Award for Best Supporting Actress in *Steel Magnolias*. "It was quite shocking," she said. She'd had a bad day filming, and the phone in her trailer kept ringing. She wasn't interested in talking to anyone, so she'd pick up the receiver and slam it back down without saying a word. "Then I got a bouquet of flowers with a note that read, 'Congratulations on your nomination.' . . . I was really excited, and I wanted to tell somebody. It was not embarrassing, but you don't want to be overly bold. So I told [Joel Schumacher], and he announced, 'We have somebody here who is a Golden Globe nominee.' So they started calling me Miss Golden Globe."

Take *that*, Miss Panthera!

On January 20 she and Kiefer attended the ceremonies. It was their first public appearance together; few outside their close circle knew they were involved. Julia had referred to "my boyfriend" in several interviews, but she hadn't said who he was. Julia won the Golden Globe; despite the stature of her costars, she was the sole member of the *Magnolias* cast to win an award. "I almost fell off my fucking chair!" she said with a laugh. "It was the most shocking night of my life. I was so unprepared. I heard a recording of my acceptance speech later, and I had to laugh. I was such an idiot." One of the things she said as she accepted her award dressed in a man's Armani suit: "I want to thank my beautiful, blue-eyed, green-eyed boy, who does everything for me."*

*Sutherland has one blue and one green eye.

She hadn't dared hope for similar acknowledgment from the august Academy of Motion Picture Arts and Sciences—after all, it had taken her brother seven years to get *his* Oscar nomination. "I had pretty much blocked it out of my mind, because you can only find disappointment in an expectant mind, right? And then the call came early in the morning. It didn't register with me until about two o'clock that afternoon. And I just got the giggles, and I couldn't stop laughing."

Filming on *Flatliners* wrapped on January 23, and Julia and Kiefer took some R&R in Tucson, Arizona. It didn't last long. Kiefer soon had to begin shooting *Young Guns II* in New Mexico. In February, Julia had commitments to publicize the movie now titled *Pretty Woman,* set to open on March 23.

Three days later, she and Kiefer attended the Academy Awards, where she lost the Oscar to Brenda Fricker from the Daniel Day-Lewis film *My Left Foot* (Day-Lewis was named Best Actor). In a month, Julia was scheduled to begin filming her seventh feature, *Sleeping with the Enemy,* in which she would play an abused wife. Her salary for the project: $1 million.

Elaine Goldsmith had been able to negotiate that rarefied paycheck because by now everyone in Hollywood knew that in *Pretty Woman,* Julia Roberts would make the kind of impact that a newcomer in the right role makes only once or twice a decade. Of the "hundred or so" movies (in Julia's words) that Garry Marshall could have put together from the footage he shot, he had assembled, in five months of postproduction, a charming fable in which Cinderella winds up with a fabulous wardrobe, a penthouse, and Prince Charming.

The only dark elements Marshall kept in were an early scene in which Vivian walks past a police investigation of a prostitute's murder (featuring Hank Azaria in his second film appearance), and the scene in which Jason Alexander, as Edward's lawyer ("the wicked witch of this Cinderella story," Marshall said), attacks Vivian. Otherwise Marshall told an upbeat, even inspiring story in which a likable, bright, feisty young woman in a hopeless profession wins a ticket to respectability and love—to the cheers of preview audiences. Disney executives were thrilled, and the word was out that this movie would make Julia Roberts a very big star.

Until a few months before it opened, the picture was still being called the "Untitled Garry Marshall Project." Marshall briefly considered "On the Boulevard" but then decided the popular practice of naming a film for a hit song (and using that song in the movie) was a good idea. "If you get the name of a picture out there in a song, you've got a leg up," he explained. The studio made three suggestions: the Frank Sinatra classic "The Lady Is a Tramp," Tom Jones's "She's a Lady," and Roy Orbison's "Oh, Pretty Woman." Luckily for Julia, Marshall chose the last rather than the first. He wanted to use the song at the beginning of the movie, but his editor, Priscilla Nedd, felt it worked better over the scenes in which Vivian is transformed into an elegantly dressed young lady after a shopping spree on Rodeo Drive.

For the rest of her career, Julia Roberts will be known as "America's Pretty Woman." Asked some years later how she felt about that, she laughed. "I started out as Julia 'Eric Roberts's sister' Roberts. Then I was Julia *'Mystic Pizza'* Roberts. So getting saddled with 'Pretty Woman' is not the worst moment of my life . . . It's better than 'Mediocre Woman.'"

Or Julia "The Tramp" Roberts.

CHAPTER SEVENTEEN

Kiefer kept telling Julia that she should "own things." He had bought a "small" farm in Whitefish, Montana (reportedly three hundred acres), where he tried his hand at raising animals and riding horses, something he and Julia loved doing together. He and a friend began building with their own hands a log cabin against the side of a mountain.

In a more cosmopolitan frame of mind, Julia bought herself first a BMW convertible, then a $1.4 million house in the Hollywood Hills. Patrick Goldstein, a *Los Angeles Times* writer, accompanied Julia, her business manager, her agent, and several Realtors on a house-hunting tour for a profile the newspaper planned to coincide with the opening of *Pretty Woman*. Goldstein was lucky enough to see the house Julia would buy, as she admired its outdoor Jacuzzi and spotlighted fountain, wondered at a refrigerator with a glass door, and stood in the bedroom, gawking at its 360-degree panorama of the surrounding hills and city below.

As Julia and Goldstein rode back down the rain-slicked Hollywood Hills, she said, "Hey, the furniture's gotta go, but what a great house, huh? It's beautiful." Goldstein asked if she planned to make an offer. "Make one?" she replied. "I already did! I'm gonna buy it. They told me if I wait till tomorrow, it'll be gone. My boyfriend is gonna *die* when he hears I bought a house . . . I remember telling him, 'Why do I need a house?' And he said, 'Well, you gotta have a place to park the car!'"

Julia was so busy in the spring of 1990, however, that her belongings sat in her apartment for three months before they were moved. While Julia was in South Carolina filming *Sleeping with the Enemy*, Kiefer supervised the move and the redecoration of the house, to the point of personally organizing Julia's clothes closet. When she returned, she and Kiefer settled into a domestic routine that, she averred, suited her just fine. "Kiefer and I spend a lot of time quietly together," she said, "because things can get so loud and heady that it's nice just to be home and read and talk and not say anything."

On the other hand, both were known to enjoy a good time, a drink, a cigarette, a sexual flirtation. Kiefer, particularly, was known as a party animal. Earlier, Joel Schumacher had paid him a dubious compliment when he said, "He's always been very mature. If Kiefer was out all night partying, which a lot of eighteen-year-olds do, he would drive to the studio at five in the morning and sleep by the security guard's booth. And he'd tell the guard to wake him up so he'd be on time for his seven A.M. call."

Just how much partying Kiefer did with Julia will likely never be known, but one raucous evening was memorialized on a videotape that, much to Julia's embarrassment, was later aired on *Inside Edition*. The tape, shot by Scott Schiflett, a bass player who was at a July 1990 party in Maui, Hawaii, shows Julia pulling down a man's pants and screaming "Right on!" to other party guests. In the next moment Kiefer splatters her face with chocolate frosting, then proceeds to lick it off. Soon the couple do their own version of "dirty dancing," after which Kiefer takes several swigs of a drink before belching and then kissing a man. He looks into the camera and shouts, "This is what happens, kids, when you're an alcoholic—you sweat!"

Julia first saw *Pretty Woman* when she sneaked into a test screening in Sherman Oaks, a suburb of Los Angeles. "I saw it with an audience, and I was in the very back. I had no idea what we were actually going to see when we got there. I was cracking up. It made me laugh so hard. I thought it was really charming."

When the film opened on March 23, all the high expectations were realized, and then some. Its opening-weekend box office proceeds, $11 million, were respectable but weren't an indicator of how well it would finally do, especially considering the reviews. Sheila Benson in the *Los Angeles Times* found the picture politically incorrect. "You'd be crazy to deny the pleasure of Roberts in motion," she wrote, "but is this the sexual climate in which to make Eliza Doolittle a hooker? Whether or not Vivian carries multicolored condoms, her 'buffet of safety' in her thigh-high boots, and doesn't kiss on the mouth, is it possible not to think of her as a ticking sexual time bomb?"

Audiences didn't agree. As Richard Schickel put it in the same newspaper's profile of Julia, "There was nothing inherent in what she—or

Richard Gere—did that pushed the film over the $150 million mark. It took off because the public wanted to plug into the fantasy." Schickel was only half right. Audiences were enchanted with Julia Roberts, men and women alike. "Like Audrey Hepburn, Marilyn Monroe, and Natalie Wood," said Richard Fischoff, a senior vice president at TriStar, "Julia has translucence. When she smiles, she lights up the screen."

The film's audience grew by word of mouth, helped along by the press's fervent interest in a girl who looked likely to become the biggest female star since Barbra Streisand. Ultimately, the film grossed $178.4 million in the United States alone ($241.2 million in 2003 dollars), making it the fourth highest-grossing movie of the year, behind *Home Alone* ($285.8 million), *Ghost* ($217.6 million), and *Dances with Wolves* ($184.2 million).

Pretty Woman was by far the highest-grossing romantic comedy in years, and most of the credit for its success was laid at the leather-booted feet of Julia Fiona Roberts. What was even more remarkable— and what observers also credited to Julia—was the film's overseas box-office receipts, which topped $280 million and made *Pretty Woman* the number three box-office attraction of the year worldwide. The reason actors such as Bruce Willis and Arnold Schwarzenegger pulled down paychecks in excess of $10 million in this era, while successful actresses were lucky to get $1 million, was that the action films the men made translated well into foreign markets and usually cleaned up worldwide, even when they did only mediocre business in the United States.

Julia Roberts in *Pretty Woman* changed all that. Now everyone in Hollywood wanted her in their movies, and they were willing to pay seemingly ridiculous sums to put her there. Elaine Goldsmith was able to get Julia a $3 million salary for *Dying Young*, and $2 million plus 2 percent of the gross over $100 million for the role of Tinkerbell in Steven Spielberg's Peter Pan movie, *Hook*, even though her performance would require under a month of work.

Julia first got an idea something big was afoot when she got a call from Elaine on her way to the airport for the flight to South Carolina to film *Sleeping with the Enemy*. "Elaine said that *Pretty Woman* had done well and had great numbers, which meant nothing to me," Julia told a reporter. "I went, 'Oh, that's fine, whatever that means.' I didn't have a clue! Then I went back to work. *Pretty Woman* didn't come to the town I was working in while I was there. . . . I was just working and completely unaware of it. . . . I wasn't there for the moment-to-moment rise of this movie—which was probably a real blessing, because I maintained a *selfness* of just being a girl and working. . . . Elaine would call and give me reports on this movie's status. It was hard to believe what she was telling me, because I wasn't there to experience it. That lent a lot of relief to what could have been a heady situation for me."

That was a luxury Julia would wish for as the craziness of the next two years unfolded.

Julia's head slammed into the marble floor. She grimaced in pain and burst into tears. "The take went horribly wrong," Julia told a reporter about a scene in *Sleeping with the Enemy*, which she was filming in Abbeville, South Carolina. "The idea was I was going to get punched, hit my head on the floor, and then get kicked by Patrick [Bergin, the actor playing her abusive husband] in a sandbag by my leg—which, with the camera angle, was supposed to look like my stomach. The first time I tried to break my fall with my hands, and it looked all wrong. For the second take I really pulled my hands back and just fell. My head bounced on the marble floor like a basketball. I can't tell you how much it hurt." Julia said she suffered a black eye but was determined to complete the scene. "I [wanted] to carry on because I was damned if I was going to shoot the scene again. Then Patrick came up, missed the sandbag, and kicked me right in the stomach. At that point my life could not have been worse."

An observer of Julia Roberts's career choices to this point could be forgiven the suspicion that they betrayed a streak of masochism. In her first eight films, she had been sexually attacked in two, suffered a diabetic seizure, died, nearly died in a medical experiment, and suffered brutal abuse at the hands of her husband. She explained her choices thus: "When I read anything, I look for a combination of elements that prove to be exciting and challenging. I probably shouldn't do it, but I know I have to. *Sleeping with the Enemy* said to me, 'Risk it all with the potential to gain everything, or walk around haunted and empty.' If I feel really happy and [at the same time] like I'm going to throw up when I close the script, that's usually a good sign."

She almost didn't get the role. Kim Basinger had committed to it, and Julia was interested in another project, *Class Action*. She called an acquaintance, Joe Roth, on his third day as head of 20th Century–Fox, and asked for the job. "It was the first and only time a star had personally called me about a role," Roth said. He told her she was too young for

Class Action but called her back two weeks later to say he thought she'd be good for *Sleeping with the Enemy,* which Basinger had asked to be released from so she could do *The Marrying Man* with Alec Baldwin, whom she subsequently married.

"We thought we might be in big trouble when [Basinger] decided not to do it," recalled Leonard Goldberg, *Sleeping*'s producer. "*Steel Magnolias* was just coming out, and Julia was basically an up-and-coming young actress. We were trading maximum star power to work with a near-unknown; we did so because Julia seemed really right for the role, and we figured we'd end up with a better film, if not a more marketable one. Now, of course, we look like geniuses."

Before Julia's signing was finalized, she met with the film's director, Joseph Ruben, who was making his eighth film and had scored a hit with *The Stepfather* in 1987. Like most of Julia's prior directors, he was captivated by her. "It was a shyness. That's the part that makes her so fascinating on-screen—all the contradictions, being both very shy but very much out there at the same time. She's both very sexy and very innocent, too. . . . There's an incredibly warm aspect to her, but she can be very cold when she's angry."

Sleeping with the Enemy, based on a novel by Nancy Price with a screenplay by Ron Bass, is the story of Laura Burney, a young woman trapped in an abusive marriage who fakes her death as a means of escape. Her husband discovers the ruse and tracks her down to the city where she has established a new life, a new name (Sara Waters), and a new relationship with a college drama teacher. This sets up a climactic—and harrowing—confrontation.

The filming proved close to a living hell for Julia. There was the frighteningly realistic brutality she suffered through. "I had to stand on my own, and it really drained me psychologically," she said. "It's not easy playing someone who is being tormented and abused. I got thrown around a lot, mentally and physically, and during rehearsals I would often have to walk out and get some air. It was just too intense."

Other aspects were unpleasant as well. For one early scene, Julia's character has to run out of the ocean and into her house, soaking wet, in just her underwear. "It's freezing cold and I'm in my panties and I'm running around and they keep hosing me with water and I'm freezing." She was miserable and exhausted by the constant retakes. Finally she hit on an idea to speed things up. She told all the crew, including the director, to strip to their underwear. "I thought it would be a great show of, you know, love and solidarity if we were *all* in our underwear," she said.

Some of the crew, offended, left the set. But others, including Joe Ruben and cinematographer John Lindley, complied.

"It was very funny," Julia said, "because there was this one camera guy who was the sweetest, quietest guy, and he was kind of just over there, fooling with the camera, you know, being very quiet. I looked over, and he had on these, like, hot-pink boxer shorts. You know, like *wham!*"

Ruben, who felt he didn't command enough respect with his pants off, later said he should have told Julia "to shut up and get on with her work. But I was at a low ebb, and Julia was so cold, and having such a hard time, and somehow her request did not seem unreasonable. With the benefit of hindsight, I think it was very unreasonable."

The emotional and physical battering she took during the filming spilled over into her off-screen relationship with Patrick Bergin, a ruggedly handsome thirty-six-year-old Dubliner making his fourth film. They chatted amiably when they first met, but as filming progressed, the violence and terror Bergin's character visited on Julia's made things tense. "We weren't necessarily friendly toward each other," Julia said. "I mean, when you come to work, and somebody kicks the shit out of you for three hours, you don't really feel like finding out where he is and saying good night."

Julia and Bergin sometimes improvised scenes of violence so realistic that they frightened Joe Ruben. "They knew they were in control," he said, "but I didn't." Julia added, "It was an enormously harrowing experience. There were whole weeks where I'd have to arrive at the set at five A.M., start crying, and be the victim of these terrible fights."

As upsetting as Julia's nervous state was for her, the director thought it helped her performance. "Julia was already there emotionally when she came on the set, almost to the point of breaking apart. She comes prepared; she comes ready to play."

There wasn't respite for Julia even away from the set. Unlike Natchitoches, where Julia enjoyed the locals, the food, and the constant support of her costars, the towns of Abbeville and Spartanburg offered few comforts. "[One] town had no restaurants in it. I would go home and sit in this small room with my dog and say, 'So, there's nothing to eat . . . You wanna go to sleep?' I didn't feel like I was on location anymore. I didn't feel like I had a job. I felt like this hell was where I lived." Julia's mood deteriorated further when she and a black crewman went to a restaurant in Abbeville called Michael's. To her astonishment and outrage, the management would not let the black man in. As they left, Julia yelled, "You shouldn't call this place Michael's—you should call it Bigot's."

"I was enraged—I was out of my mind," Julia said. Yolanda King saw Julia's reaction as very much in character. "I can see her doing that, I mean, just being outraged—the righteous indignation. I can see it pouring forth from her. And rightly so."

Later, Julia told *Rolling Stone*, "The people were horribly racist, and I had a really hard time." The townsfolk of Abbeville didn't take kindly to that and took out a quarter-page ad in *Variety* defending themselves, with the headline PRETTY WOMAN? PRETTY LOW. Julia issued a statement saying she had not meant to condemn everyone in Abbeville; she had been referring to this one incident. "I was born in the South, so in no way am I trying to create a stereotype. I was shocked that this type of treatment still exists in America in the nineties—in the South or anywhere else."

Julia's spirits were buoyed by visits from Betty, Nancy, and even Eric, to whom she was still speaking at this point. Mostly, of course, she looked forward to and enjoyed Kiefer's visits every couple of weeks during the three-month shoot. "Whenever Kiefer would show up, or come back and spend time, Julia's mood would always get really good," a crew member recalled. "So we were always happy when we heard he was coming back."

"They were playful together," said Joe Ruben, who was grateful to Kiefer for keeping the leading lady emotionally intact. "There was a sense of mutual support. I think they both cut through the bullshit factor . . . they make each other laugh. They both know the kind of pressures they're each dealing with, and they both have the same uncompromising attitude about their work, so they can be supportive and respectful of each other."

"There were times," Julia said, "when it was great just having Kiefer there. He would take me in his arms, hold me, and make everything better. Being in love is a great feeling."

Eric recalled sitting on a rock at the location with Julia, Kiefer, and Eric's pregnant girlfriend, Kelly Cunningham, having lunch, and saying, "*Pretty Woman* is going through the roof, Julie. How does it feel?"

"Oh, I don't know" was all Julia said in reply.

Julia has said that the locals seemed unaware of the sensation she was causing around the world. "I think the local theater was playing *Star Wars* [released in 1977]. They had no palpable awareness of what was going on with me." This at least allowed her to tool around town undisturbed in her rented Jeep, its top off, dressed in torn jeans and a black leather jacket, blasting the Eagles' "Life in the Fast Lane" or Elvis Costello's "This Year's Girl."

Toward the end of the shoot, though, Julia had a disquieting encounter that reinforced the notion that her life had drastically changed. "I was at home and really tired, and the doorbell rang. So I went to the door, and there's this guy, and I say, 'Can I help you?' He says, 'Hi, Julia, I'm so-and-so, how are you doing?' Like he was just going to chat with me! I tried to be really nice and said, 'That's really nice, see you later.' An hour goes by, I hear a knock on the door, and it's the same guy again. He said, 'I don't mean to bother you . . . ' He came back four times that day. So now there's a cop outside my door."

Flatliners opened in August and racked up a healthy $61 million at the box office, despite lukewarm reviews. With *Pretty Woman* showing legs—literally and figuratively—throughout the summer, the editors of *People* were champing at the bit to do a cover story on Julia. To their great surprise, she refused to give them an interview. They decided that her image on the cover would sell copies and went ahead with the profile as a write-around—meaning that if they couldn't interview Julia, they would speak to as many people close to her as possible.

The magazine's editor, Lanny Jones, telephoned his Atlanta correspondent, Gail Cameron Wescott, told her Julia had grown up in and around Atlanta, and asked her to get everything she could. Wescott found out that Betty Motes worked for the Atlanta archdiocese and telephoned her there to ask for an interview. Betty, unaware that Julia wasn't cooperating, agreed to meet her that day for lunch.

As the two women ate, Betty opened up to Wescott, telling her about Julia's childhood and the workshop's Showmobile. She said, "We had no teenage horror stories in our family" (something Eric would disagree with). She said she had accepted a new Mustang from Julia but turned down an offer of a house. "I told her I already had one," she said.

After the interview, Wescott persuaded Betty to let her borrow childhood photos, yearbooks, and other personal memorabilia of Julia's for the piece. She thanked Betty profusely and knew she had gotten a great scoop. Two days later, she phoned Betty again to get some additional information about the workshop. Betty was icy. "I've talked to Julia, and I've learned that she does not want this story done." She added that Julia had been "furious" when she learned her mother had cooperated.

Wescott's stomach lurched. Betty Motes couldn't take back what she had told her, but she could demand that the photos not be published. Wescott refrained from mentioning that, and to the reporter's great relief, Betty did not ask for their return. A few days later, Wescott called Betty once more to say she was sorry if there had been a misunderstanding.

"I've talked to Julia," Betty said, "and she said it's okay. She just hopes I didn't say anything wrong."

She didn't, and the article appeared in *People*'s September 17, 1990, issue. A beaming Julia graced the cover, with the declaration JULIA ROBERTS—THE HOTTEST STAR: ONLY 22, SHE'S SEXY, SPIRITED, AND MAGIC ONSCREEN. HERE'S HOW THE PRIDE OF SMYRNA, GA., CONQUERED HOLLYWOOD AND MADE *PRETTY WOMAN THE YEAR'S BIGGEST HIT.*

Wescott interviewed a number of Julia's friends and classmates from Smyrna. But, she said, "That was like the last picture show. That was the last Julia Roberts story they would be a part of. The next time we went back to all those kids, they had all been completely shut down."

As the editors had envisioned, the Julia Roberts issue turned out to be one of the magazine's biggest sellers of the year. Unsurprisingly, Julia became a staple on the cover; more than two dozen times over the next decade, *People* would use every possible excuse to put her there.

Two months earlier, Julia had unveiled a new look on the cover of *Rolling Stone,* one that shocked her fans—her luxuriantly long tresses had been hacked off to just below her ears. "I just got sick and tired of [long hair]," Julia said, "so I just had it all cut off. And you know what? Everyone freaked out. They all said, 'Don't do it. It'll be awful. You'll regret it.' But Kiefer said, 'Aw, go get a crew cut.'" Julia would have yet another surprise for her fans at the following year's Academy Awards.

Finally, in the middle of June, filming wrapped on *Sleeping with the Enemy,* and Julia returned to Los Angeles, frail and exhausted. "I just want to go in a field somewhere and pick flowers," she told a reporter. Instead, she and Kiefer holed up at the posh Four Seasons Hotel in Beverly Hills while the finishing touches were being put on the new house in Nichols Canyon. As Julia sunbathed by the pool, John F. Kennedy, Jr., who was studying for his third try at the New York bar exam, approached her. Kennedy, named "The Sexiest Man Alive" by *People* in 1988, had been, according to eyewitnesses, watching Julia for a while before he went over. "John went up to her and started to flirt," one observer said, "not even knowing who she was at first. But once she introduced herself, sparks began to fly."

People reported the two then "frolicked" in the pool; afterward they enjoyed drinks at a table nearby. One of the tabloids ran with the story, claiming that John and Julia spent two days "closeted in his lavish penthouse suite with a 'Do Not Disturb' sign on the door," and quoted Stephen Styles, whom they called a "pal" of John's, as saying, "They really had a thing for each other. . . . What they had that weekend was real passion."

That's unlikely, especially since Kiefer was with Julia. Apparently informed about the "frolics" in the water, he kept calling down to the pool area from their room to ask what Julia was up to, but he didn't ask to speak with her directly. When she got back to the room, *People* reported, they had a fight, and he "threatened to make his own date with Sherilyn (*Twin Peaks*) Fenn. Roberts, according to one source, told him to 'go ahead.'"

John's then girlfriend, Julia's *Steel Magnolias* costar Daryl Hannah, reportedly tried to reach John by phone while all this was happening, but he had asked the hotel to hold all calls while he studied.

Whatever friction arose between Julia and Kiefer over this apparent flirtation on her part was soon smoothed over, and the couple moved into the Nichols Canyon house at the end of June. "I'm crazy about him," Julia said of Kiefer. "And that's really amazing, because love has taken a beating in this world. . . . Everything is so hard-edged. But Kiefer has totally captivated me. We've hardly been apart since we met. Sometimes I actually weep when we're separated." She admitted that nurturing a love affair in the midst of her schedule was difficult. "The last few months have been crazy. I can't have a simple dinner. I don't have time to read a book. My whole life's mapped out for me."

In July, Rod Lurie, interviewing Julia for *The West Side Spirit,* noticed a diamond sparkling on her finger. "Is that an engagement ring?" he asked. "Pretty, isn't it?" she replied. "I got it at a drive-in burger place [Pink's on La Cienega Boulevard in West Hollywood]. This was a gift to me that came with no questions." (Such as, presumably, "Will you marry me?")

"There is the cliché of meeting an actor on the set and falling in love," Lurie said. "Is that what happened to you and Kiefer Sutherland?"

"Hmmm. Nothing that Kiefer and I do is a cliché. Kiefer and I are very happy."

Julia Roberts was now what Hollywood calls "a hot commodity." The upside was that she got sent just about every script with a young female lead, whether suitable to her or not: She could pick and choose among projects, directors, and costars, and get paid millions of dollars per film. The downside—which every movie star since Mary Pickford has had to endure—was a loss of privacy, having to read untruths about herself in the press, and being hounded by fans and paparazzi.

She tried hard to maintain her equilibrium. "I don't feel like a commodity," she said, "I feel like me. It's very nice that people want to see my movies—that is what the financial success of my films shows. My work has obviously entertained people. That's why I do it."

If Garry Marshall had been told by some "You can't dress her up," *Pretty Woman* proved them wrong. Julia looked gorgeous in the stunning Rodeo Drive outfits designed for her by Marilyn Vance-Straker; with her svelte figure and height, she could have been a model after all. Off-screen, Julia preferred not to be bothered. She went out in torn jeans and T-shirts, denim overalls, and baggy granny dresses, her hair often looking like it had been styled the night before by her pillow. Even at high-profile public events, she sometimes looked less than stylish; the man's-suit look that Bob McGowan had found "sexy" wasn't when the suit was three or four sizes too big for her and turned her figure into a shapeless lump.

She professed amazement at what many people expected of her since *Pretty Woman* opened. If stars like Ava Gardner, Joan Crawford, Marilyn Monroe, and Elizabeth Taylor always anticipated press and public interest and almost never appeared outside their homes looking less than flawless, Julia Roberts was part of a new breed of movie stars who felt they owed the public perfection only on-screen and—usually but not always—at public events. "There are people who see me in a grocery store and think that I should be, like, wearing Chanel or something," Julia said. "They can't respond to the fact that I'm in cutoffs and a T-shirt. As if it's part of my job to always look impeccable. Which isn't ever gonna happen! Ever! Or like when I get off a plane, and people write, 'Darling, find a hairdresser.' It's like, 'I've been on a plane for eighteen hours, sleeping. My skin is sucked dry, my hair is a mess. What do you *want* from me?'"

Obviously a good deal more than she was willing to give. As a result, she earned the dubious distinction of topping Mr. Blackwell's dreaded worst-dressed list for 1991.

While her sartorial nonchalance did not endear her to fashionistas, it made the public like her even more. She was clearly still one of them, despite all her special qualities and overwhelming success; the good ol' girl from Georgia who used to love watching *Hee Haw* with her grand-parents, they felt, really hadn't changed that much.

Many of the biggest female movie stars in history have had several aspects to their personalities, apparent contradictions that made them all the more intriguing to the public. Marilyn Monroe's sex appeal was potent, but it was leavened by sweetness and playfulness. Grace Kelly had a cool elegance, but with a passion burning hotly underneath; Bar-bra Streisand could look classically beautiful one minute, homely the next, and her breathtaking singing might be followed by rollicking Yid-dish shtick.

Julia felt the warring elements of her personality contributed to her success—and her ability to handle it. "Several personalities live within me," she said in 1992. "An experienced woman, an adolescent, a young woman discovering sensuality, and an innocent girl. I think it's been the simple possession of multiple personalities that has allowed me to with-stand the pressures of the fast rise in my career."

CHAPTER EIGHTEEN

The stardom of Julia Roberts, her power in Hollywood, and the rabid attention of her fans and the media increased exponentially with the release of *Sleeping with the Enemy* on February 10, 1991, not long after her appearance as the first woman on the cover of *Gentleman's Quarterly.* "I don't think you could get any hotter," Kiefer said of his fiancée, "or you'd spontaneously combust."

Despite mixed reviews—most of the naysayers questioned the credibility of several of the story's plot points rather than Julia's acting—the film grossed over $100 million in the United States, making it the third smash hit in less than a year that could be attributed mainly to the presence of Julia Roberts. It was obvious to even her most skeptical detractors that Julia Roberts was no flash in the pan. As Leonard Goldberg had felt when he hired her, Julia *was* perfect for the role of Laura Burney. Audiences sympathized with her from the first scene simply because she was Julia Roberts, whose likability and vulnerability had been demonstrated so fetchingly in her previous films. When her husband, who seems initially just a neat freak, brutally strikes and kicks her, the viewer is viscerally shocked, and a heavy sense of dread, fear, and suspense hovers over the remainder of the film.

In case his viewers might want a taste of the earlier, upbeat, unterrorized Julia Roberts, Joe Ruben added a scene in which Laura/Sara, in a theater prop room on campus with her new boyfriend, prances before a mirror trying on hats and feather boas as Van Morrison's "Brown Eyed Girl" plays in the background. Some critics lambasted the scene as exploitative, another example of movie-star image taking precedence over dramatic integrity. But the scene is charming, and it can be defended as a narrative device to emphasize the carefree abandon Laura finally allows herself after years of constant anxiety.

The range of emotions Julia conveys in this film—from faking happiness with her husband, to fearing both him and the new man in her life, then joyously welcoming the new relationship, to once again fearing her husband when he shows up—is wider than any role before had asked of her, and her growth as an actress is apparent. If Herb Ross was right that he'd had to draw subtext out of Julia "falsely," it's doubtful Joe Ruben had the same problem.

Shortly after filming on *Steel Magnolias* had wrapped in 1989, Sally Field and her production company, Fogwood, optioned the rights to Marti Leimbach's first novel, *Dying Young*. Sally thought the lead character, Hilary O'Neil—a blue-collar San Francisco girl who goes to work for and falls in love with Victor Gaddes, an aristocratic young man dying of leukemia—would be perfect for Julia. She persuaded 20th Century–Fox to pick up the project. "I told them I had this girl who would be wonderful," Sally recalled, but the studio wanted to hold out for a star. Casting was put on hold until a script was ready. The screenplay, by Richard Friedenberg, his first, wasn't completed until after *Pretty Woman* opened. Sally went back to Fox and told them, "I repeat, 'There's this girl I know who would be wonderful for this part,'" Sally said. "The good thing was that I didn't have to say, 'You don't know her yet.'"

Fox's chief, Joe Roth, was thrilled to have Julia—so thrilled, in fact, that the studio agreed to pay her $3 million. It would be her eighth feature film; in two years, Julia's salary had risen over 3,300 percent. Roth rationalized the huge salary thus: "When you have Julia's name on a marquee, you have the biggest female star in the world, one of less than ten people in the world who can 'open' a picture just because she's in it."

Julia called Joel Schumacher and asked him to direct *Dying Young*. He was pleasantly surprised by the call. "This was the first time a star had ever asked me to direct, and I don't think I would have made that particular movie if Julia hadn't asked me. I'm in love with Julia." Fox signed the impressive young actor Campbell Scott, son of the revered George C. Scott and Colleen Dewhurst, to play Victor. Dewhurst and Vincent D'Onofrio (a *Mystic Pizza* alumnus) would also be in the cast.

With Julia secure in her director's affections and happy with her costars, filming began in the California coastal community of Mendocino on November 12, 1990. The crew built a seven-thousand-square-foot house on a bluff overlooking the ocean, where Hilary and Victor go for an idyllic stretch after he tells her his cancer is in remission.

Compared to *Sleeping with the Enemy*, *Dying Young* proved an uneventful shoot. There were reports that Julia was tired after making five movies in under two years (and could catnap at any time, in any position), but there were no reports of fainting spells and no on-set tribulations between director and star. The hardest part of the experience for Julia was the overwhelming melancholy of the story. She told Julie Lew of *The New York Times*, "Yesterday I shot a scene with Campbell that was very sad, and I didn't anticipate it to be that sad. That's the hardest part of doing things like this; you don't anticipate how much will really happen." There were few scenes to lighten things up; one had Hilary laughingly rubbing Victor's bald head.

As shooting progressed, Schumacher became unsettled to find that *too* much was happening in his movie. In the novel and in the original script, Victor commits suicide at the end, and Hilary goes off with Gordon, a handyman who lives nearby (D'Onofrio). But as Schumacher tightened his focus on the two main characters, he scaled back the smaller roles, including those of D'Onofrio and Dewhurst. The director had insisted from the outset that Victor not commit suicide, but he did shoot a final scene in which Hilary chooses Gordon over Victor.

During the filming, Julia learned that she had been nominated for a Golden Globe, as Best Actress in a Musical or Comedy, for *Pretty Woman*, and shortly afterward another Academy Award nomination came her way, also for Best Actress—which she learned of while vacationing with Kiefer at his Montana ranch.

After further location filming in San Francisco and the Napa Valley, the picture wrapped on February 8, 1991, the same day *Sleeping with the Enemy* opened. As Schumacher labored over postproduction, the Hollywood rumor mill began to churn. The word was that *Dying Young* was in trouble: Fox officials, it was said, were unhappy with the downbeat title, which they were afraid would scare viewers away (and make them think it was Julia's character who died); they were unhappy with the ending, which they felt would disappoint Julia's fans; and they waffled about the release date, which originally had been set for summer 1991.

Schumacher tried to come up with a new title. He considered "All for Love" and "Forever Young" (perhaps that's how that title wound up on some of Julia's filmographies), but they didn't seem to reflect the story line. Fox executives agreed to keep the title, but after a disastrous preview, they insisted the director shoot another ending. "Audiences were horrified," an insider told a British reporter. "Julia Roberts is very popular. They don't want to see her in a bad light. [The] new ending has her comforting her lover on his deathbed."

Then there was the matter of the release date. When the studio changed it from June to "undated fall," observers saw trouble. "It was assumed that if the studio liked the picture," Schumacher said, "it would be a summer movie. But when the studio saw the dailies, there was discussion about whether it wouldn't be better placed in the fall or at Christmas, when the serious pictures come out. Later, when Fox saw the movie all put together, they said, 'This is a love story. It should come out as soon as possible.'" The studio set a final release date of June 21.

On the third weekend of February, all hell broke loose at the Roberts-Sutherland manse in the Hollywood Hills. The tabloid newspaper *Globe* hit the stands with a story entitled CAUGHT! KIEFER 2-TIMES PRETTY WOMAN JULIA ROBERTS. Accompanied by photos of a clearly uncomfortable Kiefer and a pretty brunette companion, the story detailed his intimate tête-à-têtes with the unidentified woman in the wee hours at a Sunset Strip restaurant.

Reports said that Julia and Kiefer had a knock-down-drag-out that resulted in his leaving—or being thrown out of—the house. He moved into a $105-a-week room at the seedy St. Francis Hotel on Hollywood Boulevard, near Western Avenue. Its location was telling: across the street from Hollywood Billiards, where, in January, he had met the woman in question—busty twenty-four-year-old Amanda Rice, aka "Raven" in her strip act at the Crazy Girls club on La Brea Avenue in Hollywood. Rice, who bore a resemblance to the actress Demi Moore, said in an unpublished 1991 interview, "Kiefer plays there [at Hollywood Billiards] a lot. He asked me to play a game with him, and I did."

Raised in Hawaii, Rice had danced in Washington, D.C., before moving to Los Angeles, she said, "to act." While she studied that craft, she gyrated to catcalls at Crazy Girls, where Kiefer came to see her shortly after they met. "I heard he asked someone, 'Does she have a boyfriend?'" Rice recalled. Told that she didn't, Kiefer said, "Well, she does now."

Rice admitted that she had heard Julia and Kiefer were engaged, but when she questioned him about it, "he told me specifically that he was not engaged." He *was* wearing a ring Julia had given him at Christmas, but, Rice insisted, "He said they would not be married, that being with her the last six months or so was hell."

Rice quite naturally was thrilled to be courted by a movie star, especially when he took her, her five-year-old son, Kelly, and his daughter, Sara, to Disneyland for a daylong outing while Julia filmed *Dying Young*. Rice admitted that Kiefer had given her son "a lot of things, a toy gun and a rifle." He also gave her several thousand dollars. "He wanted me to buy myself gifts, but I have to tell you, I spent every dime on bills."

Rice would not say that she'd had a sexual affair with Sutherland, but she did admit to "a relationship." And, she added, "He's great to be with. We had long walks. We had meals together. Spent hours and hours playing pool—and, oh yeah, he gives great foot massages."

According to Fran Padilla, the manager of the St. Francis Hotel—which had no telephones in the rooms—Kiefer received messages from Julia and from his friend Michelle Pfeiffer. One of Julia's said, "There's always a rainbow after the storm." Apparently she was ready to forgive him, and Kiefer moved back into the Nichols Canyon house at the end of February. According to Rice, "Julia knew that Kiefer had gone out with me, but she believed it all to be totally innocent. I heard she told someone, 'He has better taste than that.'

"She's sort of a bitch," Amanda Rice added.

The weekend after the *Globe* story broke, Julia appeared on the cover of *People* once again. This time she was pictured with Kiefer, and the headline blared, JULIA IN LOVE—"THIS IS IT!" ROBERTS SAYS OF HER ROMANCE WITH KIEFER SUTHERLAND. The story reported that Kiefer had given Julia the diamond ring the prior February, but quoted her denial that it was an engagement ring. Kiefer later gave Julia a very personal—and seemingly lasting—gift for her twenty-third birthday: a tattoo on her left shoulder blade of a red heart within a black Chinese symbol meaning "strength of heart." An artist at Sunset Tattoo did the honors, and, Kiefer said, "It was a real private, wonderful moment."

"My love for Kiefer will last as long as this tattoo," Julia gushed. "We're together all the time," she told *USA Today* early in February. "We work together, we're in love with each other. That's a life. You can't ask for more."

The *People* piece did not mention the reports of Kiefer's dalliance with Amanda Rice, but it did raise a red flag—Julia and Kiefer hadn't worked together since *Flatliners*, and their careers seemed headed in opposite directions. The story quoted an unnamed friend of the couple: "There is definitely a problem, and the problem is work-related. Kiefer is not getting offers for roles, and Julia's phone is ringing every two minutes. But she is madly in love with him, and she wants the relationship to work."

On Monday, March 25, Kiefer escorted Julia to the sixty-third annual Academy Awards, where she was up for Best Actress in *Pretty Woman*. Observers and fans were taken aback by Julia's latest hair incarnation, a short platinum-blond dye job. Although she had won the Golden Globe, she faced tough competition from Kathy Bates in the film version of Stephen King's novel *Misery*.

Bates won—deservedly so, most agreed, so Julia wasn't too disappointed. Millions of viewers across the country not only saw Julia present a Best Song nominee but also watched her interviewed by Barbara Walters on the annual Walters Oscar special.

Julia spoke emotionally to Walters about how much she missed her father and added, "But at the same time, he's— There are no physical parameters now in our relationship. We're together all the time. He's completely accessible at any minute of any day, you know, so, not knowing anything different, it's the perfect father-daughter relationship."

"I'm not sure what you mean," Walters said.

"I mean that if he were, I don't want to sound too voodoo or weird, but if he were alive, would he be here right now? Able to watch me? Maybe not. But he's here now, you know, and I can go home and go, 'Dad, I shouldn't have said that to Barbara Walters, you know, it was horrible.' So it's kind of, he's always kind of watching. I feel a force, maybe, you know, something's there . . . I just think I have a little extra guidance somewhere that maybe other people don't have."

She also spoke of Kiefer and said they would be together forever. Walters, twice married, asked her if she *truly* believed that. "Yeah," Julia replied. "Forever love. I believe in that, and I believe that this is it. We live together and we are happy and we are in love with each other—and isn't that what being married is? He is the love of my life. He is the person I love and admire and respect the most in the world. Kiefer is probably the most wonderful, understanding person I have ever met."

On April 18, Julia attended a thirty-fifth birthday party for Eric at his home in Los Angeles. In February he and his raven-haired girlfriend,

Kelly Cunningham, had made Julia an aunt for the first time with the birth of their daughter, Emma. But the party, in Eric's recollection, was not a happy occasion. "[Julia had] cut and bleached her hair blond," Eric told Fred Schruers in *Premiere* in 1996, "and I criticized her. She had a fit that I had no respect for her as an actress. This was done for Tinkerbell in Spielberg's *Hook*. She had a fit! I didn't respect her. I change my hair all the time, why can't she? And who the fuck do I think I am? I hurt her feelings. I have no kindness in my body, etc., etc."

The rift between Eric and Julia was now complete and became increasingly public as the years went on. Julia responded to Eric's version of the final breakdown of their relationship in an interview with David Hochman for the October 1996 issue of *Us:* "That's not how it happened. Certainly, I don't put so much importance into my hair that someone disagreeing with my particular choice in hairdo is gonna ruin our relationship. That seemed a pretty silly explanation. . . . Right now the best thing I can do is stand apart from it."

Around this time Julia was involved in a daring rescue of an accident victim that could have been a scene in one of her movies, as she described it to Rosie O'Donnell on her show. She was driving home from the gym, barefoot and with a loose dress over her gym clothes, when she saw one car slam into another, which flipped over and landed on its roof in a yard along the roadway. Her first reaction was to call 911, but she didn't have a cell phone. "I put my car in park and jumped out and ran over, and there was a young man in the car, and I said, 'Are you okay?'

"He said, 'I think so,' and I said, 'Okay, I don't think I'm supposed to do this, but I'm going to pull you out of the car,' because he was upside down and all bunched up, and there seemed to be an odd liquid coming from the car which concerned me." She pulled the man out of the car, and when he said his neck hurt, she got on her knees and wedged his head between her thighs to keep it stable. "I said, 'Okay, we're just going to breathe.' So I just talked to him, and I was rubbing his ears, and we were doing Lamaze breathing; I was doing all the medical shows I've ever seen on television and the things that people say to comfort."

Paramedics arrived and took the man to the hospital. Julia drove home and then "freaked out" about what had happened. Not long afterward, she received a note from the fellow, telling her that the night before the accident, he and his girlfriend had watched *Pretty Woman* because he had never seen it. "He said that when he had this accident, he looked up and saw me hanging over him with all this bright [golden] hair, and he said he was sure he was dead."

On April 30, Julia's publicist, Pat Kingsley, announced that Julia and Kiefer would marry on June 14 in a "small and private" ceremony. "I've been immensely blessed in the discovery of this person," Julia said in the prepared statement.

Thus began what Elaine Goldsmith would call "the Fellini summer." Almost immediately the "small and private" plans changed drastically. *Dying Young* was set to open a week after the planned wedding date, and 20th Century–Fox wanted Julia to get married in grand Hollywood style—and thus give the movie a priceless publicity boost.

The couple agreed, and in early June, studio chief Joe Roth instructed crews to build a "fantasy wedding set" on Fox's Soundstage 14 to simulate a southern-garden setting right out of *Gone with the Wind* (or *Steel Magnolias*), complete with magnolia trees flown in from Smyrna, white trellises, and fresh green sod. The cost was estimated at half a million dollars.

Julia chose as her bridesmaids Elaine Goldsmith, Risa Shapiro, the makeup artist Lucienne Zammit, and Deborah Porter, an actress friend, all of whom ordered $425 white Manolo Blahnik shoes dyed sea-foam green to match their $3,200 dresses, designed by Richard Tyler. Julia's maid of honor would be her sister, Lisa.

At the Tyler-Trafficante salon in West Hollywood, Julia chose a custom-made $8,000 two-piece wedding dress with a long jacket that would turn into a minidress after the long skirt and train were removed. The wedding cake, a four-tiered affair, would be trimmed in violets and sea-foam-colored ribbons of icing.

Kiefer planned his bachelor party at Dominick's restaurant on Beverly Boulevard in West Hollywood, where his cake would be a replica of a fifteen-pound turkey. Apparently he had wanted a Thanksgiving-style dinner served at the wedding, but Julia preferred beef. "Kiefer has a thing for turkeys," a source close to the cake told *People*.

Everything seemed to be going along well until the turkey hit the fan. On May 7, Amanda Rice gave an interview to the London newspaper *The Sun*, in which she claimed that she and Kiefer had had a sexual relationship. Worse, she revealed things about Julia, and about Kiefer's relationship with Julia, that Kiefer had told her. According to Rice, Kiefer complained that Julia was self-centered, demanding, had a poor self-image, "bites her nails to the quick," has "tiny breasts" and "no butt," and was an "ice princess" in bed.

Rice went on: "Kiefer said making love to her was like making love with a corpse. After we made love one night, Kiefer told me he could never wed Julia because she was so demanding, so bad in bed, and just wanted him there for her every whim. I told him, 'Kiefer, if you ever want to get out, come back to me for twenty-four hours, and I'll make you forget you ever met her. I've got a great new pair of boobs, and I'm available anytime you want me.' I wouldn't be surprised if he gets in touch with me. He needs some lovin'."

The story was picked up in the United States by *The National Enquirer*. As copies of the multimillion-circulation tabloid were put up next to supermarket checkouts in every city and town in America, Julia was on yet another movie set and having a difficult time. Her new film was Steven Spielberg's extravaganza *Hook,* based on J. M. Barrie's play *Peter Pan.* The film, set to be a TriStar release starring Dustin Hoffman as Captain Hook; Robin Williams as a grown-up Peter Pan; Maggie Smith as an elderly Wendy; and Julia as Tinkerbell, was budgeted at a staggering $56 million. Reports said that Julia would receive $7 million of that. Her actual salary was closer to $2 million—still a hefty sum for what originally was slated as a few weeks' work, especially since Julia (through her then–production company, Sabajka) would also receive 2 percent of the film's gross proceeds over $100 million.

When she was offered the part in the fall of 1990, Julia was excited about working with a director and costars of such strong reputation, as well as playing a fairy who had been one of her childhood favorites. "They have her depicted as a very fresh character," she said. "She's very clever and witty and speaks her mind. I just sat down with Mr. Spielberg two nights ago, and he was telling me some of the new ideas, which are really great."

The picture was originally scheduled to begin principal photography in January 1991, and Julia would have had to report in February, immediately after completing *Dying Young*. She soon saw that this would be too tight a schedule. She was tired and didn't relish jumping from one project directly into another. "I didn't think I had the muscle to do it. Better to pull out than to go in halfhearted and let everyone else down."

But when Julia learned that the start of filming had been put off a few months, she had Elaine Goldsmith (who had moved from William

Morris to International Creative Management) call Spielberg and the studio executives. No one else had been cast, so Julia was signed to play Tinkerbell. In April, shortly before she was scheduled to appear on the set, she told a reporter, "I get fitted for my wings in a week. *Fitted for my wings! I love that kind of shit.*"

Because of the star power attached to *Hook,* rumors swirled out from the project almost immediately. There were reports of soundstage catastrophes and cost overruns, but most of the negative rumors centered around Julia—for the first time in her career. She was under a great deal of pressure in her private life, and the burdens of creating a seven-inch flying pixie taxed her. Julia spent most of her time waiting for setups to be completed—sometimes for as long as six hours—or suspended in an uncomfortable harness in front of a blue screen. The screen would allow the movie magicians to place Tinkerbell in whatever setting she was supposed to appear. Most of the time Julia had no costar to act against. Steven Spielberg read most of her cue lines; occasionally Robin Williams helped out, but she never acted with Dustin Hoffman.

Reports said that the crew called Julia "Tinkerhell" behind her back, that she fussed and complained so much that Spielberg "lost his temper" with her, that she had thrown a shoe across the soundstage in anger. Even the film's publicity notes—a genre not renowned for hard-edged reporting—spoke of the difficulties Julia faced. "The unpredictable sets of Neverland would prove, at times, to be physically and artistically demanding. Most of her work consisted of long days inside hot soundstages reacting to actors and action that could not be seen—just approximated—while often hanging in the air suspended by a flying harness or prancing about an oversized set filled with gigantic props."

One report stated that Julia, tired of waiting yet again for a setup, had announced, "I'm ready now," and Spielberg had countered, "We're ready when *I* say we're ready, Julia." Other reports indicated that TriStar executives were unhappy with the dailies they'd seen of Julia, finding her thin, wan, and unhappy-looking, with little of the effervescence she was known for. Herb Ross, of all people, came to Julia's defense—sort of. "Julia is timid, frightened, and inexperienced, but a talented young actress," he said. "Her sudden tirades and infrequent overbearing actions could be the result of overwork. She's had a lot to deal with this year."

The situation became so bad that *USA Today* reported, shockingly, "Don't be surprised if Julia Roberts is dropped from Steven Spielberg's in-the-works movie *Hook.*"

CHAPTER NINETEEN

After just three days' work on *Hook*—and five days after the *Enquirer*'s Amanda Rice story hit the newsstands—Kiefer carried Julia into the emergency room of Cedars-Sinai Medical Center in West Hollywood. She was suffering from a spiking fever, dizziness, headaches, and dehydration. Doctors immediately admitted her under the pseudonym Fiona Douglas (Kiefer's mother is the actress Shirley Douglas) and began a battery of tests, including a CAT scan.

The tests ruled out everything from a repeat bout of meningitis to AIDS, and after news of Julia's illness leaked to the press, a hospital spokesman, Ron Wise, said that Julia had "a severe viral infection." Doctors rehydrated her and administered a broad-spectrum antibiotic through an intravenous tube.

Dressed in surgical blues, Kiefer maintained a twenty-four-hour vigil at Julia's side, sleeping on a pullout bed next to hers. ("Kiefer was a real bud when Julia was sick," Amanda Rice later said.) He remained at her side on May 21, when she was discharged. But the rumor mill was whirling at an ever more furious pace. Because of Julia's sickly appearance, whispers had begun to circulate even before her hospitalization that she was addicted to heroin; afterward, the rumors said she was in for detoxification. When the reports appeared in print, Julia vehemently—and angrily—denied them. "I was exhausted. I had a fever, bad fever. That was the worst symptom. It was, like, 104. That's why I was in the hospital so long. People should be allowed to be sick without enduring tales that they've got a needle stuck in their arm. I had the flu. I was sick. Fuck off!"

Julia's recovery was apparently rapid. Within days Army Archerd reported in his *Daily Variety* column that Julia and Kiefer had celebrated their upcoming nuptials at the Moonlight Tango Café in the San Fernando Valley, where Julia had led a conga line.

. . .

Wedding preparations continued apace. On June 2, Elaine Goldsmith hosted a bridal shower for Julia in her Marina del Rey home. The gifts included several pairs of lacy undergarments and at least one garter belt. Betty Motes was there; she stayed at Julia and Kiefer's to help with the wedding details.

As June 14 approached, construction continued on the wedding set at Fox's cavernous Soundstage 14. Gold-engraved invitations had been sent to more than two hundred of what *People* called "Hollywood's glitziest and ritziest," including Joel Schumacher, Garry Marshall, Richard Gere, Bruce Willis, Dolly Parton, Shirley MacLaine, Sally Field, Daryl Hannah, and Emilio Estevez.

Amid the magnolia-draped trellises, fifty intimate tables for four were set with centerpiece vases that would each hold a dozen fresh-cut roses. A gourmet meat supplier had an order for two hundred filet mignons; a liquor store would provide a hundred bottles of the finest champagne. The party-rental company readied the linens, dishes, and silverware. The designs for the buffet-table ice sculptures were finalized. And even though the soundstage would prevent the kind of press helicopter flyovers that had marred some outdoor celebrity weddings, Fox earmarked $100,000 for extra security to assure that uninvited guests—especially media—were kept at bay.

Then, three days before the celebration, as unexpectedly as an earthquake, the Los Angeles catering business suffered a nearly crippling economic blow. The wedding was called off. It was Tuesday, June 11—twenty years to the day after Julia's parents had separated. The shocking news that the most anticipated wedding since Prince Charles's to Lady Diana would not take place went out like a seismic wave and made headlines virtually everywhere.

Immediately, reporters and photographers massed around Julia's home, hoping to catch a statement or a photograph. But anticipating the onslaught, on Monday night she and her mother had gone to Elaine Goldsmith's, where, Betty said, "We thought we'd be safe." It didn't take long for their whereabouts to be discovered. The next day, Betty said, "We looked out the window . . . and we could not believe it. There must have been a hundred and fifty photographers ringing the house. They were flying over in helicopters. I went out there and said, 'C'mon, you guys! All she did was break off an engagement. People are starving in the world, you know? Go home!'"

. . .

So what happened? *Newsweek* ran a pop quiz: "(a) He got blasted at his bachelor party and bedded a hooker. (b) She's cracking up. He's in rehab. (c) He had a fling with a G-stringer. She has a lesbian lover. (d) Her career is in hyperspace. His is on hiatus. (e) They're still getting hitched, but wanted to hoodwink the media. (f) All of the above. (g) None of the above."

The London *Daily Mail* weighed in with a few other permutations. One was that Amanda Rice wasn't the only other woman in Kiefer's life. As Rice put it, "He told me, 'I've had a couple of flings since I met Julia. But you're different, I really like you.'" The paper also reported that Julia and Kiefer had had "major rows" over money, and that Kiefer had balked at signing a prenuptial agreement. The *Mail* story went on to express concern over Julia's physical and mental health and speculated that she might have to take a year off from filmmaking to regain her equilibrium. "In recent weeks there have been signs that she is ominously near the edge. Los Angeles radio host John Nicholls said, 'I saw her driving her white BMW to a store in the middle of town. She parked in a red zone and got out barefoot, wearing a bathrobe. She had no makeup on and looked terrible. But she seemed oblivious to passersby.'"

The article then speculated, as had *USA Today*, that Julia might not complete the few weeks of work she still had to do on *Hook*, and it quoted one of Spielberg's Amblin Entertainment executives as saying, "Julia's thin, pale, tired and sick."

The *Mail* story concluded, "Hollywood contract lawyers say that if Julia does drop out of *Hook*, one condition would be that she has psychiatric counseling. 'It's as much for her benefit as the studio's,' one expert explained. 'Her whole career could be on the line.'"

Conventional wisdom settled on the notion that Julia had jilted Kiefer primarily because of his dalliance with Amanda Rice. A friend of Kiefer's, however, put the blame on the distaff side. "Well, what would you think if someone who goes on every talk show and says how much she loves you did something like this? He's shocked!" It soon became clear that this sexual cotillion wasn't just an *affaire à trois* but an *affaire à quatre:* Julia had become involved with another man, and Kiefer found out about it.

Between her bridal shower and the cancellation of the wedding, Julia had flown to Arizona with her sisters, Lisa and Nancy, Elaine Goldsmith, and the actress Ally Sheedy to be pampered at the posh Canyon Ranch health resort in Tucson. On the plane, Julia unexpectedly ran into the twenty-three-year-old actor Jason Patric, the dark-haired, blue-eyed, square-jawed son of Jason Miller (Father Karras in *The Exorcist*) and grandson of "The Great One," comedian Jackie Gleason. The two had met briefly through Kiefer, who costarred with Patric in *The Lost Boys*. But on this short flight, sparks flew.

Serendipitously, they were headed to the same place. At Canyon Ranch on Sunday night, June 9, they enjoyed a supper of chicken piccata and peanut-butter yogurt. Afterward, an eyewitness told *People,* they slipped off, with Jason seemingly "comforting" Julia.

Word got back to Kiefer, who promptly disinvited Jason from the wedding. Julia had been having second and third thoughts about getting married for a number of reasons—Amanda Rice and Kiefer's prodigious alcohol consumption chief among them—but she was terrified by how big the event had grown, how badly she would disappoint everyone if she canceled it, and how embarrassing the fallout might be. But after being with Jason, her feelings crystallized: She was more sure than ever that she would be making "the biggest mistake of my life" to marry Kiefer Sutherland. She returned from Arizona intent on telling him she thought it would be in their best interests not to get married.

"But the next time I talked to Kiefer," Julia later told *Entertainment Weekly,* "he called *me* on the telephone . . . and proceeded to tell *me* what I was going to tell *him,* which is he did not want to marry me. . . . I was a little surprised that he said this before I had a chance to say it, so I said nothing. But he was far more nasty about it than I was going to be. He hung up the phone and called back a few hours later and said, 'So, is it on or is it off?' At that time I said what I was going to say before."

Julia felt a tremendous sense of relief, but she knew she would have to face the horrors of Hades where the press was concerned. The reality proved worse than her darkest fears. "That's when the avalanche began," she told *Entertainment Weekly.* "People love scandal, people love drama. . . . And I feel like Kiefer, for whatever reasons, tried to make it seem like *he* was the victim of the situation. . . . But he shouldn't try to make himself look better by taking shots at me. Somehow it turned into Kiefer being left at the altar. Well, I just don't understand that, quite frankly."

Julia said she had received much fan mail of the "hang in there, girl" variety, suggesting that many people saw Kiefer's dalliances as the problem. "I think it was a mix," Julia said, "that people were confused. I think a lot of things were thrown into the pot that confused the issue, what with Kiefer and—what do I call her, *this girl*—" The *EW* interviewer offered assistance: "We're talking about 'the stripper' . . ."

"Yeah, that's what she was!" Julia said with a laugh. "And once that came out, I sort of swallowed my pride a little bit and said, 'Okay, the woman *is* the last to know.' I mean, this had been going on for a very long time. So then I had to [realize] I had made an enormous mistake by agreeing to get married to begin with. Then I made an even greater mistake by letting it all get so big. At that point I realized that this had all been turned into an enormous joke, and that it wasn't going to be respectable, it wasn't going to be honest, it wasn't going to be simple. And it could have been all those things."

Steven Spielberg demanded that Julia appear at a press conference with him on Thursday, June 13, on the Fox lot to counteract rumors that all of the turmoil in her personal life had adversely affected the production of *Hook*. Director and star put on their best faces, hugged, and denied anything was amiss behind the soundstage walls. A studio employee present at the time said that Julia "seemed fine and was very happy, not mopey and sad, as she had been before." An unrecognized clue to her newfound happiness rested on her head: a baseball cap with NOTRE DAME stitched across the front. Notre Dame's Fighting Irish is Jason Patric's favorite college football team. Later that night, Julia was spotted going into Jason's West Hollywood duplex apartment. She didn't leave until the next morning, driving off in her BMW.

On Friday—the day the wedding was supposed the take place— Kiefer moved his belongings out of the Nichols Canyon house and into an apartment. At the same time, Julia and Jason enjoyed turkey burgers at the trendy West Hollywood health-food café Nowhere, on Beverly Boulevard.

A few hours after lunch, Jason and Julia boarded a flight at Los Angeles International Airport for London. They were on their way to Dublin. Julia had been granted time off from *Hook* for her honeymoon, so apparently she decided to take one—with Jason rather than Kiefer.

As they sat next to each other in first class on the one-hour Aer Lingus flight from London to Dublin, London's *Daily Mail* reported, the two beautiful young movie stars "were practically making love."

Part Four

LEAVE IT AND LOVETT

"If I'm not intact, I'm worthless.
I think it's time for me to go away for a while.
I just want to slow down."

—Julia, 1992

"I had a very strong reaction to meeting him, different from the way I've
ever reacted to any person on the planet."

—Julia on Lyle Lovett, 1992

CHAPTER TWENTY

Dublin, June 17—Just days after calling off her much-ballyhooed wedding to actor Kiefer Sutherland, America's "Pretty Woman," Julia Roberts, 23, has fled to Ireland with handsome *After Dark, My Sweet* star Jason Patric, who is celebrating his twenty-fifth birthday today.

Pursued by a frenzied band of paparazzi, the couple was seen kissing and cuddling at the £400-per-night Shelbourne Hotel. Julia ran her fingers through Jason's hair and shared an intimate meal with him, and later a late-night snack. A witness said, "They made no secret of their romance. They were all over each other like a couple in love." A hotel employee added, "The engagement ring was off her finger. She looked very drawn. She had lost a lot of weight. Her hair was pale orange, like a dye job gone wrong."

At sunset, the pair was spotted holding hands on Dublin's Grafton Street, an exclusive shopping district. Julia wore a blazer, jeans, and cowboy boots. At 1:30 A.M., when Julia and Jason returned to the hotel (in which they booked separate rooms), they dashed inside to escape photographers. They checked out of the hotel at 4:30 A.M. and are now thought to be staying at a farm on Ireland's west coast, owned by Julia's friend Adam Clayton of the rock band U2.

With press reports like the distillation above, celebrity watchers sensed a pattern. For the fourth time in four years, Julia Roberts had fallen madly, truly, deeply in love with a fellow actor who had heart-throb good looks and an intense, moody personality. Once again Julia had become involved with a man whose parents were a part of the theater world. Jason Patric Miller's mother, Linda—Jackie Gleason's daughter—appeared in the 1978 Jill Clayburgh film *An Unmarried Woman;*

his father, in addition to the Oscar-nominated turn as Father Karras, won a Pulitzer Prize for writing *That Championship Season*. As with two of Julia's three previous boyfriends, Jason's parents had divorced early in his life (he was six), and, like Kiefer Sutherland, Patric had dropped out of high school (at sixteen). He had moved with his brother from Queens, New York, to Santa Monica, California. "My brother and I were on our own for about three months," he said, "and then my mom moved out here as well. When she moved, we all got back together, and I finished my two years of high school and decided to give acting a shot."

Perhaps more than any young actor before him, Jason Patric abhorred the "publicity game." He gave interviews with great reluctance (if not truculence) and refused to discuss his personal life in any detail, particularly his brief marriage (1988–90) to Robin Wright, the future Mrs. Sean Penn. Of his celebrated grandfather, who died in 1987, he would say only, "He was a very talented man. But he was never part of my life." He had even less to say about his father, whose last name he dropped when he became a professional actor. "Growing up, I was always called Jason Patric, especially when I was bad," he said. "It's also mildly Oedipal. You have to kill the parents in order to become yourself."

Liz Smith, writing about Jason and Julia in her column of June 21, 1991, reported that his manager, Dolores Robinson, had said her client "is a completely private person and doesn't care about being in columns or having any publicity."

"So have you got that?" Smith asked. "This means we must sit down, shut up, and not pry into the relationship of Julia and Jason. Of course, it also means that Jason Patric has himself mixed up with the one woman in the entertainment world who will guarantee he gets more 'publicity' than he has ever heard of." Jason later admitted that "I knew [dating Julia] would be trouble. But for me . . . it was the ultimate nightmare."

He got his first hint when, after two weeks of sightseeing in Ireland, he and Julia returned to the United States on June 25 only to be greeted at the end of that week by both their faces on the cover of *People*—Julia for the third time in under a year and Jason for the first, along with an inset picture of Kiefer and the bold headline THE BIG BREAKUP!

The editors gleefully pointed out in a sidebar called "Tale of the Take" that the four Kiefer Sutherland films released in 1990 (including *Flatliners*) had averaged $26.2 million at the domestic box office, while Julia's last four films (including *Flatliners*) had averaged nearly four times that amount. Still, a Hollywood insider told the magazine, "The problem is not money, or other women, but Julia. Every time she gets close, she just shies away."

Certainly Julia had little to draw on to make her feel confident about the possibility of success in marriage. (Or from those of her string of paramours, with the exception of Liam Neeson, whose parents remained together.) Although at this time she repeatedly expressed her desire for a husband and a family, she had gone through four live-in relationships and two engagements in four years without tying the knot. When a relationship began to grow unpleasant, when the initial flush of passion and romantic possibilities faded, Julia's abhorrence of confrontation would lead her to abruptly end the relationship, sometimes through a surrogate like Elaine Goldsmith to avoid unpleasantness.

Writers who had characterized Julia as "coltish" on-screen started to call her "skittish" when it came to matrimony, and the image of Julia Roberts as a romantic flibbertigibbet began to take hold. She took offense. "My relationships happened over three years in my life, not on some wild, outrageous weekend," she retorted. Speaking specifically of the aborted wedding, she said, "It became something that was taking on speed, that everyone was going to have to know about. So it was a much bigger decision than just having to say to somebody, 'Let's not do this' . . . and that also probably delayed my ability to realize what I had to realize—that I can't give a *shit* about some lady in Boise who thinks I made the biggest mistake in my life or that I'm a bad person because I've done this. This is *my* life. I get to do it *one* time. And this is a decision I made for me. I have saved my life by doing this."

Kiefer moved to his Montana farm to take stock of his life and his career. "I'm not a calm person," he told Peter Stevenson of *Details*. "In fact, I'm rather obsessive. I can be terribly irrational, I have a temper." He said that Julia had shown him "how fun life can be if you weren't working all the time. I'm forever indebted to her for that. It was the first time that something else in my life interested me other than work. Although the attention was kind of embarrassing and frightening for both of us, because it wasn't the nicest kind of attention. It made you feel so estranged from everything."

Kiefer admitted to Steve Pond in *Us* that alcohol had been a problem for him. "I've gone back and forth with drinking too much quite a few times in my life. I think it would be fair for *me* to say that there have been times when I have gone on binges where I have drunk too much. Absolutely. It's also fair to say that that's finding less of a place in my life now than ever."

While Julia and Jason were in Ireland, *Dying Young* opened in the United States. Its reviews proved largely favorable, especially for the acting of its two stars and Schumacher's nonexploitative handling of the material, but the ending was roundly criticized. In *Newsweek*, David Ansen summed up the critical consensus when he called the film "an ultra-glossy Hollywood tearjerker that, given the maudlin possibilities, is a lot less offensive than you might fear. . . . But is relative tastefulness what anyone wants in a weepie? A movie like this has only one not-so-noble reason to exist—to make us sob. And it just doesn't deliver the goods. Even the forbidding title turns out to be misleading. How can a movie called *Dying Young* deny its audience a death scene? That's not just chicken, it's dramatically dumb."

That critics would object to a tacked-on happy ending wouldn't have surprised anyone. What caught the Hollywood community up short was what Ansen had intimated—that despite the negative reactions of preview audiences to the original ending, moviegoers felt equally unfulfilled by the revised conclusion. The success of *Pretty Woman* had recently reinforced the wisdom of happiness at all costs and—forgetting that the death of Ali MacGraw's character in *Love Story* did little to harm that film's revenues—Fox executives felt they had made the right decision.

They hadn't, as even Julia had to agree. "The movie that we made I was very proud of," she said, referring to the version with the original ending. "The movie that I ultimately saw didn't move me the way the film that we had made did." *Dying Young* earned a third less at the box office than each of Julia's prior three films. Although she protested that $33 million "is a *lot* of money," it was far less than the industry had come to expect of her vehicles. Worse, it left the film unprofitable in America. (Overseas revenue and video sales helped it turn a profit eventually.)

For the first time, doubts about Julia's commercial infallibility crept in. Martin Grove, in *The Hollywood Reporter,* wrote, "They said Julia Roberts could open any film. They said she could open the phone book. *Dying Young* proved they were wrong." The timing couldn't have been worse, coming as it did amid the chaos in her personal life and the rampant rumors of her "emaciation," "exhaustion," "breakdown," and "drug problems." Several press reports of the film's lack of "boffo b.o." seemed tinged with glee, as though Miss Roberts had finally been taken down a peg or two.

This shocked and hurt her. The press and some members of the public, she said, will build up a personality "to a level which is above them. And that's when they get uncomfortable, and they turn you—*me*—from being just like them to someone who *isn't* like them, which is this sort of *celebrity*, this thing that is perceived as superior. And then they get offended. 'Well, what makes *you* better than me?' This brings discomfort, which brings rumor and gossip and everything else to bring you not only back to where you started, but lower than that, so they can say, 'Well, see, she was never better than anybody else. She's dirt on the floor now.'"

Steven Spielberg's *Hook* was beleaguered by production problems that summer. Already over budget and two weeks behind schedule by late June, Spielberg had not been pleased that Julia took off to Ireland. She was technically within her contractual rights to do so, but Spielberg (who admitted to a "twenty-year fear of working with movie stars" and suddenly was directing three very big ones) didn't need the aggravation. Julia apparently did not tell Spielberg or anyone else when she would be back at work, because the film's production designer, Norman Garwood, said, "There was a lot of tension arising from the will-she-or-won't-she-show-up question. The producers seemed really worried, and some of the worrying spread down to us. We would have to work on one set instead of another to time it with her arrival."

This uncertainty led Spielberg to decide that if Julia didn't reappear, ready to work, by July 1, he would replace her. He brought Michelle Pfeiffer in for costume fittings just in case. On June 26, however, Julia was spotted in the studio commissary, barefoot, having lunch with Jason, from whom she seemed unable to bear a day's separation. Although still gaunt, she was clearly much happier than she had been weeks before. Still, Julia's ill temper during her previous weeks of filming left Robin Williams, at least, concerned about her frame of mind. A cast member said, "Robin said to me, 'I hope Julia is going to be kind to all those kids who come up to her and expect her to be Tink. Tinkerbell is magical.'"

Julia's mood had definitely improved, but her working conditions had not. She still had to wait hours for setups to be completed, or hang for hours strapped in the harness, acting opposite her director, who admitted, "I'm no actor."

Julia defended her unhappiness with the situation. "I'm a normal person. If I sit in my trailer for six hours doing nothing. I'm going to say, 'What the fuck is going on?' I don't think that's an outrageous question. I don't think that's temperamental, either." And, she admitted, "I don't think I'd do a search and destroy for other parts like this, to be hanging on a wire for hours."

One incident illustrated that Julia was still on emotional tenterhooks when it came to Kiefer Sutherland. Walking from her trailer to the set one afternoon, Julia heard someone call out, "Hey Kieffo, get over here!" She stopped, turned around, ran back into her trailer, and told the set coordinator, "Get him out of here! I don't want to see him! Call security. How did he get on the lot?"

"Who?" asked the perplexed crewman.

"Kiefer!" Julia replied.

"Kiefer? They were calling *Kieffo*. You know, Dustin's stunt double."

A friend of Julia's who spoke on the condition of anonymity revealed that Julia underwent psychotherapy "for a little while after the Kiefer thing." Julia has acknowledged this but intimated that it had as much to do with how quickly her life had evolved as it did with the breakup. "It was a rather brief stint that led me to a place where I could take care of myself. . . . Whatever you feel is going to help you get through the day a little bit better or a little bit calmer, just go for it, whether it be chanting or running or going to a therapist."

Amazingly, in the midst of all this meshugas, Julia took a day off from *Hook* to film a cameo in Robert Altman's film *The Player*, based on a novel by Michael Tolkin. "Julia Roberts would be *perfect* for this!" had become such a standard phrase in writers' pitches to studios that Altman decided to use it as a running gag in this brilliant, scathing, deliciously dead-on Hollywood satire-cum-mystery starring Tim Robbins, Greta Scacchi, Whoopi Goldberg, Lyle Lovett, and sixty-five Hollywood celebrities from Jack Lemmon to Cher—as themselves.

In a marvelous joke, a pretentious British writer (played by Richard E. Grant) pitches a dark film about a woman who is executed before the district attorney (who prosecuted her and has fallen in love with her) learns she is innocent. "No stars!" the writer insists. "No happy endings! This is *reality*!" A studio executive (Robbins) thinks it's such a terrible idea that he foists it off on a rival while stressing that a dark ending and no stars is just what the story needs. He is sure it will flop and lose the hapless man his job. The punch line at the end of *The Player* is a screening of that movie's final scene, in which a vigil led by Susan Sarandon fails to stop the woman's execution. Strapped into the electric chair is Julia Roberts; she breathes in the gas and dies. Rushing to rescue her is the district attorney, played by Bruce Willis. He uses a shotgun to blast out a window to disperse the gas and—Oh my God! She isn't dead yet! He saves her, and she says, "What took you so long?"

"Traffic was a bitch," he replies. Everyone at the screening agrees that the movie will clean up at the box office.

Robert Altman professed complete satisfaction with Julia's performance. "She just came in, sat in the chair, and passed out." Julia looks thin, pale, and tired in the scene, but since she was playing a woman who had been languishing on death row, the look seemed appropriate.

Whether it was appropriate for Tinkerbell was another matter.

Later, when she was asked about making *Hook,* Julia chose to stress only the positive aspects of the experience, even the isolation of working in a harness on a separate stage. "We had fun," she said. "We had 'whippets'—if you hold it upside down or something, you can spray air [laughing gas] from a whipped-cream can, and it gives you a buzz or a rush or something. All I know is it never worked right for anybody, because they were always spraying whipped cream all over the place. . . . I mean, it was just people being stupid."

Hook opened nationwide on December 11 to largely negative reviews. Peter Travers, in *Rolling Stone,* thought the film had been "engineered for merchandising potential and the widest possible audience. . . . What's missing is the one thing that really counts: charm." Other critics thought the movie's storytelling "a mess" and saw its big-budget, big-star gloss as counter to the gentle spirit of the play that inspired it. "This enormous wheeze comes over like the proverbial movie with a 40-million-dollar set and a five-cent script," Angie Errigo wrote in the British magazine *Empire.* She added that *Hook* "may hold its interest for under-fives but will leave most others cold."

Julia's notices were equally poor. Critics mostly agreed with Travers's feeling that "while Roberts does her best playing a flickering special effect, she's given so little to do that she could be accused of loitering." A writer for *The New York Times* commented that Julia spent most of the film looking like "a confused horsefly." And many reviewers noted that her personal problems during filming showed on film: Tinkerbell looked skinny, wan, and on the verge of tears through much of the movie.

Even Julia, her mother indiscreetly revealed at an Atlanta preview, "saw it the other night and wasn't very pleased with it." But *Hook* was intended as a children's film, and, released three weeks before Christmas, it had the intended box-office impact: receipts of $119 million in America and $181 million internationally. (Thus earning Julia and her production company an extra $4 million.)

On March 29, 1992, the CBS newsmagazine *60 Minutes* profiled Steven Spielberg. When Ed Bradley asked the director about the rumors of discord between him and Julia, he replied carefully, "It was not a great time for Julia and I to be working together." When Bradley asked if he would work with Julia again, Spielberg hesitated, said, "This is a *60 Minutes* question, isn't it?" and then softly replied, "No."

Julia, who seems capable of defending herself vociferously, rebutted Spielberg quite strongly a year and a half later in *Vanity Fair*. "[Spielberg] took these hesitations as if he had to choose his words very carefully when asked about me. I watched and thought, *Is this the same man I had whipped-cream fights with on the set?* A friend of mine actually shot a video of my last day of filming on *Hook* . . . and it was very funny. I was up on a picnic table with these gigantic mushrooms doing my thing, and Steven and everybody were way down below, and he kept going up and talking into the video camera and going, 'You are just the greatest Tinkerbell!' . . . It was so nice. So to watch that and then to unknowingly turn on my television and watch him on *60 Minutes* . . . that's surprising."

To another interviewer, Julia said, "All I can say is that I remember the great times Steven and I had on the set. If he remembers our experience differently, that's his right. I may have been tense, and there was a lot going on in my personal life at the time, but I didn't think it was detracting from my acting."

CHAPTER TWENTY-ONE

After completing *Hook* on July 31, Julia returned with Jason to the Canyon Ranch health resort in Tucson for a week of rest and recuperation. In the beautiful foothills of the Santa Catalina Mountains, the couple enjoyed massages, mud and salt baths, aromatherapy, and seaweed treatments. They took classes in yoga, tai chi, chi gong, and meditation; they attended nutrition workshops and healthy-cooking classes. Julia and Jason weren't interested in the strenuous outdoor activities such as tennis, hiking, or biking; Tucson is very hot in August. When they weren't being pampered, they mostly relaxed by one of the spa's three outdoor pools.

After a short trip to New York City, they returned to Los Angeles, but rather than move into Julia's luxurious house in Nichols Canyon—which held too many memories of Kiefer for her—the twosome encamped in Jason's small one-bedroom duplex on North Stanley Avenue in the less-than-fashionable eastern half of West Hollywood, between Melrose Avenue and Santa Monica Boulevard.

That summer, *People* magazine put Julia on the cover of its special "50 Most Beautiful People in the World 1991" issue. "The mouth is too big," the article said. "The nose flares. A slight horsiness infects her laugh. But the sum of the parts do not add up to Mr. Ed but rather a Botticelli goddess, traipsing naively through spring. . . . Fresh, buoyant, sensuous, Roberts has just enough of the pixie in her to make anyone believe in fairy tales."

Advertising Age reported that Julia was the number one magazine-cover subject in 1991, which didn't make Jason Patric's quest for privacy any easier. But if he disliked the publicity burdens of stardom, he apparently loathed its material trappings as well. Although he earned about $500,000 a film at that point, his home resembled more an impoverished college student's than a movie star's. Bedsheets and blankets covered the windows instead of curtains. According to one of Jason's friends, the actress Jami Gertz, "There's an old secondhand couch. I go in there and I'm disgusted." Another acquaintance of Patric's said, "It's like he's a rich kid but doesn't want to appear like one, you know? So he goes out of his way to look and live like he's poverty-stricken."

To all appearances, this was just fine with Julia. The woman whose net worth would soon approach $5 million happily shared this bohemian nest with her man, cleaning, shopping, and cooking for him, sitting on that Salvation Army–issue couch to watch television, schlepping out the trash wearing shapeless granny dresses or torn jeans, her hair once again done by Mr. Pillow. This delighted the paparazzi, whose photographs of her looking awful accompanied tabloid stories with headlines like JULIA'S RED-HOT FLING WITH JASON IS SLUM-THING SPECIAL!

Parked in Jason's driveway, Julia's new silver Porsche also attracted attention in a neighborhood blocks away from where homeless people slept and hustlers worked Santa Monica Boulevard. After Julia discovered two guys with a tow truck trying to steal the $78,000 vehicle, she put the Porsche in storage and allowed Jason to buy her a used Volkswagen bus. A friend said, "People were begging her to take millions of dollars to make a movie. But all she wanted was this ramshackle, broken-down old thing."

That and to be left alone by practically everyone, including her agent. For nearly the next two years, the hottest actress in Hollywood did not step in front of a movie camera. The next time she appeared on the cover of *People,* which had become the popular barometer of her life and career, was the February 8, 1993 issue. Its headline asked, WHATEVER HAPPENED TO JULIA ROBERTS?

"Roberts's absence from the screen," the article said, "has hardly gone unnoticed in Hollywood where, as *Variety* editor Peter Bart observes, 'The trend is for big stars to make movies more frequently, so that each new part poses less of a career risk.' The January 18 issue of *Variety* ran a story about Roberts in its 'Lost and Found' column, a department usually reserved for dropouts, comeback kids, and Living Trivia. The actress's publicist was not amused. 'We are sick and tired of people saying there is something wrong with her career,' she said."

Julia would later say that she had decided to "take some time off" even before the "Fellini summer," but its craziness had served to harden her resolve. "I still can't imagine I went through that," she said. "The worst thing was the feeling that everyone was watching me. It was the ultimate humiliation. I felt a total lack of privacy at the one moment in my life when I needed to be alone." Feeling as though all the pressure might undo her, Julia decided she simply had to pull back. "If I'm not intact," she said, "I'm worthless. I think it's time for me to go away for a while. I just want to slow down."

Julia has contradicted herself on the reasons for her hiatus. She has said that it was a matter of not finding scripts that interested her. But she told *Rolling Stone* that it was "just really not having enough confidence in myself. I know the things that were fractured about my life and not what I wanted them to be; that I was fully participating in them not being exact." About her choices of men, she said, "You mistake someone else's confidence for your own. But what it really comes down to, ultimately . . . [is that] if you don't find yourself that interesting, then you'll never believe anyone who claims they do." Asked if she meant she didn't like herself, she said, "I think I've always been one for self-examination and self-scrutiny, and out of that instinct, which I guess is part of my gene pool, I kept coming up with things that I wasn't necessarily happy with about myself."

As one of Julia's closest friends, Elaine Goldsmith sympathized with her client's desire to flee the spotlight and try to reestablish a "normal" life. But she was also an agent working within a corporation, and her number one client wasn't earning the corporation any money. Goldsmith hoped to entice Julia out of her self-imposed retirement as soon as possible with an irresistible movie role. As one producer recalled, "It was odd, because every three months I'd get a call from Elaine, asking if I had any projects for Julia. She'd tell me, 'She wants to work. Have you got a comedy, a drama?' I'd send out the scripts, and Julia would reject them all. Then, like clockwork, Elaine would call and the cycle would start again."

Any thought Julia may have had of leading a relatively normal life by retreating from filmmaking soon evaporated amid the onslaught of paparazzi that beleaguered her and Jason wherever they went. During their trip to New York City in the second week of August 1991, the couple had been surrounded by "shouting, menacing-looking guys with metal objects pointed at them," as Liz Smith dramatically put it, as they left Morgan's Hotel to have dinner with the director James Foley at Nick and Eddie's restaurant. A group of photographers followed their cab, jumping out at stoplights to snap them through the taxi windows. (The photos show the two of them cowering in the seat, hiding their faces.) Rushing out of the cab in front of the restaurant, Julia had her foot run over and lost her shoe.

The restaurant's manager, Scott Henkle, packed her ankle in ice. "Even veteran observers of the paparazzi star wars say Sunday night's scene . . . was beyond the pale," Smith wrote. "Photogs taunted Julia and Jason, trying to goad them to 'react' . . . attempted to force open the door of the cab they hailed . . . staked out the restaurant . . . and then after dinner paid a taxi to leave before Julia and Jason could get in." Smith also reported that angry patrons of the restaurant formed a "human barricade" allowing the couple to hail another cab. Ultimately Scott Henkle drove Julia back to Morgan's, while Jason returned separately.

The next day Jason told Jeannie Williams of *USA Today*, "Enough is enough. People have a right to privacy." He wanted to pummel the men who were hounding them, he said, but he realized that such an action would only make things worse by generating terrible publicity. "If I was a construction worker, as opposed to an actor, I would have every right to get out and defend my girlfriend."

"This ugly incident," Liz Smith concluded, "will only serve to make Jason and Julia more reclusive and less inclined to cooperate with any of the press—so who's the winner?"

Indeed, the perverse pas de deux Julia Roberts and the press were dancing had already become a vicious cycle. Julia would not cooperate with photographers, and they, resentfully, made her life miserable. Most paparazzi are satisfied if a star stops, smiles for a few minutes, and lets them get their shots. Julia rarely did that, even at public events like premieres. Bob Scott, a Los Angeles–based photographer, recalled that "Julia's basic pattern when we cornered her at the airport or at a restaurant was to freeze like a deer caught in the headlights, and then run at top speed away from us. Once we were waiting for her to come out of a restaurant on Melrose, and when she saw us, she just ran, along with her sisters, the three blocks home to Jason's house, and left their car at the restaurant. The night of the premiere of Jason's film *Rush* [in December 1991],* they *ran* by the photographers at the theater and

---

*In *Rush*, Patric very convincingly played a junkie, which fueled rumors that both he and Julia had substance-abuse problems. Now it was Jason's turn to angrily deny the reports. When a reporter at the *Rush* press junket asked if his research for the movie had involved actual drug use, he said, "I wanted to whip it out, piss in her coffee, and say, '*You* check it out!'"

didn't pose, so we decided to throw an after-screening party at their house on Stanley. About twenty photographers lined up on their driveway waiting for them to come home, as if it was a red-carpet! The neighbors all came out to see what was going on. When the limo pulled up, Julia *ran* into the house first; then Jason got out *screaming* and cursing at us. He got the garden hose and started spraying us. It was a hoot."

Apart from the unabated paparazzi interest, Julia found her hiatus refreshing and rejuvenating. "The last two years I was just having the best time," she said afterward. "I got to spend a lot of time with my friends and family. I read books [F. Scott Fitzgerald and Anton Chekhov are among her favorite authors], wrote poetry, listened to music [Mozart, Bach, Elvis Costello, the Beatles], and traveled around. I just had a quiet time, a normal, ordinary life."

In January 1992, without Jason, Julia visited her mother and half sister, Nancy, in Smyrna. She stopped by Campbell High School one afternoon to see Nancy in a play and popped her head into a class being taught by David Boyd, the English teacher who had been so impressed with her reading of Cassius in *Julius Caesar*. "Well, Coach Boyd, I see some things never change," she said with a big smile, then popped right back out. "I had about five students chase her down the hall," Boyd recalled, "to bring her back." Julia chatted with the slack-jawed students for a few minutes, then said she had to be off.

In February, Julia traveled to India to spend two weeks at one of Mother Teresa's missions for children in Calcutta. "Going to India was extraordinary," she said. "It really sort of puts you back into place, not that I feel I ever got too far from a place of perspective and grounding, too far away from where I started. But at the same time, it really snaps you into a place of perspective that doesn't really exist in the day-to-day world."

Julia returned once more to Smyrna in May, again without Jason. She visited one of her old watering spots, Miss Kitty's, a country-western bar, to hear one of her favorite bands, Confederate Railroad. Dressed in black cowboy boots, jeans, and a baggy T-shirt, she sat with friends on an upstairs balcony. A waitress noticed that Julia wasn't her usual outgoing self. "She seemed a little insecure and sorta hid behind her hair like she didn't want anybody to recognize her." When she was approached by several people, she and her friends left. This surprised veteran members of the club's staff, since Julia had been in several times since she became a celebrity and had always had a great time, usually hitting the dance floor to join in the Texas two-step.

The following month Julia took Jason on a five-day cruise to Cabo San Lucas as a twenty-sixth-birthday gift. In July she returned to Canyon Ranch for more pampering, and in August she flew to Hawaii for the first time since the infamous party video with Kiefer was shot, this time accompanied by Elaine Goldsmith and Susan Sarandon, who had become a good friend through Tim Robbins.

After Julia returned from Hawaii, the Hollywood trade papers were trumpeting the news that she would return to the screen in Alan Pakula's film version of John Grisham's novel *The Pelican Brief.* Filming was not set to begin until the following summer, so Julia Roberts would remain "missing" for nearly another year.

In September, Julia attended the christening of Tim Robbins and Susan Sarandon's son, Miles Guthrie. Guests noticed that she wore a bandage over the spot on her left shoulder where the birthday tattoo from Kiefer had been. Julia had declared that her love for Kiefer would "last as long as this tattoo," but in fact the artwork outlasted the romance by fifteen months. That same month Julia appeared at the premiere of *Bob Roberts,* a political satire Robbins wrote, directed, and starred in. Jason was not with her, prompting rumors about problems in the relationship. A few days later, the couple was spotted at a Michigan/Notre Dame football game in South Bend, Indiana, wearing Fighting Irish caps and loudly cheering on Jason's favorite team.

Julia and Jason watchers saw a different side of their relationship when both attended a taping of an MTV Bruce Springsteen Unplugged special at Warner Bros. Studios on September 22. At a backstage party after the concert, Julia fell into conversation with Bon Jovi band member Richie Sambora, Cher's boyfriend at the time.

Apparently unhappy with Sambora's monopolization of his girlfriend's time, Patric began tossing pieces of licorice candy to distract Julia. She ignored him. He got up, walked over to where Julia and Sambora were sitting, grabbed her hand, and told her, "Let's go." Julia pulled her hand away and replied, "You don't own me." But in a few minutes, she left with Jason, and the couple showed up to hear Springsteen at the L.A. Forum the following night. Jason went to Springsteen's performances over the next three nights as well, though Julia didn't accompany him.

. . .

In October 1991, Eric Roberts had gone to court in an attempt to remove Kelly Cunningham from the home they had shared in Rhinebeck, New York. In court papers, Eric claimed that Cunningham had been "vicious and physically abusive" toward him. "Kelly grabbed a cordless telephone with a sharp broken metal antenna and smashed it against my face," he declared. "I could have suffered a severe eye injury. The injury was so bad I had to go to Northern Dutchess Hospital to have my wound closed with stitches. And she was holding our baby, Emma, who could have been dropped and hurt. . . . I am in fear of Kelly's physical force. I am simply unable to defend myself."

In a sworn deposition, a friend of Eric's, James Pollock, said that during her relationship with Eric, "all [Kelly] would talk about were the things she wanted Eric to purchase for her. In fact, she became more distasteful to me because of her grabbiness, her hardness and her unrelenting demands for money, clothes, jewelry and the type of farm which Eric could not afford. Any denial by Eric to a demand made by Kelly would result in a violent outburst. . . . Last September [1991] Eric told me that Kelly had a vicious argument with him because he took her to look at a Volvo station wagon. She insisted on a Jaguar convertible, which is double the price and not nearly as practical for a child. That evening, at eleven P.M., I received another telephone call from Eric with Kelly screaming in the background, 'Get the hell out . . . Get the hell out of this house . . . I hate you, you will never see your daughter again!' Then I heard a grunt or groan. . . . Eric told me: 'She kicked me in the balls. I don't know what to do, J.C. I've got to get out of here.' "

By June 1992, Kelly had moved out of the Rhinebeck house and into Eric's new apartment on West Seventy-eighth Street. Again, she refused to leave. On Saturday, June 7, while Kelly was in California, Eric came to the apartment with a moving van and a locksmith. He removed everything inside, then had the locks changed. A friend of Kelly's told Richard Johnson of the New York *Daily News,* "Kelly called the cops, and they said they can't do anything because the lease is in his name."

Two years later, Eric and Kelly's bitter rift would still be making news—and so would the ever-widening one between Eric and Julia.

In the fall of 1992, the Hollywood trade papers reported that before Julia began *The Pelican Brief,* she would return to the screen in *Shake-*

speare in Love, an original story by Marc Norman and Tom Stoppard (*Rosencrantz and Guildenstern Are Dead*). *The Hollywood Reporter* claimed that Julia's agents were asking "a king's ransom" of $4 million for their client's services, which would have been a budget-buster for the modest project, but Universal Pictures executives were seeking cofinancing. She had loved the script, a charming romantic fable about the young bard suffering writer's block as he tries to complete his latest play, tentatively titled *Romeo and Ethel.* He finds his muse when he meets the lovely Lady Viola, who has disguised herself as a man in order to join the male-only world of theater. After experiencing some confusion over his feelings for someone he thinks is a man (a common Shakespearean dilemma), Will discovers Viola's true identity, they fall in love, and his creativity returns to full flower.

Aside from the delightful script, it must have been an intriguing prospect to Julia to work with the brilliant English actor Daniel Day-Lewis, who had won the Best Actor Oscar in 1989 playing the cerebral-palsy victim Christy Brown in *My Left Foot.* He had also been magnetic and sexy as the philandering Czech doctor in *The Unbearable Lightness of Being,* and as the buff and oiled-down frontiersman adopted by Native Americans in *The Last of the Mohicans.*

The thirty-four-year-old Day-Lewis—the son of the late Cecil Day-Lewis, a former poet laureate of Britain, and the actress Jill Balcon—had expressed interest in playing Shakespeare but had not yet signed a contract. Neither had Julia, who wanted her costar to be set before she fully committed to the project. She flew to London sometime in the early fall to meet with Day-Lewis and, presumably, to persuade him to sign on. By the time the dust had settled, production of *Shakespeare in Love* was indefinitely scuttled, Julia's relationship with Jason Patric was over, and she had begun a new romance.

CHAPTER TWENTY-TWO

On the chilly evening of January 18, 1993, neighbors of Julia and Jason on North Stanley Avenue heard shouting in the street. Several rushed outside to find the two movie stars screaming obscenities at each other in front of the television actress Jasmine Guy's house, a few doors down from Patric's.

"Jason was almost falling-down drunk," a neighbor reported, "and although Julia wasn't drunk, it was obvious she'd also been drinking. Anyway, Jason kept accusing her of having slept with Daniel Day-Lewis, yelling, 'You fucked him! I know you fucked him!' Then Julia yelled back at him, 'I can fuck anyone I want to!'"

With that, Julia hopped into her VW bus and drove off. She was never seen with Jason Patric again, and reports said that it was Elaine Goldsmith who called Jason to say Julia would not be back. He was so distraught by the breakup that he couldn't sleep in the bed he had once shared with Julia. When he couldn't sleep on the couch, either, he left the duplex apartment for over a month. A friend of the couple reported that Jason had gone so far as to enter Julia's Nichols Canyon house looking for love letters or other evidence of an affair with Day-Lewis.

Perhaps to spite Julia, Patric almost immediately began an affair with the lovely French actress Isabelle Adjani, who had just come out of a five-year relationship with Day-Lewis. She had borne him a son, Gabriel-Kane, earlier in the year and complained that Day-Lewis was with Julia when their son was born. "I felt incredible sadness and disappointment," she said.

After about a year, the usually tight-lipped Patric opened up to *Entertainment Weekly* about his involvement with Julia: It had been "a nightmare," he said, and had "ruined this carefully constructed life of privacy and work I'd known for six years. It was like—pah!—in a week." Patric said he felt that Julia was to blame for the excessive paparazzi interest.

"This was a person who very much put herself in the public eye and the public life. I think everyone has a right to privacy, but once you use your personal life to advance your fame, you don't really have the right to say no to the press."

Patric didn't agree that Julia might have been too young to handle fame. "She was no younger than the nineteen-year-olds in Vietnam or any soldier—or mothers who all of a sudden have three kids at twenty-one and no money. You know, it gets down to the point of character."

Jason's comments stung Julia. She responded, "Saying that I called all this attention to myself in order to advance my status really hurt me. It is grossly inaccurate. Worse, it was said by someone I know—and we get hurt most by the people we care about."

Early in March, Julia watchers were stunned to read in the New York *Daily News* that she had paid for a lawyer to represent Kelly Cunningham in a custody battle with Eric over their daughter, Emma.

In 1992, Eric had married Eliza Simon, the daughter of the screenwriter David Rayfiel (*Three Days of the Condor, Havana*) and an actress and casting director. He sued Kelly for custody, charging that she had denied him unsupervised visitation rights with the two-year-old girl. "The subpoena demanded that Cunningham show up at court at 8 the next morning," the story read, "but since she doesn't have the money for a lawyer, she was panicked. You'll be relieved to know that Julia Roberts stepped in and rushed to Cunningham's defense—finding her not only a great lawyer but one willing to show up in court at a moment's notice."

Kelly said she refused Eric unsupervised visits "because of his past history of violence. . . . Because he has a ready-made family [with Eliza] and figures Emma should now live there doesn't change anything. My God, you can't take a child from its mother because you simply want to."

The judge handed down a temporary decision that granted Eric monitored visits. Shortly, Eliza appeared on the television magazine show *Hard Copy* and discussed the court battle, Eric and Julia's disagreements, and their upbringing. "There was tension in that home," she said. In a *Rolling Stone* interview in July, Julia responded: "Eric tells his stories, his wife tells her stories. What I find most fascinating about Eric's wife and what she says about me and how I feel about things and what I do about things is that I've never met her. . . . My brother knows especially what our problems are. He's very clear. He can choose to relay them however he sees fit."

Eliza responded in a three-page single-spaced letter to *Rolling Stone,* which the magazine published part of: "The only reason I went on *Hard Copy* was to make it clear Eric never tried to get physical custody of his daughter. . . . Although Eric has made several attempts to plan a time to talk things out with his family (mostly for the purpose of owning his share of the hurtful behavior of the past), these attempts have been ignored."

Eliza sent the same letter to Julia. "I've pushed Eric to face how he harmed and alienated you. . . . When he gets real blue and negative and helpless, it can be extremely infuriating. . . . But it passes. . . . I wonder if you and Lisa have considered your father, and how much it might pain him . . . to know of his children's unwillingness to ask and listen to each other's realities."

Julia didn't respond to the letter and later professed weariness at this seemingly unsolvable family drama. "The thing is, we all have issues in our life—baggage issues that we inherit from our families. And I've sort of gotten to a place where I'm dealing with them and resolving them. But at a certain point, you run out of steam to keep going back to some old issue that you keep thinking will get resolved 'if you would just help a little.' I don't know. I wish Eric great success with his recovery. I *do,* because it's been long in coming."

It was around this time that Eric stopped using cocaine—because he suffered a heart attack he attributed to his use of the drug. "I had to stop," he said. "The first couple of years were rough. But Eliza stuck with me. I've been through periods when no one stuck by me, including family. I learned that you can't rely on anyone. Eliza is my family now."

Whatever the extent of Julia's relationship with Daniel Day-Lewis, the two were successful in keeping themselves away from paparazzi cameras. This was something Day-Lewis had become expert at; during his five-year affair with Adjani, they were apparently never photographed together.

Shakespeare in Love had brought Julia and Daniel together, but the project proved ill fated for them. Reports from London said that by mid-October 1992, two hundred production people were working on the film, sets were being built at Pinewood Studios, and Julia had already had costume and hair tests when Day-Lewis decided to pass on the project. The reason, his representatives said, was that the handsome six-foot-two actor had just finished *The Age of Innocence* and was committed to playing Gerry Conlon, an Irishman wrongly imprisoned for an IRA bombing in London. (That film, *In the Name of the Father,* was released late in 1993.)

Reports in the London newspapers speculated that Day-Lewis's real reasons for turning down *Shakespeare in Love* were pique at being offered two-thirds less money than Julia, and his lack of faith that so American an actress could adequately portray a British aristocrat. Whatever his reasons, once Day-Lewis left the project, Julia did, too. She turned down potential costars Sean Bean, an ascendant Yorkshire actor; Ralph Fiennes, who had just starred opposite Juliette Binoche in *Wuthering Heights;* and Colin Firth, another rising star.

At ten-thirty A.M. on October 20, the film's line producer called together the two-hundred-member crew at Pinewood Studios' Stage B and broke the news that the production was shutting down. It was a bad blow for an already suffering British film industry. Julia's new publicist, Nancy Seltzer, told *Daily Variety* on October 23 that Julia "has never been committed to *Shakespeare in Love*," meaning that she had not signed a contract. "She ultimately decided that it was a film she did not feel comfortable making." Elaine Goldsmith added, "I think the frustration comes with everyone wanting to go forward with this project and not being able to find the right person once Daniel Day-Lewis passed."*

Day-Lewis's agent, Julian Belfrage, told the London *Evening Standard,* "Julia's reason for not doing it is that she adores Daniel and doesn't want to do it without him. I think she thought that by leaving, she might persuade him to reconsider. But now that Hollywood is blaming Daniel [for the demise of the project] he will never do the film."

According to one insider, Julia's affection for Day-Lewis was "the talk of the [British] film industry," and Day-Lewis had let it be known that he would be "very happy to do a screen test and go out with Julia, even sleep with her, but he was not going to put his professional career on the line to do a film with her." Why Day-Lewis felt doing a film with Julia was a risky career move remains unexplained.

If Hollywood blamed the collapse of *Shakespeare in Love* on Day-Lewis, the British newspapers were merciless in their criticism of Julia's decision to abandon the film. London's *Evening Standard* raked her over the coals in a Neil Norman piece headlined HAS JULIA COOKED HER GOLDEN GOOSE? "Roberts packed her bags and flew back to L.A., leaving

---

*The movie was released in 1998 with Joseph Fiennes (Ralph's brother) and Gwyneth Paltrow in the leads. It won seven Oscars, including Best Picture, Best Actress (Paltrow), and Best Supporting Actress (Judi Dench as Queen Elizabeth I).

a bewildered and suddenly redundant production crew behind her in England. It won her few friends. But Roberts has never shown much evidence that she has read and inwardly digested *How to Win Friends and Influence People.*"

Norman went out of his way to further (and often inaccurately) lambaste Julia, even turning Robin Williams's humor against her. "At a press conference in London [for *Hook*]," he reported, "Williams was asked what it was like to kiss Julia Roberts. . . . His mouth puckered up in an obscene parody of osculation. 'We used stunt lips,' he said. 'She does have a very interesting mouth. She's the only person I know who wears underwear on her lips.'

"With friends like these, who needs enemies?" Norman asked, clearly unfamiliar with Robin's brand of humor. He went on, "The *Shakespeare in Love* episode marked the culmination of a bad year for Roberts, public-affection-wise. She has spent the intervening time turning down scripts or walking off productions when she couldn't get her way. Questions were asked: is this any way for a grown, responsible woman to behave? Of course not. But why on earth should anyone expect her to behave like a grown, sensible woman when people are willing to pay her $7 million to pretend to be somebody else?"

Julia was shocked and hurt by the vehemence of the backlash. "I can't say I'm completely unbothered, untouched, unscathed . . . that's just not true," she told Katie Couric on *Today.* "But at the same time it sort of empowers what they are doing, to get bothered by it."

As Julia's absence from the screen stretched into mid-1993, more and more observers began to wonder, as Norman had, whether her career had self-destructed. As one former studio head told *People,* "This definitely has gone beyond the range of normal movie-star behavior. We've reached the point where a lot of people are wondering just what in the world is going on with her?"

Julia admitted that her meteoric rise had left her not only frightened but disoriented and full of self-doubt. "I went through sort of an elongated confidence dilemma," she said several years later. "Even now, in a kind of absurd way, I still have an element of that. As if tomorrow they could say, 'Okay, time's up. Go back to Smyrna,' you know? You find yourself living out your dream, and at the same time, you wonder, *How did I get here?* Then you add in all the interviews and people taking your picture on the street . . . all that kind of stuff scared the shit out of me. When you're twenty-one years old, you're still trying to get your own legs as just this gawky girl in the world."

It would seem that Julia was trying to get her romantic legs firmly on the ground as well. Liz Smith reported on March 9 that "Julia Roberts has been in London, visiting her old flame, Daniel Day-Lewis, and he is the man in her life these days." Julia was with her fifth lover in five years, a track record that seemed almost pathological, even by Hollywood standards. Observers wondered whether she was terrified of commitment, afraid of repeating her mother's mistakes, or simply hadn't gotten over her "boy-crazy" phase, in spite of having achieved worldwide fame, adulation, and wealth.

What seemed evident was that Julia Roberts was, as an intimate later said, "needy" when it came to masculine attention. Her father, in his custody petition when she was five, had said, "She's an innocent child who needs tenderness, and she's definitely not getting it. I do not want her to suffer as an adult for anything that happens to her as a child." Eric has made clear that he feels that's exactly what happened to his sister, who seems to need the self-validation of an exciting new romance and looks around for it—or allows it to happen—when her current relationship begins to sour or turn stale.

In Day-Lewis, Julia yet again had a love interest who was a handsome, intense actor, one whose father had died early in his life, whose childhood had been unhappy, and who left school as a young teenager to become an actor. Day-Lewis had an Irish passport, and Julia enjoyed visiting him in both England and Ireland. In February several British papers reported that Julia had purchased a $60,000 cottage in Mayo, "Ireland's loveliest county," as a "love nest" for her and Day-Lewis, who had spent childhood vacations nearby. The Sun reported on March 10 that Julia had been "spending a fortune on trans-Atlantic flights" and "used a variety of disguises to snatch secret weekends with Daniel."

"I can only hope," the Sun writer said (apparently with sincerity), "that Ireland refreshes her career—and that the good country air will improve her romantic luck." A rare sighting of the couple took place one afternoon in May 1993 in the Strawberry Beds pub in Chapelizod, an area of Dublin. "They were having a great crack, she was all over yer man," the barman, Francis Heffernan, told Day-Lewis's biographer Garry Jenkins. The two had arrived in a red Mercedes, both dressed in jeans. "He was drinking Guinness, and she was drinking lager," Heffernan added. "There was a lot of laughing and whispering going on."

According to a woman whom the London Daily Mirror said was a friend of Julia's, the actress "was besotted [with Day-Lewis]. Despite her fame, Julia is still only twenty-five years old and basically just a small-town girl from Georgia. The whole idea of this handsome man from across the Atlantic is all so terribly romantic to her. She is in awe of his talent, and overwhelmed by his sexual magnetism. But Daniel is trying to keep this thing quiet. He's very private. It's the real thing for Julia. She seems to spend half her life with jet lag."

In a few days, another British paper reported that "dashing actor Daniel Day-Lewis is NOT in love with Julia Roberts, his friends revealed yesterday. But the *Pretty Woman* star has fallen head over heels for the Irish performer. . . . The friends said thirty-five-year-old Daniel was fond of Julia—'but he doesn't want to get involved in anything serious.'"

One of Day-Lewis's associates said years later that Julia was "madly in love" with the actor, but he was "obsessed with his career. He doesn't *want* to get married. He doesn't *need* to get married." Day-Lewis himself told a reporter, "Marriage has no meaning for me as an idea. It's not a concept I think about."

By the time Julia began filming her comeback picture, *The Pelican Brief*, in June, she and Day-Lewis were no longer an item. The reason for their breakup may well have been his aversion to marriage, because marriage was something that *she* was thinking about. She admitted as much several years later: "It's a symptom of childhood, this Cinderella theme that marriage is the beginning of the Happy. People think if you get married you'll be happy. . . . When you're a little girl, Barbie and Ken are happy, so are Mickey and Minnie—they've been together forever." But as she prepared for rehearsals, Julia Roberts was an aspiring bride with no groom in sight.

Before she started filming, Julia took a trip to Costa Rica with her close friend Susan Sarandon, Sarandon's daughter, Eva, and her brother Terry Tomalin. "Costa Rica is a really beautiful place," Susan recalled. "I was telling Julia about it, and this little trip just evolved." The trip, she said, made her realize that Julia is "very flexible, and scorpions love her. We had to sleep on the ground, and when it came time to eat, there was one set of utensils. So we would make pasta and have to eat it with a knife or a spoon. Not everybody can deal with those circumstances."

Still, it was fun, Julia said, and she was equally impressed with Susan's adaptability. "Susan handled everything, and at dinner I noticed that the level of conversation was always that much more interesting. Susan would ask our guides questions that I never would have thought to ask."

A few days into the trip, Susan's brother noticed that most of the music Julia had brought with her was by Lyle Lovett.

CHAPTER TWENTY-THREE

Julia wanted to kiss Denzel Washington. "That's a call-your-girlfriends, right there," she said of costarring in *The Pelican Brief* with Washington, the handsome actor later named the "Sexiest Man Alive" by *People* magazine. "He's the best, because to be that talented and that funny and that sweet and that profoundly brilliant and that gorgeous is just almost too much to bear. And I wanted to kiss him in that movie, and I just want to say that right now, I voted for the kiss, I wanted the kiss, I was ready to kiss him."

There were, however, several factors militating against an on-screen lip-lock between Julia's character, Darby Shaw, a Tulane law student whose life is endangered when she writes a brief theorizing (correctly) on the identities of the assassins of two Supreme Court justices. Denzel's character, Gray Grantham, is an investigative reporter whom she enlists to help her. In John Grisham's novel, Gray Grantham is Caucasian, and although Darby's law professor/lover is killed in a car bomb intended for her at the beginning of the story, Gray and Darby are romantically involved by the book's end.

Tom Rolf, the film's editor, recalled that it was Denzel who nixed the idea of so obvious an indication of romance as a kiss. "He said, 'The sisters will never forgive me,'" Rolf recollected. Washington spoke from painful experience. In his 1989 film *The Mighty Quinn*, Denzel had kissed Mimi Rogers, and during a test screening, there were loud boos from the black women in the audience. Denzel asked the studio to delete the kiss, and they complied. He vowed not to do any more interracial love stories, and since Hollywood executives were largely uninterested in producing black love stories, there wasn't much romance in Washington's screen life.

Julia, with her inbred lack of prejudice, didn't understand the problem. "This movie is not about who's black and who's white," she said.

Ironically, many observers who saw the film's lack of romance as either a cop-out or an example of racism blamed Julia. "I have taken so much shit over the years about not kissing Denzel," she said some time later. "It was his idea to take the damn scenes out."

Julia said on *Inside the Actors Studio* that one of Denzel's objections had nothing to do with race. Rather, he felt that too short a period of time passes in the film after the death of Darby's lover to make her involvement with any other man sympathetic. "What it came down to, we had to count pages of the script. Denzel thinks at least a month has to go by before you, like, put a move on this lady. So we're counting days, and we're going, 'Seventeen, oh, come on, thirty, come on, thirty' . . . but it was twenty-two days or something, and it didn't stand a chance."

Still, Julia said, at the end of the film, the two characters are "totally lovers," even if it isn't obvious. "At the end of the movie, when you see me watching Denzel on TV . . . I want everybody to know, that's his cabin, okay, passage of time. We are now lovers, just so you know. Go back, rent it, watch it again, you'll be able to tell."

On a warm New York morning in early June 1993, Julia Roberts stepped onto a movie set for the first time in almost two years. A week earlier, Elaine Goldsmith had thrown her a send-off party in Hollywood, attended by Nick Nolte (with whom Julia had committed to costar next in *I Love Trouble*), Billy Baldwin, Shirley MacLaine, Vincent D'Onofrio, Oliver Stone, and Joe Roth, the former head of 20th Century–Fox, with whom Julia had entered into a production deal.

"I feel ready to blow the door open," Julia told the *Hollywood Reporter* columnist Army Archerd, referring to her new film, for which she was being paid $8 million, the highest salary in Hollywood history for a woman, despite her long absence from the screen. She added that she didn't have "a single regret" about the hiatus and that she had spent the two years being "a homebody" and trying to lead "a quiet, simple life." Obliquely addressing her reputation as a serial man-killer, she said, "I'm not mean to anyone."

Tom Rolf said that despite all the rumors about Spielberg's difficulty with Julia, and all the dark speculation about the reasons for her long layoff, the *Pelican* crew wasn't apprehensive about working with her. "No, I don't recall that. I think people were 'chuffed'—that's an old British expression [meaning 'delighted'] that they were involved with the picture that Julia was coming back on. There *was* some discussion, a little uncertainty, but I don't think anyone was really nervous about doing a picture with Julia Roberts, that's for sure."

Julia, however, found herself racked by insecurities when she arrived in New York to begin filming under the direction of the respected Alan J. Pakula (*All the President's Men, Sophie's Choice*). "I hadn't worked in two years, and I truly got to that set and I thought, *What if I've forgotten how to act? What if they say 'Action!' and I just stand there?* I really was apoplectic. I was inconsolable. [But] Alan Pakula is fantastic. He really gave me confidence. [And] I was working with Sam Shepard, who I worked with on *Steel Magnolias,* so I had that comfort of someone I knew."

Julia needed more comfort on several occasions during the filming. While she worked on location in New Orleans, letters began arriving addressed to her in care of Warner Bros. Studios from an anonymous man who professed to be her most devoted fan. Before long, the letters took on a more ominous tone, suggesting sadomasochism and forcible sex. The studio turned the letters over to a private-investigation firm, which deemed the man dangerous and suggested Julia get full-time protection.

Initially, Julia balked at twenty-four-hour guards, but a frightening incident in New Orleans changed her mind. During a lull in filming, she walked about a block to get a cup of coffee. A crowd of fans mobbed her and soon pinned her against a wall. She was near panic until a passing patrolman dispersed the crowd. Later, Julia said, "All that kept going through my mind was that the man who's after me could be in this crowd. I didn't dare focus on anyone. I just kept pleading, 'Please, move back. Please give me some room to breathe. You're scaring me.'" From that point on, plainclothes guards kept a close eye on Julia, traveling with her to locations for this film and her next as the stalker's threatening letters continued.

The movie's most emotionally charged scene also took its toll on Julia. In the scene, she and Sam Shepard leave a restaurant on the Vieux Carré. He's had too much to drink, and she doesn't want him to drive. He tells her she'll have to walk home and gets into the car. As he turns the ignition, the car explodes, killing him instantly. Pakula's camera watches Julia as incomprehension, shock, disbelief, fear, and grief cross her face in a matter of seconds. "I spent more time thinking about that scene than anything else," she said. "I minorly obsessed, because it had the potential to be this great moment. And yet it's this extraordinary challenge of, how do you relay X number of emotions in X time? Those were an exhausting few nights."

Pakula found himself impressed by Julia's emotional investment in the scene. "She goes into some dark part of herself. After the first take— which was excellent, very full emotionally—I went over to her. It was like holding a fluttering bird. She could hardly talk. Her eyes were full of tears. 'Is there anything else you want?' she said. I hesitated, and she looked into my eyes and said, 'You want less.' I said, 'Yeah.' We did it again, and she contained it. It amazes me when actors do that, because in one place they're in an uncontrolled emotional state, and in another they're thinking about it as a part."

Another scene challenged Julia as well. She said, "One day we were doing a very intense scene, and I thought, *I can't do this again.* Up to the last minute, I was in denial that I was going to have to do this, and I said to Denzel, 'What am I going to do?' And he said, 'Act.' Well, it really put it in a whole different perspective. I'm just going to have to *act.*"

The tensions these scenes created in Julia often made her weary. "I fell asleep on our camera operator," Julia recalled. "We were sitting next to each other, and I just sort of dozed off on his shoulder, and he was so polite and sweet about it that he didn't— He was supposed to be working, and he sat there paralyzed for like twenty minutes while I just slept."

Julia learned a new way to relax while making this film: knitting. "I learned from a lovely guy who was the standby painter [on the picture]. He also taught one of my girlfriends how to knit. I sit knitting, and people come up and say, 'Oh, I want to know how to knit.' By the end of the movie, there's always a knitting circle that has grown. The nice thing about knitting is that it's something that you can do and also be completely social. I can sit on a set between shots and chat with people and just knit away." Julia now knits on every movie set to pass the time.

On June 21, after a month of filming, the principals of *The Pelican Brief* held a press conference in their new location, Washington, D.C. Reporters found Julia a vastly different woman from the sullen, suspicious star who had met the press in December 1991 to promote *Hook.* She was relaxed, even friendly, and her sense of humor had returned. Asked if she felt rusty after two years off, she replied with a grin, "I don't feel rusty. Do I *look* rusty?"

She didn't. In fact, the glow and the smile that had made Julia a superstar were again in full flower; her hair, once again long and a light brown, fell insouciantly around her shoulders. Clearly, the time off had done her a world of good. "I think I came back with some renewed vigor . . . I've been giddy."

The assembled reporters dutifully jotted down the quote—"I've been giddy"—without knowing its full import. *Time* magazine offered a hint in an item about the press conference in its July 5 issue. "If Hollywood were a milk carton, Julia Roberts would be pictured on its side. 'Colossal star missing from feature films. Last seen: *Hook*, 1991.' Look no further. At a press conference to inaugurate the Washington shoot of her thriller *The Pelican Brief* . . . Julia invited reporters to focus on her work—a plea that clearly went unheeded. Days later, a New York tabloid focused instead on her rumored romance 'with quirky balladeer Lyle Lovett.' "

Lyle Lovett? The gangly country crooner with the craggy face, drunkard's-path grin, and towering hair that *People* described as a "thatch of nuclear-radiated alfalfa sprouts"? It couldn't be. The Pretty Woman's gallery of lovers to date had featured only some of the best-looking men in the world.

Julia denied she and Lovett were romantically involved. When a reporter asked if she was "seeing" him, she replied, "That's funny . . . I mean, I do *know* Lyle. He played here in D.C. and a whole bunch of us went. We went on this big bus because there were about twenty-five of us from the crew. And you know how they always have the destination spelled out on the front of those buses? Ours said: 'Lost.' It just seemed so perfect."

For once, a star's denial of a romance rumor seemed plausible. But as readers thumbed through their new issue of *Time* a week later, they learned that Julia and the offbeat, introspective singer-songwriter had already exchanged wedding vows.

CHAPTER TWENTY-FOUR

Julia was determined that this wedding would be the antithesis of the one she had planned with Kiefer Sutherland. Instead of a lavish set constructed on a Hollywood soundstage, the site would be the small, rustic St. James Lutheran Church in Marion, Indiana, population thirty-two thousand, chosen because it was near Noblesville, a suburb of Indianapolis, where Lovett and his Large Band were performing as part of a summer concert tour. Instead of two hundred of Hollywood's "glitziest and ritziest," seventy-five people attended, the only glitz provided by the newlyweds themselves and Julia's friends Susan Sarandon and Tim Robbins. Instead of wearing matching designer gowns, the attendants (Deborah Porter, Sarandon, Lisa Roberts, Paige Amsler Sampson, and Elaine Goldsmith) were attired in whatever they could throw together on seventy-two-hour notice; instead of wearing Manolo Blahnik shoes, Julia went barefoot—the better to feel the rose petals strewn along the aisle.

Most of all, she made certain this wedding would be private. The day before the nuptials, she gave a three-hour interview in the Jefferson Hotel in Washington, D.C., to Kevin Sessums for a *Vanity Fair* profile. "In the course of our conversation," he later wrote, "she took three brief phone calls on logistical matters, which made sense since I'd been told she was getting on a plane so she could spend Sunday with her mother. The next day she flew to Indiana and married Lyle Lovett. I, meanwhile, considered a career in refrigerator maintenance."

When Sessums had asked her about the rumor that she and Lovett were dating, she denied it—"and, proving what a wonderful actress she really is," Sessums said, "she did not blink." Julia later admitted, to Sessums and to others, that the questions she and her publicist had started getting about Lovett had "panicked" her with flashbacks to the Sutherland debacle. "We were to get married six months later," she told Roald

Rynning of *Time Out,* "but I was sitting in my kitchen in Washington after a day's filming, and I panicked about the press finding out and people digging around in our trash."

She also told Sessums, "I called my oh-so-composed fiancé and explained how I was feeling. 'So what do you think about maybe getting married this weekend?' And he said, as only a perfect gentleman can say, 'Whatever you want, honey.' "

In an effort to make this startling marriage seem less impetuous, Julia's representatives suggested that she and Lyle had met while working on *The Player* in 1991, and their relationship had evolved from there. The problem with this story was that Julia and Lyle never appeared together in *The Player,* nor did their shooting dates coincide. In fact, Lyle's girlfriend at the time, Allison Inman, recalled that she and Lyle had looked forward to meeting Julia, but "we were gone the day Julia shot her scene."

So just how did this odd couple come together? Lovett has said that someone told him several years earlier that Julia was a fan of his music (his vocal timbre and intelligent, introspective songs are reminiscent of Bruce Springsteen with an occasional twang). "I thought that was really something," Lovett said, "and wanted to write her a note, but I was too chicken." He returned Julia's admiration in kind; an associate of his said that he carried a video of *Pretty Woman* around with him on tour "and must have watched it a hundred times before he ever met her."

Then, early in 1993, Susan Sarandon's brother Terry Tomalin, a reporter for the *St. Petersburg Times* in Florida, interviewed the singer and told him about Julia's having all his albums with her during their trip to Costa Rica. This time Lovett made the call, and after Julia's breakup with Daniel Day-Lewis, they met in New Orleans on June 8. "I had a very strong reaction to meeting him," Julia said, "different from the way I've ever reacted to any person on the planet . . . Lyle is the sweetest man in the universe. He has this incredible calm and sense of self. A lot of people might think he's not very emotional; it's totally the opposite. He thinks more deeply than anyone, but he has a way of adapting to the world. I wish I had his laid-back attitude; maybe I wouldn't have so much trouble dealing with what other people think about me."

Unlike Julia's last four paramours, Lovett—a thirty-five-year-old Texas native—was not the product of a broken home (his parents, Bill and Bernell, had been happily married for thirty-seven years), not a high school dropout (he earned degrees in journalism and German from Texas A&M University), and not a pretty boy. With five failed relationships in five years, Julia had had her fill, for the moment, of gorgeous young actors. Lovett must have been a very appealing change of pace.

Unkind observers dubbed the couple "Beauty and the Beast," and even Lyle found himself awestruck that Julia returned his affections. On his 1992 album, *Joshua Judges Ruth,* Lovett had written no fewer than five songs about unrequited love. "Meeting Julia has made everything make sense for me," he said. "It sort of justified all the hopefulness I had always felt."

A longtime acquaintance of Lovett's, Sandy Lovejoy, told *People* that "What women look for in a man he's got in spades. He's sweet, kind, and gentle and really a catch. And I bet you he'd do anything to make a woman happy." Allison Inman, with whom Lyle remained on good terms, said, "He met a person [Julia] who was crazy about him and really believed in him and understood him . . . I think he needs somebody to really have confidence in him, and she did. I think she's just so crazy about him that it's just done a lot for his self-confidence. . . . He did express that to me, you know, he felt kind of bad for a while, and then he met someone who was so good to him."

In a rare comment about Lyle's looks, Julia said, "I like his hair, but if you spend any time with him, his hair is not as big as everyone makes it out to be. Whenever people write about his hair, they find a picture where his hair is the biggest. I've seen pictures from years ago, and I say, 'Honey, wow, that's high, you know?'"

Early in June, the brand-new couple had been spotted at the Café Brasil in New Orleans, listening to the New Orleans Klezmer All Stars, an acoustic band that plays funky Jewish folk music. "They were nuzzling and dancing together," a fellow audience member recalled. "Everyone knew something special was happening between them."

On her weekend filming breaks in June, Julia could be spotted backstage at Lyle's concerts in Memphis, West Virginia, and New York City. Lovett began to dedicate songs to "Fiona" or "my very special friend," but of course no one in the audience knew who that was. "Fiona likes to think I wrote this song for her," Lovett said at New York's Paramount Theater before he began "She Makes Me Feel Good" ("She's got big red lips / She's got big brown eyes / When she treats me right / It's a big surprise".)

The New York press didn't figure out until after Lovett left town that the womanish man who introduced Lyle's version of "Stand by Your Man" was actually Julia in drag. When reports began to appear that something might be up between the two, they decided to move up the wedding to June 27—and to keep it as secret as the Manhattan Project.

And so, at 11:45 on a drizzly Sunday morning, less than two hours before the scheduled ceremony, Lyle Lovett and Julia Roberts applied for a marriage license at the Grant County Courthouse. Unlike other states, Indiana does not require blood tests or a waiting period, only proof that the bride has been vaccinated against German measles. The court clerk, Karen Weaver, asked, "Are you the *real* Julia Roberts?" When Julia softly replied in the affirmative, Weaver signed the license. Later, she said that they were "nice people. I was very impressed but not awestruck. I was awestruck when I met Dan Quayle."

At three o'clock (an hour and a half late, to accommodate tardy guests), Julia's sister, Lisa, walked down the aisle of the church as the organist played "Jesu, Joy of Man's Desiring," followed by Julia's brides-maids. The only decorations were bouquets of red, yellow, and purple flowers tied to the ends of the wooden pews.

As the flower girls—Susan Sarandon's eight-year-old daughter and Deborah Porter's five-year-old daughter—scattered rose petals from wicker baskets, and the ring bearer—Susan and Tim's four-year-old son, Jack Henry—followed behind, a cellist began to play Mendelssohn's "Wedding March." Julia walked down the aisle on the arm of an old friend, the actor Barry Tubb, called her latest love interest only weeks earlier by the tabloids.

"She looked gorgeous," Deborah later said, although some guests were surprised by the simplicity of her loose, floor-length white sheath dress. "It looked more like a slip that should go *under* a wedding dress," said one of Lyle's relatives. "You could see her belly button [through it]!" In fact, the dress—designed by Rei Kawakubo of the New York boutique Comme des Garçons and priced at two thousand dollars—had been a gift that Lyle sent to Julia on the *Pelican Brief* set. "When we originally decided to get married [in the fall]," Julia said, "I was talking to this girl-friend of mine who was doing wardrobe, and she was going to help me make my wedding dress. Then when it came down so fast and furious, I was just looking for anything white! And I fortunately had this beauti-ful dress that he'd given me that I'd never worn before."

Julia wore, around her head, crossed at her neck, and trailing down her back, a floor-length piece of tulle that held her hair back off her forehead and rivaled any scarf worn by Isadora Duncan. And she was, amid the scattered rose petals, barefoot. Lyle wore a conservative black suit (one he usually wore for his concerts), a gray tie, a gardenia in his lapel, and his hair as high as ever while he waited at the altar with his best man, the film director Wayne Miller, for Julia to join him.

The twenty-minute ceremony was conducted jointly by Lyle's family minister—Pastor DeWyth Beltz of the Trinity Lutheran Church in Lyle's hometown of Klein, Texas (named after Lyle's great-great-grandfather)—and the Reverend Mark Carlson, pastor of St. James. "When I knelt down," Julia said, "I could feel the air on my feet, and I thought, *I bet everybody at this moment is looking at the bottom of my feet*, and then I thought, *Oh my God, I hope my feet are clean.*"

After they were pronounced husband and wife, the newlyweds joined their guests on a three-bus caravan to the Deer Creek Music Center in Noblesville. Outside the amphitheater, a large green-and-white-striped tent had been erected. The celebrants dined on roast turkey (Kiefer would have enjoyed that), prime rib, grilled shrimp, a five-tier wedding cake, and champagne.

As Lyle kneeled down to peel Julia's pale blue garter off her leg, she turned to the guests and said, "He makes me so happy . . . he's so good to me." When Julia threw her bouquet into a crowd of grasping bachelorettes, Elaine Goldsmith caught it.

"It was like a great *event*," Julia later gushed about the wedding, "the way someone who's never been to the Oscars would imagine it to be. . . . I was trying to maintain my composure, because I was really giddy."

The newlyweds left the reception early, because Lyle had to prepare for that evening's show. Julia didn't even have time to change out of her wedding dress before she came onstage at the Deer Creek Amphitheater and announced, "Ladies and gentlemen, my husband . . . Lyle Lovett and his Large Band!" She then did as the song says while Lyle sang "Stand by Your Man," and when he finished, she kissed him to the cheers of ten thousand Lovett fans. "Welcome to the happiest day of my life," Julia said.

The news that Julia Roberts was now Mrs. Lyle Lovett was so improbable that when Nancy Seltzer called the Associated Press to make the announcement, the reporter she reached wouldn't believe it wasn't a hoax. "I could not prove to them who I was," Seltzer recalled. "The AP asked me to name my clients, so I did. Then I said, 'What about Julia's agent, Elaine Goldsmith? She's right here.' But then we couldn't prove who *she* was, either." Finally, Seltzer got Susan Sarandon on the line, who succeeded in convincing the reporter that this was on the level. "She had too many details," the man said.

And so the news was out. YA GOTTA LOVETT! screamed one of the headlines.

People found itself, even more than usual, deeply immersed in the drama of Julia Roberts's life. When its editors learned that she had been spotted disguised as a man at Lyle's New York concert, and then got wind that the couple might wed, they assigned Steve Kagan, a Chicago photographer, to attend Lovett's concert in Noblesville and see if he could get some shots of the newlyweds. Kagan met up with Janna Wilson, the writer assigned to the story, and they drove to the concert late Sunday afternoon. Wilson had gotten press passes, which wasn't difficult, because the concert wasn't sold out.

When they arrived and asked for their press badges, however, Kagan was told that all photo-press access had been revoked because "they just got married." Kagan's head swam. Here he was in the middle of what could be the celebrity story of the year, Julia was very likely to be with Lyle at the concert, and they wouldn't let him in. Kagan asked if he could *buy* a press ticket. "No, there are no press tickets," the woman at the box office said. Then she added helpfully, "But you can buy a [regular] ticket if you want to."

Wilson and Kagan did so, but they then ran into a man from MCA, Lovett's record label, who got them complimentary tickets and told Kagan to just "make his own way" once he got inside. "Security is really lax here," the man said. "Just wave your [general] press pass if you have to. Go in and tell them you're official and shoot."

Kagan was dismayed when he saw that his seat was toward the back of the venue, not close enough to the stage to take the kinds of pictures he knew *People* would want, even with a telephoto lens. But as Roseanne Cash's opening act concluded, Kagan saw that a number of seats ahead of him remained empty. He moved up closer to the stage, discreetly took out his camera, which was loaded with black-and-white film, and waited.

When Julia came out in her wedding dress to introduce Lyle, a shot of electricity coursed through the crowd. Kagan snapped away unnoticed, because he used fast film that required no flash. He moved closer to the stage twice more during the concert, and by the time Julia came out again near the end of the show, in a new, country–style print dress, to sing a duet with Lyle, Kagan was only four rows from the stage. He switched to color film and started to shoot again.

At that point a uniformed guard spotted him and told him to stop. Kagan explained he was with *People* and hoped that would be enough to placate the guard. It wasn't. The young man ("a high-school kid," said Kagan) asked him to step outside. "I probably could have just walked away or said no, and he wouldn't have been able to do anything about it." But Kagan, thinking he'd just be escorted out of the concert, complied. He at least had shot his pictures.

Instead, he was led to a room at the back of the concert hall and grilled for an hour by three men wearing black suits who asked him who he was, how he got in, how he got his cameras in, and why he was taking pictures. Kagan didn't know who the men were, but he assumed they were representatives of either Lyle, Julia, the Deer Creek Music Center, or some combination of the three. Kagan explained that the representative from MCA had given him a tacit okay to shoot, and he showed the men the rep's business card. The interrogators were unimpressed. "He doesn't have the authority to do that," one of them told Kagan. "*We* do, and you're going to have to give us your film."

Now Kagan's heart really sank, but his resolve didn't budge. "No, I can't do that," he replied. He had not been kept out of the concert, he argued, and the film was his property. "Okay," the man said. "We're going to have to call the sheriff." Minutes later, Kagan found himself confronted by Lieutenant Gelhausen, a six-foot-two officer of the Hamilton County Sheriff's Department who had a large revolver dangling from his belt. After the two sides explained their viewpoints, Gelhausen said he would call the county prosecutor for advice. When he returned, he said he would have to take the film "into evidence" and let a judge decide to whom it belonged.

Kagan reluctantly turned over the film. "I don't know what they were afraid of," he said. "Maybe it was just a matter of control, or maybe they thought Julia might have looked a certain way onstage that they didn't want portrayed. I don't know, I've gone over it in my mind, why they had such a severe reaction, and I still don't know."

Back in his hotel room at two in the morning, Kagan called *People*'s art director, M. C. Marden, and told her what happened. The next day Marden conferred with the magazine's attorney, Nick Jollymore, who told her that they could either sue for the return of the film or give it up. This was the first time in nearly twenty years of publication that *People* had faced such a situation. The magazine very badly wanted the pictures; the wedding was *big* news, and Julia Roberts was one of their best-selling cover subjects.

The week's Wednesday cover deadline loomed. If the magazine didn't get the photographs by then, they would be worthless. On Monday afternoon Time-Life's general counsel Harry Johnstone exhorted Jollymore to "Sue the bastards!" The magazine enlisted the help of a First Amendment specialist in Indianapolis, Robert Johnstone, who filed a suit in federal court at noon on Tuesday.

"Johnstone was good," Kagan recalled. "He started making phone calls right away [to the Deer Creek lawyers], asking questions like 'What kind of insurance do you carry? What are the limits of your liability? Do you know how many millions of dollars it would cost if you hold up an issue of *People* magazine?' So they got real scared, thinking they could be liable for huge damages."

Johnstone also told the Hamilton sheriff's department, "You took film from somebody. You have no criminal proceedings against that person, and you have no court order, no civil proceedings. What right in the world do you have to our property? Keep in mind that the film could be worth millions of dollars because of the difference a cover can have in the sales of the magazine." The sheriff decided he wanted nothing more to do with the matter and gave the film to the Deer Creek officials. Their lawyers told Johnstone, "We have the film, you want it, Lyle Lovett wants it, we don't know who to give it to, and we're going to put it in the court tomorrow."

Steve Kagan, who had missed a Monday doctor's appointment in Chicago and was still wearing the jeans and short-sleeved shirt he'd packed for what he expected to be a one-night stay in Noblesville, testified for an hour Tuesday afternoon in the courtroom of Judge Sarah Barker at the Indianapolis federal courthouse. Meanwhile, back in New York, *People*'s editors learned that there were intimate, posed color photographs of Julia and Lyle's wedding, taken for the couple by Peter Nash, that were under the control of Julia's publicist. When the editors contacted Nancy Seltzer about using Nash's pictures, she asked for approval of *Kagan's* photos. "If you'll let us see Steve's pictures," she said, "I'd be more than willing to let you have them, but I want to go over them to make sure that if you use [one] on the cover, it's a nice picture."

This situation was one *People* had faced more and more frequently: a publicist who wanted to control every photograph and every bit of copy about her client. As always, they refused the request but continued to cajole Seltzer to allow publication of Nash's pictures.

Shortly, Nancy Seltzer relented and allowed the editors access to Nash's photographs. What they didn't yet know, but Seltzer did, was that Judge Barker had just ruled in *People*'s favor. Seltzer knew that Nash's photographs would probably be the best and that without them, the magazine would have to use Kagan's or others she had no control over. Her hand had been forced.

"In general," Judge Barker said in her opinion, "when a person's picture is used to illustrate a non-commercial newsworthy article, his interest in the use of his likeness or image must be evaluated in light of constitutional interests found in the First Amendment." The marriage of Julia Roberts and Lyle Lovett, she concluded, "was a newsworthy event of widespread public interest," and thus *People* had the right to publish the Kagan photographs.

Even though the editors now had actual wedding photos, they still needed Kagan's pictures by the deadline, since they would be the first of the couple after the wedding and would round out the article. Clutching the brown paper bag of film, Kagan parked his car in an Indianapolis garage and flew to Newark Airport on Tuesday night. He got in at one in the morning, found out there was a taxi strike, and had to take a bus into Manhattan. After a few hours' sleep at the Waldorf-Astoria—the only hotel he could find a room in at that hour—he put his well-worn jeans and shirt back on and walked the film over to the Time-Life Building. It was then that he learned about Peter Nash's wedding photos.

"My pictures were of value in getting those pried loose," Kagan said, "but all of a sudden their value, in terms of a story, diminished. They were important pictures because they were the only ones of the two of them together, right after they got married, but they came up with all these wedding pictures of Julia barefoot in the church and all that stuff, which are much better picture-wise and for the story—but they didn't help my cause any."

The magazine published two of his shots—one of Julia onstage, holding Lyle's face in her hands, and another of the outside of the St. James Lutheran Church—in their July 12 issue. The cover headline read EXCLUSIVE PHOTOS—JULIA'S WEDDING ALBUM!

It was the biggest-selling issue of the year.

Julia and Lyle spent their wedding night in a luxurious suite at the Omni Indianapolis North Hotel in Indiana, where they repaired immediately after his performance. As soon as they reached their room, Lyle phoned down for a bottle of Dom Perignon. The hotel employee who delivered it recalled that "Lyle answered the door, and I could hear Julia giggling in the background. He tipped generously and obviously couldn't wait to get back to his bride."

There was no immediate opportunity for a honeymoon. The next day Lyle was on his way to Ohio for the next leg of his tour, and Julia flew back to the Washington location of *The Pelican Brief*. The cast and crew had been as surprised as everyone else by the marriage. As Tom Rolf recalled, "When Julia got married, it blew everyone's mind. She took off for the weekend and came back a married woman. We had no inkling. We all felt that Lyle Lovett was the strangest choice she could have made. A very nice fella, but still . . . But he was a very talented man, and, thank God, not everything is about the way you look."

On Tuesday, Julia's first day back on the set, Alan Pakula threw the bride a party to which everyone wore T-shirts that proclaimed, on the front, WELCOME BACK, MRS. LOVETT and on the back, HE'S A LOVELY BOY . . . BUT YOU REALLY MUST DO SOMETHING ABOUT HIS HAIR. During a scene in which Julia speaks to John Heard on the telephone, the camera operator, Dick Mingalone, popped into the shot carrying Cupid's bow and arrow. As Julia began the scene, she expected Heard's voice on the other end of the line, feeding her his lines. She recognized Lovett's voice instead but never broke character. Pakula had given Lyle the lines and arranged for him to call. When she completed the scene, Julia beamed: "That's my husband."

Julia enjoyed a mutually respectful relationship with Pakula, who had directed such renowned stars as Liza Minnelli, Jane Fonda, Warren Beatty, Meryl Streep, and Robert Redford. "She gave everything," Pakula said of his star. "By the end she had earned the respect of the entire crew. Julia responds to the other actors, which is what the best people do."

According to Tom Rolf, there was *some* friction between actress and director. "Pakula would get frustrated with Julia because she would be very adamant about her feelings about saying a line a certain way. They'd butt heads a little bit. He loved her, and he was very supportive of her always—but they were a couple of adults who were passionate about what they were doing, and there would be some dialogue between them. I'd say the disagreements were settled about fifty-fifty. They respected each other too much to get into an argument, but there would be *discussions*."

Near the end of the shoot in late August, a close brush with danger once again left Julia emotionally shaken. While she and Denzel shot a scene in hundred-degree heat in an underground garage, an explosion rocked the building, and a ten-by-twelve-foot chunk of brick wall crashed down within feet of the actors. "There was a tremendous rumbling," a crew member said, "a booming vibration like a tornado, and then the bricks in the wall just blew out. Julia was terrified. She thought she was going to be buried alive."

Julia, Denzel, and the crew fled up four flights of stairs to get out of the building. A spokesman for the production, Jeanmarie Murphy-Burke, said, "We were ordered out of the building by fire marshals and were kept out until they were sure we could return safely the next day." The explosion had been caused by huge air conditioners that the crew had brought in on flatbed trucks to make what they had come to call "the hell hole" more comfortable for filming. They had attached the coolers' exhaust pipes to the garage's circulatory system. But the building's exhaust vents had been boarded up as a precaution against vandalism, and when the air conditioners were turned on, their exhaust had nowhere to go. The buildup of pressure finally blew out the section of bricks.

"Denzel and the director tried to comfort Julia," the crew member said. "She was totally traumatized by what happened. When Lyle showed up, she collapsed into his arms. He hugged her tightly until she stopped shaking and the blood returned to her face."

In the days before the incident, Julia and Lyle (whose tour had ended) had been spotted around Washington, holding hands and kissing, and sharing a box of popcorn while watching Woody Allen's *Manhattan Murder Mystery* at a theater near the Maryland house Julia had rented for the duration of filming.

After the scare, the couple stayed home more often, and Lyle escorted her to the set every morning. "He even walks her down the four flights of stairs [into the parking garage] with his arm still around her," the crew member said. "The guy's worried. [He] told a member of the cast that he's really frightened for her. If he had his way, she'd quit the film and go home with him. But Julia's a trouper—she'll brave it out."

After filming ended, the rush was on to complete postproduction in time for a Christmas release. Tom Rolf recalled that the pressure of the schedule was exacerbated by a major problem. "We didn't have a final scene—there hadn't been a decision about how to end the movie. A *week* before we were supposed to be in the theaters, we still didn't have an ending. It was a panic. I know that Pakula had sent out about twenty different location people all over the world—everywhere from the Indies to Africa to Fiji, the Taj Mahal, you name it—to try to find a location for an ending sequence. And with all of that input, we ended up shooting it in Santa Barbara—you can see the offshore drilling rigs in the background, which you shouldn't be able to see." Julia was filming her next picture when she was called in to shoot the final scene, in which Darby watches Gray on television. And, as she had said, "We are now lovers, just so you know."

When *The Pelican Brief* opened on December 17, it was met with mixed reviews. Brian Lowry of *Variety* called it "a taut, intelligent thriller that succeeds on almost every level. . . . With all the descriptions of a long-legged . . . beauty in the book, it's not hard to figure out who Grisham had in mind, and Roberts is simply terrific, expressing Darby's initial bewilderment, followed by resourcefulness and steely resolve." (Grisham did indeed have Julia in mind as he created Darby.)

David Ansen disagreed in *Newsweek*. "Let's face it, *All the President's Men* this movie is not . . . the dialogue has no sparkle and [Pakula] dampens down his actors, as if a lack of juice were verisimilitude . . . Washington underplays suavely; it's almost impossible to muffle his charisma. But Roberts's fans, who have been waiting for her return to the screen for two years, may not feel they're getting maximum wattage for their bucks. The role requires her to be reduced to a state of whispery panic most of the time. She does it well, but what a waste. Why strip the vivacious Julia of her best colors?"

Julia's fans didn't seem to mind. *The Pelican Brief* grossed over $100 million in the United States alone, assuaging any fears that Julia's absence from the screen had dimmed her star power. The word in Hollywood was that the Pretty Woman, as an actress and a newlywed, was once again on top of the world.

CHAPTER TWENTY-FIVE

The marriage of Julia Roberts and Lyle Lovett evolved unconventionally, even by show-business standards. Their conflicting professional schedules not only prevented them from taking a traditional honeymoon but kept them apart for most of the first year of their marriage. "We've never spent more than seven days together [in a row]," Lyle told an astonished reporter five months after the wedding.

A week after the wedding, they had been able to steal a long weekend over the Fourth of July. Julia joined Lyle on his tour, first in Minnesota, then Illinois, allowing them three uninterrupted nights. In Chicago they holed up in a posh suite at the Ritz-Carlton Hotel, with a panoramic view of Lake Michigan. Lyle told the hotel to hold all telephone calls, and asked that only management deliver room service, to avoid the possibility of a susceptible bellman or waiter blabbing to the tabloids.

As she had on their wedding night, Julia attended Lyle's concerts. He inserted the name Fiona wherever he could in his songs, and when he returned for his encore, Julia accompanied him. To the thrill of the crowd, they once again sang a duet, and then Julia gave her husband what one observer called "a big, wet kiss."

The next day Lyle was off to the next city on his tour, and Julia was back on location. The pattern continued through their first year of marriage; Julia went from film to film, as she had early in her career, with precious little time between shoots; Lyle toured, wrote songs, and attended recording sessions. "With Julia making a film," a friend of Lovett's said, "the spotlight is on her. But Lyle is just as busy." A relative of Lovett's added, "Lyle is a workaholic."

Perhaps the most unusual aspect of the Lovett marriage was their separate residences. Lyle still called home the five-room clapboard farmhouse his grandfather had built in rural Klein, Texas (outside of

Houston), in the 1920s, where he had spent many happy hours as a child. Lyle had the house, complete with its cast-iron claw-foot bathtub, a wood-burning stove, and pressed-tin ceilings, moved next door to his parents' home, a mile away, when it was threatened with razing by developers. "Lyle loves this house," his uncle John Klein said. "The favorite gathering spot is the wrap-around porch in the front. A lot of weddings and celebrations were held on that porch, while sheep, pigs, and beef roasted in barbecue pits dug in the yard."

By contrast, in April 1993, Julia had purchased (through a trust she had set up in 1990, managed by attorney Barry Hirsch and accountant Victor Meschures) a four-bedroom penthouse duplex in a seven-story building in the posh New York enclave of Gramercy Park. She paid close to $400,000 for the apartment and spent another $100,000 on extensive redecorating, curving walls, raising ceilings, and painting the walls in pastel blues and greens.

On the same day she purchased the apartment below hers for $173,000, reportedly for her sister, Lisa. In January and February 1994, she scooped up two more units in the building—which was built in 1957—one for $171,000 and the other for $450,000. Finally, in 1995, she snatched up yet another unit, this one for $365,000.

Julia had sold her Nichols Canyon house and rented another in Los Angeles, where she and Lyle stayed when both were in southern California. At those times, Julia said, she and her husband were able to "pretend to be a normal couple. . . . We get up in the morning, we have breakfast, he goes off to work, I go off to work, we come home at night. 'How was your day, dear?' That whole gig."

Such domestic regularity was rare, but Julia told reporters that not only did her separations from Lyle not hurt the marriage, they actually helped it by keeping her and Lyle in an ongoing state of bliss. "It's like we're on a perpetual honeymoon," she said a few months after the wedding, "especially when we spend five or seven days apart. Because then it starts all over again. He opens the door and [I] go [*gasp*], 'Oh my God!' How many wives are lucky enough to say that every time their husband opens the door, their heart skips a beat?"

Marriages that take place just weeks after two people meet can provide unwelcome surprises for one or both as they get to know each other. Julia and Lyle may have had many things in common, but they had just as many divergent interests and tastes. Julia's appreciation for the finer things in life had come a long way since her days in Smyrna, as evidenced by the penthouse apartment and her fondness for throwing small nouvelle cuisine dinner parties of grilled fish and vegetables, after which guests would read poetry aloud. Lyle was in many respects a steak-on-the-barbecue man whose idea of a high time was tending to his chickens, hanging out with his good-ol'-boy buddies, and tooling around Klein in his pickup truck.

When Julia was with Lyle in Texas, she adopted a country-girl style, expanding on the barefoot persona she'd adopted for the wedding. She wore calico dresses or denim overalls, her hair in a ponytail, tended to the chickens, and cooked Lyle dinner.* The cliché, however, is "barefoot and *pregnant*," and after a year of marriage, there was no news that Julia was expecting. Over the past few years, she had told reporters several times that she very much wanted to have children. According to Lyle's family pastor, DeWyth Beltz, Lyle felt the same way. "I've had long talks with Lyle, and he wants to have as large a family as possible. He's an only child who wanted brothers and sisters—now he wants several kids. He's only lived in two houses in his life—his parents' house and his grandparents' house. . . . Lyle's told everyone that's where his family is going to be raised. He wants the kids to grow up around their cousins, and Julia knows how he feels." For whatever reason, it was not to be.

Differences aside, Julia professed that the more she got to know Lyle, the more she loved him. "He's like the universe god," she said a few months after the wedding. "[At] one with things, you know? . . . [He's] unflappable—but it's not like he's a man without extreme feelings. I think it's quite obvious in his music that he's very emotional and has a really interesting take on things. At the same time, there's a fluidity to him that is nothing short of refreshing, if not just . . . *staggering*."

That fluidity allowed Lyle to accept with more equanimity than had some of her previous paramours the glare of the spotlight that followed Julia everywhere. "I know all this fascination isn't about me," admitted the performer, whose career, although steady, had not made much of a mark on America's consciousness beyond country-music fans. "But I don't take it personally in any way. I don't think anything I'll do on a public scale will be as newsworthy [as his marriage to Julia]. . . . You have to keep focused on the reality of the relationship and not on the publicity."

---

*Julia's cooking skills had improved from the days when she telephoned her mother in a panic from Los Angeles to get running advice on how to cook a Thanksgiving turkey.

By all accounts, Julia reveled in her role as Mrs. Lovett. She left telephone messages as "Julia Lovett," knitted Lyle a sweater that he proudly wore, and said she felt "liberated" by her marriage. "I feel like this really pleasant calm has descended [on] my life. . . . It has to do with recognizing your own ability to make a perfectly correct decision. I think that's quite a feat: to look at something you've done and say, 'This is completely right.' Every time I talk to him, or every time I look at his picture or listen to his music, or think about him, I think, *Wow, I'm so . . . I'm so smart!*"

Julia would come to feel that she had made less than a smart decision by agreeing to her next movie. Perhaps she should have been forewarned by the fact that this was her thirteenth film, or by the title: *I Love Trouble* was an original script by husband-and-wife writing-directing team Nancy Meyers and Charles Shyer (*Father of the Bride, Baby Boom*) and the first production in Julia's development deal with Joe Roth's Caravan Pictures, to be released by Disney/Touchstone. Meyers was set to produce and Shyer to direct the story of Sabrina Peterson, an ambitious cub reporter in Chicago who butts heads over a big story with Peter Brackett (Nick Nolte), a crusty, womanizing, egotistical veteran on a rival newspaper. (Think Katharine Hepburn and Spencer Tracy in *Woman of the Year* or Cary Grant and Rosalind Russell in *His Girl Friday*.) Julia has said that Russell and both Hepburns (Katharine and Audrey) were among her strongest influences as a teenager.

Julia, not yet twenty-six, liked the snappy battle-of-the-sexes dialogue in a script that harked back to the movies of her mother's adolescence. She looked forward with pleasure to working with Nolte, the handsome, blond fifty-two-year-old action star who had earned a 1992 Oscar nomination playing an emotionally tortured football coach in Barbra Streisand's film version of Pat Conroy's *The Prince of Tides*. Julia's character's name, Sabrina, seemed to give homage to Billy Wilder's 1954 May–December romantic comedy of that name, starring Audrey Hepburn.

On paper, the project looked like a sure bet. "Julia Roberts in a romantic comedy? I think it might work," Joe Roth said with a knowing laugh. Julia felt the same way—until about a month into filming, in the late fall of 1993, when she came to two unsettling realizations: first, that the movie was turning out less like *Pat and Mike* and more like a Hitchcock suspense-thriller wanna-be. Second, that unlike Tracy and Hepburn, she and Nick Nolte, as one writer put it, "shared all the chemistry of lemon juice and cream."

"If you read the script," Julia said later, "you'd know why I did the film. It was clever banter, forties-style, hard-driving, a little wacky, a little screwball, a little adventure. But throughout the making of the movie these things weren't supported enough by our leaders. It became a nineties movie that didn't really know what it was."

The adventure aspects of the script gave Julia pause when the time came to film them. "Doing the action scenes where I was supposed to be scared wasn't really difficult, because I *was* scared. I relied heavily on our stunt supervisor, Jack Gill. I just figured that if they had the nerve to ask me to do this, I might as well have equal nerve and actually do it."

As far as Julia's rapport with Nolte was concerned, reports in the *Los Angeles Times* indicated that she found his machismo attitude so off-putting that "tempers flared between them . . . with a few Roberts tantrums along the way," during which Julia "would deride and insult her co-star. He became so annoyed with her attitude that he would do things to agitate her even more. The discord was so intense, the sources say, the two played more to stand-ins than to each other."

It's considered bad form in Hollywood for costars to disparage each other before a movie opens, especially if they're in a romantic comedy, because the controversy can hurt the film's box office. And Julia rarely badmouths anyone unless provoked. When the time came to promote the film, she spoke of Nolte as diplomatically as she could but didn't hide the fact that he wasn't her favorite costar: "From the moment I met him, we sort of gave each other a hard time, and naturally we got on each other's nerves." While saying that Nolte can be "completely charming and very nice," Julia added that "he's also completely disgusting. He's going to hate me for saying this, but he seems to go out of his way to repel people." To another reporter, she said, "His sense of humor is . . . effective and funny, but . . . he's very disgusting in a kind of boyish, throw-a-spider-on-the-girls-to-make-them-scream kind of way. Like, Nick would talk about smelly feet and think it was funny. I'm trying to be sort of tactful. . . ." Later, Julia admitted that "it's no secret that Nick and I didn't get along like a house on fire."

When there's no chemistry between an actress and her leading man, Julia said, "You work your ass off. And nobody will ever appreciate it. Because you don't say to the press, 'Wasn't the chemistry great?! And, you know, I hated him!' Instead, you're sitting at home going, 'Where is my Oscar for endurance?' "

Paul Hirsch, who edited *Steel Magnolias* and worked on this film as well, saw the friction between Julia and Nick. "When she had to play the love scene [with Nolte], she told Charles Shyer she was going to do only one take, and reportedly she [had to drink] a bottle of wine first in order to get through it. They shot only one take."

Which, according to Hirsch, was very unusual for Shyer. As an editor, Hirsch found *I Love Trouble* "a difficult shoot. Charles and Nancy would huddle around the video monitor after a take, and he might say to her, 'What did you think?' She'd reply, 'I thought that was great.' He'd say, 'Me, too. I can't think of how it could be better.'

"Then they'd say to Julia, 'Okay, one more just like that!' They shot and shot and shot. Twenty takes of a waiter taking an order in a restaurant. We had four editors, including Walter Murch, whom Charles didn't want to hire at first. He only did it when I insisted." The seemingly endless takes maddened both Julia and Nick, especially when Shyer and Meyers asked them to improvise their dialogue again and again. "It drove them nuts," a source said.

Julia has had nothing negative to say about either Meyers or Shyer. For his part, Shyer had only praise for Julia. "Julia's got 'It,'" he said during filming, "that indefinable thing. She comes through. She makes a connection. Audiences relate to her. Sometimes when I'm looking through dailies trying to find a specific take, I forget what I'm looking for because I get caught up in just watching her."

Unfortunately for the film's commercial success, Julia's "It" factor wasn't enough to make *I Love Trouble* palatable to critics or audiences. At a screening of the finished print, Touchstone executives watched with dismay as the hoped-for fizz between Roberts and Nolte flatlined. They made a last-minute decision to market the film as a suspense thriller rather than a romantic comedy. "It's gone from a Hepburn–Tracy *Woman of the Year* to *The Pelican Brief* in a very short time," an executive at a competing studio gloatingly told the *Los Angeles Times*.

The mix lay uneasily on the screen, and the critics weren't kind. "This unhappy vehicle lets its two stars down, individually and as a team," wrote Lisa Schwarzbaum in *Entertainment Weekly*. "Roberts doesn't have enough to do to keep sharp. Nolte doesn't have enough to do to stay soft. The chemistry experiment doesn't work; the two could be acting on separate soundstages. The jokes are thin, the comedy is spotty, and the elements of suspense are scattered chaotically. . . . When it could have made news, *Trouble* rehashes an old story."

Many critics once again complained that Julia wasn't playing a character like Vivian Ward. Kenneth Turan in the *Los Angeles Times* wrote, "For the second time in two movies Roberts finds herself thoughtlessly misused. An actress with an unbeatable smile who can effortlessly project warmth and good cheer, she spends far too much of this movie looking somber and glum when she isn't the focus of sporadic insipid ogling. Unless everyone concerned wakes up and remembers what her celebrity is based on, Roberts's career could end up in considerable trouble itself."

Thus Julia found herself in a classic Hollywood conundrum: Should she take roles that played shamelessly to the strengths that had made her a star (for which she would, no doubt, also be critically lambasted by many) or take risks that might jeopardize her box-office appeal? It was a professional dilemma that would play out fascinatingly over the next several years.

I Love Trouble sputtered at the box office when it opened in June 1994, earning only $7.8 million its opening weekend, and a total of $30.6 million in the United States, making it Julia's least successful big-budget movie. She has been quoted as calling the film "a disaster," but she has also said, "Quite frankly, I can *watch* the movie. . . . There were things about it that were funny. I didn't walk out of there saying, 'What a hideous disaster! *What* was I thinking?! . . . Where I feel disappointment is that the original concept of the movie sort of trickled away." Another time she was far more blunt: "I don't know what I've already said about *I Love Trouble* other than that it was a piece of shit."

In February 1994, Julia had flown on Disney's corporate Learjet from the Los Angeles set of *I Love Trouble* to Aspen, Colorado, where Lyle was doing sound checks for two sold-out concerts at the Wheeler Opera House. When Julia arrived late in the afternoon, Lyle politely asked everyone—from roadies and assistants to his band members—to leave the auditorium. He then gave an acoustic concert to an audience of one: his wife.

At that night's performance, Julia once again joined Lyle onstage for a song—this time along with John Denver—and the Lovetts had a midnight supper at the members-only Caribou Club. "They just laughed and talked until closing time," a neighboring diner said. "They seemed very close, very affectionate."

The next day, as usual in this modern marriage, Julia returned to L.A., and Lyle was back on the road. "I'm not lonely," Julia protested when a reporter asked about her infrequent husbandly companionship. "I have plenty of friends in New York and lots of things to do. Some people think of togetherness in terms of physicality. I think that when you have a great love, and you're secure in that, it doesn't matter how far apart you are. Lyle and I actually spend a lot more time together than people imagine. I feel wherever I go separate from him, I now, by virtue of our being married, represent both of us."

One of the ways married performers can spend time together is to appear in the same production. Robert Altman offered the Lovetts this opportunity when he hired them both for his new film *Prêt-à-Porter* (released as *Ready to Wear* in the United States), a send-up of the Paris fashion world that began filming in the French capital in March, shortly after Julia completed *I Love Trouble*. It would be Lyle's third film, all of them directed by Altman. Julia took a substantial salary cut to work again with Altman, whose films were always relatively low-budget art-house productions.

Lyle would play Clint Lammereux, a Texan traveling with a former *Vogue* editor; Julia would be a *Houston Chronicle* fashion writer, Anne Eisenhower, forced to share a hotel room with an American sports-writer (Tim Robbins) whose editor orders him to stay in Paris to cover the murder of a fashion executive just before the unveiling of the spring collections. Among the other stars in the film—playing desperate magazine editors, ditzy reporters, flamboyant designers, past or present models, and assorted hangers-on—were Sophia Loren, Marcello Mastroianni, Danny Aiello, Anouk Aimée, Kim Basinger, Lauren Bacall, Linda Hunt, Rupert Everett, Teri Garr, Sally Kellerman, and Richard E. Grant.

Julia and Lyle had no scenes together except, as she put it, "some airport stuff that the whole cast is in at the beginning of the picture." Almost all of her scenes were with Tim Robbins, and the two of them had a lot of fun during filming, which shows on the screen. For the second film in a row, Julia was playing a reporter who initially loathes another reporter and then falls for and sleeps with him—in this case, only when she's had a few drinks. This time the chemistry worked, and Julia and Tim's story line is the most effective and enjoyable one in the movie. Almost all of Julia and Tim's scenes together took place in the hotel room.

Julia said that kissing Tim—one of her closest friends—was one of the hardest things she'd ever had to do in a movie. "He's like my brother! So we made up this gag about Casper the Friendly Ghost that actually made it into the movie. He pulled the sheet over his head, so we were kissing *through* sheets for about four hours. Gave me, like, *major* sheet burn on my lips!"

When Altman directed *The Player,* many of the sixty-five actors doing cameos asked him what he wanted them to do. "I don't know," he told them. "You're playing yourself. Just be yourself!" He apparently didn't give Julia and Tim much more direction than that on this film. "Tim and I would have lunch," Julia recalled, "and he'd say, 'Okay, so what are we going to do today?' We didn't know! We had this not terribly original story—boy meets girls, boy fucks girl, boy loses girl—and so we tried to make it kookier and funnier in very subtle ways and very, very silly ways. It's like, his fly is open and my pants are down to my knees—most people won't even notice, but we thought it was hysterical. Bob trusts that you don't have to 'milk it.' [But] you have to shoot from the hip. Playing drunk and giggly can be badly done. But with Anne Eisenhower, all her defensiveness, the bravado of being a woman in a 'career,' turns into the opposite, and she's deeply silly with a drink in hand. She's actually funny."

Altman was delighted by the pair's on-screen dynamics. "They remind me of Clark Gable and Claudette Colbert in *It Happened One Night,*" he said. He reserved special praise for Julia. "She's smart, very, very smart. And confident. She knows what she's doing. She's way, way beyond the platitudes. I mean, she's really got it. And I'm not talking about ticket sales, about box office. I'm talking about performance."

Lili Taylor, who had costarred with Julia in *Mystic Pizza* and was also in *Ready to Wear,* said she noticed a major change in her old friend. "During *Mystic Pizza* she was innocent, almost naive," Taylor said, "and had a bit of that sparkle thing in the eye. When I saw her again, she was *much* older—and wiser. Sometimes you lose that sparkle to gain life experience."

When Julia arrived at the Paris airport she ran into Lyle's arms and very publicly embraced him. They repaired to a $2,000-per-night hotel suite, where they remained for over twelve hours. Then they were spotted walking hand in hand along the Champs-Élysées. They later dined alone in romantic bistros and always referred to each other as "my husband" and "my wife."

"It's a true romance," Altman said of his two stars. "It'll survive long after the trashy media wagon has moved on." But those who pay close attention to these things thought they noticed discordant notes in the love symphony. Julia didn't always wear her wedding ring. She didn't accompany Lyle to an Altman tribute in New York City on April 18, even though she was also in Manhattan. One report indicated that Lyle stayed in a hotel rather than at Julia's apartment.

When Lyle flew back to Paris a few days later for more work on *Ready to Wear,* Julia stayed in New York. Early on the morning of April 29, she called her publicist to warn about the possibility of an impending firestorm. "What's going on?" Nancy Seltzer asked warily.

"Well, um," Julia replied, "I went out last night. . . ."

CHAPTER TWENTY-SIX

Later, Julia would call the episode she had warned Nancy Seltzer about the "low point" of her year. The headline in the April 29, 1994, edition of the *New York Post* neatly summed up the problem: JULIA'S GOT A HOT DINNER DATE—& YOU CAN BET LYLE WON'T LOVETT.

The story described how Julia had spent the prior evening "on the town with her brand-new honey—hunky heart-throb actor Ethan Hawke. Hollywood's most dynamic new duo were . . . holding hands and staring into each other's eyes as if there were no tomorrow. Hawke, 23, and Roberts, 26, sipped Dom Perignon into the wee hours." Along with the story ran photos of Julia and Ethan, the star of *Alive* and *Reality Bites,* dancing and embracing at Lola, a restaurant in Manhattan's Flatiron district.

"Their passionate pairing seems to confirm a published report [in *The National Enquirer*] that Roberts has separated from Lovett," the story went on. It concluded with a quote Julia reportedly gave a friend: "Lyle's an OK guy, but there's really nothing between us. I have my career and he has his. Our first anniversary is coming up. But I don't want anyone planning a party for us. The marriage is over."

Nancy Seltzer swung into damage-control mode. She denied there was any truth to the reports of a romance between Hawke and her client, and asked rhetorically in *USA Today,* "Why can't she have friends? Why can't she go to dinner? Why can't she have a dance with someone?" She went on to explain that Julia and Ethan were accompanied by Miramax Films executive Harvey Weinstein (one of the producers of *Ready to Wear*) and the producer Cary Woods. They discussed, she said, "a movie they're considering doing together. Julia also danced with Harvey Weinstein."

Julia called a reporter from *Vogue* who was preparing a profile of her to deny the rumors of a split between her and Lyle. "I have a deep, tremendous love for Lyle," she said. "I think he is one of the poetic geniuses of our time." When the reporter asked if she believed that marriage should be monogamous and last forever, Julia gave an answer—but then called back and asked that her (presumably noncommittal) reply not be printed. It wasn't.

Later, Julia spoke out further, to Ned Zemas in *Vanity Fair*, her words and her tone indicating that despite years of battles with the press, her skin remained thin. "I danced. Is that a felony? The facts are simple. I, actually for the first time in a long time, went out to dinner. Just me with some people I've worked with. Talked about some writers, everything is going gangbusters. The band strikes up—'Hey, you want to dance?' We all had a good time. So, since when is that bad? I love to dance. And I will continue to dance. In fact, I will just say right here and now that up until the time I go to work—and maybe after I'm already at work—I plan on doing as much dancing with as many people as possible. I will dance until I drop. How about that?"

Julia later complained about untruths about her in the press to *Rolling Stone*'s David Rensin. "On Monday I'm pregnant. On Wednesday I'm getting divorced. On Friday I'm having affairs. That's the media version of my week. And my version is that I got some chores done, I had a few meetings. I worked out five times. I ate good and didn't have any potato chips. I've been fleeced, lied about, raked over the coals, misrepresented, misconceived, and misquoted enough. But Lyle knows the truth. Essentially, our marriage is a storybook romance."

Whew. Storybook or not, the Lovetts continued to spend most of their time apart. Late in April, Julia checked in to the Lenox, Massachusetts, branch of the Canyon Ranch health resort with her sister, Lisa, and an assistant. Observers noted that Julia wore no wedding ring. No one overheard her talk of Lyle, but one fellow spa-goer did hear her reminisce about the home gym she and Jason Patric had enjoyed when they lived together.

On May 12, Lyle flew out of Paris after completing his stint in *Ready to Wear*. Later the same day, Julia flew *into* Paris to do some additional work of her own on the film. Six weeks later, the couple spent their first wedding anniversary on separate coasts; Julia in New York to publicize *I Love Trouble*, and Lyle in Los Angeles to shoot a video for his new album, *I Love Everybody*. (At least there was a lot of love floating around.)

But perhaps not enough *loving*. During a stop in Cohasset, Massachusetts, on his 1994 summer tour, Lyle joked to the audience, "You know, it's a common misconception that musicians get a lot. My concern is not for the musician who, you know, doesn't get any. Because it's one thing to not get any, but to not get any and have people *think* you are, well, that's tragic."

As Lyle's U.S. tour continued, Julia flew to London for the June 2 start date of her new film, the director Stephen Frears's film version of Valerie Martin's novel *Mary Reilly,* for which she was being paid $10 million, yet another record salary for an actress. The well-regarded 1990 novel, a *New York Times* Notable Book of the Year, retold Robert Louis Stevenson's 1886 Gothic horror story, "The Strange Case of Dr. Jekyll and Mr. Hyde," from the point of view of an Irish servant girl in Jekyll's Edinburgh home. She fears and loves both the doctor and his evil alter ego, Hyde.

"This is going to be Julia's Oscar!" Elaine Goldsmith enthused, and few accused the agent of hyperbole. *Mary Reilly* was a prestige project, to be directed by the acclaimed British director of *Prick Up Your Ears* and *Dangerous Liaisons,* with a screenplay by Christopher Hampton, one of England's most esteemed playwrights. The Jekyll/Hyde tale, based on a dream by Stevenson and written and published in ten days, has fascinated readers (and moviegoers) for over a century with its themes of good versus evil and its pulsing undercurrents of repressed Victorian sexuality. Two months after the November 1993 announcement of Julia's signing by Sony/TriStar, John Malkovich, one of the most acclaimed young actors of his generation, came aboard to play Jekyll/Hyde. Rounding out the cast were Glenn Close as Mrs. Farraday, Michael Gambon as Mary's loathsome father, and George Cole as Jekyll's butler, Mr. Poole.

Julia found herself drawn to the mixture of vulnerability and strength in the character of Mary Reilly. "Mary is a good servant because she's so incredibly grateful for her job. She thinks she is safe in the house. . . . Mary had a very violent childhood, but she has developed an inner strength that comes from an attitude that what's done is done, no sense lingering in the past. And that attitude and her infinite goodness draw Dr. Jekyll to her. The more he learns about her and her wretched past, the more intrigued he is at her ability to prevail in such a positive light."

Stephen Frears was determined to give his film and its characters the look and feel of a Victorian Gothic. The streets of Edinburgh would be dark and misty, the lighting in Jekyll's mansion low and menacing, the laboratory labyrinthine and threatening. Julia, eschewing any vestige of her movie-star image, would be dressed in long-sleeved, floor-length, high-necked servant's garb and bonnet for almost the entire film, her makeup ghostly pale and her eyebrows lightened. "This role does not call for any ounce of glamour I could ever possess," she said. It took hair, costume, and makeup people two hours every morning to turn the Pretty Woman into a pale, waiflike household menial. "I really like the look," Julia said. "I felt it was incredibly authentic, and very naked and stark and appropriate. I enjoyed that I couldn't get away from it. Every time I looked in the mirror, there she was . . . I was thrilled to pieces to get to do something where no one was at any point going to say, 'Could you just give us a smile?' "

This would, as it turned out, become a major problem for *Mary Reilly*, and it was an issue that made the producers initially skeptical about hiring Julia. "She was a movie star," one of the producers, Norma Heyman, said, "so undoubtedly people were concerned. But she just bewitched Stephen. She's an extraordinary creature. I remember her walking past me on the way to the set. You just wanted to put your arms around her and say, 'It's going to be all right.' She just exudes vulnerability and a need for affection in this role."

The author of *Mary Reilly* was one of those concerned about Julia playing Mary. As Julia recalled, "I read this little interview with Valerie Martin . . . and they said, 'What do you think about Julia Roberts?' And she said, 'I think she'll be fine.' But then she goes on to say that John Malkovich was her 'first choice' and that Stephen Frears is 'just perfect.' And I thought, well, 'fine' looks pretty shrively next to 'first choice' and 'just perfect.' "

Julia's "vulnerability and need for affection" had worked for *Sleeping with the Enemy*, but Joe Ruben had still felt a need to insert that "Brown Eyed Girl" bit to remind audiences why they fell in love with Julia Roberts. In *Mary Reilly*, Julia never so much as raised the corners of her mouth; instead, she appeared throughout either meek or terrorized, her eyes alternately downcast or wide with terror.

The production encountered a number of other problems as shooting progressed in the early summer of 1994. First among them was that Frears and Hampton were unable to decide how to end the film. In the Stevenson and Martin stories, Jekyll kills himself to stop Hyde, but the writer and director weren't sure this was a satisfactory conclusion to what was, in Martin's retelling, essentially a love triangle. Should Mary's good side choose Jekyll, or should her repressed libido opt for Hyde? According to Corie Brown in *Premiere*, neither Hampton nor Frears could decide. "Then came an epiphany. The ending didn't matter. This was a woman's conflict. Roberts's performance would lead them to the truth about *Mary Reilly*, the truth about women. Her choice of facial expressions, the way she moved her body, would make the ending inevitable. Julia Roberts directing herself to an Oscar? Quite a leap forward for the Pretty Woman. Isn't it the studio's job to decide these tricky story points before spending $39 million? Apparently not. The studio signed off on Frears's plan to shoot his movie, edit it, and then reconnoiter the cast and crew to shoot whatever final moment . . . well, revealed itself."

Sony producer Ned Tanen and his producing-partner wife, Nancy, were less sure, and they pressed Frears and Hampton to give the film a more definitive dramatic arc as soon as possible. While Frears had expressly requested Tanen as one of the *Reilly* producers, he couldn't abide Nancy and barred her from the set and story meetings. Ignoring this decree, both she and Tanen continued to press Frears about the ending; they pushed him to fire Hampton and hire a writer who would better define Mary's character. When Nancy came into a meeting between Frears and Hampton and said she didn't want *Mary Reilly* to be another *Age of Innocence*, the writer and director both walked out and threatened never to return unless she was removed from the production.

Instead, when Ned fell ill and was unable to work, Nancy's influence grew. She began to express her opinions more strongly than ever, about everything from Julia's appearance ("She looks like shit!") and the character's motivation ("Give her an inner life!") to the most minute of the director's visions ("That's a lousy camera angle!"). Finally, Frears appealed to studio president Marc Platt, who decided the best course of action was to fully back the director. For better or worse, *Mary Reilly* would reflect Frears's vision.

As filming progressed, it became evident that relying on Julia's performance to decide the ending had been a silly notion, and the studio pressured Frears and Hampton not just to decide on an ending but to retool the entire script. Over the course of five months of filming, Hampton churned out no fewer than two dozen rewrites. "The studio asked for a different ending every week," he complained.

Before long, *Mary Reilly* had the reputation of a troubled production. Rumors swirled that Julia was unrecognizable as Mary; that the lighting was so dark, aspects of scenes were hard to make out; that Frears had had to reshoot many scenes; that he had filmed three different endings and couldn't decide which one to use; that Julia and Glenn Close had had a dustup over the use of a golf cart around the set. Most of the rumors were untrue, but the only one Julia definitively denied was the one about the golf cart. "We never had a golf-cart altercation in any way," she said with a laugh. "She never asked me about my golf cart. She never wanted to borrow it. She never admired it."

In October, after over five months of filming, principal photography wrapped, and Julia returned to New York. She was happy to be done. "It was six months in another country, and I got really homesick. Besides, English food is not high on my list of favorites." Even worse was that the pervasively bleak mood of the film and the character had seeped into her psyche. Back in Manhattan, she did little at first to restore her appearance. When her friends saw her short-cropped hair and bleached eyebrows, they were shocked. "I looked like some kind of bizarre mod alien. My friends were like, 'What the hell has happened to you?' I went and got myself all pasted together, my eyebrows colored in. I felt like Groucho Marx."

Three months later, Frears called the cast back to film a new ending. Julia wasn't happy. "If there is a certain set where bad things happened on a regular basis, you'd say, 'Oh, God, I don't want to go back there.'" Jekyll's laboratory, for instance, was "*Creepsville,* man! Nothin' nice about that place! Like, jars with embryos and fingers and eyeballs."

Over the next eighteen months, the negative perceptions of *Mary Reilly* grew as the film's release date was postponed *seven* times while the director and the studio haggled over its final cut. Frears had assembled a movie that reflected his original vision—a thoughtful, modestly paced, atmospheric psychological thriller with the novel's ending of Dr. Jekyll's suicide. When this version was greeted by a lukewarm preview response, studio president Marc Platt told Frears to recut the film to pick up its pace, change the ending, and make Mary's repressed libidinous desires for both Jekyll and Hyde more overt.

Frears was already at work on a new film and told Platt to recut the film himself. After four months of work, Platt reworked *Mary Reilly* into what he considered "a more black-and-white version, about good and evil," as opposed to Frears's "gray version, a film about ambiguity." Platt was convinced his cut would be far more commercial; Frears abhorred it, Platt said. "He doesn't take criticism well."

Frears prevailed, and it was his vision for *Mary Reilly* that ultimately played across theater screens in February 1996, nearly two years after the start of shooting. By then Julia had completed three other films, done a guest stint on television's most popular sitcom, *Friends,* divorced Lyle Lovett, and had a love affair with *Friends* star Matthew Perry.

CHAPTER TWENTY-SEVEN

C AUGHT!
    It was a tabloid headline that had reverberated through Julia's life once before. This time, however, the front-page photos didn't reveal her fiancé in a compromising situation with another woman, but her husband. "Lyle Lovett is cheating on Julia Roberts with a sexy blonde— and *The Enquirer* caught the lovebirds red-handed in a Texas hotel," the newspaper reported. The story went on to describe the woman as an aspiring country singer, twenty-six-year-old Kelly Willis, with whom Lovett had apparently been involved for several months. On October 5, 1994, Lyle and Julia had attended the Country Music Association Awards in Nashville, appearing as much in love as ever. "Lyle and Julia sat next to each other at the awards and were kissing up a storm," an observer said. "They put on a terrific show of being totally in love."

Two days later, Julia was absent as Lyle performed at Austin's Paramount Theatre. During the show, he brought Kelly, dressed in a form-fitting black dress, onstage and introduced her to the thousand people in the audience as "my favorite singer." He then kissed her and whispered something in her ear. The twosome proceeded to sing a duet of Lovett's song "I Love Everybody."

After the concert, reporters with inquiring minds (who always haunted Lyle's concerts in the hope of spotting Julia) shadowed both Kelly and Lyle when they left the theater together at twelve-thirty A.M. The singers ran through a driving rain to Lyle's Chevrolet Suburban. One of Lyle's assistants drove Kelly to her Toyota Tercel, parked at the other end of the lot, and then drove Lyle to the Four Seasons Hotel. Kelly drove to her home, two and a half miles from the hotel. It seemed like the end of the story—but neither rain, nor snow, nor heat, nor gloom of night can stay these intrepid journalists from the scent of scandal. Their wait outside Kelly's house was rewarded when, at one A.M., she emerged, now casually dressed and carrying a bag, and drove over to the Four Seasons. She wasn't spotted again until eleven A.M. in the hotel lobby.

A similar scenario played out the following night. This time Kelly showed up at Lyle's suite 741 at four A.M. A DO NOT DISTURB sign remained in place for twelve hours, until the couple came out of the room, carrying baggage and guitars, only to find a photographer snapping their picture. Lyle started toward the lensman, who fled. Down in the lobby, Kelly fretted. "Oh my God! What am I going to do? Someone just photographed me and Lyle in the hallway! I better get out of here."

Kelly's live-in boyfriend, Bruce Robison—who, at six-seven, towers over the six-one (including hair) Lyle—was furious. "Lyle Lovett stabbed me in the back," he reportedly told a friend. "He's stolen the woman I love and torn my life apart. I'd love to wring his scrawny little chicken neck and cram his big beak of a nose down his throat!"

Julia made no comment on the story, which was published in late October, but her apparent reaction to it aired on television on October 26, when the gossip show *Inside Edition* showed a videotape of Julia wiping her eyes and seemingly pouring her heart out to Jason Patric on a bench in New York's Central Park. "Jason was trying to console her as best he could," an observer said. "He sat and listened, but he seemed truly distressed about seeing her in such a state."

The show's producer, Brian Hendl, said, "The photographer said Julia was sobbing uncontrollably before he started shooting the tape. But by the time the camera was rolling, she was still wiping away tears and trying to pull herself together."

Julia had little time to "pull herself together" for her new film. In a matter of days, she was due on the Beaufort, South Carolina, location of *Grace Under Pressure,* a film based on a screenplay by Callie Khouri, who had won an Oscar in 1991 for her script *Thelma & Louise,* the seminal postmodern female buddy picture.

Khouri has not said whether she had Julia Roberts in mind when she created the character Grace King Bichon, but she might as well have. Grace is a nervous, slightly frazzled rural Georgia woman, a former equestrian whose girlhood dream was to be a large-animal veterinarian. She lives in close proximity to her family: her father, Wyly (Robert Duvall), the tough wheeler-dealer for whom she manages the family stables; her mother, Georgia (Gena Rowlands), genteel and (at first) acquiescent to her husband; her sardonic sister, Emma Rae (Kyra Sedgwick); her daughter, Caroline, a budding equestrian herself (Hayley Aull); and her husband, Eddie (Dennis Quaid), a handsome good ol' boy with, as Grace learns early in the story, a cheatin' heart.

Julia was pleased to be playing an older character than she ever had—a woman married for about ten years, the mother of a sentient child. "Choosing this role had a lot to do with not doing the same stuff over and over. It's also about getting older and having increasingly more to offer. You start to mature, and the roles mature with you." (Julia was not yet twenty-seven.)

Julia got along well with the cast, the crew, and her director, the Swede Lasse Hallström (*What's Eating Gilbert Grape*), who seemed on the surface on odd choice to direct a piece of southern Americana. "Lasse is terrific," she said. "We had so much fun working together, and I just knew that he would be the perfect director for this, because I think that his movies show great sensitivity and great understanding of family. [He's] very Swedish, as is Sven Nykvist, our cinematographer, and you know, the two of them sitting in a corner talking to each other was always a great visual. A lot of 'O' sounds, like 'Hejdo, playdo,' you know, it sounded like they were kidding around, and nobody knew what they were talking about. [But] Lasse was very clear about what he want[ed], very specific."

Julia got along much better with Dennis Quaid than she had with Nick Nolte. "We had a lot of laughs!" Julia said. "He came late to the production. We had to do this big dance scene, and so we started off not even acting together but *dancing* together! And actually, it's a great way to get to know somebody, because you are forced into an intimate situation, and you have to rely on each other." Asked if she found Quaid to be a good kisser, Julia replied, "Well, not everyone you get to kiss is a good kisser, and if you go around saying who the good kissers are, then people can pretty much figure out who the bad kissers are. . . . He's not one of them."

The scene in which Grace follows Eddie and finds him in a restaurant with a woman she had seen him kissing resonated for Julia. "I was in a relationship years ago," she told Oprah Winfrey. "I remember following the guy. I was in my twenties, and I see him make a left turn going to the other girlfriend's house, and later, when I asked him about it, he said, 'That wasn't even me in the car. You're delusional.'" Julia never said who this boyfriend was—pick a suspect.

After location work in Beaufort and the nearby Davant plantation in Ridgeland, South Carolina, the company moved to Perry, Georgia, where Grand Prix Championship scenes were filmed at the Georgia National Fairgrounds. The weather chose not to cooperate. Pat Dozier, a Georgia grandmother, answered a call for extras and was hired at fifty dollars a day as a stand-in for the actress Anne Shropshire, who played Aunt Rae. "I've never seen it pour in southern Georgia that much," Pat recalled. "Nine out of ten days, it rained. Julia really hated the rain. She said, 'This red clay has ruined every piece of clothing I own. They've tried to clean them, but it's impossible, and I'm going to throw them all away—especially the white ones.'" Julia undoubtedly had flashbacks to the clay-splashed rainy days of her girlhood in Smyrna.

Although Julia's character was an equestrian, and Julia is an experienced rider, only one brief scene at the end of the film shows her atop a horse. "Julia loves horses," Pat Dozier recalled, "and one day she went up to one of them and started talking to it. He reared up his head, as horses will do, and knocked Julia down. And she got a very bad bruise on her face. They had to call off her filming for about three days. And even though she and Lyle Lovett were separated, he flew right in and stayed until they could cover up the bruise with makeup and she could go back to work."

The separation of Julia and Lyle was not yet public knowledge. It wouldn't become so until Nancy Seltzer issued a press release on March 28, 1995, the day after the sixty-seventh Academy Awards, a time when Julia must have hoped the Oscar excitement would overshadow the announcement. It was not to be.

Rather than feature "Oscar styles" as its main cover subject, as it usually does, *People* featured a photo of Lyle and Julia smiling at the December 1993 *Pelican Brief* premiere, with the headline BYE BYE, LOVETT. The lead photograph for the article, "One Last Sad Song," showed a morose-looking Julia wearing sunglasses, riding in the back of a car on March 29 in London, where she had gone to film the final scene of *Mary Reilly*.

Most observers greeted the news with an "I told you so" shrug. From the outset, few had expected this odd coupling to last. There had been so many clues: the geographically challenged couple's frequent separations; Julia's dance-floor clinches with Ethan Hawke; Lyle's apparent hotel trysts with Kelly Willis; his several appearances with his former girlfriend Allison Inman; his "romantic" dinners with another old flame, Ashley Judd; Julia's hand-in-hand seashore stroll with Richard

Gere (Nancy Seltzer said they discussed a *Pretty Woman* sequel; whether they also "smooched" depends on which account you read); and Lyle's response to a Buffalo, New York, audience member's shouted question, "Where's Julia?"

"She's . . . she's everywhere," he replied in a weary voice. Later, according to *The Buffalo News*, he gave a "small speech" about his marriage: "No matter how well you may have planned, things don't always come out as you intended."

He and Julia had obviously tried to make the union work; there were all those efforts to "pretend to be a normal couple." The prior September, Lyle had said that he and Julia discussed having a child after she finished *Mary Reilly*; and just a few weeks before the separation announcement, he had said that their life "is a lot more normal than people might think by keeping up with the tabloid media. I'm just really happy to be in a great relationship." Despite all their protestations to the contrary, the relationship was too unconventional, too long-distance, too "showbiz" to allow the kind of bonding that helps a young couple ride out the rough patches and settle into a love based more on fact than fantasy.

Julia admitted as much. "It doesn't necessarily mean you should be married to everyone you have a good friendship with and love, you know? I think we just had problems. We weren't supposed to be married. . . . There was nothing wrong, there was nothing bad, nobody did anything. It's not even that complicated. It's sort of inexplicable.

"I do think, however, that there's a certain kind of 'show' that is part of the early stages of every relationship. It's what attracts you to someone. As you get more deeply involved, you no longer want the show, or need it; you want the real person. . . . If I never get married again in my life, though, I'm glad that I got married to Lyle. It was a hoot. We had a great wedding, and we had a great time. It was a great adventure."

Julia denied reports that one of their major problems was that Lyle wanted children and she didn't (at least not right away). She felt it was unfair for observers to view the breakup as a sign of weakness in her and Lyle's feelings for each other. "When people look at relationships, they think that to stay in a relationship, to work at it, is to be strong and to give up on it is really weak, you didn't try or whatever. Well, lots of times, it's the easy choice to stay. It's the weakness in a person or a situation that keeps you together."

When she was asked if the breakup was "hard," Julia replied curtly, "No." But then she added, "It wasn't easy. I mean, it wasn't effortless, but we're friends, so it's not a feud. It wasn't a big punch-out or anything. It's not a day at the beach, getting divorced, but . . . we maintain our relationship in a really positive way."

Lovett, as songwriters will, poured out his feelings about Julia and the breakup in his songs. In 1996 he released an album entitled. *The Road to Ensenada.* Listeners could debate which of the sometimes bitter sentiments expressed in the lyrics referred to Julia, but in some cases there was no doubt—as in the song "Fiona," in which Lyle says the title woman's father is "in heaven," her mother "won't like you," her sister's "pretty," and her brother's "crazy." He concludes with the advice not to "cross" her or "boss" her, because if you do, "Here come a cup and saucer."

Despite the album's explicitness, Lyle and Julia did remain friends. She kept a black-and-white photograph of him on the wall of her office. They spoke often, and she frequently sought his advice on various issues. She denied a report that she required Lyle's approval of any new man in her life, but she did admit that their ongoing friendship affected her potential relationships. "I have what I call the Lyle barometer. If a guy cannot deal with the fact that Lyle and I are such good friends, then okay, we just don't go any further."

Even though her marriage had been a failure, Julia looked upon it as a positive experience that had strengthened her. "I know that I am a strong person. I know that I'm not a person who can do something and not do it fully; I know that I am a person of great convictions. And I have a very close relationship with Lyle Lovett. It's not going to just go away."

But a large part of that relationship *had* gone away, and that realization, Julia admitted, sometimes caught her up short. While she and her sister, Lisa, were shopping one day, one of Lyle's songs came over the store's sound system. "We both sort of looked at each other," Julia said, "and went on buying lip balm or whatever the hell we were doing. And then I walked out of the store, and I was like, 'Jesus, *that* on top of the rest of my day!' "

As his sister's marriage crumbled, Eric's endured a very public crisis as well. On February 8, 1995, he had been arrested by Los Angeles police on a charge of spousal battery. He and Eliza had been married three and a half years, and he had settled into a steady if unspectacular career, making—as he put it—"Grade B *Mad Max* movies." He remained a volatile and emotionally tortured man; his marijuana habit had worsened. "To be frank with you," he told *Premiere* in 1996, "I would roll out of bed, open up my script to break down whatever I was working on that day, and as I started my day's work, I'd roll my first doobie."

Eliza felt that the cannabis use was Eric "self-medicating for depression, only it made it worse—made the gaps, the vicissitudes, much wider. When Eric gets depressed, he gets bleak." He also, on occasion, would get abusive. He was not generally in a good mood at this point, having recently lost his latest custody battle with Kelly Cunningham over their daughter, Emma.

On this February morning, Eric was particularly "agitated" (as Eliza put it) because he was preparing to play his first romantic movie lead in years—but the object of his love was a man, Gregory Harrison, in the AIDS drama *It's My Party*. Not only would Eric, who had built up a hyper-masculine screen image, kiss Harrison in the film, but he was also faced with the emotional challenge of playing a dying man. "It's a big gamble," Eliza said at the time, yet she was the only one of Eric's advisers who told him he should do it. On this morning he was having second thoughts about the project, and after a contentious telephone conversation with his agent, he grabbed his script bag and prepared to leave the house. Eliza tried to stop him. "He was really agitated. My experience with him is, when he's agitated, he doesn't drive well."

Eric got into his car, Eliza said, and "I stood by the car, and he got out of the car and walked past me." Back in the house, Eliza tried again to stop him from leaving. Eric said, "She grabbed the back of my pants, so I dragged her across our living room, heading out the door. Trying to get her hands out of the back of my pants, I swung my script bag and hit her and then left."

This time Eric started the car and screeched down the winding turns from their house (which had once belonged to Judy Garland) toward Silverlake Boulevard. Eliza was terrified Eric would harm himself or others. "I called 911. I had never called 911 before. But at that moment I was frightened. I didn't think Eric was going to hurt me; I was frightened for *him*."

Eric went on, "I'm driving down the block thinking, *I'm out of my mind here.* So I go back and say, 'Honey, I love you, I'm sorry—why don't you come with me to rehearsal?' She says okay and goes to get her shoes." As they prepared to leave, two LAPD officers appeared at the door. "They put me in handcuffs—man, I was under arrest."

"Eric was real cooperative," Eliza said. "I was flabbergasted."

He spent three hours in a holding cell (during which he was pitched screenplay ideas by a fellow detainee, asked to sign autographs, and razzed as a wife-beater), and had to post a $50,000 bond for his release. The assistant city attorney interviewed Eric and Eliza together (she said she didn't need to speak to the attorney alone), and they explained that Eric had not battered his wife. A spokesman for the city attorney's office later said, "It was found there was not sufficient evidence to prosecute."

The bad publicity, however, did little to change the minds of those in Hollywood who considered Eric bad news—including Eliza's family and friends, who pressured her to leave him. "But I sat down with myself and thought, *Is there an escalating pattern of abuse here?* There wasn't, which is why no charges were brought."

The couple did go into therapy, an experience Eric said has "done me good." Part of what he learned in the sessions, he said, was that "the behavior that is abusive comes out of a child in us that feels frightened. . . . A big grown man, when he's in that child state, is a big grown man doing it; he's not a hurt child. . . . I didn't want to abuse anybody. . . . Whenever I would get in those states, what I was doing was repeating what was done to me."

In its June 1994 issue, *Harper's Bazaar* ran a profile of Julia by Jay McInerney, the novelist who began his career with *Bright Lights, Big City*. One passage in the article characterizes well what it is about Julia Roberts that millions of moviegoers have taken to heart. Early in the morning, with Julia at Manhattan's Subway Inn (a bar near Bloomingdale's), McInerney caught her leaning against the jukebox. A man whom McInernery estimated to be in his mid-sixties, "skinny and rangy," stood up, approached Julia, and asked her to dance to a Willie Nelson song. Julia smiled and agreed. McInerney described the ensuing scene:

He is extremely courtly, holding Roberts at a certain respectful distance, not looking at her as he dances her in slow circles in a kind of fox-trot. She follows his lead with every evidence of enjoying herself. At the end of the song, he bows, excuses himself, and marches off into the three A.M. murk of Manhattan.

CHAPTER TWENTY-EIGHT

In May 1995, Julia made a six-day trip to Haiti as a goodwill ambassador for UNICEF, a position that had last been held by the late Audrey Hepburn. Her brief tenure in the role would have to be called a mixed bag, marred mainly by Julia's well-honed distrust of the press. The visit was intended to bring public attention to the plight of Haiti's impoverished children, but Julia treated photographers—in this case from reputable news outlets, not tabloids—as unwelcome intruders. In a sweltering slum classroom, she thought one photographer too pushy and reportedly called, "You—in the orange shirt! *Out!*"

Julia offered a different version of what happened. "We were at this vaccination post," she said, "and these kids were singing these songs for me, and this guy was sort of wedged between these two kids, when he should have been standing on the other side. Not only did the children find it distracting, I found it disgusting. So I had the guy who was standing next to me, who happened to be from the UN, make him move to the side."

For a cocktail reception in Julia's honor—to which she wore overalls—the UN press office invited Associated Press photographers to cover the event. When the photographers arrived, security guards covered their camera lenses and pushed them away. The next day, at a barbecue, all press members found themselves disinvited. It was not the UN press office that had ordered them banned. The UN Children's Fund apologized to the media; they attributed Julia's behavior to her "shyness" and "inexperience in her new role." Julia herself didn't feel compelled to apologize, saying only that the negative publicity "at least brings attention to the plight of the poor children of Haiti."

Back in the U.S., Julia testified before members of Congress about the trip to help raise awareness of the Haitians' plight. "When I was there, I was in a classroom and I sort of thought to myself as I was being stared at by all these beautiful faces—they don't know who I am, they must wonder what I'm doing here. So I asked them, 'Do you know what I'm doing here?' And this little boy in the back stood up and said, 'You're here because you love us.' And he was right, and the only reason I stand here terrified in front of you people is because I love them.'"

In June, less than two months after her separation from Lyle Lovett had dominated the news, Julia surprised her high school classmates by showing up at the tenth-anniversary reunion of the Campbell class of 1985 with her friend Paige Amsler. "We went as dates," Julia said, "and she was pregnant. So I was her date, protecting her from people touching her stomach who didn't like us in high school—so don't touch us now!"

"Julia sort of snuck in and snuck out," a classmate who preferred anonymity recalled, "doing nothing to draw attention to herself. She was dressed very modestly compared to the rest of us. She wore a very nice jacket and skirt set—it was elegant. Everyone just *had* to talk to her. My husband and I were talking to some friends, and somehow she ended up near me. She looked up, saw me, came over, and called me by my full name. We talked for several minutes, celebrating old times, before she was whisked away by others who wanted a moment with her. My husband was shocked that she knew or even remembered me. I told him as I had before—she's a true Georgia peach!"

Despite her celebrity, and her friendliness to everyone at the reunion, Julia was no more able to win the top spot in a popularity contest that night than she had been in high school. As classmate Jamie Hiatt recalled, "Julia lost the 'Most Eligible Bachelorette' award of the evening to someone who had been more popular in high school."

Julia found the reunion experience somewhat disturbing. "People were saying, 'Oh, yes, you were always the funniest, and you always told great stories, and you were kind of like the actress in high school,' which I never was. So it was bizarre . . . people tell stories, and I just don't even know who they're talking about." (Perhaps they recalled her triumph as Cassius in Coach Boyd's English class.)

The following month Julia flew to Dublin to shoot a small role in the director Neil Jordan's epic true story of early-twentieth-century Irish freedom fighters, *Michael Collins*. Her ex-lover Liam Neeson played the title role. She would play Collins's lover, Kitty Kiernan, who is also loved by Collins's best friend and fellow revolutionary Harry Boland (Aidan Quinn).

Jeff Berg, the head of Julia's talent agency, ICM, had telephoned Jordan to convey Julia's interest in playing Kitty. Jordan told Berg that the part was relatively small, and he couldn't pay Julia anywhere near what she usually got. Berg said that neither would be a problem. On March 10, 1995, Jordan met with Julia in the ICM offices in Manhattan. "Of all the actresses I have met for the role," Jordan wrote in a diary of the production, "she is the one who knows most about it. I didn't realize she had spent so much time in Ireland. She is quite wonderful and as usual some instinct takes over and I offer her the part." Jordan realized there would be objections to casting such a big star, especially in a tertiary role—but, he thought, what was done was done.

Julia liked Kitty, whom she considered "a perfect balance of complexity and simplicity. She comes from an interesting family, and when she becomes involved in the lives of Michael Collins and Harry Boland, it brought out an untapped source of strength and compassion. And certainly she was no fool. She had both of these men in love with her, and I think she enjoyed that. But I think that ultimately she was truly and deeply in love with and devoted to Michael Collins. . . . I don't think you see that much in films—a love based on something so pure and simple. She loved him for her whole life."

Dublin likely renewed for Julia thoughts of Jason Patric, with whom she had made her first trip there in 1991. "The first time I ever came here," she said, "it just got me. I felt very at home here. . . . I sometimes think I'm the reincarnation of an Irish fishwife or something. . . . The people are so friendly and easygoing, and things seem to go at a *life pace*. They're not sleeping, but they're not all in a panic to get where they're going."

She, however, was near panic, because the next day would be her first of filming. "I'm anxious. Very anxious." She was still practicing her brogue and learning her lines. "Tomorrow was going to be the perfect first day for me. A really big scene, and I have one line. And now there's supposedly a storm coming, so I have the potential for a trial-by-fire first day."

The director found himself a tad concerned about Julia's reunion with Liam Neeson, particularly since Neeson was now married to Natasha Richardson and had a one-year-old child. "I think it was very natural for me to be worried at the start," he said, "with these two having been in a relationship. But I spoke to them about it, and we all quickly realized that Liam was terribly wrapped up in that baby of his and that Julia has a very mature attitude."

Julia said she found Neeson's presence "an enormous comfort factor. It takes a special dynamic to be able to parlay a failed romance—for lack of a better word—into being pals." The love scenes were easier as well, she found. "I realized how much more challenging and perhaps impossible it might have been to achieve that sense of knowledge with someone I had only known for a couple of weeks; so it really served me very well, knowing him. Plus it was good fun, you know?"

On July 26, Jordan recalled, "Julia [made] her first entrance. . . . The press are everywhere, generally in ridiculous disguises. We drag photographers from under Julia's trailer, from the rooftops, but it's impossible to keep them away."

One of the things that had impressed Jordan when he met Julia was her knowledge of a song Kitty was to sing in the film, "She Moves Through the Fair." Julia was nervous about singing for the first time onscreen, especially since when she does, Michael Collins exclaims, "She's a voice like an angel!" She said, "I could not have been more terrified. I'm not a singer!" Still, she does a creditable job with the song—she sang it, Jordan recalled, "Just the way my sister did."

By August 3, Jordan looked on in awe as Julia played Kitty "with a simplicity that makes the eye of the camera melt." The next day he shot the scene of Kitty buying a wedding dress for her marriage to Collins, which would be interspersed with scenes of his simultaneous death. "The minute Julia put on the dress," he recalled, "a pall of gloom falls over her. I don't know what it is, don't want to ask. I think she has a problem doing emotionally depressing scenes. It's understandable, but the way it upsets her is unsettling."

Ireland did rekindle an old flame for Julia, but it wasn't Liam Neeson. It was Daniel Day-Lewis, who gave her a heart-shaped Irish claddagh ring she wore on the fourth finger of her right hand. Asked about it by a reporter during the filming, she gazed at the ring "with a faraway look" and said, "Yep, my heart's pretty full these days." But she wouldn't reveal who had given it to her. Asked if another marriage might be in the works, Julia said, "Well, you can never say never. I believe in love, if that counts for anything. And I'd like to have kids one day. If I'm married when that happens, terrific. If not, that's fine, too."

The tabloids reported that even before she started to film *Michael*

Collins, Julia and Daniel had "set up housekeeping" in her Manhattan apartment. "Julia and Daniel are trying to keep their living arrangements hush-hush," one newspaper quoted a source, "but Daniel is virtually living there, and Julia couldn't be happier. . . . Julia couldn't give a hoot about what anyone thinks of her love life, but she lost Daniel once and she doesn't want that to happen again."

While Julia worked in Ireland, *Something to Talk About* (the retitled *Grace Under Pressure*) opened in the United States to positive reviews. "With refreshing, full-bodied characters, smart dialogue, and a gifted cast in both lead and supporting roles, this is about as good as comedies of manners get in the mid-'90s," said Cathy Thompson-Georges in *Entertainment Today.* Roger Ebert thought that "Julia Roberts only occasionally reminds us that she's Julia Roberts as she portrays Grace . . . this is an intelligent, quirky human story that finds room not only for the remarkable expanse of Julia Roberts's character but also for several other well-developed characters."

The movie took in $50.8 million in the United States, a respectable amount but only half what *The Pelican Brief* had earned. Once again some reviewers criticized Julia for not being "sunny" enough. Kenneth Turan, in his *Los Angeles Times* review, asked, "When is Julia Roberts going to allow herself to smile more than briefly in a major motion picture? Although it is heartening to see her involved with this kind of quality material, her long-ago sunniness remains a distant memory."

Julia addressed the issue by asking, "Isn't it okay to do something when there's not a lot to smile about? Should I smile just because people want to see me smile? But on the other hand, if I kept on doing romantic comedies like *Pretty Woman,* kept on smiling and having fun, people would be like, '*Gag!* Enough! Do something! Tell a story!' It's an interesting catch-22."

Julia completed her scenes in *Michael Collins*—during which she did little smiling—in early September. After a well-received preview in Pasadena on January 9, 1996, Jordan decided to shoot some additional scenes, among them a prelude and several involving Kitty, including one in which she learns of Michael's death. (In the first version, the film cut from his death to Kitty having the bridal wreath placed on her head in the wedding shop, and it ended there.) On February 8, Julia shot her new scenes, and one week later, a preview of the new cut was screened in New York, with Julia, Liam, Julia's friends Brad Pitt and Gwyneth Paltrow, and Neil Jordan's friend Vanessa Redgrave "all hiding in obscurity in the back," according to Jordan. "Vanessa comes out after the screening profoundly moved, actually weeping. Have a party of sorts afterwards and it feels like a premiere. So the cut must be finished."

While Julia clearly did not enjoy being married to Lyle Lovett enough to remain his wife, she must have liked her taste of his rural brand of living. If her New York penthouse represented her sophisticated movie-star persona, there was also the southern Julia bursting to get out some of the time. To placate the barefoot belle in her, in September 1995 she purchased (through her Astral Trust) a fifty-acre ranch with an adobe house in Taos, New Mexico. The property featured an indoor pool, garages, a greenhouse, stock sheds, barns and corrals, and fountain gardens. The price? $2.2 million.

According to *The Albuquerque Tribune*, the seller, William West, had to sign a confidentiality agreement and could not say whether Julia Roberts had bought his property. Several Realtors in the area also signed similar agreements. A neighbor, Wesley Jackson, said the property was "gorgeous, it's all irrigated. It's real nice pasture land." He added that the seven-thousand-square-foot Territorial-style four-bedroom, four-bath house might need some renovation.

When a reporter from the *Tribune* contacted Victor Meschures, the CPA said he could not confirm that he represented Julia Roberts, then added, "I wish I could." But the news was out among the townspeople. Dozens of them had spotted Julia taking pictures of the land, shopping in supermarkets and at Wal-Mart, eating in cafés and purchasing thousands of dollars of antiques at local galleries.

Content with her new home, Julia has since bought five adjacent acres and added outdoor tennis courts and a plowed dance floor at the edge of a field "in case I get the urge to dance." She has seven horses and six dogs on the property, which she calls "the little commune of my dreams." During the summer, when she's not filming, she clambers on top of her blue Ford tractor and tills the dirt for sunflower plantings. In the fall she plows them under, preparing for winter. She has retiled several of her bathrooms and learned to weave on a loom in her bedroom.

Apparently, however, not all Taosenos appreciate Julia's brand of neighborliness. "No one here in Taos likes Julia Roberts," said one resident, Angelina Maceas. "She's a snob. She has entire stores closed when she shops, so she doesn't have to deal with anyone from the public. I have some friends who were doing work on her property, and she told them all to leave because she said they were gawking at her, which they said wasn't true.

"She's not very gracious when people go up to her or ask for an autograph. She just turns away when people approach her."

CHAPTER TWENTY-NINE

Julia's next film, *Everyone Says I Love You,* was a musical comedy, but her character, an unhappily married psychiatric patient, still didn't allow her much opportunity to sparkle. The prospect of doing the picture, indeed, put her in an almost perpetual state of insecurity. Once again she had accepted a relatively small role (a mini-trend that puzzled many observers), and as such it shouldn't have presented too daunting a challenge. But this was a small role in a Woody Allen picture (his first musical). "First of all, he's *Woody Allen,*" Julia said, explaining her trepidation, "so you're completely nervous and just want to die. And of course the first time I met him I was sick, so I was off to a good start, because he was like, 'Get away, Typhoid Mary'—it was just a cold."

Adding to Julia's anxiety was the fact that she would again have to sing. One of the director's most delightful efforts, the film tells the tale of a wealthy Upper East Side Manhattan couple (Alan Alda and Goldie Hawn), their extended family, which includes his addled father, their daughter (Drew Barrymore), her fiancé (Edward Norton), a son and two other daughters, and Goldie's ex-husband (Woody Allen), who has had a series of failed relationships since their marriage ended. In the style of thirties and forties musicals, Allen planned to have characters burst into vintage songs like "Just You, Just Me," "Enjoy Yourself, It's Later than You Think!" and "Makin' Whoopie" throughout the movie.

Julia's plotline concerned Woody's efforts to woo her character, an art historian named Von, by learning her likes and secret romantic fantasies from a friend of one of his daughters, whose mother is Von's psychiatrist. The young women eavesdrop on Von's sessions and give the information to Woody, who arranges to meet Von during a trip to Venice and amazes her with their compatibility.

Julia was convinced that as much as the director might want her for the role of his beautiful love object, she simply wasn't a good enough singer. The film's editor, Sandy Morse, vividly recalled the day that Julia came to the cutting and screening room for a meeting with Allen during preproduction. "Woody suggested that Julia take a moment to record her vocal range with me and my assistant, Kent Blocher, so that Dick Hyman [the film's musical director] would have a clearer idea how to arrange the song 'All My Life,' which was her solo." Sandy and Kent had recorded a number of the other actors to save them the trouble of scheduling a meeting with Hyman "and to make the process seem more casual."

Allen "left the room so as not to embarrass Julia," Sandy recalled. "Kent set up the mike, and I suggested to Julia that she choose any song of her liking as a sample of her singing. She sang the Irish folk song that she had sung in *Michael Collins*. It was a lovely, simple song and probably a very good reflection of Julia's singing. Then I asked her to sing several notes up the scale, to determine the limits of her range.

"The whole thing took a matter of perhaps three or four minutes. But the moment she finished singing, Julia said, 'I just lost the part, didn't I? He'll never want me now. I'm not good enough,' and started to *cry*. I was absolutely stunned. Her voice was gentle and light but certainly nothing to be ashamed of. My heart went out to her. I walked across the room to her and gave her a hug and said, 'No, you're absolutely wrong. I guarantee you Woody wants you and doesn't care how good your singing voice is. For him, that's the point. He wants everyone to break into song in a casual continuation of the dialogue and doesn't want the cast to sound like a bunch of trained singers. The key to him is that everyone should sound natural.'

"She seemed consoled, though still ill at ease about what she was getting into. It was a very endearing moment for me, a very human moment that only makes me appreciate Julia's performances more."

None of the actors in the cast, which also included Lukas Haas, Gaby Hoffmann, Tim Roth, and Natalie Portman, could sing much better than Julia, with the exception of Goldie Hawn, who vocalized rings around all of them. Julia wasn't the worst of the lot, however—that, unsurprisingly, was Woody himself.

Although Julia found Allen "sweet and charming," his reputation as one of the great American directors kept her "terrified," she admitted. "The very first day [on location in Paris]," she said on *Inside the Actors Studio*, "I knew I was going to be fired. I was doing a scene and we had camera problems and it was getting late and I knew that Woody had a dinner reservation and he was hungry and we had to do this scene and it was just the two of us. The camera finally gets it right, but I was like, 'Oh, I was terrible.' Then he said it, too, just like that, he doesn't mince words, 'You were terrible.' *Oh my Lord!* So I go back to my start mark, shoulders shaking, and I just proceeded to screw it up over and over again. I pronounced words wrong, and at that point I was just completely falling apart. And then by some miracle, on the last take, just before the dinner reservation, it was great. He was like, 'Okay,' and he left.

"Well, I go home that night and I'm thinking, *They're going to deport me from this country, Woody's going to have me carried out in the night.* The next day I had to go to work, and it's the scene where I had to kiss him, and I thought, *Oh, great, now I'm going to be a bad actor, a bad kisser, he's totally going to fire me.* I was convinced of it."

In the scene, Woody's character fervently blows on Julia's shoulders, something he has learned turns her on. "I just know how funny it is," Julia recalled, "but I'm trying to be really straight-faced and this is rehearsal and so I'm thinking, *He's blowing on my shoulders, this is my fantasy for men to do this to me,* and I whip around and I gather him up in my arms and I'm also towering over him, so I'm looking down on this sweet face of Woody Allen with his little glasses, and he's looking up at me and he goes, 'You're hurting me.' And I hadn't even kissed him yet!"

Despite all her fears, Julia's experience on this film turned out to be a pleasurable one. She enjoyed the Paris and Venice locations and came away adoring Allen, who returned the affection: "She's bright, beautiful, and a pleasure to work with," he said.

During her sojourn in Venice, Italian press reports linked Julia romantically with a "hunky gondolier," Mario Fontanella. During the shoot, the twenty-eight-year-old Fontanella had ferried Julia from her hotel, the opulent Gritti Palace on the Grand Canal, and along Venice's waterways. The two were apparently spotted kissing and dancing cheek to cheek "until dawn" at a disco, and holding hands during breakfast at a pastry shop below Mario's apartment.

Apparently Julia's romance with Daniel Day-Lewis was once again a thing of the past; as soon as she left Italy, so was the relationship with Mario, who reportedly placated his angry fiancée with a gift of expensive shoes she had craved. But Julia had been busy on the romantic front in Italy. She was also reported to have had a fling with her Italian bodyguard, classically handsome thirty-five-year-old Lorenzo Sylvan, the owner of a private investigation agency. According to the local press, the pair were spotted four nights in a row at the Sotto Voce Pizzeria in Lorenzo's home area of Mestre, a suburb of Venice. They either delighted or scandalized the locals with lavish displays of affection, kissing, hugging, and walking hand in hand, appearing to all the world as if they didn't care who saw or photographed them. "Now all of Mestre is talking about this love story," said a local. But, as with Mario, as soon as Julia returned to the United States, it was *ciao bello* to Lorenzo—and on to yet another romance back in the States.

In November 1995 Julia met Matthew Perry, one of the stars of the hit television sitcom *Friends,* at a party. There was a definite spark between them, and he casually—and with little hope that she would agree—suggested that she appear on the show, along with Brooke Shields and Jean-Claude Van Damme, for a one-hour special episode to be aired after the Super Bowl on January 28, 1996. Julia said she would love to: *Friends* was one of her favorite shows.

While her agents made the arrangements, Perry plucked up the courage to ask her out on a date. "I assumed she wouldn't even take the call, but I heard that some of her assistants were cute, so at least maybe I'd be able to talk to *them.*" Julia did take the call, which left Perry feeling like a lovesick high-school kid. "You pretend to be very poised and sure of yourself, and then when you get off the phone, you run across your house and vomit."

Julia was impressed that Perry had the nerve to ask her out. "Nobody ever asks me on dates," she said. "Ever . . . and I can't recall ever asking anybody out. . . . Maybe this is part of my problem." (*Problem?* One image of Julia Roberts that had not taken hold in the public's imagination was as a dateless wallflower.)

Julia professed to be "very nervous" before the date, but they had a fine time. Perry was happily surprised by Julia's verbal dexterity as they parried throughout the meal. "Matt said she was incredibly funny. That impressed him a lot," said a source on the *Friends* set. "It was her sense of humor that really won him over." Julia returned the compliment. "He's a smart, very funny, talented, handsome man—and he's on my favorite show," Julia said. To a girlfriend, she cooed, "He's cuuuuute!"

Perry still wasn't sure if there would be a second date until he started getting phone calls and faxes from Julia on the set; she had asked an assistant to get his numbers. "Matt couldn't believe Julia was interested in him," said the source. "When faxes started coming through, he thought it was a big joke, a hoax. When he discovered that it was really her, he flipped. They started having three-hour-long phone calls and got into a lot of romantic stuff you wouldn't normally see until a couple got together. They would talk about long walks in the rain and gushy stuff like that." One of Julia's faxes, reports said, read, "I love a man who can fax me five times in one day."

In December, Julia taped her appearance, playing Susie, a highly sexed grade school classmate of Perry's character, Chandler. She reappears in his life, persuades him to wear her panties to a double-date dinner, then seduces him in the restaurant's restroom before pulling a big surprise on him. Julia seemed to have a lot of fun with the part, and with Perry. Julia's sister, Lisa, joins her in two scenes, including the dinner, playing Cathy, a movie production assistant. (Lisa's acting has been infrequent, and most often she appears in Julia's vehicles.)

The electricity between Perry and Julia was evident on-set. "At first everyone thought the chemistry between them was purely professional, because of their roles in the episode," a crew member said. "Pretty soon it became obvious that there was much more going on." When Perry's mother visited the set, Julia peppered her with questions: "Was he this funny when he was young? Was he always this cute?" According to the source, "Matt and Julia were larking around like teenagers. There was a lot of pushing and playful shoving, but they were also very shy and coy toward each other, and it appeared their relationship was very new."

The couple was spotted outside Perry's Hollywood Hills home early one Sunday morning in January, Julia barefoot, Perry in socks, reportedly "snuggling." They were also seen dining in a Malibu restaurant, enjoying a barbecue at a mutual friend's beach house, and driving through the Hollywood Hills in his black Porsche convertible.

The tabloids, of course, pounced on the story and published photographs of the twosome making out in a public place. The writer J. Randy Taraborrelli, who has profiled Julia several times, said, "Now, that was a sight. I loved that. It was like she was telling everyone, 'You want a show? Fine. Here's a show for you.'" But a friend of Julia's said that she regretted the action when she saw the pictures. "I think she thought, *What the fuck am I doing? Am I nuts? I mean, didn't I learn anything from the experience of all that attention over Kiefer?*"

When Julia sat down for a number of media interviews in February 1996 to publicize *Mary Reilly*, which was finally being released, she found herself fielding more questions about Perry than Mary. "I find him terribly, terribly interesting. . . . I love being engaged in conversation with the man, because he's so terribly clever. Wit is the key, I think, to anybody's heart, because who doesn't like to laugh?" Still, she added, "He hasn't given me his letterman's jacket or anything, if that's what you mean. We're not *pinned;* I mean, we live in two different places."

"She's just a fascinating girl," Perry summed up from his end. Then he deadpanned, "She's always borrowing money from me, that's the only downside."

Julia may have welcomed the diversion from the subject of *Mary Reilly,* which quickly established itself as her most ignominious failure. She gamely tried to hoist up the film, the character, her interpretation, her appearance in the role, her costars, and her director. Of Mary she said, "She has somehow risen above the circumstances of her childhood to become a rather joyful, happy girl, appreciative and content, not a victim at all."

One of the main problems with the film, however, is that Julia doesn't play Mary that way. Critics blasted the picture as lugubriously paced and unremittingly dreary, and bemoaned both the lack of a single smile from Julia or a strong enough characterization to make Dr. Hyde's interest in her believable. A scene like the one in *Sleeping with the Enemy* in which Julia vamped before the mirror (perhaps one of Mary dancing an Irish jig, unaware that her master is watching) would have humanized her, given the film a few moments of lightness, and shown Mary as the "rather joyful, happy girl" Julia had described.

Most critics were merciless. In *Newsweek,* David Ansen said that "Roberts captures Mary's skittishness and panic—better than she sustains her brogue—and gamely deglamorizes herself. But she doesn't have the technique to plumb this character's psychosexual depths: she's too pallid to hold center stage." Owen Gleiberman of *Entertainment Weekly* graded the film C-minus and wrote, "Anyone eager for a glimpse of the famous Roberts smile—those luscious wax lips come to life—had better look elsewhere. In *Mary Reilly,* the lips are taut and nervous, drawn into a stoic line of woe . . . the passion we see isn't light or dark—it's just dead gray."

The film, and Julia, did have defenders, among them David Thomson in *Movieline.* "Now, I don't mean to be discovering a lost masterpiece. I'm not suggesting that it's anything but a mess. But it has an atmosphere, a nightmarish sense of place and décor, and in Julia Roberts it finds (or digs up from the grave) a real actress, someone who has willed herself into a quite alien creation: a downtrodden, fearful, unattractive Irish servant girl who may be London's best chance for keeping the peace between Jekyll and Hyde. . . . That is what makes *Mary Reilly* worth watching."

Julia had asked an assistant as they went over portraits of her as Mary, "Do you think that people will accept me looking so radically different?" The assistant replied, "Well, the kinds of people who are going to have a hard time with it are the kind of people whose favorite movie is *Dumb and Dumber*." Unfortunately, far more moviegoers than that stayed away. The film earned a dismal domestic box-office total of $5.6 million, which barely covered half her salary. (Even *Satisfaction* made more money!) Perhaps the reason, as David Thomson put it, was because "Mary looks like a ghost—the whole film feels set in a morgue. . . . Indeed, this is a face from Dachau; Rodeo Drive is not even a memory." The abject failure of *Mary Reilly* further cemented the impression that moviegoers prefer their Julia Roberts unencumbered by fear, death, depression, or tragedy.

The box-office receipts of *Dying Young, Mary Reilly* (and later *Michael Collins*) cast serious doubt on Julia's ability to "open the phone book." She realized that she could not keep taking offbeat, dark, or minor roles and remain a commercial force in Hollywood. "Maybe it's a backhanded compliment," she said, "but people like it better when I'm happy."

There had to be a meeting ground, a way for her to play an interesting, complicated character and still give audiences enough of the Julia Roberts sparkle they obviously missed. In the spring of 1996, she found just such a character in Julianne Potter, a lovably neurotic food critic in *My Best Friend's Wedding,* a witty romantic comedy by Ronald Bass (*Rain Man, Sleeping with the Enemy*) that she hoped would provide her with a huge comeback—the second of her eight-year stardom.

For this film, she would be paid $12.5 million, despite the string of disappointments that preceded it; the salary once again made Julia the highest-paid actress in the world. (The extra $500,000 was said to be designed to do just that, since Demi Moore had recently been paid $12 million for *Striptease*.) Julia has often pooh-poohed the endless fascination with her paycheck. "I'm probably the last person in the world who should be rich," she said. "I don't do anything with the money. Being paid all this money doesn't make me do a better job of acting . . . It's nice that I've been able to bridge the gap between the boys and the girls, and just because I was the one who was able to do it first doesn't mean I'm the most deserving of it. . . . The penis is costing so much extra, I think. [And] I've never understood that."

Julia's relationship with Matthew Perry was over before it really got started. Although she had gushed about him during publicity interviews for *Mary Reilly*, by the time that film was released on February 23, Liz Smith was reporting their breakup and rebutting reports that Julia was "terribly upset" about it. "Somehow, I doubt that," Smith wrote. "They had what—five or six dates? It didn't seem enough time for anyone to get seriously involved."

Apparently they were seriously enough involved for Perry to come to the realization that he and Julia had different concepts of cleanliness. He was quoted in the *Long Beach Press-Telegram* that Julia "leaves her panties on the bathroom floor and toothpaste all over the sink." *Woman's Day* magazine further quoted Perry, through a friend: "The occasional item you wouldn't mind. But it's panties, bras, tights, tops, skirts—the lot. She's the untidiest woman I've ever known. . . . She won't lower herself to pick up a duster . . . and she can't cook!"

Julia downplayed the seriousness of the affair. "I wouldn't call that a relationship. We were friends. We *are* friends. Went out on a bunch of dates, had fun, but the 'love affair' never existed. For that to happen, I think people being in love with each other probably helps."

Julia's friend, quoted earlier in this chapter, said that Julia and Matthew remained close. "I mean, she's still in touch with him. You know, he's got like this little drug problem that she's been helping him with. She cares a lot about him, but being involved with him made her decide, no more celebrities [as boyfriends]. It's too much trouble, you know? She wants to be low-key, I think."

CHAPTER THIRTY

Julia began filming *My Best Friend's Wedding* in Chicago in the summer of 1996. Ron Bass's original script turned on an intriguing conceit: former lovers-turned-best-friends Julianne and Michael vow that if neither marries before the age of twenty-eight, they will wed each other. A few weeks before the witching birthday, Jules (as her friends call her, like many of Julia's friends do her) gets a call from Michael (Dermot Mulroney) to say he is getting married that weekend to Kimmy, a beautiful, intelligent millionaire's daughter (Cameron Diaz), and he wants Jules to be there for him. Julianne, realizing she is in love with Michael and cannot bear to lose him, tries every devious trick in the book to prevent the wedding.

Early in the casting process, Matthew Perry was considered to play Michael, but the end of his relationship with Julia probably put the kibosh on that. Asked to comment, Ron Bass said, "I don't remember exactly, but I'd say that the time we were looking at him coincided with, uh, those rumors."

The desperate, manipulative, deceitful Julianne could have been a very unlikable character, but as usual, the casting of Julia Roberts was the best $12.5 million the film's producer, Jerry Zucker, could have spent: The affection audiences have for her, and her ability to convey vulnerability even while scheming was exactly what the role required. The character's complexities appealed to Julia: "I thought she was great and I loved her misguided sneakiness and I understood it. This is a woman ruled by her emotions; she's come to this crisis in her life and there's no linear thinking, it's like PMS multiplied a thousand times in the course of four days."

Asked if she had ever been as desperate for a man as Julianne, Julia brought up Joe Thompson, although not by name: "I've never had the 'I'll do anything' philosophy, but I had a crush on a boy in high school who took me on one date and then couldn't have cared less. Well, he's living his own life now, isn't he? Some magazine called his mom and said, 'Julia Roberts said she had a big crush on your son,' and she was like, 'My son has moved to Vermont and made a good life for himself, and he wouldn't want to have a life with some starlet from Hollywood.'"

The "starlet"* now had enough power to choose her own directors, and for *My Best Friend's Wedding*, Julia wanted P. J. Hogan, an Australian. He had written and directed another comedy about nuptial chaos, *Muriel's Wedding*, a hilarious sleeper hit in 1995. "*Muriel's Wedding* was so powerful, and I had such a good and sad time watching that movie," Julia said. "I thought, *Here's a man who really understands the balance between comedy and the sincerity of the more somber moments in life.* . . . He knows when you can take it all the way to the point of ham and then knows when you have to bring it down and be more subtle."

Hogan met with Julia holding only a perception from her early career. "I hadn't seen her most recent films," he admitted. "So when I met with her the first time, the force of her personality was something of a revelation to me, and I wanted to get that on film."

Julianne appealed to her, Julia said, because "I wanted to be able to smile and laugh and wear big hair again. I had fun with that look." And she had fun making the movie. With a solid script and four gorgeous, talented costars acting at the peak of their form (led by the rollickingly mischievous Rupert Everett, who well nigh steals the picture), Hogan presided over a happy set, despite the heat and humidity of a Chicago summer. Stories abounded about Julia's behavior, but this time they weren't about flying shoes or bitter exchanges with the director. She was said to have given gifts to everyone whose birthday fell during filming—fourteen in all. When she grabbed a bullhorn at the end of one wearying day, some of the crew feared a diva-style tongue-lashing. Instead, she called out, "Happy birthday!" to a startled coworker. "It was so cute!" said Bonnie Deutsch, an extra. "Then she turned around to [a group of Chicagoans watching the filming], and she thanked them for supporting us and letting us tie up all the traffic. Everybody just

---

* The word *starlet* has recently come to be misused in the press. It means, in effect, a "small star"—someone who is just beginning to attract attention. To call Julia Roberts a starlet at this stage of her career is as absurd as saying—which some have—"starlet Marilyn Monroe."

thought that was wonderful. She said, 'We just want to thank you. We know this is a hassle for you, but we're thrilled to be here.'"

Julia took perverse delight in a lot of Julianne's over-the-top behavior. "Oh, well, she's horrible . . . She's sooooooo manipulative, and she's trying to be so sneaky and devious . . . I mean, I used to make jokes when we were working. . . . P. J. would [say] cut, and I would turn and say, 'Evil . . . has a *face*.' That's what the one-sheet will be, a big picture of me that'll say, 'Evil . . . has a *face*.'"

Julia brought her German shepherd–husky mix, Diego, with her on location and ensconced him at the swanky Citizen Canine doggy bed-and-breakfast. The owner, Steve Malone, recalled that Julia brought along "regular old basic dog food" for Diego, unlike other masters, who ask him to serve their pets everything from Mexican food to Chinese takeout. And Julia "waited in line like everyone else," Malone added. "She didn't expect any star treatment."

Out on a walk down Michigan Avenue with Diego one afternoon, Julia stopped to say hello to a policeman, Jim Meier, who was collecting money for the Special Olympics. She apologized about not having any money with her but promised to return. Meier recalled thinking, *Yeah, right,* but the next day Julia showed up again and dropped a hundred-dollar bill into Meier's plastic bucket. "I promised I would come back," she said, "and here I am."

A few people recognized her, and shortly a crowd began to gather, calling her name and taking pictures. Rather than panicking, as she had in the past (it couldn't have hurt that a policeman was standing right next to her), Julia posed graciously and even spoke to a few of the gawkers. After several minutes, she easily glided away and back toward her hotel. "We love you, Julie," Jim called out. "Keep up the good work!" Julia turned around, flashed her famous smile, and called out, "I'll try!"

Julia's good cheer and equanimity may well have been a by-product of her latest romance. Late in 1995 she had hired as her personal trainer the handsome, muscular thirty-five-year-old fitness guru Pasquale (Pat) Manocchia. A former professional hockey player, Manocchia owned Manhattan's La Palestra ("The Gym"), a preventive-medicine spa catering to such celebrity clients as John F. Kennedy, Jr., Liam Neeson, and Joan Lunden, who also had Manocchia hired as a fitness consultant for *Good Morning America*.

Julia's friend, quoted anonymously earlier, said of Manocchia, "What a nice guy, a charming man, quiet. And a hunk. What a bod on that one! He was here in L.A. with her, and I walked in on him in his shorts, and I was like, 'Wow!' He's got that six-pack thing going on his stomach. Julia loves that. She's into the physical thing with guys, which is why Lyle Lovett was odd for her. He has no body whatsoever. Now, Jason Patric, that's a body. I love him, he's so nice. Pat's nice, too, though."

"He looks like a little Mafia guy," Julia said of Pat with affection. In early May, Julia met Pat's mother when the couple dined with her at the World Café on Manhattan's Upper West Side. The threesome could be seen through the French doors on Columbus Avenue, but fellow diners were politely informed by the management that no autographs would be signed. Julia wore jeans, a denim shirt, and her hair in a ponytail. Pat paid cash for the meal, and after they left, the restaurant's manager told a reporter, "They more or less wanted to be seen by people. His mom *really* wanted to be seen. She was loving the attention."

"It takes a brave man to ask me out," Julia said, explaining one part of Pat's appeal. "The thing is, any poor guy who invites me out to dinner practically takes his life in his hands, because by the time the salad is served, we're halfway down the aisle." Right on cue, rumors surfaced that Pat and Julia were marriage-bound. "They talked about getting married" around the time Julia met Pat's mother, Julia's friend said, "but then they decided not to. They like things the way they are. He gave her a gold and diamond ring, but it wasn't an engagement ring, it's an 'eternal ring.' I don't know what that is exactly, but it's sweet, isn't it? Pat is her first sensible love affair because it's occurring at a time in her life when she's a lot more mature and confident. She can be herself. . . . That's a big thing for her, not caring what a guy thinks, just walking around with no makeup, that kind of thing."

The "eternal ring" Pat gave Julia, of course, just sparked more engagement rumors, and several tabloids reported that the couple planned a Thanksgiving wedding. (There would be that turkey-dinner option again.) But, as Julia's friend said, "They're perfectly happy with things the way they are. There are no wedding bells that I know of."

One report intimated that Julia agreed to date Pat only after she got Lyle Lovett's approval. Julia's friend said, "She was at my place reading the tabloids when she read that. She laughed out loud and said to me, 'Oh, my. Poor Lyle. Why would people think he has nothing better to do than endorse or veto my romances? It's so fucking ridiculous.' " Engagement or no, the relationship with Manocchia remained serious through most of 1996. "I only date him," Julia told *Us* magazine.

. . .

Julia had had her share of tense shooting situations, but her experience with *My Best Friend's Wedding* was practically perfect. "There are times," she said, "when the chemistry isn't natural and it's almost an impossible thing to manufacture. In this instance, it was just a blessing from top to bottom." One of the film's most enjoyable scenes takes place in a karaoke bar, where Cameron Diaz's rendition of Burt Bacharach's "I Just Don't Know What to Do with Myself" is so bad that instead of humiliating herself (as Julianne had hoped), she wins the crowd over with her sheer chutzpah and sense of fun. As part of their preparation for the scene, Julia and Dermot Mulroney went to a karaoke bar in Chicago and signed up to sing a duet of Sonny and Cher's "I Got You Babe."

"Without even thinking," Julia recalled, "Dermot put himself down as Tom, and I used the name Nicole because I was registered in my hotel under the name Nicole Diver. When we heard ourselves introduced as Tom and Nicole, it finally dawned on us what we'd done. Dermot chickened out after a few lines, leaving me to do the whole song alone. I think I've ruined Nicole Kidman's reputation forever—and she can sing!"

A documentary on the filming of *My Best Friend's Wedding* might suitably be called "Everyone Says They Love Julia." Her director and costars had nothing but the nicest things to say about her, which can sometimes be PR blather but in this case seemed genuine, and Julia returned the good feelings in full. She had a particularly fun time with Everett, an openly gay actor with spot-on British comic sensibilities.

Everett improvised a bit of business by pawing Julianne in a taxicab to make Michael jealous. Julia thought it was hysterical and worked well for the scene. But Everett, a cutup, kept at it after the cameras stopped rolling, and Julia finally slapped his hands away. "Julia did get pissed off at me" about that, Everett admitted. "She does not like people touching her tits. I did it again when we were playing around."

Copped feels aside, Julia professed to be "so proud of everybody in the movie. Everybody worked so hard, and they were so charming. Rupert Everett is the funniest thing to ever hit the planet. Truly, I mean, so funny that there were scenes where we'd be doing stuff, and I would be laughing so hard that you can't even understand what I'm saying! 'Cause I'm trying to get through the scene, but I'd just be peeing in my pants! I'm gonna take so much credit for this," she joked. "Even though there's no reason I should. I was actually teasing P.J. about all the ways in which I'm gonna take full and complete credit for the movie—if it's funny. But if it sucks, it's all P.J."

Julia had good reason to hope that *My Best Friend's Wedding* wouldn't suck. Nineteen ninety-six turned out to be the worst year of her career in box-office terms. *Michael Collins,* released in October and budgeted at $50 million, received lukewarm reviews and grossed just $11 million in the United States. Although Julia had found Kitty Kiernan "a perfect balance of complexity and simplicity," the character is woefully under-developed in the finished picture. She's a woman lacking discernible motivation whose affections transfer from one man to another without adequate explanation and whose feelings about the Irish rebellion are left to the audience's imagination. "All we know about Kitty," *Newsweek*'s reviewer complained, "is that she always shows up wearing a new, and improbably smashing, outfit."

Everyone Says I Love You was released two months later to excellent notices. "In perhaps the film's most inspired casting," said Duane Byrge in *The Hollywood Reporter,* "Julia Roberts is wonderfully appropriate as Allen's woefully inappropriate romantic ideal." Despite its abundance of charm and good notices, the film took in just $9.7 million in the United States, a disappointing sum even for Woody Allen, whose films appeal to a smaller, more discerning audience. (By comparison, his *Hannah and Her Sisters* grossed $40 million in 1986.)

From a commercial standpoint, Julia's career looked bleak. Though her films were once routinely expected to rake in at least $100 million, her last four had averaged $19.3 million—a figure bolstered consider-ably by the $50.8 million take of *Something to Talk About.* Commenta-tors wondered whether the longevity of her stardom would more closely approximate Farrah Fawcett's than Audrey Hepburn's.

The state of Julia's career became fodder for media hand-wringing. An *Us* article quoted an unnamed "major film director" who said, "This is a case of a totally mismanaged career. She's surrounded herself with the wrong people, she's made bad script choices, and she's let her pri-vate life totally color her persona—all of which has taken its toll on the public. I don't think people are in love with Julia the way they once were."

Julia took umbrage: "I was looking for things that were different, for things I hadn't done before." In the cases of *Michael Collins* and *Every-one Says I Love You,* she said, "It was a nice change of pace not to be in the lead, and also I enjoyed not having to work quite so hard." As for criticism of her management, Julia defended her advisers. "I've had the same agent for ten years, Elaine Goldsmith. We're very close friends, so certainly whenever I read a script, it's something she's already read, and we'll talk about it. But it comes down to me. I'm the one who's ultimately responsible for my behavior and decisions. I've done things that Elaine didn't find as interesting as I did, and I've passed on things she thought were probably smart things to do."

Anyone giving Julia Roberts advice about the smart thing to do on the evening of September 7, 1996, undoubtedly would have told her not to set foot in a "grungy biker bar" called Hogs & Heifers in Manhattan's Meatpacking District. Once she *had* gone inside, they probably would have advised her not to jump up on the bar, take off her black Maidenform 34B bra from under her blouse, gyrate with it hanging from her mouth, and then dance suggestively with the club's scantily clad barmaid Margaret Emery to the beat of the Charlie Daniels Band's "The Devil Went Down to Georgia."

Julia may have imbibed a little too much that evening to keep her naturally raucous instincts under control. "She can drink like a fish," said a close friend who spoke on the condition of anonymity. "I mean, we get drunk. She's a lot of fun."

Under the next day's headline POST PHOTO EXCUSIVE, Julia's least favorite New York newspaper ran four photos of her latest wild night, two showing her mouth tantalizingly close to Ms. Emery's, another revealing her distraught expression once she realized she was being photographed, and another of her holding hands with two hunky men as she left the bar.

"Post lensman Gary Miller caught the two [Julia and Margaret Emery] dancing together on top of the bar. . . . 'I saw their tongues come out and they started to kiss. There was one big, long, tongue-to-tongue kiss that lasted between thirty and fifty seconds. Then Roberts pulled the other girl close and started licking her neck.'"

As often happens in New York, the *Daily News* took great delight in debunking its rival paper's story. Their "Rush & Molloy" gossip column quoted Emery: "Julia Roberts did not kiss me. . . . [Thirty to fifty seconds is] a long time for a kiss. I don't know if I would do that even with a guy." The column went on to report that Julia was at the club with Pat Manocchia after attending a celebration party at Beema Grill with Lyle

Julia does "my Stepford smile" as she arrives at the Screen Actors Guild annual meeting on January 10, 1993. An ailing Audrey Hepburn had asked that she accept the guild's Lifetime Achievement Award for her. (Chris Martinez/AP)

Julia glows at a June 1993 press conference during filming of *The Pelican Brief*. She said she was "giddy," but few guessed what that meant until six days later, when she shocked the world by marrying Lyle Lovett. (Marcy Nighswander/AP)

The night of the wedding in Marion, Indiana, on June 27, Julia joined Lyle onstage at a concert in Noblesville. She introduced him while still in her wedding dress; then, near the end of the show, she came out to sing a duet with him. (Photo by Steve Kagan)

The kiss Julia gave Denzel Washington in *The Pelican Brief* was far more chaste than she would have liked. "I wanted to kiss him in that movie. I voted for the kiss. I was ready to kiss him." It was Washington who nixed the idea—because, he said, "the sisters will never forgive me." (Author's collection)

Mr. and Mrs. Lovett pose in a hotel room shortly after their wedding. For them both to be in the same place at the same time was a rarity; between his concert tours and her movies on location, Lyle said, they were together seven days in a row only once in the first five months of their marriage. (Globe Photos)

Julia and Ethan Hawke party in a Manhattan restaurant on April 28, 1994. Reports described how she had spent the night "on the town with her brand-new honey. . . . Hollywood's most dynamic new duo were holding hands and staring into each other's eyes as if there were no tomorrow." Lyle was reportedly not happy with the news, but Julia denied any impropriety. (Mike Alexander/*New York Post*/Globe Photos)

Julia and Nick Nolte seem as disconnected in this photo as they did in most of their aptly named 1994 film, *I Love Trouble*. The two stars did not get along. "He's very disgusting in a kind of boyish, throw-a-spider-on-the-girls-to-make-them-scream kind of way," Julia said. (Author's collection)

Ready to Wear brought Julia together with her friend Tim Robbins, with whom she spent nearly all of her screen time in this hotel room. Julia said that kissing Tim was the hardest thing she'd ever had to do in a movie. "He's like my brother! So he pulled [a] sheet over his head—we were kissing through sheets for about four hours. Gave me, like, major sheet burn on my lips!" (Author's collection)

In *Something to Talk About* (1995) Julia played a wife and mother whose husband (Dennis Quaid, with her here) philanders. This dance scene was the first the actors filmed. Julia said, "It's a great way to get to know somebody because you are forced into an intimate situation, and you have to rely on each other." (Author's collection)

In April 1995, Julia had announced that she and Lyle Lovett would divorce. In November she guest-starred on the TV sitcom *Friends*. She began to date one of its stars, Matthew Perry. Paparazzi caught the couple reenacting this scene from the show in front of his house. (Author's collection)

"This is going to be Julia's Oscar!" her agent had enthused about *Mary Reilly,* the film version of a novel about a servant girl in the household of Dr. Jekyll (John Malkovich, here). Instead, it became her most ignominious failure to date upon its release in 1996. Critics and audiences found the film, and its tragic ending (pictured here), too dreary. (Author's collection)

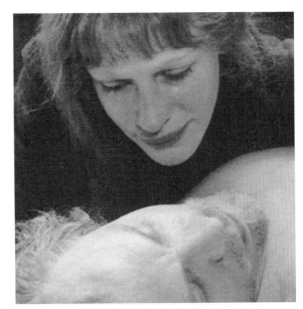

On May 17, 1996, Julia attended the Haitian Flag Day Awards banquet at the John F. Kennedy Library in Boston. With her is Sonny Thelusma of Haiti. A year earlier, Julia had made a six-day trip to Haiti as a goodwill ambassador for UNICEF. (Steven Senne/AP)

Julia reteamed with Liam Neeson for the 1996 epic of Irish freedom fighters, *Michael Collins*. Her role was small, but she liked her character and found Neeson's presence "an enormous comfort factor. It takes a special dynamic to be able to parlay a failed romance...into being pals." (Author's collection)

At the Manhattan biker bar Hogs & Heifers in September 1996, Julia jumped up on the bar, took off her bra under her blouse, and danced suggestively with a barmaid. The photographer said that Julia and the woman exchanged "one big, tongue-to-tongue kiss that lasted between thirty and fifty seconds." Julia's publicist said, "The only person who got a kiss that night was Pat Manocchia." (Gary Miller/*New York Post*/Globe Photos)

Mr. Manocchia, with Julia here at the premiere of *Michael Collins*, is a personal trainer and health-club owner. "What a nice guy," said a friend of Julia's. "And what a bod on that one! He's got that six-pack thing going on. Julia loves that." There were rumors of an engagement, but the romance ended within a year. (Walter Weissman/Globe Photos)

Julia was thrilled to work with Woody Allen in 1996 on *Everyone Says I Love You* but was terrified of singing in the film, which she does in this scene. Woody's editor recalled that during a test session, "the moment she finished singing, she said, 'I just lost the part, didn't I? He'll never want me now. I'm not good enough,' and started to cry." (Author's collection)

My Best Friend's Wedding in 1997 proved a blockbuster for Julia, her first hit in four years. She took delight in her character's scheming ways. Here, she is devastated when her plan to mortify her rival in a karaoke bar backfires. Dermot Mulroney and Cameron Diaz smooch at left. (Author's collection)

Julia looks radiant at the premiere of *The Ice Storm* at the 35th annual New York Film Festival on September 26, 1997. (Henry McGee/Globe Photos)

Julia gives the Harvard Hasty Pudding Club some "satisfaction" as she plays the bass guitar during her appearance to accept the club's Actress of the Year award, February 13, 1997. Earlier, Julia had led a parade in a sea-green 1965 Buick Skylark convertible. She was flanked by two Harvard men in drag, a club tradition. (Elise Amendola/AP)

Julia comforts Mel Gibson in an early scene from *Conspiracy Theory*, 1997. The director never got a handle on whether it was a comedy or a thriller, and his uncertainty shows in the film. The result was akin to a Monty Python spoof of *The X-Files*. (Author's collection)

Julia and her friend Susan Sarandon played rivals for the affections of Susan's children after a divorce in *Stepmom* (1998). In this climactic scene, Susan has made the conciliatory gesture of asking Julia to be present in a family portrait. (Author's collection)

Hugh Grant and Julia in a tense scene from the otherwise light and sparkling romantic comedy *Notting Hill* (1999). Julia denied that the character, the world's biggest movie star, was in any way like her. Grant retorted, "She's either lying or deluding herself." The film was a huge hit. (Author's collection)

Nineteen ninety-nine's *Runaway Bride,* the unofficial sequel to *Pretty Woman,* gave moviegoers another two hours of the Julia Roberts–Richard Gere magic, and this time there was the added pleasure of a wedding finale (pictured). The movie, although not as good as the pair's earlier teaming, proved a hit. (Author's collection)

Julia's new lover, the Latin heartthrob Benjamin Bratt, escorts her to the New York premiere of *Notting Hill,* May 12, 1999. The two had met more than a year earlier and almost immediately fell in love. (Trevor Gillespie/Getty Images)

A week earlier, Julia had appeared on Ben's smash hit TV series, *Law & Order.* She played a scheming killer who tries to seduce his character. (J. Barrett/Globe Photos)

"Romeo and Julia" arrive at the premiere of *Runaway Bride* in Westwood on July 25, 1999. The golden couple seemed headed to the altar, and their engagement was reported several times. A patron at their regular restaurant observed, "Julia is his favorite dish. He rarely looks at the menu, he's so smitten with her." (Mark J. Terrill/AP)

Erin Brockovich tells off her lawyer (Albert Finney) in a scene from the movie that would win Julia an Oscar. Although she inhabited the character of the real-life, trash-talking environmental crusader, she found it hard to get used to scanty, low-cut outfits like this one. (Author's collection)

Two of the most beautiful people in the world—and Hollywood's biggest stars—teamed for the first time in *The Mexican* (2000), an unusual combination of heist caper and character study. Fans of Brad Pitt and Julia were disappointed, though, that they had so few scenes together. This is one of them, and it comes at the very end of the movie. (Author's collection)

Andy Garcia, George Clooney, and Julia in a scene from *Ocean's Eleven,* the 2001 remake of the 1960 movie. Julia's role was small, but she played Clooney's ex-wife and Garcia's girlfriend—relationships that help set the plot in motion. (Author's collection)

Brad and Julia seem to glow at the premiere of *Ocean's Eleven* in Westwood on December 5, 2001. The picture went on to make more money than any Julia Roberts film since *Pretty Woman*, and earned her more than $20 million in profit participation. (Kevork Djansezian/AP)

Julia and her new man, Danny Moder, share a drink while strolling the streets of Malibu, spring 2002. The affair with the married Moder created ill will between Julia and his family. (Fame Pictures)

On June 6, 2002, Julia appeared before the U.S. Congress to plead for increased funding for Rett syndrome, a disease that afflicts mainly baby girls. (D. Cook/AP)

The reason Julia Roberts will never get fat: a scene from *America's Sweethearts* showing her character before she lost sixty pounds. John Cusack (shown here), Catherine Zeta-Jones, and Billy Crystal also starred. The film was Julia's fourth hit in a row. (Author's collection)

Then there was *Full Frontal,* Steven Soderbergh's $2 million experiment shot in eighteen days. With Julia here is Blair Underwood; the scene contains a reference to the Julia/Denzel kissing dilemma in *The Pelican Brief.* The film's box-office take, a dismal $2.5 million, made it Julia's worst commercial failure. (Author's collection)

After a series of cameo appearances and popcorn movies, Julia returned to gravitas with *Mona Lisa Smile* (2003), in which she plays a free-spirited professor who changes her students' lives. Here, she and John Slattery horse around. (Arnaldo Magnani/Getty Images)

Julia, as a CIA operative in George Clooney's film version of Chuck Barris's "unauthorized autobiography" *Confessions of a Dangerous Mind,* realizes that Barris (Sam Rockwell, background) has given her a poison drink she intended for him. The 2002 film won good reviews but never found its audience. (Author's collection)

Three months after their surprise wedding in Taos, New Mexico, Mr. and Mrs. Danny Moder attend a screening of *Punch-Drunk Love* in Manhattan, October 5, 2002. Julia reportedly paid Danny's ex-wife $400,000 to expedite the divorce that left the couple free to marry. (Arnaldo Magnani/Getty Images)

The Moders return to their Gramercy Park apartment after a shopping trip in November 2002. Despite rumors that the marriage was in trouble, the couple celebrated their first anniversary over the Fourth of July holiday, 2003. "I was born to love this man," Julia said. (Mario Magnani/Getty Images)

Lovett and his girlfriend, Elizabeth Vargas, following Lovett's concert at Madison Square Garden. (It was Manocchia and a bodyguard with whom Julia left the club.)

The next day the *News* reported that the *Post* had censored a Liz Smith item that "pooh-poohed" the incident. "You can read the item in *Newsday* [a Long Island newspaper that also carried Smith's column]," the *News* informed its readers. It also turned out that while few would disagree with the description of Hogs & Heifers as "a grungy biker bar," it had, for some reason, become a magnet for celebrities like Harrison Ford, Brad Pitt and Gwyneth Paltrow, Ashley Judd, Drew Barrymore, Daryl Hannah, and Elle McPherson. All five of the women, as had Julia, performed the traditional bra strip and added their own to the eight or nine hundred hanging from two antlered deer heads on the walls.

"This bar is famous for having women dance on the bar," Julia said. "The other thing this place is famous for is that you have to take off your bra if you want to dance. So I took off my bra, but I pulled it down the sleeve without taking off my shirt. I don't strip as a general rule. I've been offered millions to do it, so I'm not going to do it for free in a bar."

As for the alleged lingering tongue kiss between Julia and Margaret Emery, an in-depth investigative analysis of the photographer's contact sheets by this author revealed no lip-lock. After a deep sigh, Nancy Seltzer told Liz Smith, "I was awakened at six A.M. in California with the news of Julia's so-called wild night, and now I have to spend the rest of my day saying, 'No, Julia isn't gay; she was just having fun, out dancing with friends.' . . . Her friends dared her to get up on the bar and dance, and she did. . . . It wasn't any big deal. The only person who got a kiss that night [from Julia] was Pat Manocchia."

Julia addressed the unexpectedly arisen question of her sexual preference matter-of-factly. "I really love women. I really appreciate the efforts and struggles and intelligence of women. You know, there are girls' girls and there are boys' girls, and I think I've always been a girls' girl—regardless of my capacity to appreciate men, to be interested in men, to be captivated by men." When an *Us* writer asked Julia what woman she would most like to have sex with, she answered the question as forthrightly as she would have any other: "Hillary Clinton, because I don't think she's getting her fair share. But really, I don't know, Sophia Loren, maybe. Actually, Julie Christie. She's the one."

Part Five

GOLDEN MEN

*"I don't have to win, because I have
my own golden man at home."*

—Julia, referring to Benjamin Bratt,
when asked how she felt about the
possibility of winning an Oscar

CHAPTER THIRTY-ONE

Julia stood in the bedroom of a suite at the Sherry-Netherland Hotel in New York, where she was conducting a business meeting, and dialed Elaine Goldsmith-Thomas.* She heard the door open. She turned and saw Mel Gibson standing in the doorway with a lamp shade on his head.

"I was trying not to be noticed," Mel later explained. Gibson, his frequent director Richard Donner, and the producer Joel Silver (the *Lethal Weapon* films, *Father's Day*), had come to New York to persuade Julia to costar with Gibson in *Conspiracy Theory*. The story, by Brian Helgeland (whose screenplay for *L.A. Confidential* would win an Oscar in 1998), was about Jerry Fletcher, a paranoid taxi driver with an obsession about conspiracies on everything from fluoride in the water supply to the "Got milk?" campaign. He desires (stalks, actually) the beautiful Alice Sutton, a Justice Department employee, and she becomes reluctantly involved in a dangerous cat-and-mouse game when one of Jerry's theories turns out to be true.

Julia had told Joel Silver that while she was intrigued by the script, she wouldn't be able to do it because the start date was only two weeks after she completed *My Best Friend's Wedding;* she would be too tired to "give 110 percent." Silver, however, is not a man who takes *no* lying down. When he, Donner, and Helgeland were talking Gibson into doing the movie in his office on the Warner lot, Silver threatened to bring in a set carpenter to nail the door shut until the actor said yes. "It was a little frightening," Mel said. "They were looking at me like carnivores." After an hour and a half, "I found the situation so bizarre and funny that I said, 'Yeah, let's go.'"

* Elaine, who caught Julia's bouquet at her wedding to Lyle Lovett, soon thereafter married Daniel Thomas, an attorney.

Next the team set their sights on Julia. She agreed to the meeting "just to talk to them about dates and how long they were going to shoot in New York—things that I, wanting to sleep, felt were important. So I think we're going to have this conversation, but within minutes they're saying, 'Well, are you gonna do it?' Mel was sitting in the corner looking very suave and intimidating, and so finally I realized, *Wow, they're not going to let me leave until I give an answer.* They promised me the moon and said they'd work around my nap time. I said, 'Well, I really need to make a phone call,' and I went into the back room. There was this flock of people back there, all with, like, tape measures and clipboards ready to pounce on me the minute I said yes." When she saw Gibson with the lamp shade on his head, she naturally asked, "What are you doing?"

"I'm a lamp. Ignore me," Mel replied.

"Obviously, he'd been sent to do some reconnaissance work and find out who I'm calling and what I'm saying," Julia said. "So I kicked him out, I made my phone call, and I walked back in and said, 'What the hell?' And Joel Silver said, 'Was that a yes?' and I said 'Yeah.'"

With that, a brass band came out of another room "and just started playing in my face," Julia recalled. The band symbolized Joel Silver's joy at having Mel Gibson and Julia Roberts as the stars of his latest movie (and, obviously, his confidence that Julia would agree). The production designer of *Conspiracy Theory*, Paul Sylbert, recalled Silver telling him the good news about Julia coming on board. "Joel said, 'I can just *smell* the money.'"

Silver would be spending a lot to earn a lot. Mel Gibson's salary of $20 million, Julia's $13 million (another record), the film's villain Patrick Stewart's $5 million, and Richard Donner's $5 million alone amounted to more than the entire budgets of most other films. Silver, in fact, had to fight with Warner Bros. co-CEO Terry Semel to pay Julia what her agent asked for, in light of her recent box-office failures. "I kept saying to Terry, '*My Best Friend's Wedding* is going to be a big hit,'" Silver recalled. "It's such a strange, weird world we live in—I'm selling them on a TriStar movie so they'll put her in ours."

Semel agreed to pay Julia's asking price, but according to Paul Sylbert, "we had to cut this and cut that in order to get enough money out of the budget to afford Julia." The producers managed to whittle the budget down to $70 million.

That Mel Gibson! The lamp shade, Julia soon learned, was merely an appetizer. On the first day of filming in late October, he handed Julia a package, beautifully wrapped with white tissue and purple ribbon, as a welcoming gift. "A present from Mel Gibson," Julia recalled thinking. "I'm the luckiest girl alive." She opened the box, and "years come off my life. I scream, my heart's pounding in my chest—it was a dried rat about this big, with a big long icky tail."

"I thought she'd like it," Mel deadpanned. "I liked it, and you can only buy things for people that you think they'll like. But I wasn't prepared for the vigorous reaction it got. She screamed, and I was, like, thirty feet away by then, outside the van, in New York City with the traffic flying by, and the buildings reverberated with her screams."

A few days later, Mel gave Julia another package, and she warily opened it. "It was another rat," she said. "No, it was the same rat," Mel corrected her. Julia said, "I had hidden it, and he found it and gave it to me again. Then my birthday came up shortly after that, and he gave me another package with a card imploring me to open it, 'Please, please, I promise it won't be a rat.' It was a beautiful, soft leather Filofax billfold." But Julia could give (almost) as well as she got. "This is so childish . . . I came into work one day earlier than he did and snuck into his trailer and I saran-wrapped his toilet bowl."

When Mel went to use the toilet, he apparently wasn't paying much attention. "I was tap-dancing like Gene Kelly in *Singin' in the Rain*. I was thankful it was just number ones."

The hilarity just wouldn't stop. During a scene in which Mel shakes Julia's hand, she felt something squishy in his palm. "Her face was just priceless!" Mel cried gleefully. Julia went on with the scene, apparently unfazed. "I'm acting my little heart out, but I know there's some foreign matter between us. Then he pulls his hand away, and I look down and there's a slew of muck [hairstyling gel, Mel said] and a huge cockroach in the palm of my hand. Of course everyone knew this was going to happen, so the camera is following me everywhere as I go screaming."

In the midst of all this frivolity, Richard Donner was making a tense, expensive thriller. He got what he expected from his stars, who provided total professionalism when required. "I was surprised," Paul Sylbert said of Julia's dedication to the film. "I had worked with her brother on *The Pope of Greenwich Village,* so I knew he was a very serious worker, and I just had a feeling that she might come in on the moviestar side of things with all that smiling. But she was very committed. And Mel is a very committed guy, and she caught the theme, and maybe it was just the combination."

Richard Donner, Sylbert felt, "is a very nice man. [But] he was very confused by the movie—very uncertain about it all the time. And the writer kept saying, 'They're gonna kill it. I know they're gonna kill it'—meaning the producers would get in there and screw it up. And Donner would say, 'I've never been in a situation where I didn't quite know what the movie was.' "

Donner couldn't figure out whether he was making a comedy or a thriller. If it was a thriller, should it be tense and gritty, or more of a "popcorn" movie? Joel Silver's position was never unclear. According to Sylbert, "Joel would say things like, 'Every movie I ever made that made money, a car went through a window'—and he tried to get us to do that. It was originally in the script, but Donner shot it down. That's the way Joel thinks—there are these elements people love in movies, and they'll pay to see them. And you shouldn't disappoint those people. It goes with popcorn—it *is* popcorn."

Mel Gibson faced the difficult task of giving his wacky taxi driver plausibility, and he felt Julia's casting made the job easier. Jerry, he said, "is a stalker, he's obsessed. He dressed like a child molester. And he's a complete lunatic. There's a lot of aspects that are kind of repellent, and I couldn't get how any woman would tolerate hanging around him. . . . I thought the answer lay in what [Julia] did—it needed a mix of strength and vulnerability and compassion. I think Julia did very well. She invited the right seedbed for that kind of work."

Joel Silver agreed that the empathy Julia instantly summons from audiences would be key to the success of *Conspiracy Theory*. "Mel says she's the queen of subtext, because there's always so much going on behind her eyes. She's the eyes and the voice of the audience as she watches this crackpot suffer and discover truth about himself, and, like them, she slowly falls in love with Jerry."

Donner offered an example of what Silver meant. "There was one little scene where Alice comes into the hospital and, knowing Jerry's fears about being killed in his sickbed, spots a body on a gurney in the corridor. For a moment she thinks it's Jerry, and as she pulls back the sheet, someone says the FBI wants to see her. As usual, I had written a series of notes—guilt; my career down the tubes; why does the FBI want to see me?—so if she was floundering, I'd have something to throw at her. But she came in on the first take, did the whole thing, and as she leaned back against the wall, I saw every one of my ideas roll across her eyes. She's a great little actress. . . . She carries around some emotional baggage, like we all do, yet she never lets it shake her."

Some of Julia's "emotional baggage" became clear during the scene in which Alice mourns at Jerry's grave. Thoughts of her father's death likely helped her into a state of racking sobs, and when Donner yelled, "Cut!" Julia couldn't turn off the tears. The director consoled her, and an observer on the set said that "it was obvious to everyone that she was grief-stricken, and her tears were for someone other than Mel's character."

As she had with Denzel Washington, Julia lobbied for more romance between Jerry and Alice. But Donner felt the relationship should be maternal rather than carnal, and the couple merely share a peck or two. "I always wanted more," Julia said. "Put me and Mel in a movie, and people are going to be waiting for a little smoochy." Resigned to not getting any, she added, "I hope people realize the value of the reality we give them, rather than waiting to see us smooch."

When a reporter asked her to compare kissing Woody Allen to kissing Mel Gibson, Julia's diplomacy could have won her an ambassadorship to the UN. "Hmmm. I kissed Woody more. I only did a little smoochy on Mel, the way, you know, I kiss my mama or something. My kiss with Woody was a bit longer. I was able to assess more. And it was very nice. But the Mel smooch was good, you know. They're just different. It's like an apple and an orange. One's a smooch and one was more of a kiss."

Got that?

Once again, the filmmakers of a Julia Roberts picture were at sixes and sevens about how to end it. They filmed two endings and left it to test audiences. Not surprisingly, they went for the ending that Donner felt was "less pure" and Helgeland thought would "kill it," but one that—to the delight of Joel Silver—left open the possibility of a sequel.

Conspiracy Theory wrapped production on February 7, and Julia repaired to her Taos ranch for the rest she had wanted since finishing *My Best Friend's Wedding.* "I think this place represents my lessons learned," she has said. "I think that anybody who came here would say this is a girl who understands and appreciates the quality of life." It would be hard for anyone to argue with that, watching Julia guide Cadillac, one of her seven horses, through a barrel course on the property (she owns a barrel-rodeo championship contender, Two For Perks). She learned barrel-dodging as a child at her grandfather Tom's horse ranch. "When I was a kid, the barrels were steel oil drums," she said. "My knees were always a wreck. But I was proud of them."

Julia's property boasts an awe-inspiring view of New Mexico's Sangre de Cristo Mountains. When she's not riding, she frolics with her six dogs, tills the land, dances to the music of a boom box on her dirt dance floor at the edge of the lower forty. At this point in her life, Julia realized the value of downtime more than ever. "Now I'm able to realize the luxury that all that hard work can provide me. The luxury of just being totally relaxed."

Julia's relationship with Pat Manocchia ended after about a year, apparently on good terms. In the spring of 1997 she met an attractive twenty-eight-year-old aspiring actor, Ross Partridge, at Kevin Spacey's Los Angeles house. Partridge, a bartender in New York, walked Spacey's dogs in Manhattan, and Kevin thought he had the looks and talent to make it in Hollywood. He moved Partridge into his guest house in L.A. When Julia saw him, she asked Spacey, "Who's that gorgeous guy?'

"That's Ross," Spacey replied. "You two would be perfect for each other." Julia agreed, and that night she and Kevin dined at Le Colonial restaurant, where Ross tended bar. "The bar was busy," an observer noted, "but Ross gave Julia his full attention." Julia asked Ross out on a date, and the two hit it off well enough for her to ask him to stay with her in New York while she promoted *My Best Friend's Wedding*.

Ross had been cast in several small roles, including one in *Jurassic Park: The Lost World*, but Julia helped him gain representation from the same manager who handled Chris O'Donnell. "The more time I spend with Julia," Ross told a friend, "the more I fall in love."

An intimate of Ross's who spoke on the condition of anonymity found Julia "such a natural person. I loved her personality, I loved everything about her. She was so sweet and so caring. Ross always referred to her as 'a real bohemian.' But he said that she never got a chance to really be one because of all her managers and handlers telling her what to do—you know, how a movie star should behave. There was a lot of tension around her—she had one foot in and one foot out of the world. I don't think Julia has ever been able to be Julia in her own heart of hearts, you know? She was always at loggerheads about what she wanted to be. [She and Ross] were really devoted to each other, and intellectually they were good for each other. I don't think Julia has been with any man who was equal to her intellectual level except Ross, who's very bright. She needs mental stimulation, and I just don't see that she's gotten that from the men she's been with. Ross is also very down-to-earth and stable, which I'm sure appealed to her." (In fact, several of Julia's beaux were at least her intellectual equal.)

Within a few months, the tabloids had Julia and Ross engaged, but the affair never reached that point. By October, familiar problems had begun to arise. "He was getting absorbed into her world," Ross's intimate said, "and it was very hard for him to continue in his world and do what he wanted to do. He was so fearful about that, and it put pressure on them. Plus, Julia's needy. She has to have constant attention, and she wants her man to be at her side as much as possible. What really did the relationship in was when Ross refused to go to Borneo with her for a documentary on orangutans she planned to host. Ross is a loner—he likes to be alone. And with Julia, there was always an entourage, and he knew it would be even worse if they went on that trip. He didn't want to be in the spotlight. It was not a good match."

Ross was so devastated when Julia broke up with him in the spring of 1998 that he went to stay at his childhood home in Kingston, New York, with his mother, Enid. "He was so depressed over Julia," Mrs. Partridge told one of his friends, "he couldn't get out of bed for days at a time. If he was a horse, I'd have shot him to put him out of his misery."

My Best Friend's Wedding was due for release in June 1997, and Julia was anxious about its reception. She was pretty sure it would be a success, but one never knows; and if it failed to live up to expectations, her status in Hollywood could be seriously jeopardized. She was determined to do everything she could to bolster the movie's box office. In March she attended the Las Vegas ShoWest convention, an assemblage of cinema owners, where the studios try to create excitement about their upcoming features. Julia, of course, was the big attraction, and some in the audience thought her presentation betrayed a tinge of desperation: "My hair is a lovely shade of red [in the movie] and very long and curly the way you guys like it," she said. "For the love of God, please see this movie!"

She needn't have worried. TriStar was so certain they had a hit on their hands that they scheduled its opening for the same day as the guaranteed blockbuster *Batman & Robin*. While that film did come in first over the weekend, *My Best Friend's Wedding* took second place with receipts of $21.6 million, a record for Julia, and ultimately pulled in more than its rival: $126.8 million in the United States (as opposed to $107.2 for *Batman & Robin*) to become Julia's biggest hit since *Pretty Woman*.

My Best Friend's Wedding is a film that announces its desire to be loved under the opening credits, as a girl group made up of a bride and her three attendants sing a campy version of Dusty Springfield's "Wishing and Hoping." It also, much like its heroine, wears its heart on its sleeve. The good news for Julia was that the film's contrivances work well enough to carry viewers along on a wave of good cheer without making them feel manipulated. She gets to smile largely and often, and that was exactly, as many critics had observed, what the public wanted from Julia Roberts. "Hold those career obituaries for Julia Roberts," Rex Reed wrote in *The New York Observer.* "The naysayers will have to lunch on humble pie when they see the 'Pretty Woman' in her new comedy."

For once—and to the filmmakers' credit—a Julia Roberts film did not have a manufactured happy ending. Julianne does not get her man, but she realizes that she has been a selfish boor and lets Kimmy have him.

"One of the things that makes *My Best Friend's Wedding* such a terrific romantic comedy," Mike McGranaghan of *Aisle Seat* wrote, "is that it refuses to play it safe. It would have been so easy to make the character of Kimmy an unlikable shrew so that the audience would easily cheer for Julianne. Instead, the movie deals honestly with the situation—two women both want the same man and only one can have him. I give Julia Roberts credit for playing a character who is not always likable. . . . The film is smart enough to know that a complicated scenario is far more enjoyable than one in which we can see the outcome a mile away."

Conspiracy Theory, on the other hand, left most viewers unsure of their reaction. Richard Donner's uncertainty about the film's tone was evident almost immediately. Was it supposed to be a tense thriller about governmental intrigue or the story of a nutcase in a wool cap who balances bottles on his doorknob so he'll know if someone's trying to get into his apartment—perhaps to steal his milk, which is in a locked Thermos inside a locked refrigerator.

Much of the movie plays like a Monty Python spoof of *The X Files,* with Mel as John Cleese playing Mulder, and Julia as Jamie Lee Curtis playing Scully. Jerry seems too bizarre to be taken seriously by the audience, much less Julia's supposedly intelligent lawyer whose office he haunts, holding guards at bay with a gun when they try to deny him access. Hearing the commotion, she says the one intelligent line the script provides her: "That guy is a restraining order waiting to happen."

But does she get one? *Nooooooo*. She comforts him as he lies on the floor after the guards take him down and tells them to let him in (for the eighth time—he's been counting). He tells her about his latest theory: a conspiracy to kill the president with earthquakes created by NASA from outer space.

Film schools emphasize a concept called "the willing suspension of disbelief." This amazing ability of the human brain allows us to accept that a gorilla can climb the Empire State Building, that Keanu Reeves can kickbox while flying through the air, or that Madonna can act. This power is often sorely tested in motion pictures, especially teen slasher flicks, after which the most-often-asked question is "Why would she do something so stupid as to go back into that house?" The answer, of course, is that if she didn't, the movie would have no plot. So in *Conspiracy Theory* we have the intelligent actress Julia Roberts playing an intelligent character who welcomes into her life a man any sensible New Yorker would swim across the East River to avoid.

If the beginning of the movie put audiences in an unreceptive mood, the labyrinthine mishmash of a plot that ensued hardly improved matters. At one point Julia looks at Mel in horror as he rants about something, and one finds oneself thinking that her expression could reflect her feelings about having agreed to appear in this movie. (Not good for verisimilitude, another film school concept.) To top it all off as nicely as a cherry bomb on a birthday cake, *Conspiracy Theory* tacks on a patently absurd happy ending in which Jerry—who is supposed to be dead after taking three bullets in the chest—and two cronies (whom we thought were bad guys but turn out to be good guys) sing "Can't Take My Eyes Off of You" as they ride in a car and watch Alice ride a horse on her father's farm. At that moment Alice notices Jerry's union pin (which he had given her and she had placed on his grave) pinned to her saddle. She smiles with the joy of knowing that eventually she and Jerry will be together in romantic bliss.

This poppycock gave audiences a joyous finale and set up the possibility of a sequel, but it obliterated any trace of seriousness to which the film ever aspired. "I know Joel had to do with changing the ending," Paul Sylbert said. "Months before we started filming, Joel called me from Paris to say he had heard some old pop tunes that he wanted to get in the picture, because they were gonna be big, and that's how that dopey song they're singing at the end got in the movie. He thought he was gonna sell a lot of records."

Conspiracy Theory was the number one box-office hit the weekend it opened, but in the end Joel Silver didn't smell much money—the movie made $136 million worldwide—a loss because of its production budget of $70 million.* Few blamed Julia for this, and from here on, she would stay at the peak of the box office (except intentionally, when she played small roles in quirky "indie" films) and at the apex of her power as the highest-paid actress in history.

*Because of the high cost of publicizing and promoting potential blockbusters, in order to turn a profit, such films have to earn about twice as much as they cost to make.

CHAPTER THIRTY-TWO

On a chilly November evening in 1997, Julia dined with some friends at Raoul's, an elegant French restaurant on Prince Street in Manhattan's SoHo district. At some point in the meal, she looked up to see a six-foot-two, dark-haired, olive-skinned, Latino man with a chiseled face, smoldering brown eyes, and a body that might have been the model for the Oscar statuette. "It was like something hit me over the head with a bat," she was quoted. (She later denied having said exactly that, but one may safely assume the effect was similar.)

Julia recognized this singularly beautiful specimen of manhood as Benjamin Bratt, the costar of one of her favorite television dramas, *Law & Order*. He was also one of Hollywood's most eligible bachelors. Julia felt so atwitter at the sight of Bratt that, though she was still involved with Ross Partridge, she made the first move. As Bratt recalled it, "The maître d' came over and said, 'Julia Roberts would like to buy you a drink.'" Bratt was skeptical. "It's a restaurant I frequent, and I thought one of my friends was playing a joke on me. I didn't want to impose on her, if that was the case, so I walked out without saying a word to her."

The next day Bratt started to worry that if it *had* been Julia who sent the note, he had not only blown a priceless opportunity but must have seemed dreadfully impolite, which was definitely unlike him. He sent a note to her explaining the situation, but by then Julia was on the West Coast. It took several more months to set a dinner date.

During their first meal, Julia was thrilled to find that Bratt's beauty wasn't only skin-deep. His intelligence, his passions, his elegance, and his old-world courtliness all impressed her deeply. "He's very good-looking," she said, "and his handsomeness pales in comparison to his kindness. That is all a girl could ask for, really." The first time they kissed, Julia recalled, "I wondered if I was smart enough to know that it was the first kiss I'd ever had from the last person that I'll ever choose to kiss every day."

Julia later offered some insight into why she fell in love with Ben Bratt. She told a reporter that while she and her girlfriends were answering a questionnaire about love and sex in a women's magazine, she said to them, "Think about it. Think about the chances that you actually meet somebody who is, superficially anyway, appealing enough to want to eat food with. And then think of the small miracle of having interesting repartee while eating that food. And then imagine that you have a similar sense of humor, and a similar concept of the world but different enough to keep things lively and interesting. Then add to that that you like the way they dress and the way they kiss, and then, God forbid, that you finally get down to it, and oh my God, you make love to this person—and it's fabulous! What are the chances? They are minuscule! *Minuscule!* It's amazing!"

Equally amazing was that yet again Julia and a new paramour shared parallel early-life experiences: Bratt's parents had divorced when he was four, just as Julia's had. Born in San Francisco on December 16, 1963, he was the third of five children of Peter Bratt (the blond English-German six-foot-five son of the Broadway actor George Bratt) and his wife, Eldy, a five-foot-two dark-skinned Peruvian Indian.

Five years after the divorce in 1967 (Ben's mother accused her husband, a sheet-metal worker, of often being drunk and abusive), Eldy took her brood of five to Alcatraz Island, which the American Indian movement had occupied in November 1969 as a protest against their treatment by the U.S. government. At nine, Ben didn't understand the politics, but he liked living there. "It was the ultimate playground. It was cool in the haunted-house sense." Eldy brought the kids back to the mainland a year and a half later and "struggled mightily," Ben said, "with basic needs. It wasn't uncommon for our water or our electricity to be turned off." Once Ben reached his teens, he decided to live with his father. "I think I was rebelling against my mother's free-spiritedness," he said. "I needed a firm hand."

His dad provided that. "He didn't let me get away with shit. In my recollection, he was the booming voice of God." It was Ben's grandfather, who had worked onstage with James Cagney and was a published poet and photographer, who encouraged him to be an actor. Ben resisted at first, because acting didn't "fit my high-school image." He did it "almost on a dare," he said, and "the real prompt was that I would have a great opportunity to make out with the girls behind the curtain."

He studied acting at the University of California at Santa Barbara, from which he was graduated with honors, then continued in a master's program at the American Conservancy Theater. He got his first break when a casting director needed a Latin-looking actor to play a sheriff's deputy in a TV pilot called *Juarez*. The show was never picked up, and neither was another, *Lovers, Partners & Spies*, but the money Bratt earned made an impression. "For a starving kid, for a welfare kid, I was rich. I thought, *This is some racket. Forget the degree, I'm going to stay down here and see what I can do!*"

Just as his career was taking off, Bratt suffered personal heartache when his father, for reasons Bratt won't or can't explain, broke off all communication. "I've made attempts to get in touch with him," Ben said years later, "and he won't respond. It's a deep pain for me."

In 1990, Bratt joined another drama with a short life, NBC's *Nasty Boys*, produced by Dick Wolf, who later created and produced *Law & Order*. Bratt's debut film roles came that same year, first in *Bright Angel* and then in *Chains of Gold*, starring Joey Lawrence and John Travolta, in which Bratt played a vicious drug dealer. He gained wider public attention with two 1994 feature releases: In *The River Wild*, with Meryl Streep, he portrayed a Native American ranger; and in *Clear and Present Danger*, he was the field officer for American soldiers sent by the CIA to infiltrate the Colombian countryside. Soon after, he was cast as the lead in the ABC miniseries *James A. Michener's Texas* (1995). That year was also Bratt's first as the conservative, nattily dressed chick magnet Detective Reynaldo Curtis on *Law & Order*, which made him a very big television star.

In 1997, Ben starred in and helped produce the well-received low-budget feature *Follow Me Home*, directed by his brother Peter and featuring Alfre Woodard and Salma Hayek. His reputation as a committed and elegant actor and "a really nice guy," as Dick Wolf put it, grew in Hollywood. His romances were kept quiet. From 1990 until 1996 he dated documentary filmmaker Monika McClure. After actress Jennifer Esposito made a guest appearance on *Law & Order* in 1996, she and Bratt began a relationship that ended eight months later. The night he saw Julia Roberts in Raoul's restaurant, he was eminently available.

Once her romance with Bratt had flowered, one of Julia's friends described her as "incredibly happy. The relationship is so special that none of us wants to comment." Julia told reporters that they shouldn't ask her about him because she could go on for a week about how wonderful he was. "I like everything about him. We are together and we love each other."

A sentiment to which the patrons at Le Madri, a restaurant near

Bratt's Seventeenth Street apartment in Manhattan, could attest to. Every few weeks the lovebirds dined there, often arriving late and taking a table as far as possible from the crowded bar. Julia usually ordered pasta with truffle sauce. As for Ben—well, a regular patron said, "Julia is his favorite dish. He rarely looks at the menu, he's so smitten with her. They're very lovey-dovey, sitting back there and kissing all night long. They're definitely very much in love."

Not surprisingly, Julia's latest foray into giddy romantic bliss met with journalistic skepticism. *People*'s cover story JULIA AND HER "LAW" MAN noted that "Roberts and long-term relationships are not the safest bets." Another publication put it more cattily: "We've heard all this before." Of course, Julia was aware that many eyes rolled heavenward whenever she waxed poetic about a new beau. "I am happy, but sometimes I have a reluctance to say so because people infer from that that sometimes I wasn't happy, which confirms their 'Well, I knew that all along' kind of attitude. But I am happy, and that applies in increasing amounts."

Despite her long string of failed romances, Julia insisted in 1999 that relationships "are workable. But if you really want it to work, you can't say, 'Well, I'm leaving because I'm sick of the press.' Or 'I can't work if I'm with you!' That's a cop-out. Some men and women can't handle it. I'm here telling you it can be done. There are people with open hearts and minds who can see the difference between a real person and some manufactured image. Not that it's easy. Not that I haven't been in situations where it's like, 'Whew! This is going to be a heartache.'"

Unlike most of her previous relationships, this one never became live-in; Julia and Ben kept their separate Manhattan apartments. And there was, as always, the challenge of maintaining two robust careers. Bratt's kept him in Manhattan, where *Law & Order* is filmed, while Julia's films took her to such locations as London and Maryland during the first two years of their romance.

Still, Bratt called the relationship a "normal" one that they "balance by keeping it real. By keeping those things that are important to you close to you, those simple things that everyone wants: peace, love, security, privacy. You'd be amazed at just how normal our lives together are. We can walk around the streets of New York and San Francisco [where Bratt and Julia often visited his family], and no one really bothers us. We don't walk about with bodyguards, because that in itself creates a scene. We behave as what we are—just human beings."

Indeed, Julia had been able to keep the romance out of the public eye for longer than ever before; the *People* cover story didn't run until January 1999, over a year after she and Bratt met. To explain why the paparazzi didn't dog her the way they had with Kiefer, Jason, and Lyle, Julia said with a laugh, "I think he's just a badass and everybody's scared." Then, more seriously, she added, "But as a team, I think we've done very well dealing with the attention, and I also think that people, for whatever reason, are more respectful than they used to be."

Asked the inevitable question, Julia said that marriage was "not on my wish list. Red Ferragamos would be on my wish list. You don't wish for things like [marriage]—you just let life evolve. I don't see marriage and children as an aspiration. Why is the media so impatient? It's like, 'Marry, have kids, get on with it!' Doesn't anybody understand that life just kind of flows?"

Certainly Julia's career was flowing, as was the cash it generated. The success of *My Best Friend's Wedding* upped her asking price to $17 million, which TriStar executives fell over themselves to pay her for costarring with her friend Susan Sarandon in *Stepmom,* a Bette Davis–style weepie to be directed by Chris Columbus (*Home Alone, Mrs. Doubtfire*). The original script, by Gigi Levangie, concerned Isabel (Julia, who turned thirty during the filming), who becomes involved with a divorced older man, Luke (Ed Harris, who turned forty-seven during filming), and has to deal not only with his children, who resent her, but with his ex-wife, Jackie (Susan, who turned fifty-one during filming). Jackie shares custody and thinks Isabel is such an incompetent surrogate that with her the children are in danger. This battle-of-the-same-sexes becomes more complicated (and moist-eyed) when Jackie is diagnosed with cancer. Finally a rapprochement is reached when Jackie realizes that Isabel truly cares about the children and will be their only mother once Jackie is gone. In a touching final scene, Isabel is taking a family portrait of Jackie, Luke, and the children when Jackie asks her to put the camera on the timer and join them in the photograph.

Julia disliked the title. "*Stepmom* sounds like a booger movie. It makes me think *horrible evil person will slash your throat at night.*" Columbus at first assumed it was a comedy, perhaps thinking of *My Stepmother Is an Alien* (which, in fact, began as a drama about child abuse). Sarandon found the title "misleading," since Isabel doesn't marry Luke during the film's running time. The creative team batted around other possibilities, most of which, Columbus felt, "sounded like bad soap operas. No one could come up with a title that everyone agreed on." So *Stepmom* it was. "I'm trying to find solace in the idea that I've seen some *really* shitty movies with amazing titles," Julia said. "So maybe we'll prove that a shitty title does not a bad movie make."

Stepmom was the first film in which Julia costarred with an actress of equal stature since she herself became a superstar. Some observers expected (and perhaps hoped for) estrogen-fueled fireworks. As Sarandon succinctly put it, "If you make a movie with a male star, everyone assumes you're fucking. If it's a female star, everyone assumes you're fighting."

"Actually," Julia added, "Susan and I were kinda hoping that people would say we *were* fucking. Now, *that's* delicious cocktail-party fodder. But this? *Boring.*"

This was the fact that Roberts and Sarandon, intimate friends since 1992 and co–executive producers of *Stepmom*, got along just fine. They had long hoped to find a film they could make together, but scripts with one strong female lead are rare enough in Hollywood, much less two. Elaine Goldsmith-Thomas happened upon Gigi Levangie's script, and both Julia and Susan were intrigued by the story but found the script "flawed," according to Julia, and "unrealistic," according to Susan. (Levangie couldn't understand the latter criticism: "I *am* a stepmom," she said. "I wrote this from personal experience.")

The interest of Roberts and Sarandon (who had won the 1995 Best Actress Oscar for her role as a nun who counsels a condemned man in *Dead Man Walking*) loosened up more development money from Tri-Star and allowed the producers to hire three writers to take another crack at the script. Finally, Ron Bass, one of the hottest scenarists in Hollywood after the success of *My Best Friend's Wedding*, was hired to do final rewrites. Levangie didn't mind the extra cooks stirring her broth. "Having Ron Bass [hired to rewrite] means your movie gets made," she said.

Julia found the job of executive producer a tad taxing. "Before *Stepmom*, if I read a script *twice* by the time a movie finished shooting, that was pretty impressive. Though I'm *incredibly intrigued* by development, it's not my favorite thing in the world. Every time a new version came in, it was like, 'Oh, *this* again.'"

After Bass's fourth rewrite, Julia and Susan committed to the film, and they chose Columbus to direct. Then, the director said, the *real* rewriting began, and everyone participated. "In the early drafts," Sarandon said, "Julia and I instantly became best buds. When you get sick, you don't start chatting about your ex-husband's sexual prowess." That approach also left little room for the characters to change, a bedrock tenet of storytelling.

Even after filming began in New York in the fall of 1997, the script continued to evolve, helped along by the actors and the director. As Julia recalled, "There were times when I said this scene doesn't seem right, and [Chris Columbus] would say, 'Well, what doesn't seem right?' And I'd say, 'I just want it to be better. I want it to be more forceful. I think she should be more aggressive. Or whatever.' It's easy to make this wish list, but you don't always get what you want. But the next day we'd come into rehearsals, and he'd pass out little scenes for everybody. Pretty amazing."

Don McAlpine, the film's cinematographer, recalled that "Chris had a bit of a challenge, because he was working with two leading ladies who had promoted this project and were executive producers and wanted to contribute a lot to it. Now, this wasn't in a bad way, but it made it difficult because oftentimes he'd have a particular idea expressed in three different ways, including his own, and he had to try and resolve that in the best way he could. I think he wasn't intimidated by that, but rather exploited it and used it to the advantage of the film, which is exactly what he should have done."

"I was a little concerned," Columbus admitted, "that I would have to deal with egos and some of those other issues. I didn't have to deal with any of that. There was no phony quality about Julia, just sort of a meter that we used to call her BS meter. She always knew if something was false or phony, and part of that I think comes from living in New York for so long."

Don McAlpine called *Stepmom* "a fundamentally easy shoot. I try to keep out of politics whenever possible. I'll walk away from a situation I see developing that's not going to benefit me or my job. But this was probably less than most films I've worked on in regard to 'discussions' and problems. Chris Columbus is a very skillful diplomat, which every director has to be, and he worked it out very well." Often cinematographers will hear definite ideas from a film's leading lady about how she should be lit or from which angle she looks best. With two powerhouse female stars relying on him for how they appeared on-screen, McAlpine could have been forgiven some trepidation. But he found neither Julia nor Susan particularly vain.

"Susan was playing a woman dying of cancer," McAlpine recalled, "and that presents a conundrum, because you certainly don't want to paint a death mask from day one, but you do have to progress to that. Susan didn't demand that she be lighted a certain way or look younger or anything like that. But there were times where I felt the script [had moments that] demanded that she look as good as she could and others where obviously she shouldn't."

Although well known for her lack of vanity, Sarandon did say it was difficult to play a dying woman. "Let's put it this way: It's never great for your ego when you finish getting made up and come out looking worse than when you went in."

McAlpine admitted that with his first look at Julia Roberts, he felt "a little disappointment." But he soon found that "her whole strength for me is her ability to switch—she has this wonderful face that looks, I wouldn't say average or ordinary, but certainly not a classically glamorous face. But when she switches to smiling or other qualities that she's got, the effect is very dramatic. That, to me—amongst a lot of other skills she's got—is the reason she's a big star."

McAlpine felt his main job in lighting Julia was to "anticipate a little bit where the story was going to put her in that elevated, switched-on mode, and light her so that the audience would get the best of that. And other times, when she was in a less positive phase, you could use less light or develop a camera angle that wasn't that flattering. I tried to work all the way through the film to exploit this quality that she has." Julia didn't always agree with McAlpine's decisions in this regard, but she never approached him directly with her views. "She never attended the dailies," he recalled, "but her makeup and hair people would always be there. And sometimes I'd hear comments from them that I knew were from her, expressing her concern. Sometimes they were helpful and sometimes they weren't. But I never suffered any direct instructions. Some of the times when I'd let the light diminish on her, they'd comment that she should be more brilliantly lit all through the movie. I'd just tell them what I thought, and it would just go away once I explained what I was doing. It was a dramatic movie, and it had to have variations—it wasn't like a glamorous musical."

Even with her close friendship with Susan Sarandon, Julia found herself insecure about working with such an esteemed actress. "I remember the first big rehearsal day with Susan. Suddenly, I thought, *What if she thinks I suck?* That was the first time it occurred to me, *Gee, this could be bad.*" Sarandon didn't deny that she wasn't sure what working with Julia would be like. "If she'd been unprofessional or unable to deliver, there'd have been a problem." Needless to say, there wasn't. Still, Julia found it strange to have bitch fights with one of her best friends, in character. "It seemed like *banter* when we were revising dialogue. . . . But in rehearsal it quickly became Susan as the aggressor. I think she absolutely enjoyed herself."

Sarandon admitted it: "I kind of never get the chance to be nasty, so I was really happy to be mean and bitchy." Julia was less pleased. She remembered wondering, *Why do I think my life is spinning out of control?* "Then I'd realize, *Oh, it's because I've been shat on all day.* . . . There were times where Susan would walk off the set [after a confrontational scene], and I'd say, 'A little too good. Just a little too good.' She's this great force and this great presence." Still, Susan said, neither of them took any of the nastiness personally. "The fun of being an actor is you don't play yourself."

As Julia's thirtieth birthday approached, she said, "there was this weird buildup, starting with *In Style* magazine, that just infuriated me. I was on their July cover with the cover line JULIA TURNS THIRTY. I was like, 'Yeah, in *October.*' So I started feeling all this pressure. I don't see Brad Pitt with that cover line. But each day that my birthday got closer, I began to feel this bliss to the point where I thought if I had known how great thirty was, I would have done this when I was twenty-five!"

Julia said that at her ripe old age, "I can enjoy taking responsibility for my life now, whereas when you're younger, responsibility is more daunting, and you're sort of afraid of making the wrong choices. There is probably nothing that I can't deal with. Put me in any situation, with any sort of crisis—personal, professional, direct, indirect—that I caused or need to fix, and I can deal with it. I have a full capacity to cope."

At a Six Flags theme park in New Jersey, two hundred of Julia's friends and coworkers threw her a birthday bash on a weekend off from *Stepmom;* they ate chicken fingers and pizzas and showered her with gifts. Jena Malone, the thirteen-year-old actress playing her stepdaughter, gave her a rubber ducky "so she would remember her childhood," and a book of advice on how to survive turning thirty. Against her better judgment, Julia let herself be talked into getting aboard a ride on which "you free-fall and swing back and forth," as Malone put it.

"Everyone wanted her to do it because she was the birthday girl. [But] as she came down, she was crying, she was so scared."

"I was like a pig in mud," Julia said of turning thirty. "I just loved it. . . . My twenties were wonderful, but when I turned thirty, it was maybe the happiest day of my life. I felt so *justified*. I felt like I had earned this great big reward of being thirty." There could be little doubt that Julia Roberts had come into her own after almost ten tumultuous years as a movie star. She still had some insecurities borne of her childhood, but she felt better able to surmount them. She might still blatantly avoid a photographer or a fan, but just as often she could be gracious and accommodating. "She used to have that deer-in-the-headlights quality," Garry Marshall summed it up. "Now she stops the car."

Don McAlpine remembered the experience of working with Julia quite favorably. "You just can't help but love her. She certainly was a person to know. I was thrilled I had a chance to get acquainted with a fine actress and a really fine person. Off the screen, Julia is a lot like she is on the screen, and she exploits it on the screen all the time. . . . I got to know her fairly well, and it was amazing to see this wonderful, beautiful woman being just as delightful off-screen as on-screen."

Julia's friendship with Susan Sarandon had provided her a great deal of support and quickened her maturity, she said. "Have I gone to her house and boo-hooed about my pathetic life? Of course I have. Did she fix it? She probably made me laugh. There are some friends who, when I'm in the midst of a crisis, double the crisis because they are so frenetic in their help. Susan is never like that. There is a calmness to her."

On giving advice, Susan said, "I find that what really helps is when someone asks questions, because I then see things from a different perspective. The fastest way to ruin a friendship is to tell somebody what to do, especially about leaving somebody." On another subject altogether, Susan also neatly summed up Julia's sex appeal. "Julia really tells you with her body language that she is letting life in. I think that's what people read as sexual, an openness that says, 'I can get in trouble here, I can get heartbroken, but I'd still rather try.' Julia has this in person and she has it on the screen, and I think that when people see her, they think, *There's a chance for me!*"

After she completed *Stepmom*, Julia had a chance to spend some quality time with Ben before she left for London to film *Notting Hill*. Prolonged separations and busy filming schedules would remain a perennial problem for the couple. As Julia told Liz Smith in *Good Housekeeping,* "There is a balancing act to it, but that's true for any two people with busy jobs—you know, who's going to get the groceries today or who's going to be able to run this errand. Everybody's balancing something. But you find the time and the space wherever you can." Julia reiterated in this interview that she "definitely wants kids," and said of Benjamin, "When people meet [him], even for only a minute, they get a strong sense of his kindness and his stature as a person. And that's very accurate."

Bratt was equally effusive about Julia, and optimistic about overcoming the unique problem their careers presented. "All I have to say about Julia couldn't possibly fit into two or three sentences. She's an incredible woman." Although he had said before he met Julia that "long-distance relationships do not work," now he felt that he and Julia would cope by traveling. "Wherever she goes, I'll follow, and vice versa. We are together. Despite all the complexity and chaos that appear to exist in her life, she's also a very simple person. Simple in the most beautiful ways: generous, soulful, giving, humorous, loving—all those things that are important to me."

So when would they set the date? Bratt said they had no plans, but added, "We both know we're in it as deep as it gets. And knowing that is enough."

CHAPTER THIRTY-THREE

Whenever the recollection of his first meeting with Julia Roberts intrudes on Hugh Grant's memory, he is sure to feel fresh mortification. It was 1992, in London, and Grant, then thirty-one, a handsome actor with the charming air of someone who has just rolled out of bed, was among those auditioning for the title role in *Shakespeare in Love*. Although he had been acting for twelve years and appeared in fifteen television and feature films, including *Maurice* and *Impromptu* (in which he played Frederic Chopin), his star-making role in *Four Weddings and a Funeral* was still two years away.

As Grant recalled it, "I was a very, very unemployed, pathetic actor at the time. I remember being so intimidated by the fact that [Julia] was in the room that I got myself in a sort of kerfluffle and missed the chair when I sat down. I sat on the *arm* of the chair, then had that very awkward inner debate about whether to say, 'Actually, I've missed the chair,' or to pretend that I was really a slightly quirky sort of character who *always* sits on the arm."

Julia, apparently sensing his nervousness, told him to come back in two weeks for the audition. Neither Julia nor Hugh appeared in the movie, but by 1997, when they met again to discuss *Notting Hill*, Grant was a star (with a dollop of notoriety after his 1995 arrest with a prostitute in a car parked off the Sunset Strip in Los Angeles). This time it was Grant who was already attached to the project, since the *Notting Hill* script had been written by Richard Curtis, author of *Four Weddings and a Funeral*.

Julia had very much enjoyed that film. "I went and saw it with my sister. And I was having a real class-A piece-of-shit kind of day. It couldn't have been worse. I couldn't have *felt* worse, couldn't have *looked* worse, could *not* have wanted less out of life than I did at that moment.

"So we go, and it was as if the Bad Day Man had been sitting on my chest and got up during this movie. So something funny happened, and normally I'd go, 'Ha ha ha.' But that day I was like, 'HAHAHAHAHA!!!' People were turning around, you know? Like, *that* girl's having a good time . . . I would laugh hysterically, and then get quiet and then laugh again. Squealing, screaming like a pig."

Curtis's new script concerned Anna Scott, the most famous actress in the world, and her unlikely romance with William Thacker, a shy travel-bookstore owner she meets while on a press junket in London. Curtis said the idea for the story came to him amid insomnia. "When I was lying sleepless at nights, I would sometimes wonder what it would be like if I just turned up at my friends' house, where I used to have dinner once a week, with the most famous person at that time, be it Madonna or Princess Diana. It all sprang from there. How would my friends react? Who would try to be cool? How would you get through dinner? What would they say to you afterwards? That was the starting point, the idea of a very normal person going out with an unbelievably famous person and how that impinges on their lives."

Although Curtis has said he did not model Anna Scott after Julia but rather a combination of Grace Kelly and Audrey Hepburn, Julia was the first choice of everyone on the film: Grant, Curtis, and the film's director, Roger Michell (*The Buddha of Suburbia*). As Ned Zeman wrote in *Vanity Fair*, "Who better to play the world's most mythic, inaccessible, and intimidating star than the world's most mythic, inaccessible, and intimidating star?"

Michell doubted they had much of a chance to land Julia, especially since the film's $38 million budget could not support her asking price of $17 million. But they sent the script to her anyway and were much encouraged when Elaine Goldsmith-Thomas told them it was the best romantic comedy she had ever read. Initially Julia was excited to read the script. It had Elaine's strong recommendation and was written by Curtis, who in addition to *Four Weddings* had penned some of the funniest British television series—*Blackadder, The Vicar of Dibley, Mr. Bean,* and *Spitting Image* among them. But when Elaine gave Julia a three-sentence summary of the characters and plot, her reaction was "Ugh. Why do I want to play some big movie star? It just sounded boring." Elaine pressed her to read it, and "Within the first few pages, from that moment when they first meet in the bookshop, and then when they bump into each other in the street, I was right in there. Richard Curtis is my hero with words."

Though the script sparkled with wit, Julia wouldn't commit until she'd met with Curtis, Michell, and their producer, Duncan Kenworthy. All three men were reduced to nervous schoolboys by the prospect of meeting La Roberts at the Four Seasons Hotel in New York on July 31, 1997. "The three of us had one room," Curtis recalled, "and we all went off—me to the bathroom, Duncan to the lobby, and Roger in the bedroom. We emerged ten minutes later wearing suits for the first time *ever*. It was an extraordinary experience to see the real Julia Roberts waiting at the dining room table. She was ten years younger than some of us—twenty years younger than one of us—and yet so obviously in charge that it was alarming."

Although the men thought the meeting had gone well, Julia remained noncommittal. She did invite them to attend her appearance on *The Late Show with David Letterman* that evening. After the taping, Julia gave Michell a kiss and said, "Good luck with your film." Michell was sure she was actually saying, "Don't call me, I'll call you."

For Curtis, the drive back to the hotel was "the worst ten minutes of my life. I just sat in the back of the car, winded and horrified, and finally said, 'You guys *did* hear what she said?' " But two days later, Julia committed to the project, accepting far less than her usual fee, which she herself has called "an absurd salary." She would like, she said, "to be known as someone who just wants to do things that are interesting and appealing and quality. If the people making that don't have money, I would want them to know that it's not a given. But if it's the studio asking me to do something I think is good and they've got a bazillion dollars, well, they have to pay me. Because that's the way the market works. It has nothing to do with me as a person."

Filming began in London's Notting Hill neighborhood (where Curtis lives) on April 17, 1998. Grant said he was "tense as a toad," his embarrassment over the first meeting with Julia unabated. "I think the emotion you have when you first meet someone tends to linger with you. I was all ready to be scared, and I must say, the fear never quite left me." Nor did it leave the rest of the creative team. When Michell thought Julia was wearing too much makeup, he dreaded telling her and barely managed to whisper, "Ummm . . . would you mind terribly washing your face?"

On the other end of the equation, many American actors are intimidated by British actors, who are generally wet-nursed on Shakespeare and apprentice, as Patrick Stewart has put it, "with years of stage work before ever seeing a camera." Julia was no exception. She was further daunted by the almost preternatural connection between Grant and

Curtis. As Kenworthy put it, "Hugh is one of the only actors who can speak Richard's lines perfectly, like an expression of Richard's inner rhythms." Michell added, "Hugh does Richard better than anyone else, and Richard writes Hugh better than anyone else. I think that's a writer/actor marriage made in heaven."

Julia was also impressed by the cast of British character actors assembled to play Thacker's friends, including the wonderful Emma Chambers, who played Honey and is so funny as the zany Alice Tinker in *The Vicar of Dibley*. "I am just in awe of the performances in this movie," Julia said.

Julia may have added to the trepidation her coworkers felt by arriving in London with her weight-training equipment, a treadmill, a hairstylist, a makeup artist, and a personal dresser. But the *Notting Hill* cast and crew found out the same thing her other colleagues had. "She was not superstar-ish," said the film's hair and makeup designer, Jenny Shircore, who had also worked with Julia on *Mary Reilly*. "Julia talks to any- and everybody. She's interested in our lives."

Julia did sense one problem with her costar's awe of her. "I know he's a lovely guy, but he looked on me as a diva and couldn't think of me as an actress. But perhaps that tension contributed to the tone of the film." As filming progressed and they got to know each other, Julia and Grant found themselves in a mutual-admiration society. "Working with Hugh was fun," she said. "We had a great sense of fun together, a lot of banter, and an immediate rapport. From the first day of rehearsal, I just thought, *We're going to get along quite easily*—and it was true." Grant, for his part, found Julia "silly and teasable, and I couldn't have liked her more."

Julia found out about a little-known quirk of Grant's during a kissing scene. "Even if I don't really like the actress," Grant explained, "I always get a stirring. In the past I've had to ask the director to hang on for take three because I have to wait for this stirring to subside. There was one scene where I had to walk the room and wait for everything to settle down. It can be very embarrassing." A source on the set said, "Julia couldn't believe what was happening during their love scene. It was very embarrassing for her and doubly so for Hugh."

Despite the friendliness and the "stirrings," Grant later took Julia to task for her insistence that she and Anna Scott had nothing—*nothing, I tell you!*—in common. "She's either deluding herself or lying," Grant said rather bluntly in an interview. "There were times in this movie when she'd deliver a speech I felt was coming from somewhere deep in her soul." It's undeniable that Anna says certain things in the movie that make one think of Julia, but in most cases she's talking about the problems that any superstar faces.

Assuming her quotes were accurately reported, Julia has contradicted herself on this subject. A *Vanity Fair* profile said that she worried after reading the script that everyone would think she was just playing herself. Then she came up with the rationale, "Well, since everyone will think it's about me, I'll just take a little European vacation and *be me* for three months."

Later, she said, "I don't know whether this is stupidity or naïveté, but it never occurred to me that people would think I was playing myself. But I've had seventy-five people in two days say, 'Are you playing yourself? What are the similarities?' And I'm stunned. I mean, first of all, how boring to play yourself, and second of all, what hubris to think I'm that interesting that I should be the main component as the female lead in a movie." Perhaps it was neither stupidity nor naïveté but modesty. Whether it should be thought of as genuine or false depends on one's perceptions of Julia.

Adding to the probability that the thought did occur to Julia is another quote from *Vanity Fair* about the filming: "I thought I was going into familiar territory, but ended up doing twice the effort because I wasn't prepared for effort." In the final analysis, Julia Roberts and Anna Scott have a lot in common—and plenty that distinguishes them from each other. The differences gave Julia some trouble, especially the plot point that Anna is hiding out from the press after tabloids publish nude pictures of her taken years earlier. "I didn't agree with what she did," Julia said. "Didn't agree with how she got into this mess—I would never have been in that situation. . . . Didn't agree with *any* of that stuff."

Whenever Julia spoke to the director about her sense of discomfort with Anna's actions or motivations, Michell would reply, "Anna Scott— *different person.*" Julia also thought early on that her character should be funnier, especially since she was surrounded by all those droll Brits. "Julia's part *was* underwritten at first," producer Kenworthy admitted. (Michell said there were ten drafts of the script before shooting began.) In the final version, Julia doesn't have as many funny lines as the others, but the ones she does have are priceless—and often cleverly tied in some way to Julia's own past.

In one of the movie's many hilarious scenes, Anna, eating ice cream, tells William that she has provisions in her contract about nudity. (As does Julia.) "You have a stunt bottom?"* William asks her. When she says yes, he asks, "Are there people who are tempted to go for better bottoms than their own?" Anna replies, "Yeah, I mean, I would . . ."

The morning after Anna and William sleep together, Anna repeats the famous line Rita Hayworth said after starring as the smoldering temptress in the 1946 film *Gilda:* "Men go to bed with Gilda, but they wake up with me." Julia must have worried that audiences would hear "Men go to bed with Pretty Woman, but they wake up with me."

"I hate to say anything negative about what Richard wrote," she said, "but I *hated* that line. To me, it was nails on a chalkboard. I don't really believe *any* of that." Julia lost the argument, however, and the line remained in the film.

Most of the cast and crew found the Anna–Julia conundrum "surreal," to use both Grant's and his character's term. After watching dailies of the film's first shot of Julia, in which Anna Scott arrives at a glamorous Hollywood premiere, smiling broadly, as Elvis Costello croons "She," Curtis recalled, "We said, 'Fuck! *That's* who we're dealing with.' It's very easy when you're dealing with a very reasonable, lovely, relaxed, thirty-year-old woman to forget that she's also Julia Roberts— who, for ten years beforehand, you could never have gotten within a hundred yards of. It was a freakish moment when we realized that the woman we were dealing with was actually both those things: this relaxed person and this untouchable, iconic object of which there are so many photographs."

Hundreds of paparazzi who beleaguered the *Notting Hill* locations hoped to add to that treasure trove. When Ben Bratt came to London to see Julia during a break in *Law & Order* filming, the f-stop brigade went into overdrive, which only added to the bizarre nature of the entire exercise.

When Ben arrived in London for another weekend visit about a month later, Julia surprised him by hiring a car to take them to Heathrow Airport. They boarded a private jet for the romantic isle of Capri in the Mediterranean Sea, where Julia reportedly spent $150,000 to lease a private boat. Friends said that Ben had taken to calling Julia "Scattercash" and that he said he'd never seen a woman spend money like she did.

*Grant saying this line with his British intonation is worth the price of admission.

A photographer caught them lunching at an outdoor café, Julia wearing a fisherman's cap and checking her guide to Naples, Ben feeding her something across the table, and the two of them kissing over a bottle of mineral water. The Australian magazine *Woman's Day* published the photos along with the headline JULIA GOES FROM AISLE TO ISLE. The article began, "*Belissima!* That's the only word to describe Julia Roberts in the company of her new husband, *Law & Order* star Benjamin Bratt, as they honeymooned on the beautiful Italian island of Capri."

Wrongissima! Happily, the American press checked out the rumors and ascertained they were incorrect before similarly placing their feet in their mouths.

A key scene in *Notting Hill*—and the notion that inspired Richard Curtis to write the script—is a birthday dinner for William's sister, to which he brings Anna without telling anyone in advance. It's extremely funny: William's sister freaks out; other guests are cool; others awkwardly pretend to be cool; and one of them genuinely has no idea who Anna Scott is. "What do you do?" he asks her. "I'm an actress," she replies, and the guest says he imagines the work is hard and the wages "a scandal."

"They can be."

He then asks her what sort of acting she does.

"Films, mainly."

"Oh, splendid. Oh, well done! How's the pay in movies? I mean, the last film you did, what did you get paid?"

"Fifteen million dollars."

He looks at her, stricken. "Right. So that's fairly good, then."

In a marvelous example of life imitating art imitating life, *Marie Claire* magazine asked Julia to re-create this scene at an actual dinner party in Manhattan shortly before *Notting Hill* opened. They found a thirty-two-year-old unmarried bookstore clerk, Sasha Jarolim, who was told only that the magazine would like him to invite six friends for dinner and they would provide him with a date. When Julia showed up, early as planned, Sasha's recognition was "overwhelming and instantaneous.... [But] Sasha is surprisingly composed—that is, until she smiles. . . . Sasha visibly melts. 'I was dumbfounded. All I could think about was *Move your tongue, don't make a jackass out of yourself, and act as cool as possible.*'"

Julia admitted feeling some anxiety herself, which, the magazine noted, revealed itself in her demeanor. "She has difficulty maintaining eye contact with Sasha. Sitting on the opposite couch, her body seems to be at odds with itself. While the upper torso is stiff and practically static, her lower extremities are in constant motion, the elegant legs endlessly crossing and recrossing themselves."

The first guest, Brian, a math professor, did a comical double take when introduced to Julia. She asked him what kind of research he was working on. "Differential equations," he replied. "That was my second guess," said Julia with a straight face. The next guests, Denis and his girlfriend, Alida, reacted differently. Denis, usually a cool character, stuttered when he met The Star. "When people meet me," Julia said, "the nervousness manifests itself in a thousand different ways. Some shake my hand too long, some stammer, others tremble. Denis was cute. He did a little bit of each." Alida remained relatively levelheaded but couldn't resist asking Julia for her autograph, which she insisted was for her sister.

Megan, like Alida, played it cool. She and the others assumed that Julia and Sasha were a new item. Megan thought, "*Wow—things like this can really happen in New York!* I began daydreaming about how this relationship was going to work, how Sasha was going to deal with the paparazzi, the changes to his lifestyle."

Denis thought his friend "had a shot" at Julia, too. "I mean, he does kind of look like Lyle Lovett in a weird way—minus the hair, of course." (The name Ben Bratt doesn't seem to have come up during the evening.)

While the guests grew more comfortable with their celebrated dinner companion, Julia remained surprisingly nervous. As the hors d'oeuvres were served, she excused herself and went into a bedroom. She later told the magazine editors that she had stood in the bedroom and muttered to herself, "What am I doing? What am I supposed to be doing?" As if preparing for an acting exercise, she told herself, "It's your basic Julia-Roberts-in-a-roomful-of-strangers situation. It's a bizarre paradox. I feel like I should be driving the scene in some way. . . . But at the same time I want to be natural and somewhat inconspicuous."

Inconspicuous? The magazine reported that "every time she passes one of the guests, they instantly track her out of the corner of their eye, as if she were a heat-seeking missile." But in a comical moment straight out of Curtis's script, one guest, Suzanne, whom the magazine described as "laconic and cerebral," turned to Julia at dinner and asked, "And what do you do for a living?" Mouths dropped, and Julia, herself taken aback, replied, "I'm an actress."

"Anything I might have seen?"

"How about *Pretty Woman*?"

"It suddenly registers," the magazine reported. "Suzanne literally wilts. 'She's not very good with faces,' her fiancé, Jim, offers sheepishly. 'Please don't take it personally.' Julia manages a smile. The table erupts in laughter." (Later, Julia said that she was impressed with Suzanne's lack of recognition "because I thought, *Well, this is a woman with a really interesting life, and she must read a lot of really great books and have such an interesting job that she doesn't spend time going to the movies and reading magazines and things of that nature,* so I was quite fascinated by her.")

As the dinner drew to a close, Julia tapped her wineglass and made an announcement: "I'd like to thank you all for participating tonight in the reenactment of a scene from my new movie—*Notting Hill.*" After Julia left, the guests expressed reactions ranging from disappointment at the charade, to pure delight—even if the experience had been in essence a publicity stunt—to skepticism that they had experienced the *real* Julia Roberts. As Denis put it, "You're left with: Was that really her or was she acting? I'd like to think she was genuine." Julia, through the magazine, assured them that they had seen the real her.

During an interview to publicize *Notting Hill,* Julia mentioned that she didn't have a date for the London premiere. Benjamin was in Hollywood filming the romantic comedy *The Next Best Thing,* with Madonna and Rupert Everett. It may have been better that he wasn't there.

To borrow a phrase from Richard Burton, who was describing his extramarital affair with Elizabeth Taylor in 1962, Julia's appearance at the premiere created *Le Scandale.* News of the matter barely rippled across the Atlantic to America, but the British public and press were whirled into such a tizzy by the sight of Julia that night that a 1999 biography of her published in the United Kingdom *began* with the incident, as though it represented the defining event in her life. "I couldn't believe the drama it created," she said.

What had Julia done? Stripped naked before hundreds of fans? Had mad, passionate, unruly sex with Hugh Grant on the red carpet? No, nothing so prosaic. She waved to the crowd. Now, normally this is not a gesture that would generate an undue amount of excitement. What set this wave apart from all the others throughout history was what it revealed: Julia had not shaved her armpits!

Sacre bleu! The British press went into a swivet (they're excitable), running banner headlines like DO YOU DARE TO BARE YOUR HAIR? and ARMS AND THE WOMAN. The Fleet Street papers dubbed the unshaven patch "the black forest" and redubbed Julia "Pretty Hairy Woman." Others were positively shaken by the spectacle. The *Sun* columnist

Caprice wrote, "Yuk, yuk, yuk. I shuddered when I saw Julia Roberts's hairy armpits." The *Sun* set up a toll-free hotline for readers to vote up or down on Julia's lack of axillary tonsure, and radio shows ran polls asking whether respondents approved of unshaven armpits in their romantic partners. (In one, 63 percent said no.) The *Evening Standard* noted that Julia seemed oddly out of step with her countrymen because "Yanks are fanatical about personal hygiene." The implication, of course, was that Julia wasn't simply unshaven but unclean.

Adding to the juiciness of the story—to which even the sedate *Sunday Times* devoted an inordinate number of column inches—was the supposed feud between Julia and Hugh Grant's longtime girlfriend, Elizabeth Hurley, the gorgeous actress and Estée Lauder model. The *Times* reported that the two women refused to speak to each other at the premiere. Elizabeth had arrived clad—barely—in a Gianni Versace gown of see-through Lycra slit to the thigh, looking as though she had, proverbially, been sewn into it. By contrast, Julia had worn a sleeveless red dress dotted with silver sequins that one catty fashion writer called "frumpy." The *Times* columnist India Knight provided her own unique take on the matter: "Julia Roberts comes up with the most divinely comical idea ever: Liz Hurley, Miss Ubiquity herself, upstaged by an armpit."

"From the English press, you would have thought I had chinchilla under there," an offended Julia said. "I thought that I looked pretty. I had on a pretty dress and I felt pretty. Forget that armpit thing, hon. And Elizabeth Hurley has a great figure and she always wears beautiful dresses; not dresses that I would pick, dresses that look really pretty on her. But you know what? We're apples and oranges. You can't say one is better than the next. So for them to put us on the cover and have it be 'Gorgeous Liz, Dowdy Julia,' that's not nice." Then she got in a final dig at Hurley. "Well, you can't read a newspaper through my dresses, anyway—I guess that's a strike against me."

Julia didn't think Kusasi, a four-hundred-pound male orangutan who makes his home in the Bornean jungle, would be much of a threat to her. "To get close to him didn't seem like a risk," she said, "because he usually ignores people. Everyone assumed he would ignore me. But he didn't."

Instead, Kusasi grabbed her. Badly frightened, Julia stroked the beast's arm to calm him as crew members tried to pry his hands away.

But his prehensile feet held on to Julia, and then, terrifyingly, he grabbed her neck. One of the documentarians, Nigel Cole, frantically pulled at Kusasi's grip, and Julia was able to scramble free. When Julia thanked Cole for potentially saving her life, he replied, "I'd like to think I rescued you, but he let you go."

"I don't think he meant any harm," Julia said. "He was just curious. And he has the strength of ten men in one finger, so it got a little dodgy."

Julia's visit to Borneo (which had ruptured her relationship with Ross Partridge) was part of the British documentary series *In the Wild*, in which celebrities interact with wildlife (the real kind). Previous participants had been Robin Williams with dolphins, Anthony Hopkins with lions, Debra Winger with pandas, and Goldie Hawn with Indian elephants. It was Hawn, a friend of Julia's, who persuaded her to take part in the series. After a year of trying to arrange the timing, Julia, three of her friends, and a six-person crew traveled (without Ben Bratt) to Indonesia in August 1998, just after filming wrapped on *Notting Hill*. On foot and by primitive boats called *klotoks,* the Roberts entourage traveled to Camp Leakey, a research center that rescues orphaned orangutans, an endangered species.

The celebrity guests choose the animal they want to interact with, and Julia picked orangutans because "I'm fascinated by primates, by the similarities and connections to man. But orangutans are not social, like chimps and gorillas. They spend most of their lives alone. There is an enlightenment that comes from their solitary lifestyle that I find incredibly intriguing." The show's producer, Andrew Jackson, said that the host of each episode "sets the tone, and Julia wanted to go to the extreme on everything." She insisted on sleeping in the forest so she could remain close to the orangutans. She gingerly walked across rickety logs perched over swamps, climbed ladders to treetop platforms, and braved insects, spiders, and snakes.

With the exception of the scary encounter with Kusasi, the orangutans and Julia got along famously. The first one she encountered jumped out of a tree and began playing with her hair. A three-month-old named Hughie held on to her for the better part of a day, and she bottle-fed him. "He's really sweet. He gave me a nice little love bite on my ear." (Julia had proved her appeal to higher primates around the world, so why shouldn't some of the lower ones follow suit?)

As Julia washed her clothes in the Sekonyer River, a female named Unyuk came up beside her, grabbed some soap and a shirt, and started scrubbing, too. When Unyuk's teenage son wanted to join in, his mother handed him the bar, but not before she scraped off enough to continue. "I thought, *This is a good mommy*," Julia said. "This is a sharer and a giver. When I'm a mom, I hope I remember this incident."

In the finished documentary, which aired on PBS in the United States on May 20, 1999,* Julia's encounter with Kusasi was truncated, in Julia's words, "to keep people on the friendly side of liking orangutans." But she admitted that "my head was spinning, and my heart—my microphone was in my bra—you can hear my heart start going faster and faster. Seeing it on film a year later made me laugh, because my first reaction was to pat his arm, like, 'Oh, it's okay.' You can't imagine how big he is unless you're really in front of him. Next to him, I look like I belong on a key chain. And there I was, trying to reassure him."

Julia wasn't entirely happy with Nigel Cole's decision not to show viewers the entire encounter, because "my level of being rattled in the post-encounter interview seems a little extreme. I don't want people to think I'm wimpy. I appear completely free. But in actuality, one of Kusasi's feet is holding on to my wrist below the frame."

Julia said that the decision to take part in the series was her contribution toward bringing attention to the plight of an endangered species. "I possess the knowledge that what I do provides me with a forum. I've been doing this for a dozen years."

Reviews of *Notting Hill* were mostly ecstatic. The "surprising sting" Julia showed in the film didn't please every critic. *Newsweek*'s Jeff Giles felt that Anna "becomes increasingly less lovable as we get to know her better. . . . Roberts is so convincingly uppity that you wouldn't wish her on anybody." (This is not really true. Julia as Anna Scott is endearing for most of the film; it is only when, under extreme stress and the belief that William has betrayed her, Anna reverts to movie-star imperiousness and begins to lose the audience's sympathy. But Anna and Julia win us back before the final credits roll.)

Notting Hill proved a smashing success, Julia's fourth in a row. It

*Almost exactly one year earlier, Julia had appeared on the final episode of *Murphy Brown*. The seed was sown in 1990, after she went up to the show's creator, Diane English, and one of its stars, Joe Regalbutto, in a restaurant to say how much she enjoyed the program. "It made Joe's day," English said. "In fact, it made his year." It took a while, but Julia finally guested on the show. In the episode, she flirts with Regalbutto's character, and they share a kiss. "He was counting the days until Julia showed up," English said.

grossed $363.1 million worldwide, evolving from what the creative team originally thought would be a "small picture" into a blockbuster. Any doubts about the magnitude or staying power of Julia's stardom had now evaporated. As long as a film didn't stifle the natural Roberts attributes that audiences loved, ticket buyers would flock to see it, and producers would "smell the money." It wouldn't be long before Julia's "absurd salary" would get even higher as she joined the exclusive, formerly all-male $20 million-a-picture club.

Longtime Julia watchers observed that when it came to her fashion sense, she had a chameleon-like quality: She would take on the style of her paramour of the moment. With Kiefer and Jason, she wore grubby jeans, "baby-doll dresses three sizes too big for me," had a tattoo on her shoulder and five rings through her earlobe, carried a handbag one writer described as looking like "a steamer trunk," and carried an eyeball key chain. After she married Lyle Lovett, she frequently wore shapeless cotton dresses in small prints. She hadn't exactly become his "little gal in calico," but she approached it.

Now, paired with the elegant Bratt, who looks better in a suit and topcoat than just about anyone, Julia developed an elegance that surprised the public as much as it suited her. While she was still more comfortable in jeans or sweatpants at home or walking the streets of Manhattan, she began to appear at parties and premieres in stunning creations by the world's top designers. "I'm a late-blooming clothes fanatic," she admitted. "Most girls go through this at sixteen or eighteen. I've never had to get dressed for work. I could show up for shoots in pajamas and no one would care. . . . I'm beginning to realize you can be comfortable, stylish, and—dare I say—pull off a whole sexy thing. . . . I'm in a phase where style is becoming a fun issue, a sporting event."

Julia now went for the gold. In March 2000 she appeared on the cover of *Harper's Bazaar* wearing a grape-colored silk and cashmere sweater by Prada, diamond and platinum earrings by Cathy Waterman, her hair lightened and straightened by Serge Normant. A year later, she graced the cover of *In Style* wearing a slinky, backless Vera Wang dress, her hair long and darker than it had been for some time. Inside, she posed in the hotels, bars, streets, and canals of Venice in a stunning array of outfits: a cream-colored cardigan by Malo, over a halter and skirt by Dolce & Gabbana; a short dress by Alberta Ferretti and tweed coat by Valentino; a black-and-white silk dress with long flared sleeves by Ferretti; a gray tailored-to-her-body trouser suit by Armani (she wore the jacket over her bare breasts, finally achieving the sexiness with the look that Bob McGowan had spoken of early in her career); and, most gorgeously, while riding in a gondola, a pale yellow bustier and skirt by Thierry Mugler topped with an abalone choker by Pippa Small.

In four months, Julia showed up once again on the cover of *Harper's Bazaar*, looking more elegant than ever in a skintight silk strapless black gown by Ralph Lauren, her hair dyed black (Daisy Araujo finds style). Inside, she modeled a silk georgette dress by Marc Jacobs ($1,200); a "seductive mini" matte jersey dress in black by Calvin Klein ($800); a "girlish" silk-jersey-blend black dress with white collar and cuffs by Marc Jacobs ($1,200); and the Ralph Lauren black silk strapless dress ($1,995), long leather gloves, and satin sling backs.

In a veritable blitz, this was a side of Julia the public had not seen since *Pretty Woman* (and the brief scenes in *Notting Hill* during which a glammed-out Anna Scott arrives at premieres). If there had been any doubt, it was erased: Julia Roberts had evolved from a gangly, awkward, badly dressed starlet into a superstar clotheshorse whom modeling agencies would kill to represent. She might still be "coltish," but she was now a filly Diana Vreeland would have been proud of.

CHAPTER THIRTY-FOUR

In the eight years since *Pretty Woman*, Richard Gere and Julia had been asked constantly if and when they would attempt a sequel. The stars and their director, Garry Marshall, were indeed interested in re-creating the magic they had spun in 1990, but finding a suitable concept proved daunting. "There was talk for a while of doing *Pretty Woman 2* [and a script was written], but that, to me, was a bad idea," Julia said. "Making a continuation of a movie that people are so attached to—you're totally setting yourself up for failure."

So the hope turned to finding a script that would reunite the stars in a different story, but one equally appealing, comic, and romantic. Many scripts failed to pass muster, but while Julia was in London, Gere sent her one by Josann McGibbon and Sara Parriott that he thought might work: a remake of a 1930 Mary Astor film called *Runaway Bride*. In the new version, Ike Graham, a cynical *USA Today* reporter, writes a column mocking Maggie Carpenter, a woman in a small Maryland town who has fled from four of her wedding ceremonies. Maggie writes to the newspaper listing a number of errors in the piece and threatens to sue, so Ike travels to Maryland to research the story himself. He learns about Maggie's zany and aborted nuptials and then—of course—falls for her.

Julia was rather surprised to find she liked the script Gere sent, because "we have incredibly dissimilar tastes, as our careers would attest. So it [had] never really seemed as though anything would come to pass."

But she wasn't entirely sure. Immersed as she was in the dry English wit of Richard Curtis, this small-town-America-tale seemed a tad prosaic. "So I called my boyfriend and said, 'I think it's really funny, but I can't tell.' And he could appreciate by the tone of my voice how frenetic I was. So I sent it to him Johnny-on-the-spot, and he read it just as quickly. And he called me up and said, 'This is the no-brainer of all time.' "

As usual, after Julia got involved, things fell quickly into place. Garry Marshall signed on to direct; Hector Elizondo joined his earlier cohorts to appear in his eleventh Marshall film: Joan Cusack would play one of the runaway gal's sardonic friends.

When the project was announced, some journalists tittered. As *Premiere* put it, "*Runaway Bride* could be considered a gutsy choice for an actress who has had two broken engagements and a divorce." As Julia had done with suggestions of similarities between her and Anna Scott, she dismissed any art-imitating-Julia aspects to this movie. "Look, *Runaway Bride* is a great title, incredibly evocative, but it doesn't attach to my life at all," she (unconvincingly) protested.

But, as is her wont, Julia later said something revealing about Maggie—and herself. "I think she's a little extreme, but I think that people need to be allowed to make their mistakes, because we're nothing without some of our mistakes, and I think it's very taxing to have to be judged for doing what everybody in this world does, which is make a bad choice and then make the best of it. Everybody does that, so why should she be judged for it, or why should I be judged for it?"

Julia's salary—$17 million—predictably stirred up resentment in some quarters. Liz Braun sniped in the *Toronto Sun*, "Roberts's income for the film surpasses anything earned by Demi Moore or Jodie Foster or Babs or Meryl or anybody, and why not? Look at the great pleasure her various hairstyles have given the movie-going public for years. Is there anyone coming up who might one day earn more than Julia? How about Cameron Diaz? Anyone who might surpass her in thespian talent? How about Tori Spelling? Pam Anderson? A rubber doorstop?"

Meooooow.

Filming began on location in Maryland in the fall of 1998. Garry Marshall has said that he was mightily impressed with how much Julia had matured, as a person and as an actress, and intimated that she had been much more like Margaret in 1990 than she was now. "She's got it much more together, as they say, in her craft and in her life. Back then, she was with various boyfriends, breaking up, starting over, all of that. But now she has a regular fella, you know. I think she likes that boy. I mean, sometimes he comes to Baltimore just to say hello. That, to me, says something. Where are you gonna find a guy who does that?" Both Gere and Roberts, Marshall added, "are more mellow now." Hector Elizondo said, "Life has carved them up and created character." Marshall joked that Gere had changed in another way as well: "Richard looks great, but his hair is now so white, I told Julia that if she stood close enough to him, I wouldn't have to light her."

To Richard, Julia had "changed a great deal. . . . Considering what she's lived through, I think Julia has come out pretty healthy. I see her as better than ever, creatively and personally." Julia said she noticed that "Richard and Garry sort of stayed the same and I got taller and thinner." But she felt the biggest difference in herself was confidence. "When we did *Pretty Woman,* I would have a bunch of ideas, and I would maybe once in a while express one, 'cause I was kind of afraid to look stupid. Now I'll say anything, and it can be really stupid, but I'll still share it, and maybe someone can make something better of it or maybe it's just such a bad idea . . . but I'm not daunted at the idea of people's opinions of what I say anymore."

Marshall noticed another difference. In 1990, not yet a superstar, Julia had been terrified by large crowds of fans or paparazzi. Now Marshall saw an intriguing turnabout. At the end of most days' filming on an outdoor set, Marshall would take Julia and Richard by the hand and walk over to the crowd of fans who always gathered at the periphery. "This is why it's hard to be Julia Roberts: With me, they look at me and say, 'Hi, Penny's brother, right?' Then, to Richard, they'd say, 'Hi, Richard. You're so sexy!' And then Julia comes over [quite happy to greet them], and they just kind of moan. They don't say hello or anything, they just stare, and some of them truly break into tears . . . the only other time I saw that was with Princess Diana."

One thing that hadn't changed since 1990 was the on-screen chemistry between the stars. "It's something special. You can't teach that. When those two look at each other, you really don't need the violins. It's there for some reason. I've worked with some people that you need a full orchestra, the Dixieland band, a damn parade. But they do it, and that's intangible. They're comfortable with each other. They overlap. I see her on other pictures and everything, but she doesn't fully let it out. When she's with Richard, she lets it out."

Filming of *Runaway Bride* proceeded without any major problems. As Marshall put it, "We hung out and told a lot of stories from the old days." But for Julia, it wasn't all a walk in the park. According to Marshall, "Julia had to be in great shape for this film, because we made the character quite an athlete. She kickboxes, she jumps rope, and she runs from her weddings!" Asked whether the pratfalls and goofiness required of her in this and other films came naturally, Julia laughed and said, "I'm afraid it does! I was a very clumsy child, and I realized at a certain time that that clumsiness could kind of pay off!"

As in *Notting Hill*, some aspects of *Runaway Bride* seem to have been lifted directly from Julia's life. One of Margaret's would-be weddings (which we see in flashback) mirrored Julia's planned all-stops-out extravaganza with Kiefer on the Fox lot; another duplicated the barefoot-hippie aspects of her wedding to Lyle Lovett. Life, art, art, life—who's to say where one begins and the other ends?

For all the goodwill and camaraderie among its participants, and the seemingly powerful potential for comic brilliance that *Runaway Bride* presented, it proved—artistically, at least—a disappointment upon release in July 1999. Perhaps critics, as Julia had at first, compared it to *Notting Hill*, which primed them for disappointment. In *The Hollywood Reporter,* Kirk Honeycutt wrote, "Remarkably, the actors have only gotten better-looking with age, and there's no question the chemistry between them still works for a light romantic comedy. But an overcalculated, undernourished screenplay undermines much of the effort." The *Los Angeles Times* critic predicted that the movie would leave audiences "with a bad taste in their mouths."

Daily Variety gave the film one of its few rave reviews, and more accurately predicted the success the film would enjoy: "This Paramount release can hardly miss." Indeed. Anticipation of the Gere–Roberts reunion brought Julia her biggest opening-weekend box-office gross ever, $35 million, and a domestic total of $152.1 million, $36 million more than *Notting Hill*. Once again, Julia Roberts had more than earned her "absurd" salary.

Some thought it odd that Julia and Ben still kept separate (although in the same neighborhood) apartments after nearly two years, especially since they shared one of the most important and long-lasting relationships in Julia's life. Others theorized it was the lack of constant proximity that kept the romance fresh—and ongoing.

"Julia and I don't focus on our relationship," Bratt said somewhat enigmatically, "so we'd prefer that others didn't, either. Having Julia in my life is just one part of being in this happy light that is my life these days." But at the same time he admitted, "I knew that being with Julia would make me highly visible. I admit I once had the same curiosity about celebrity couples that people now have about us." He then joked, "Julia and I have decided we are going to live our lives according to what appears in the tabloids. That means in the past two weeks we've been engaged and separated. This week Julia will be abducted by aliens. When she returns, we'll get back together."

Julia and Ben's love triumphed over a number of differences in their lifestyles. He's a homebody; she loves to socialize, especially with close friends. He loves sports; she couldn't be less interested. She's a voracious reader; he prefers watching television. "I still try to get him to read," she said, "but what can I do? He likes TV!"

"Romeo and Julia" (as people dubbed them) decided to take advantage of one main thing they had in common: acting. Julia agreed to do a guest stint on the two hundredth episode of *Law & Order*. She played Katrina Ludlow, "an evil sex killer," as Julia called her, who is arrested by Detective Curtis, whom she tries to seduce. The audience doesn't know whether she's guilty or innocent until the end of the episode. She was reportedly paid $4,500 for the appearance.

Julia found the experience "quite exciting" but "nerve-racking" in a number of ways. "Because you're trying to play this incredible murderous, sophisticated bitch in front of your boyfriend. It was kind of embarrassing, but we all had a good time." She expressed amazement over how hard—and how quickly—Benjamin and the rest of the cast had to work. "He works harder on that show than I've ever worked in my entire life. I worked four days, and I slept for a week afterwards. And I had two days in between. I can't believe he comes home from work and says, 'Where do you want to go to dinner?' It's just a miracle to me. So my respect for him has quadrupled."

Respect for Julia's acting ability increased as well when the episode aired on May 5, 1999. She was impressive, playing a nastier character than she ever had before, and she was nominated for an Emmy for the performance.

Later in the year, Bratt left *Law & Order*, both to pursue a career in movies and to move to San Francisco. "I've felt like it was time to get back home to my family," he said. "How do you walk away from the best job in the world and a group of people that you've grown to love? It's not easy, and it was an extremely difficult decision that I had to make."

On May 26, 1999, Bratt's final episode aired. Two weeks earlier, he had been named one of *People*'s "50 Most Beautiful People in the World."

Now his relationship with Julia was more long-distance than ever. But their love was strong enough to survive the separations, to hear Julia tell it. During a *20/20* interview with Julia that aired on May 12, 1999, Diane Sawyer had asked her, "For a girl who's been in love before, what's changed? Who is she now?"

"Golly, I guess I feel like I just radiate when he's nearby, maybe not so nearby, the confidence that I have and the—god, my heart is racing so hard right now. It's just a feeling of empowerment that I think we share with each other. A tremendous power within this union . . . that floors me."

"You know what I love most about this moment?" Sawyer said. "Even your ears are blushing! So does this mean marriage?"

"I had someone ask me that not that long ago, and it's funny because I'm so dazzled and caught up in the here and now that to project too far into the future is to miss the really great details of the day, and I don't want to miss anything."

The place where Ben and Julia spent the most time in a marriagelike situation was at her ranch in Taos, where they often stayed for weeks when neither was working. Julia has estimated that she spends 40 percent of her nonworking time at the ranch and the remainder in New York, where she also has her production company's offices.

Julia had poured millions into making the Taos retreat what she called "the little commune of my dreams." She often sits on the front terrace of the main house (there are five others) and watches the uniquely golden New Mexican sunsets. There is a heated indoor swimming pool in the main house; outdoors, a tennis court. (One recalls Julia's comment that she shouldn't be rich because she doesn't spend money.) "Benjamin's a great [tennis] player, and he has sort of reinspired me to play." Often the couple would take a boom box out to the dance floor on the edge of a field. "Sometimes we don't even need it." The image of Ben and Julia entwined in each other's arms, slow-dancing in the middle of a field to nothing but the sounds of a New Mexico evening, is a very pleasant one indeed.

Julia's friend Barry Tubb, himself a rancher, says that while she is unquestionably a great and glamorous movie star, "you should see her at five-thirty in the morning, when she wants to know how to switch the tractor from the disc to the planter. There's not a bit of the movie star about her then."

One summer she worked morning to night, tilling the soil along her driveway with her blue Ford tractor in order to plant sunflowers. "I wanted to make a grand, sweeping gesture," she said, and got it when the showy flowers bloomed. If the weather was inclement or Julia felt homey, she would repair to her bedroom to practice weaving on a huge loom. She also rolled up her sleeves for some redecorating work, coming up with whimsical design schemes, including Georgia O'Keeffe postcards and prints to cover the walls of one bathroom and colorful Mexican tin cutouts in another. On her bathroom counter she placed framed portraits of Clark Gable and Cary Grant. "Cary and Clark watching over me while I pee," she said with a laugh. Another bathroom wall was covered in artwork by her niece Emma, Eric's daughter, to whom she has grown quite close; the art came about when Julia could find no drawing paper for the girl.

There was little doubt that Julia Roberts, a woman who made so many halting (and very public) attempts to find herself in her twenties, was, at thirty-two, very much at peace. She was a part of the sophistication of New York when she wanted to be, or of the simple pleasures of the Southwest; she had a strong group of longtime friends, close relationships with her mother, sister, and niece (if not with Eric), and a man she couldn't stop gushing about.

"He's a force," Julia said of Ben. "He's a six-foot-two, strong, powerful energy. The first time I was actually standing in front of him, on a street corner where we were meeting, I felt like Thumbelina. He's a man. I'm all for women ruling the world, but everybody wants a man. He's a man, and that's nice. Oh my God, I've gushed about him so much, he'll be so embarrassed. Don't make me look too sappy—it's just hard to avoid when you're talking about Benjamin. He is *heavenly*."

Unfortunately for Ben, his first theatrical film after leaving *Law & Order* was considered less than celestial by the critics. *The Next Best Thing* involved a straight woman (Madonna) and her close gay friend (Rupert Everett) who have sex one night after drinking too much wine and conceive a baby. (That happens *so* often to gay men.) They decide to live together and raise the child until, five years later, she meets the man of her dreams (Bratt), who wants to marry her and move away with the child. A nasty custody battle ensues.

Julia admitted to a twinge of jealousy at the thought of her man rolling in the hay with a blond sex symbol. Ben wouldn't let Julia on the set the day the love scene was to be shot, Julia said. "So I pretended to be all furious, and he pretended to be all, 'Oh, honey, please don't be furious.' And we were very amused by the whole thing. [But] Rupert Everett is my friend, so I said [to him], 'You watch! You make sure everything goes well.'"

Julia needn't have worried about losing Ben to Madonna. He, in fact, felt a little left out of the thick-as-thieves friendship between Madonna and Everett. "Theirs is a relationship that's difficult to infiltrate," he said. "There's a conspiratorial quality to the way they are, especially between takes . . . they reminded me of the mischief-makers in high school."

Ben felt that the film's theme might "enlarge the parameters as to what comprises a family. That a practicing homosexual can be a good parent may be a concept the old order has trouble understanding—but it is utterly feasible."

Certainly the star power of its lead players seemed to give the tale (however tortured and however difficult for the "old order" to wrap its mind around) a shot at success, but the critics reacted to the picture as though it were radioactive. Shawn Levy of the Portland *Oregonian* considered it "a tone-deaf disaster of the first order, poorly acted, written with no sense of shame, clumsily staged and shot, and riddled equally with clichés, embarrassments and shocking lapses in taste, judgment and craft." Wesley Morris in the San Francisco *Examiner* wasn't any kinder: "It's so weirdly acted, shot, edited, directed, written and scored you can't believe it's happening."

The Next Best Thing brought in only $18 million at U.S. box offices. Ben could take some solace in the fact that no one blamed him for its failure. But he fared little better with his next film, a mission-to-Mars adventure called *Red Planet,* starring Val Kilmer, Carrie-Anne Moss, and Tom Sizemore. Julia flew to Australia to visit Ben on the set and offer encouragement (and more: "I just made out. That's all I did in Australia," she said). With director John Schlesinger (*Midnight Cowboy*) at the helm, Ben's expectations for the picture were high. However, there had been several mission-to-Mars movies within the last few years (one was even called *Mission to Mars*), and this one was greeted with gaping yawns by critics and audiences. "At some point near the start of the 21st century, Hollywood must have secretly decided science fiction is really just a synonym for drivel," wrote Rene Rodriguez in the *Miami Herald*.

Red Planet, budgeted at $80 million, collared a paltry $17 million in domestic box office. Ben's movie career had not begun as he had hoped it would; visions of David Caruso must have intruded on his brain.* But his next film, *Miss Congeniality*, in which he costarred opposite Sandra Bullock, made over $106 million in the United States; his film after that, *Traffic*, took in $124 million, was nominated for Best Picture, and won four Oscars, including one for its director, Steven Soderbergh, and another for Ben's costar Benecio Del Toro.

Soon, Julia would also work with Steven Soderbergh, in the true story of a single mom and legal crusader, *Erin Brockovich*. That film, too, cleaned up at the box office ($125 million in the U.S.), and was nominated for Best Picture, Best Director, and Best Actress. It put Julia among the rarefied stratum of actors who make $20 million a picture. Most important, it earned her every acting award given that year—including the Oscar.

*Caruso, who had achieved television stardom on *NYPD Blue*, left the show in 1995 after two seasons to pursue a movie career, which went nowhere. He wasn't able to reestablish his stardom until he went back to television and was cast in the *C.S.I.* spin-off *C.S.I.: Miami* in 2002.

CHAPTER THIRTY-FIVE

The inspiration for the movie that would win Julia Roberts a Best Actress Academy Award began on a Los Angeles chiropractor's adjustment table.

While Carla Santos Shamberg, vice president of special projects at Jersey Films, had her neck manipulated, her doctor told her the seemingly incredible story of another of his clients, Erin Brockovich. A twice-divorced mother of three with no legal training, she had almost single-handedly taken on the corporate giant Pacific Gas and Electric over the harm its toxic waste had caused to the citizens of Hinkley, California. She ultimately helped win the largest settlement in a direct-action lawsuit in U.S. history: $333 million.

Shamberg, the wife of Michael Shamberg, a partner in Jersey Films with Danny DeVito and Stacey Sher, was further intrigued to learn that Brockovich was something of a character—a woman who said exactly what was on her mind, often in terms that would make a sailor blush, and who wore short, flashy skirts, low-cut tops that boldly accentuated her ample bosom, and spiked heels. To make the dramatic possibilities of this story almost perfect, while Erin was playing David to PG&E's Goliath, she was struggling hard enough to make ends meet that she often went without food herself so her kids could eat.

Shamberg arranged for Brockovich, a blond, forty-year-old Kansas native who had once been crowned Miss Wichita, to tell her the story over tea. Shamberg recalled thinking, *This would make a great Julia Roberts movie.* Jersey Films had a production deal at Sony; the partners and Brockovich pitched the idea to Sony executives, who passed. Stacey Sher then ran the idea past Steven Soderbergh, who in 1989 had a huge independent success with *sex, lies, and videotape* and was directing the big-budget Jersey Films production *Out of Sight,* with George Clooney and Jennifer Lopez. Soderbergh said it was the worst idea he had ever heard.

Despite these setbacks, Jersey Films commissioned Susannah Grant to write a screenplay. Grant had written the Sandra Bullock film *28 Days* and the updated Cinderella tale *Ever After,* with Drew Barrymore. When Grant was unable to do a rewrite, Jersey hired Richard LaGravenese, one of the most highly regarded writers in Hollywood (*The Fisher King; The Bridges of Madison County*), to refashion the script. (His contribution ended up uncredited.)

When the script arrived at ICM, it found its way to Julia, who immediately expressed interest. When Steven Soderbergh read it, his feelings about the story changed. "I'm in," he told Sher. The director then flew to New York to have dinner with LaGravenese and Julia, in hopes of extracting a firm commitment from the actress.

Michael Shamberg was so nervous while waiting for word on Julia's decision that he called the restaurant and asked for Soderbergh, hoping he had good news. A waitress told him, "Honey, the guy you're looking for wasn't here very long. Everybody's left already, and they sure didn't look very happy."

Shamberg felt his stomach drop—but then he heard Julia's distinctive guffaw. He had been talking to her all along, as she did her best cocktail-waitress impression. He gingerly asked what she had decided. "When do we start?" Julia replied.

They started on May 25, 1999, on location in several small towns in California's Mojave Desert, including Hinkley, where the contamination of the water supply with the chemical chromium six took place; Boron, home to the Borox mines and the town where NASA tests rocket engines; and Barstow, where the courthouse of Judge LeRoy A. Simmons is located. (Simmons—whose landmark decision that the case could proceed put Brockovich et al. on the path to success—came out of retirement to play himself in the movie.)

Julia loved what the script revealed about Erin Brockovich. "As a person, Erin really intrigues me. I have great admiration for what she stands for. A lot of women in our culture are facing being a single mother, trying to make ends meet. They are the heroes of our times, aren't they? . . . Erin is who she is and doesn't change for anybody—which is what makes her such a remarkable individual. She can be in a situation where she's completely out of place and have no awareness of that and just focus on the issue at hand."

For all that admiration, Julia at first had a difficult time inhabiting her character. Although Soderbergh had interviewed Brockovich, Julia did not meet her until midway through filming, when Erin played a diner waitress whose name tag read JULIA. Erin's confrontational style didn't come naturally to Roberts. "I was raised in the South. I was taught to be respectful, to say 'Yes, sir' and 'Yes, ma'am.'"

Many actors acknowledge that costumes can help them find a character's center, and in the case of Erin Brockovich, they were key not only to her personality but to the plot. Julia wasn't entirely comfortable wearing skirts and blouses that made her look like Vivian Ward gone back to hooking. "I have something in my closet I call a dress," Julia said. "There's something in her closet where the whole part that covers your ass just isn't there." And Julia has never been comfortable in high heels.

The film's costume designer, Jeffrey Kurland—who had worked with Julia on *Everyone Says I Love You* and *My Best Friend's Wedding*—unreservedly loved the assignment. "Erin wears what she wants to wear when she wants to wear it, and it's always fun to dress a [character] like that. My conversations with Steven were mostly about making her true to the real Erin. [She] is an exaggerated personality, but we didn't want it to be comical or ridiculous—it had to be acceptable exaggeration. On the other hand, neither did we want to water it down so that she was no longer that woman."

Brockovich showed Kurland photographs of herself taken at the time of the story's action. "The truth of the matter is that she did wear eight-inch miniskirts and three-inch heels and plunging necklines. That's what she still wears. She looked terrific then, and she looks terrific now."

The clothes transformed Julia as none had before. "I would come to rehearsal looking like a fourteen-year-old boy and then get ready and come back forty-five minutes later, and people would be like, 'What happened to you?' I was the most entertained, I was the one fascinated by my own-ness."

One thing Julia didn't find realistic, even in Brockovichian terms, was that the filmmakers wanted her to wear miniskirts and low-cut tops during scenes where she felt such apparel was totally inappropriate. "I really felt abused by this whole wardrobe concept. The original script has her shimmying down wells in micro-miniskirts, and that didn't make sense to me, because if she's as smart as I thought she was, and she knows that she's on her way to shimmy down a well, you don't put on a micro-miniskirt."

And then there was the subject of her "boobs" (Erin's word). In the script—and apparently in real life—Brockovich's ample endowment often gained her entry into areas restricted to others. The problem was that while Julia has an enviable body, she would never be described as chesty with her 34B cup. Several options were considered, including Rick Baker–style prostheses, but finally all agreed the best approach was to simply show the cleavage Julia did have to best advantage.

When moviegoers saw Julia as Erin Brockovich, many assumed, incorrectly, that she'd had breast-enhancement surgery. "Benjamin says it took a village to create that cleavage," Julia joked. "It doesn't involve pumps or levers or anything, just a little good old-fashioned know-how." They used inserts called *cutlets,* she said. "Pads—and we cut the bras apart and put them back together in a different way to make it work. I got a little sweaty actually, in the desert; I had to make sure they stayed in their place."

"The reaction," Jeffery Kurland recalled, "was as if we had reinvented cleavage." Julia's clothes and bosom in *Erin Brockovich* call to mind the 1952 film *Niagara,* in which Marilyn Monroe's character is said to wear dresses "cut so low in front you can see her knees." As one critic observed, "Miss Monroe has very nice knees." So has Miss Roberts.

"It took a little practice," Julia said. "I was fine in the shoes until I got everything [else] going, and then there was the whole balance issue, because I was up high and I was out far."

During filming in Barstow, Julia stayed at the Holiday Inn, ate all her food from the catering truck, and bowled with the crew at the local alley. (She signed her scorecard "Lulu," but how good a game she rolled remains unrecorded.) When a piece of equipment began humming strangely just before one of her scenes, Julia jumped up and joined the others in fiddling with it to see what was the matter. "She's not the type to sit there and let everyone else do something for her," said Marg Helgenberger, who played one of the Hinkley residents affected by the toxic poisoning.

The film provided Julia with several blasts from her past: Conchata Ferrell, who played the pizza-parlor owner in *Mystic Pizza,* here played an office worker who gets on Erin's nerves ("Bite my ass, Krispy Kreme!" Erin snarls to her at one point). And Peter Coyote (from *Baja Oklahoma*) played the hotshot lawyer Erin's boss brings in as a partner on the lawsuit.

Julia loved being directed by Steven Soderbergh, whom she called "a genius." She had found that "sometimes directors, they're kind of talking you to death before you ever get to do anything. And you figure, 'Why am I here? Because you clearly have no trust in what I'm going to do.' But with Steven, you feel his trust and confidence all the time." Soderbergh returned the compliment. "I feel very lucky, like I was catching her at a real high point. . . . It's like watching Michael Jordan drive the lane. She's at her absolute peak as an artist. Technically, she can do anything. . . . What's that adjective they use on that tooth-cleaning commercial? *Effervescent*? That's what she is . . . I picture her as a little glass with bubbles in it . . . She's one of the few actresses you can compare to Audrey Hepburn without being struck by lightning."

Julia found equally enjoyable working with the veteran English actor Albert Finney (who had costarred opposite Hepburn in *Two for the Road*). Finney played Erin's boss, Ed Masry, a good man who gets along with Erin at first like oil with water but comes to appreciate, respect, and reward her. Finney and Anthony Hopkins, Julia said, were the two actors she most admired. "I feel the same way about Albert as Erin does about Ed," Julia said. "I could not have achieved what I've achieved in this movie without him by my side, without his friendship and support, and he's a man I respect and really love."

For Finney, Julia's "commitment to this really touched me. When I read the script, I thought, *Terrific part for her*—slightly different from what I've seen her do and a great opportunity to show what she's made of. After three weeks I told her how great she was in the role. . . . Working with her was enjoyable because it was volatile and unpredictable. I was proud of her as a fellow professional. That's how a trouper should be."

Julia took special joy in the actors playing her children. She would hide-and-go-seek with Scotty Leavenworth, who played Erin's son Matthew, and Gemmenne de la Peña, who played Erin's daughter Katie, and with her own niece, Emma, who visited the set several times. Leavenworth's mother, Brenda, said that Julia "came into the kids' trailers and let them go into hers. At one point she told them, 'Oh, so you just come in and trash my trailer and then leave?' And they said, 'Yup.' She would clown around. But I liked the way she handled them—just like a mom. If they get out of line, she'd be like, 'Hey, get over here!' But loving . . . She would wrestle with Scotty." Scotty, who weighs fifty-five pounds, was amazed that Julia "would pick me up, throw me over her shoulder and down on the ground—that's how strong she is."

The script of *Erin Brockovich* hewed pretty closely to the facts, but some liberties were taken to make the project more commercial, particularly with the character of George, Erin's boyfriend. The real George (whose name is Jorge) is considerably older and less good-looking than Aaron Eckhart, the actor who played him, and according to Erin wasn't nearly as selfless as he is portrayed in the film. "We had lived together for about a year when the Hinkley case first began to take over my life," she said. "To make sure I had the freedom I needed to work on it, Ed Masry's law firm hired George to be my kids' nanny. That's right, George was *paid* to take care of the kids."

Filming wrapped at the Santa Ventura Studios in Ventura, California, on August 5, 1999. While Soderbergh spent the next eight months getting the film ready for a spring 2000 release, Julia took another hiatus nearly a year long. "This was a really perfect moviemaking experience, start to finish, top to bottom, all over the place," she told Oprah Winfrey in March 2000. "That made me feel, jeez, what else could I do that would be as much fun and creative and challenging? So I haven't worked a day since."

"So what do you do with yourself?" Oprah asked.

"Um, you know, watch *Oprah,* soap operas, stuff like that."

She did a lot more, of course, whether in New York or Taos. In Manhattan, she continued to ride the subway to her Shoelace Productions office, stroll hand in hand with Ben Bratt in Gramercy Park, pick up soy milk from the local deli, shop for jewelry (her favorite place for baubles was a boutique called Me & Ro), work out at her gym, and jog almost every morning. To Billy Crystal in *Harper's Bazaar,* she described a typical day as having breakfast, "maybe walking around a little bit, work up another appetite. Then go meet my sister at her apartment. She will make me a nice little meal. And we'll watch our soap opera [*Days of Our Lives*] and catch up. But I'm a homebody. I like to clean, especially when I get home from location. I can spend weeks. And my day would finish with Benjamin taking me to a movie and dinner. A bucket of popcorn. Pretty much, I have exceeded my calorie limit in New York."

Julia and Ben found that the number of New York residents, and its high celebrity quotient, brought them more privacy than they experienced elsewhere. Unlike Los Angeles, where she had another of those paparazzi-popping-out-of-the-bushes experiences she had come to love so much. "It was late at night and it completely horrified me," she said. "Later, I thought, *Why didn't they just come up to me and say, 'Good evening, Miss Roberts. May I take your picture?'* I guess that was out of the question."

(There is an answer to Julia's rhetorical question. Paparazzi sell many of their photos to the tabloids, which aren't particularly interested in a demure photo of Julia. A picture of her looking horrified or hiding her face or running away would go much better with their story about how she's dying of a "mysterious disease," having a nervous breakdown, busting up with Ben, or whatever their Julia "tragedy" that week happens to be.)

As the release of *Erin Brockovich* approached, Universal Pictures sensed that it had a major success on its hands. An industry insider who calls himself "Dr. Richard Kimble," on the Urban Cinefile website out of Australia, reported that in two screenings the film "scored higher than *Notting Hill*. . . . It's more *Norma Rae* than *Silkwood* and apparently it's unbelievable. Zero walkouts with a score of 92 top two boxes, and 88 definite recommend. . . . Universal has an embarrassment of riches, and would like to push the movie to summer to go against the big guns, but Soderbergh was burned before in summer with *Out of Sight* and wants to stick to spring 2000. Sony (which co-owns the rights) believes that whenever this one comes out, it should be a grand slam." Indeed. Released on March 17, 2000, *Erin Brockovich* became an instant box-office smash. It tallied $28.1 million its opening weekend and went on to earn $125.5 million in the U.S. and an additional $132.9 million in the rest of the world.

The film changed the public's—and the movie industry's—fundamental perception of Julia Roberts: She *could* open a film without resorting to the romantic-comedy formula. Always regarded as a good actress, she had also been somewhat typecast as a "star performer," someone whose personality and looks were more impressive and marketable than her dramatic abilities, and an actress who needed to be sunny (and grinning widely) to attract blockbuster ticket sales. Her performance as Erin Brockovich, although undeniably big on looks and personality, also gave her an opportunity to inhabit a character as she never had before, and to show a range of emotions she had rarely attempted in the past.

Erin Brockovich was certainly pleased. She told Julia, "You got it so *right*! . . . Everything you did—the struggle, the emotion, and the *cleavage* . . . It was so great!" Most critics agreed. Julia's reviews—and those for the film itself—bordered on rapturous. Andrew Johnston in *Us* magazine wrote that Julia "gives the most convincing performance of her career. . . . Thanks to [Soderbergh's] keen instincts, what could have been a generic star vehicle pulses with the verbal wit of a screwball comedy and the emotion of a great country song. A brassy performance by Julia Roberts makes this a must-see." Leah Rozen wrote in *People:* "A powerhouse performance by Julia Roberts. . . . Without ever sacrificing a watt of her movie-star radiance, she convincingly plays a downtrodden woman who discovers, in fighting for others, that she matters. . . . Roberts rules in an impressive drama."

There were, of course, a few dissenters—Roger Ebert, for one, and Julia's brother, Eric. On Howard Stern's show, Eric said his sister was "useless" in *Erin Brockovich*. "What did she do? Wear some push-up bras! It wasn't great acting." Eric also said Julia had become "too big for her panties. . . . I got her first role for her," he added, "but she's turned her back on me for years."

In October 1999, Julia traveled to Asia to film *In the Wild: Horsemen of Mongolia,* a documentary that launched the nineteenth season of *Nature* on October 22, 2000. She spent two weeks with a nomadic family in their one-room transportable *ger,* a circular wood-framed enclosure covered with layers of canvas and heavy felt that had no bathroom, no running water, and no heat. "Mongolia isn't about cities," Julia said. "Most Mongolians are nomads. . . . A tough life, hardly changed for thousands of years. . . . What will they make of me—a girl from New York?" Naturally, they loved her. Julia and the family communicated as well as they could, not knowing a word of each other's language, and she bonded especially with the children, wrestling with them and playing games.

One morning Julia awoke to learn that the family was moving to find fresh grazing land for their horses. "Oh, that's what we're doing today," she said. "We're moving the house." The men began to unwrap the *gers* in their camp, and Julia realized it was something of a social event. "It was like a party . . . and I'm actually having a good time in the freezing cold, deconstructing a house. Who knew?"

The documentary focused on the Mongolian's close relationship with horses, on whom they rely for milk (Julia milked one herself) and transportation, and whom they race as part of the nation's religious and cultural festivals. Julia was amazed at how loyal the animals were to their "masters." Julia said, "For those horses to just be allowed to roam around, and they don't take off and leave, never to be seen again. . . . is kind of amazing. Everywhere in America, you see animals and you also see fences. . . . Here it's really about the love and respect man gives to the animal . . . [that's why] they stay together."

Before she left, Julia was told that she should expect to ride one of the horses, which would first be "broken in" for her. Although an accomplished equestrienne, Julia professed to being "scared. It's like a blind date to just get on a horse you don't know. And as we all know, blind dates can be disastrous. So I'm hoping there's a Benjamin Bratt in the horse outfit out there somewhere [who will] be nice, give me a fun day. Not buck me off. That would be terrible!" She nervously waited on the windy, barren steppe as the horse was selected for her. She then rode the animal without incident.

To promote *Erin Brockovich,* Universal Pictures embarked on a publicity campaign that brought Julia a slew of magazine articles, including the covers of *People* and *Film Review,* as well as an interview in *Rolling Stone.* The culmination was an hour with Oprah Winfrey, whose show hosted both Julia and Erin Brockovich on March 10, 2000. Julia stunned Oprah when she said she was already married to Benjamin Bratt. "Some guy asked me [at the Golden Globe Awards], 'When are you going to get married?' And I said: 'We've been married for eighteen months!' "

After clarifying that their "marriage" was a state of mind and not a legal commitment, Julia added, "I feel drunk with joy for twenty-four hours a day. Benjamin's a wonderful person, and he loves me unconditionally. He accepts me as a flawed individual and loves me anyway." Julia credited her peaches-and-cream complexion and sparkling eyes to her boyfriend. "I'm very active—besides, all that making love does wonders for the complexion. You have to do it for a while—enough to get the rosiness," she said with a laugh.

A year later, when she won the Academy Award, the whole world got to see Hollywood's queen and her handsome consort in action. They made a stunning couple, and Ben's quick response when Julia tripped going up the steps solidified his reputation as one of Hollywood's true gentlemen. Anyone in the Oscar-telecast audience who didn't know that Ben and Julia were a couple found out emphatically that night.

All could see that Julia Roberts, thirty-three, was a woman who had everything: enormous success in her chosen profession, looks that only seemed to improve with age, and her own Sir Galahad lovingly by her side. The only question seemed to be: When would Ben and Julia, after three and a half years of romance, tie the knot and start raising a Bratt Pack of their own?

CHAPTER THIRTY-SIX

Julia's next picture, *The Mexican,* costarring Brad Pitt and *The Sopranos'* James Gandolfini, took a tortuous course to the screen. J. H. Wyman, a Canadian television actor turned screenwriter, sold his second script (the first was *Mr. Rice's Secret,* released in 2000) to Newmarket Films in 1998 after every other studio in Hollywood had turned it down. The story contained two related but separate plotlines. In one, Los Angeleno Jerry Welbach (Pitt), a young messenger for the Mob who is trying to get out, must take on one more assignment: Go to Mexico and bring back a beautifully made pistol (the "Mexican" of the title), a gun that has almost mythical lore attached to it—and a number of very bad people interested in stealing it.

The second plot involved Jerry's girlfriend, Samantha Barzel (Julia), who is furious that he's taken another job and so drives to Las Vegas alone. While at a rest stop, she is attacked in a stall by an armed man who wants her to come with him. Just as the gunman, LeRoy, opens the stall door, another man, Winston Baldry (Gandolfini), shoots him several times and kidnaps Samantha, telling her *he's* LeRoy. Both men have been sent to capture Sam as bait to make Jerry turn over the pistol. Winston turns out to be unusually sensitive for a hit man, and he and Sam develop a friendship, although she remains his captive.

Jerry's sojourn in Mexico involves car theft, shootings, kidnappings, betrayals, chases, and crashes as the Mexican changes hands several times; Jerry is always desperate to get it back, because if he doesn't bring it to the man who sent him, he will be sent himself to that great firing range in the sky. At the end, all is solved (although Jerry must kill Winston), the pistol is returned to its rightful owner; and Jerry and Sam avow their undying love.

Wyman and the studio both saw the film as a low-budget, independent feature, and they signed Lawrence Bender (*Pulp Fiction*) and John

Baldecchi (*Simon Birch*) to produce. In the spring of 1999, several stars, including Ben Stiller and Meg Ryan, expressed interest in the script, and Kevin Reynolds (*Robin Hood: Prince of Thieves*) came on board as director. When no casting had been set by August, Reynolds bowed out. Then the producers got a call from a representative of Brad Pitt, *People*'s "Sexiest Man Alive" two years in a row, to say that the superstar was interested. Baldecchi's reaction? "You've got to be fucking kidding me!"

Brad sent the script to his *Fight Club* director, David Fincher, who was too busy with postproduction on that film to read it. In September, Bender sent the script to Gore Verbinski, who had directed the Budweiser talking-frogs commercials and had one film (the Nathan Lane comedy *Mouse Hunt*) under his belt. Bender felt confident that Verbinski could handle big stars as well as he had small animals. Verbinski was interested but didn't land the assignment until Fincher had again turned it down.

In the meantime, David Geffen, one of the partners in DreamWorks (along with Steven Spielberg and Jeffrey Katzenberg), had read about the script and Pitt's involvement and was amazed that it hadn't interested a distributor. When Katzenberg finished reading the script, he told the producers that DreamWorks would like to be involved. With a major studio and a superstar male lead, the female role needed someone of equal stature.

In January 2000, Pitt's manager ran into Elaine Goldsmith-Thomas at an event and mentioned the project. Goldsmith-Thomas was intrigued. "It was a combination of *Out of Sight* and *Pulp Fiction*," Elaine said. Julia's interest was equally piqued, especially by the prospect of working with Pitt, with whom she had been friends since Gwyneth Paltrow (his lady love at the time) introduced them years earlier. Pitt had first seen Julia on-screen in *Mystic Pizza*. "She was gorgeous, with a spontaneous energy that could make you fall in love with her. . . . She's a lovely woman and very intelligent."

Later that month, Katzenberg and Verbinski flew to Manhattan to meet with Julia. Katzenberg had phoned Joe Roth and asked him to "talk up" Verbinski to Roberts. "I knew that when I went to meet Julia, it was an audition for me," Verbinski said. "If she loved the movie and didn't love me, they're making the movie with *her*."

Julia liked Verbinski just fine, and now *The Mexican* had two hot stars and a director. The budget, mainly to accommodate Julia and Brad's salaries, ballooned from $10 million to $35 million. Both stars were paid $7.5 million; asked if it was hard to persuade them to lower their fees so substantially (Pitt usually got $20 million), Verbinski said no. "Because of the subject matter, which is kind of funky, because of the genre mixing, it was not a typical star vehicle. It was very different. It is a departure for both of them, certainly for Julia."

There was still one major role to be cast, that of the hit man who kidnaps Julia. At their meeting, Julia suggested to Verbinski and Katzenberg that they cast James Gandolfini, star of *The Sopranos,* one of her favorite television dramas. It seemed an inspired choice, but would Gandolfini agree to play what was essentially a gay Tony Soprano? The actor had no problem with that; he was just as interested in working with Brad and Julia as they had been with each other (and with him), despite an unnerving experience he'd had with Julia a year earlier. "I saw her at an awards show doing this [he smiles and waves his hand prissily, like Queen Elizabeth greeting her subjects from a carriage]. At that point in my life, I hadn't even thought that she would bother waving at me. So I was sitting there freaking out completely."

"He ignored me!" Julia said to Ben Bratt, sitting next to her. "I did the fan wave across the room, and he ignored me."

"I looked over my shoulder like, 'What is she doing?'" Gandolfini went on, "and my wife was like, 'She's waving at you, you moron!'"

Julia said her face "turned red, and I turned to Benjamin and said, 'James Gandolfini just ignored me.'" But she held no hard feelings over the inadvertent slight.

The Mexican began location shooting in the picturesque centuries-old desert mining town of Real de Catorce, Mexico, on April 17, 2000. The experience started out inauspiciously for Julia, who was kept awake her first night by a braying donkey under her hotel window. The hotel sent a security guard to coax the impolite *Equus asinus* to a different location.

About a month into filming, Julia had a scare in a four-by-four in which she was riding. A local resident, Eduardo Casteneda, recalled that "Julia was [being driven] back from Matehuala up the cobbled street to Real de Catorce. The road is really rough and uneven, and halfway back, the car she was in blew a tire. It could have been serious, but fortunately for Julia, the car just came to a stop, and the driver got on the radio for another car, which came and picked her up."

Other than those incidents, Verbinski recalled the filming as a largely pleasant experience. "You have some tequila every day after wrap," he said. "We cooked goat underground, and at the weekend we'd have big barbecues. When in Rome . . ."

Although Julia and Brad got along as well as might have been predicted ("He's a helluva guy," she said), Verbinski had a bit of a problem with their differing acting styles. "I think Brad is really experimental. He's not afraid to fail and will pursue something until it feels right, whereas Julia is a kind of female Gene Hackman [also in the cast]. She's a 'take two' kind of girl. If you want to do take three, you have to take a fifteen-minute break discussing why you want to do it." That Verbinski preferred Brad's method can be surmised by something he said about the "guerrilla shooting style" he was applying to the film. "For me, *Mouse Hunt* was so storyboarded. In this movie, I didn't storyboard anything. It was much more of a process of keeping it intuitive, hopefully capturing something much fresher."

Verbinski worried that audiences might not like the fact that in a movie starring Brad Pitt and Julia Roberts, the two share the screen for only about twenty minutes. He considered rewriting the script to give them more scenes together, "but they signed on because of the script, and I think it would [have been] stupid to change [it] two weeks before we started shooting just because we had two of the biggest stars in the world. It was a blessing and a curse."

Julia was concerned, too, since she and Brad didn't share a kiss until the end of the film. "When I mentioned it to the director, I was kind of trying to couch it in a way that didn't just make it sound like 'I wanna kiss Brad Pitt,' because how embarrassing." The two Hollywood hotties are in bed when we first see them, but they're just waking up, and the presumed sexual passion of the night before is no more than a hangover. Julia said she wanted the scene to look realistic, so she wore no makeup. "I'm a notorious *Days of Our Lives* watcher," she said. "So I see all these beautiful people waking up with lipstick and eye shadow on [and] that bothers me. I only like to look glamorous when it's called for. So when I shot my scene with Brad, I just did it au naturel."

According to Pitt, Verbinski did "ask us to go with it [during the few scenes of affection between Jerry and Sam], but in the love scenes, we resorted to being technical because we just kept laughing. There was no love there. Having a thing with Julia would be like having something with my sister. What's more, I'm besotted with Jennifer [Aniston, whom he would marry shortly after filming wrapped]."

As the shoot wound down, Julia faced the most emotional scenes in the film. "I remember there were ten days of hysteria during the end, and every day I was [facing] some form of fear and terror. And day after day

I had to walk onto the set and start crying for fourteen hours. After that, I sort of become the remains of Julia."

As she had on most of her films, Julia bonded with many of the crew members, a practice that had made her one of the most popular stars with the nuts-and-bolts brigade. One guy in particular caught Julia's eye: the boyishly handsome thirty-three-year-old Dan Moder, who had the unimpressively titled job of "B camera first assistant."

Julia was chatting with Pitt when she noticed Moder, wearing khaki pants and no shirt, sweat glistening on his six-pack abs. An observer on the set who witnessed what followed said that Julia peered over her sunglasses at Moder and asked Pitt, "Who's that young hunk of burning love?"

Pitt, obviously thinking about Ben Bratt, admonished her, "Now, you be a good girl, or I'm gonna tell on you!"

"Honey," Julia replied, "someone needs to strip that boy down, wash him up good, and bring him to my trailer." She then walked over to the blond, green-eyed, five-foot-nine Moder and spoke to him. A friend of his, Barry Livingston, said that "never in a million years would Danny have approached Julia. It wouldn't have crossed his mind that a famous celebrity such as her would be interested in him. Plus, he would never have jeopardized his job by coming on to any member of the cast."

Danny seemed uncomfortable at first, then appeared to warm to Julia's attention, especially when she began running her fingers up and down his washboard stomach. She later sent him a note, scribbled on a page of her script, that Moder called "pretty suggestive."

Unknown to Julia, the sexy Mr. Moder was a married man. In 1997 he had wed Vera Steimberg, a Hollywood makeup artist born in Argentina. When she learned of Moder's marital status, Julia moaned, "Why are all the good guys taken?" Danny told her that his marriage was essentially over. "I guess I have to believe him. But I don't date married men. Period." Still, with delectable Danny in Julia's line of sight every day, the period turned into a semicolon, then a comma, and then all punctuation was abandoned as the "married" superstar and the married B-unit cameraman began an affair.

Daniel Richard Moder, as all-American as Ben Bratt is exotic, was born in Los Angeles on January 31, 1968, the youngest of three children of producer Mike Moder (*Beverly Hills Cop*) and his wife, Patty. He grew up in the exclusive seaside community of Point Dume (just north of Malibu) and lived the California beach-boy lifestyle into his twenties, Rollerblading and playing beach volleyball, his light brown hair turned blond and his pale skin tanned by the nearly constant Southern California sunshine. He went to Catholic high school, during which he proved catnip for the girls, played baseball and football, and was voted the boy with the "best hair." (Locks of it do seem to fall in just the right places for maximum sexy effect.) He attended Santa Monica College, then transferred to the University of Colorado, where he earned a degree in psychology. In 1995 he worked as an assistant to his father on the Denzel Washington film *Crimson Tide*. Later his interests turned to cinematography, and he became a cameraman.

In addition to his good looks, Moder apparently has a special way with women. Patricia Hilton, who dated him for three months, described him this way: "He's smooth, a real romantic. He loves to give a girl simple gifts. I heard he gave Julia a scrapbook of their early e-mails to one another. That's just like him. In fact, he once gave me the exact same present. . . . He's the most unselfish lover I have ever had. He was completely giving, absolutely right there with me, connected in a way that I have never known with a man."

Another of Danny's exes added, "He's sexy to the point where it just oozes out of him. When you're with him, you are the most important person in the world. It's intoxicating. The contradiction, though, is that he's not a showy person. He's shy and unassuming, which makes him even more appealing."

Barry Livingston said when he first heard that Julia Roberts was "hanging out" with Danny, "I figured, well, that's it. She's his. We used to call him 'Doctor Love' because he knows how to treat a woman. Julia didn't stand a chance." Roberts family friend Tom Caldwell agreed. "She couldn't help herself. Danny came into her life just when Julia was bored to tears with Benjamin, a nice guy who no longer lit her fire, if you know what I mean."

But Julia and Ben would not break up until almost a year later, after appearing to all the world (almost literally, at the Oscars) as Hollywood's prettiest and happiest couple.

Released on March 12, 2001, *The Mexican* deeply divided critics, who either loved it or loathed it. Most complained, as expected, about the lack of Julia–Brad togetherness, but Andrew Johnston in *Us* magazine felt that the film "hits the bull's-eye" and that the scenes the two stars did have together were "all hilarious, and their separation provides each with ample opportunities to shine individually." Lisa Schwarzbaum in *Entertainment Weekly* took the "Ain't I clever?" approach to criticism by comparing Julia and Brad to the talking frogs in Verbinski's Budweiser commercials: "Brad Pitt and Julia Roberts . . . are top of the food chain—they're BRAD & JULIA, prince and princess of Hollywood, brought together for the first time in a historic union of box office royalty. And here's where worlds collide: Every now and then, when this picaresque caper loses its way, you can imagine Pitt and Roberts, each posed prettily on a lily pad, ribbiting BRAD. JULIA. BRAD. JULIA."

In fact, *The Mexican* is an entertaining, often funny film with terrific performances from its three stars—all of whom are playing to type, so why shouldn't they be terrific? The picture looks gorgeous: The time and poverty-ravaged stone streets of Real de Catorce are a cinematographer's dream, and Dariusz Wolski made the most of them with any number of beautifully framed sunrise- and sunset-lit shots. The script, though largely predictable and prosaic during Pitt's chase/caper plotline, sparkles with wit, emotion, and inventiveness as it develops the odd-couple relationship between Julia's character and Gandolfini's.

Despite the megawattage of its leads, the film fared relatively poorly at the box office: $66.8 million in the U.S., half of what *Erin Brockovich* took in. The film would seem to have all the elements of a crowd-pleaser, except one—*Brad and Julia together*. DreamWorks apparently knew that moviegoers would want to see these two beautiful and pre-eminent movie stars in a full-on romantic story, because the print ads showed them very close to a kiss and carried the tagline "Love with the safety off." This blatantly false advertising undoubtedly hurt the movie. Those expecting a different film were disappointed, and word of mouth wasn't good.

For the first time since *Pretty Woman*, Julia's clothes in a film created a mini–fashion craze. It wasn't exactly on the scale of *Bonnie and Clyde* or *Saturday Night Fever*, but several magazines did run features advising readers how they could duplicate Julia's casual-chic look in the film. Her short-sleeved pink top, for instance, was available from Scoop in New York for a mere $33; an ostrich-feather boa she wears around her neck (and dances with on a bed) could be had for $175 from Neiman Marcus; an embroidered peasant skirt was available from Urban Outfitters at $28; and Me & Ro could provide assorted beaded necklaces ($190 to $405), a silver Prabhujee cuff ($235), a tiny petal-and-bead anklet ($465), and a silver lotus-petal anklet ($310).

There was also Brad's signature look: cargo pants ($54 at Stussy) and a short-sleeved T-shirt (Banana Republic, $15.50) over a long-sleeved one from Stussy priced at $22. The costume designer, Colleen Atwood, said she shopped for many of the clothes at vintage stores, "like Decades and Jet Rag in Los Angeles, and in New York, at Calypso. . . . I covered the planet for Julia's costumes—from Alberta Ferretti to the Gap to Banana Republic." Atwood found Julia "smart and collaborative" but said Brad was "very tricky to dress because he is so intuitively stylish. You kind of just want to dress him down. Brad's orange T-shirt started quite a sensation in the town [Real de Catorce]. The kids knew who he was, in a big way."

The publicity push for *The Mexican* put Brad and Julia on the covers of *Entertainment Weekly* and England's *Empire* (which captioned a photo from the film of Julia holding a gun, "Revealed: Julia Roberts's *Thelma and Louise* audition"). It also put Julia on the covers of *Us* magazine, *Seventeen, In Style, Harper's Bazaar, Redbook,* and *People;* it led *Esquire* to run an "appreciation" of Julia, with admiring quotes from her colleagues and commentators; and it brought her back to her favorite talk show, David Letterman's. The culmination, in July, was a special issue of *Time,* "America's Best," with an extreme close-up of Julia on the cover. The magazine proclaimed her "Best Movie Star."

Oddly, Julia declined to pose for the cover of *Vanity Fair*'s annual Hollywood issue with fellow heavyweights (past and present) Meryl Streep, Catherine Deneuve, Gwyneth Paltrow, Kate Winslet, Vanessa Redgrave, Nicole Kidman, Sophia Loren, and others. Perhaps Julia had been angered by the magazine's 1999 cover story by Ned Zeman, which made the egregious error of calling her father Walter Motes and claiming that Roberts was a stage name adopted by Julia, Eric, and Lisa. (The magazine's usually fastidious fact-checkers must have been out to lunch.)

The Roberts acting dynasty welcomed a new generation in the spring of 2001, when Julia's beloved niece, ten-year-old Emma, appeared as Johnny Depp's daughter in the drug-dealer movie *Blow.* Eric knew he had a potential actress on his hands "when she was maybe four," he said.

"She was walking around the house doing English accents *well.*" Emma pleaded with her mother to let her audition for *Blow,* and Kelly relented. "I thought it would [just] pacify her, and she got the job!"

The film's director, Ted Demme, said that Emma, a fourth-grader, "was never intimidated" by difficult scenes. She wasn't entirely happy, though, with the costumes she had to wear for the eighties-era drama. "I wore these hideous outfits . . . I'd wear little dresses that pouf out. How could people dress like that?" (She did, however, approve of the 1982 Valentino gown that Aunt Julia chose for the Oscars.)

Of Julia, Emma said, "I wish I could act as good as her, but I just do my best." Demme thought her best was pretty good. "I see an enormous future for her."

CHAPTER THIRTY-SEVEN

On June 28, 2001, Julia—who, after fourteen years in Hollywood, still had the ability to shock people—*really* shocked people when she announced that she and Ben Bratt had parted. Even the most casual Julia watchers wondered, *How could this be?* Hadn't the world just seen them acting like the most loving couple on Earth during the Oscars? Hadn't Liz Smith reported on March 30 that when Ben was asked at the ceremony, "Are you going to get married?" he replied, "Well, we set the date. But no, I won't tell you when it is."

Just two months before the breakup was announced, Ben and Julia were spotted strolling down St. Mark's Place in Manhattan, eating watermelon and having a seed-spitting contest. Some cynics suggested that Ben and Julia's Oscar love-fest was an act designed not to spoil her big night, but several people close to them denied that. What *was* an act was Julia talking as though she and Ben were still together during the press junket for her new film, *America's Sweethearts.* Yet again Julia's life imitated Julia's art: In the film, a superstar couple pretend not to be estranged in order not to hurt the box office of their new film, a romantic comedy.

Julia didn't want her personal life to overshadow her film, so she basically lied—or at least didn't tell the whole truth—whenever she was asked about Bratt. Deception evidently doesn't come easily to her. When a reporter at a press conference in Manhattan's Regency Hotel on June 23 pressed her repeatedly about what made her and Ben's life together "so happy and wonderful," she murmured something about how he had taught her to "take comfort in my privacy."

"But is there some quality you admire about each other that makes it special?" the reporter persevered.

Julia replied, "I would say mutual respect and integrity."

"See, that wasn't so hard," the journalist teased.

"Well, yeah," Julia replied with steely eyes, "but your stomach doesn't hurt."

Neither Ben nor Julia has spoken in specifics about why they broke up, but the couple's friends and colleagues paint a picture of a relationship beset with several serious problems. The worst of these was Ben's desire to get married and have a family, and Julia's resistance to the idea—despite her oft-stated wish to do just that. Ben wanted her to work less, move to San Francisco, and be more of a presence in his life. Instead, she worked more than ever, making four films within two years.

A friend of the couple's told *People* that "he was putting her in conflict, having to choose between what she was doing and being on his set. With each movie [she made], he got more angry. He didn't want her to give up her career, but the reason they fought was that he wanted her to be there for him. He wasn't saying, 'Can't you be home and cook for me?' He was saying, 'I like it when you are home.' There is a deep love there, but it was like trying to fit a square peg in a round hole. He realized she was a bit of a gypsy."

Ben was also distressed a year earlier when *The National Enquirer* published cover photographs of Julia and Ross Partridge carrying on in a restaurant/bar. Julia was shown kissing Partridge and wrapping her legs around him as she sat on his lap. The implication was that the pictures were recent, but they were from the days when Julia and Ross were dating. (Pictures had also been published a year before of Julia and Jason Patric strolling and kissing in a Los Angeles park.)

Whether Ben knew about Julia and Danny Moder is unclear, but friends of the couple said that he *was* angered by the rumors that Julia and George Clooney had grown "cozy" and "canoodled" while filming Steven Soderbergh's *Ocean's Eleven*. Reports filtered out of Las Vegas that Julia and George—who played a divorced couple, still in love—had put on a steamy dancing display during a cast party at the Bellagio Hotel to celebrate the Oscar victories of Julia and two crew members on the film. "It was hot and heavy," a witness reportedly said.

As Roberts family friend Tom Caldwell implied, perhaps Benjamin Bratt was too much of a gentleman, too much of a good guy for a woman who, despite her own developing elegance and maturity, clearly still found bad boys a turn-on. "I seem to keep making the same mistakes when it comes to men," she had said before she met Bratt.

None of the many weekly magazines that ran stories on yet another "big breakup for Julia Roberts" mentioned Danny Moder—except for the *Enquirer.* "Ben . . . heard rumors that Julia had a romance with cameraman Danny Moder when she filmed *The Mexican* last year, according to another insider," the paper reported. "When contacted by the *Enquirer,* Danny's wife, Vera, denied that her husband two-timed her with Julia, but she did say: 'Of course Julia hit on him. That's just Julia being Julia.' "

In May, when Julia visited Ben on the Montreal set of *Abandon,* a thriller he was shooting with Charlie Hunnam and Katie Holmes, observers say that he pressed her to marry him and move to San Francisco. Julia apparently assured him she wanted to get married, but moving was out of the question. A friend of the couple claimed that Ben then "hit her with heavy artillery. He accused her of fooling around with Clooney and others, hitting her with rumors of affairs she'd had with old boyfriends and crew members. Julia panicked as the fight escalated. She went into defense mode and denied, denied, denied. And that's when he told her, 'The bottom line is, I don't think I can trust you. This is no way to start a marriage. Julia, we're through.' "

A friend of Julia's said, "Julia's problem with men is always the same—she can't be faithful to any one guy. And she can't resist having affairs with some of her handsome costars. But this time it's Julia who is shattered over the broken romance. Julia's never been dumped before— it was always Julia who did the breaking up."

On July 10, Julia again appeared on David Letterman's show to promote *America's Sweethearts.* Inevitably, the subject of the breakup arose, and she handled the matter with class. "I've been practicing in front of the mirror: 'Hi, I'm Julia. I'm single,' " she said. "It doesn't make me a bad person. . . . Here's the thing—I love Benjamin, he's a good man, he's a fine man. He is, to the exultation of the female single population, not *my* man anymore. Sad but true and not ugly, not because of anybody else, [just a] parting of the ways, there you go, make it what you want. . . . We're both just two kids trying to find our way in the world and . . . I've never heard it so quiet in this studio in my entire life!"

Bratt seemed deeply hurt by the failure of the relationship. Even after his April 2002 marriage to the actress Talisa Soto, a gorgeous former Bond girl with whom he costarred in the 2001 film *Piñero,* Bratt was described as "tense" whenever the subject of Julia came up. In a *Vanity Fair* cover story on him in August 2002, he said, "I learned definitively that there's a vast difference between what you want and what you need. . . . From the way I'm feeling right now, I look back and I see that it was necessary to go through whatever it was that I did to clearly understand and ultimately to enjoy the heights of this love [with Talisa]." The article revealed that Mrs. Bratt was three months pregnant. The baby, Sophia Rosalinda, was born on December 6. Benjamin had gotten the marriage and family he desired—but not from Julia Roberts.

Ben and Julia got into an exchange of salvos over a year after their breakup. She was reportedly angered by his comment—which echoed Jason Patric's—that her enormous fame had made their relationship unworkable. "It's that mosquito that buzzes in your ear when you're trying to sleep at night," he said. "It's constant and ever-present, and it disrupts any chance of peace." Julia slapped back during an interview on *Good Morning America* a few months after Bratt got married. "He's a thirty-eight-year-old man. I figure he's kind of making his choices—all for the better, because he was unhappy, and he left and moved along and found happiness . . . in a place where there are no mosquitoes!"

Julia felt fat. She had good reason to—she was being made up and put in a fat suit to look sixty pounds heavier for a few flashback scenes in *America's Sweethearts*. According to Julia, she would get tired during the long transformation procedure. "It's a very tedious process. I don't know how Eddie Murphy did it in those *Nutty Professor* movies, because it takes a really long time." The makeup men told Julia, "You know, we can [adjust your chair back] if you want to sleep."

"Why would I want to sleep and wake up sixty pounds heavier?" she replied. "I may never sleep again." The experience of seeing herself in that condition was awful enough, but walking around proved even worse. "Not to be indiscreet," Julia said, "but the boobs were *so heavy*. All day my back hurt. And I'm like, 'God, why do I feel like I'm put together wrong?'" Even playing Erin Brockovich hadn't prepared her for this. "When your whole physical body becomes so different, it affects your posture. You move strangely. I noticed that even the way I spoke was somehow different. It's *bizarre*."

Devoted Julia watchers could be forgiven an assumption that the title *America's Sweethearts* referred—just as it seemed *Steel Magnolias*, *Pretty Woman*, and *Runaway Bride* had—to an aspect of Julia. Certainly she had been repeatedly called "America's Sweetheart" by the press. But in fact, Julia did not play one of the title roles in the film—the story of Gwen and Eddie, married movie stars on the way to an acrimonious divorce who pretend their marriage is still happy. Julia instead played the tertiary role of Kiki, Gwen's mousy sister and assistant, who had been overweight but slimmed down and is secretly in love with Eddie.

When Julia's longtime friend and production partner Joe Roth heard that a Billy Crystal/Peter Tolan script spoofing Hollywood and press junkets had been put in turnaround by Castle Rock, he snapped it up. Crystal wanted to direct and play Eddie, but Roth didn't think either was a good idea. Crystal was busy directing the HBO drama *61** (about the 1961 competition between New York Yankees Mickey Mantle and Roger Maris to break Babe Ruth's single-season record of sixty home runs). Since Roth wanted to start the film quickly (before a threatened writers' strike), there didn't seem to be enough time. And Roth thought it was "crazy" that Crystal wanted to play the movie star. "I thought he should play the publicist who's behind the whole thing, the guy trying to get the married stars through the press junket without anyone finding out they're really getting divorced. I also thought everybody in the movie should be twenty years younger." Crystal agreed to switch roles, but Roth told him a final decision hadn't yet been made on the director.

Roth thought he knew the perfect person to play one of the Sweethearts: Julia. He sent the script to her marked "Part of Gwen." She liked the script, but "I didn't want to play that part, because I thought she was a bitch. I do that all day at home. I just kinda liked the girl in the corner. I thought that would be interesting. . . . Kiki had the most nuances. And, it's a bit of laziness on my part because she's the supporting role, so I don't have to work so much."

Once Julia agreed, Roth called Crystal to break the news, and added another piece of information: "How would you like it if I got Julia Roberts and I directed it?"

"If you can deliver her," Crystal replied, "then I suppose the answer would be yes." Julia thought that being directed by Roth (who had previously helmed *Streets of Gold, Revenge of the Nerds II,* and *Coupe de Ville*) would be "a lot of fun. It'll be great." With Julia in place, Tolan and Crystal felt they needed to do some rewrites. "If you have a resource as valuable as Julia Roberts," Tolan said, "you damn well better use it every second she's on-screen. You want to see her play moments of vulnerability, so we wrote those in. There are moments when she is trying to facilitate the man she loves getting back with her sister, so we had to show the conflict in her at having to do that."

They rounded out the cast with the gorgeous Catherine Zeta-Jones as Gwen; John Cusack as Eddie; Robert Downey, Jr., as Gwen's Mexican

Lothario boyfriend; Stanley Tucci; and Christopher Walken. Cusack rather than Crystal playing Eddie necessitated still more changes, Tolan said. "Billy knows how to knock a joke over the wall. John wants to come around to things a little more indirectly. I went through the script before the table reading and took every hard joke out. I had to change all the rhythms."

A potential disaster to the filming arose when Robert Downey, Jr., was arrested for drug possession. Since there was a good possibility that Downey, a repeat offender, would be in jail when filming began, he was replaced by Hank Azaria. Filming began on January 10, 2001, two days after Crystal finished work on *61**. Ty Burr and Steve Daly wrote a lively account of a day's filming for *Entertainment Weekly*.

Part of Joe Roth's new job required simultaneously dealing with an actress playing a world-renowned film star and a world-renowned film star playing an average Josephine. The scene being filmed this particular day is the climactic shouting match that takes place in the hotel's convention room, as Gwen, Kiki, and Eddie finally declare their pent-up affections and antipathies before 300 assembled junketeers. Roberts and Zeta-Jones run fresh variations in each take, playing it broad, reining it in, continuing the collegial bitchiness even when the cameras aren't rolling. "Oh, just back it up, Zeta," Roberts mock-snarls when her costar fluffs a line.

When preview audiences reacted negatively to the film's romantic finale, the stars were called back to shoot a more comedic (but still romantic) ending written over a weekend and tested (positively) in a Thousand Oaks, California, cineplex.

In a bit of counterprogramming, *America's Sweethearts* opened on July 20, 2001, the same day as *Jurassic Park III*. Sony marketing and distribution chief Jeff Blake explained the decision: "We think we're the big romantic-comedy alternative for July. We're up against *Jurassic*, but we think there's a great advantage to having a Julia Roberts comedy in that slot. Midsummer is always a great opportunity for a romantic comedy with big movie stars."

The film garnered what *The New York Times* deemed "tepid" reviews. That paper's critic, A. O. Scott, wrote, "Like a bottle of lukewarm champagne—an expensive one, judging by the label—*America's Sweethearts* opens with a promising burst of effervescence and quickly goes flat. . . . There is something potentially wonderful in seeing a star of Ms. Roberts's magnetism and popularity play the ugly duckling. . . . But the spark of romantic conviction is not there. Ms. Roberts's scenes with Mr. Cusack have a draggy, soft sincerity as both actors fall back on familiar quirks and twitches in the absence of strong writing."

Most of the critics, as is often the case, got it wrong. (The problem must be that they simply see too many movies.) *America's Sweethearts* has a lot of laughs, especially in its rollicking last half hour, during which the director of Gwen and Eddie's new movie (terrifyingly played by Walken) unveils the picture as a secretly shot behind-the-scenes documentary in which Gwen reveals she's had an affair with Azaria ("Sometimes you just have to get laid") but that "down there" he's no bigger than a roll of quarters. (She uses her lipstick case as an illustration, rolling the lipstick down a little first.)

Gwen is horrified, but Crystal's publicist is thrilled. "They loved it!" he says of the audience. "They're calling it the Blair Bitch Project!" In the meantime, Azaria is pleading with everyone who'll listen that "I ham not like coins! I ham ex-treeem-ely well-*chung!*"

Everyone in the movie is in great comic form—especially Zeta-Jones and Crystal—though John Cusack is a weak link. His performance is fine, but his character is underdeveloped and pales in comparison to the others'. Rupert Everett could have been a far better choice, but producers in Hollywood have the absurd notion that the public won't accept a gay actor playing a romantic lead opposite a woman. (That's been happening without the public's knowledge for over a century.)

Despite the reviews, *America's Sweethearts* pulled in $30 million its opening weekend, placing a strong second (as expected) behind *JP III*, which took in $50 million. The film went on to make a solid $93.6 million in the U.S. and $157.6 million worldwide. Most of the credit for the film's success, as usual, was attributed to Julia.

CHAPTER THIRTY-EIGHT

J ulia's affair with Danny Moder became public with a splash early in September 2001 when *The National Enquirer* ran a blazing cover headline: JULIA ROBERTS RUNS OFF WITH MARRIED MAN. The publication got Vera Moder on the phone. She "tearfully" told their reporter, who asked what had happened, "I don't have the whole story. Julia has the whole story. Why don't you call Julia and ask her what she did?"

A friend of Vera's said, "Vera is devastated. She's strong, but this thing is going to take a while for her to get through. . . . Vera naively thought Julia was a friend to both [her] and Danny. She had no idea Julia was planning on getting her hooks into her husband." Reportedly, Vera's first hint that something was amiss came when she discovered a cell-phone bill with a slew of calls from Danny to Julia. He protested that the calls were all "work-related," and said, "What do you think, I'm having some kind of an affair with Julia? Don't be so ridiculous! What would Julia Roberts want with me?"

When it became apparent to Danny exactly what Julia Roberts wanted with him, he moved out of the Woodland Hills, California, house he shared with Vera, rooming first with his sister Jyl. Not long afterward, Jyl, fond of Vera (as were all the Moder family) and angered because she felt Julia was "toying" with her brother, confronted the star. "What exactly do you want from my brother? Don't you realize he's married?"

"Yes, I do," Julia replied. "But Danny swore to me that he and his wife are through. I love Danny, and I believe he loves me."

Before long, Julia and Danny had moved into an apartment that a friend of Julia's, the hairstylist Bonnie Clevering, had vacated when she moved out of state. The U-shaped, two-story luxury building is on Sunset Boulevard in Brentwood. A fellow resident of the complex, who spoke on the condition of anonymity, recalled Julia and Danny keeping so much to themselves that most of the neighbors in the twenty-unit building didn't know they lived there for the first eight months. When they found out, the source said, they started calling Julia and Danny's apartment "the love nest."

This neighbor, as far as she could tell, was the only one with whom Julia and Danny were friendly. "She had a parking space here right next to her back door. She's very good at evading people—very fast. She'd say hello, but she was usually standoffish. She did her own laundry, housework, and grocery shopping. I urged her to borrow my cleaning lady, but she wouldn't. People here were astounded to see her in the laundry room or taking out the trash."

The apartment was not furnished in a manner that one would expect of a woman worth over $100 million, said the neighbor. "They slept on a mattress on the floor! They had furniture, but it was sparse— nothing you'd expect the top movie star of the world to live with. They usually ordered out for food—mainly Indian." The neighbor remembered being in the apartment shortly after Julia won her Academy Award and seeing a picture of Danny lying in bed holding up the Oscar.

The source noticed early on that the superstar next door was "extremely possessive" of her beau. "If I would meet him in the back of the building where the cars were parked, we'd chat—he was very sweet. But boy, she was right out there. A minute would go by, and there she'd be, walking down the driveway wondering, *What is he doing? Who is he talking to?* And she would join us all the time. Her eyes would just double in size when she saw him—she was so crazy about him. The first time I saw her with him, I knew she was going to marry him. Their apartment was on the second floor, and I walked up the stairs with him one day, and she ran out of the apartment and looked at him like someone who hadn't eaten in a year and he was a roast turkey. She wanted him very badly. And he never had it so good—flying on private jets and all that. He had to go to Florida while she was in Montreal, and he said, 'I have to fly commercial. If I don't travel with her, I can't go by private jet.'

"It was stressful with her here," the neighbor recalled, because the tabloids discovered the "love nest" and staked out the place. "She called the police several times because of the paparazzi. This is a quiet, lovely building. I came home one day and the police were at her door and I said, 'What's wrong?' and she said that she had driven up the drive-way—there are two, one to enter and one to exit—and she had come up the entry driveway, and someone had followed her and gone up the exit driveway, so they met head-on and she didn't like that at all. So she called [the police].

"I had seen some people lurking about the building, and I called the police and told them that Julia Roberts is living in this building and there are some odd-looking persons hiding in the bushes. Then my gardener told me he saw someone across the street taking pictures of the building. It always makes me think of Rebecca Schaeffer,* and it scares me, because I don't want anyone to harm Julia. I told her, 'If Danny isn't home and someone rings your bell, you call me. And I'll see who it is.'"

Danny and Julia expressed anger at the number of stories the tabloids ran about them. "They were in the *Enquirer* so often, and he came in here one day so frustrated. He said, 'You know, we should just go and sue everyone we know who would let this information out!' I think they decided it was his sister."

The tabloids, predictably, had a field day with the Julia-Vera-Danny triangle, gleefully reporting that most of Danny's family hated Julia and considered her a husband stealer. When Danny's mother, Patti, died of a heart attack on August 21, 2001, reports were that the family blamed Julia for causing the stress that killed her. Julia tried to extend an olive branch with expressions of sympathy and an offer to pay for and help arrange the funeral. The efforts caused more backlash than goodwill. "The Moders are fuming over Julia's brash attempt to crash their mother's memorial gatherings," a family friend said. "They feel she's incredibly callous to try to worm her way into their lives." Though it hardly seemed possible, things would get worse in Julia's personal life before they got better.

Professionally, Julia was in an indie frame of mind after winning her Oscar. She helped finance and did a cameo with Bruce Willis (their second such teaming) in *Grand Champion,* written and directed by her friend Barry Tubb as a "love letter to [his native] Texas." She also agreed to appear in a small-budget, no-frills Steven Soderbergh film, *Full Frontal.*

The story of *Grand Champion* concerns a group of children who commandeer a champion rodeo horse named Hokey before the animal can be shipped to a slaughterhouse. It was filmed in the summer of 2001 in Snyder, Texas (Tubb's hometown). Emma Roberts played one of

*An up-and-coming young actress, Schaeffer was shot and killed in 1989 by a deranged "fan" after she answered the door at her West Hollywood apartment.

the kids and made a big impression on cast, crew, and extras during the filming. For a concert scene with country star George Strait, another friend of Tubb's, she made her way through a crowd in a black and gold cheerleader costume, repeating "Excuse me, excuse me, excuse me," then jumped onstage to do the "Hokey Pokey" with Strait.

Because the film's budget was so low, Tubb couldn't afford to pay all the extras for a crowd scene. Julia tooled over to the local Wal-Mart, commandeered the public-address system, and announced, "Hello, shoppers! This is Julia Roberts. My niece is filming a movie and we need your help." Crew members reported that "the local folk dropped everything to help Julia and Emma out."

Dixie Chicks member Natalie Maines also had a cameo role and became close to Julia during filming. "[She] came in my trailer and wrote lines and she's very funny," Maines told Hollywood columnist Marilyn Beck. "I play a West Texas DJ with big hair and blue eye shadow. She was such a supporter; she was like my wardrobe girl and my stage mom. Between takes she'd come over and help me take my jacket off, sit with me and give me sips of wine. She knew I was just shaking with nerves. Thank God she was there, or I'd never have made it."

Another person close to Julia worked on *Grand Champion*: Danny Moder, who she made sure got hired as a camera operator. The cast and crew stayed at the motel-style Beacon Lodge, where Moder had Room 22. Julia stayed next door. On a circle of grass enclosed by the motel, Julia and the gang "barbecued and played music and football," said Beacon owner Shirley Schulze. "Julia was very sweet and low-maintenance. A maid would come by, and she'd just tell her to leave fresh bed linen and she'd take care of it." Though now and then Julia and Danny sat outside their rooms chatting and sipping soft drinks, their friendship, reported Schulze, seemed just that: "It was innocent."

Julia's presence was required for just a few days, but she stayed on location for almost two months, ostensibly to act as the guardian of her niece. "That was just a cover-up," an observer said. "The real reason she was there was to be with Danny. When he wasn't working, Danny and Julia were virtually inseparable."

Julia and Emma attended the "world premiere" of *Grand Champion* in April 2002 at the Paramount Theatre in Austin, after which cast and crew gathered at the Hard Rock Cafe for a hoedown. The proceeds from the premiere benefited the Austin Children's Museum. The film was never nationally distributed, a surprise, considering the participation of Julia, Bruce Willis, and George Strait. As of this writing, it is also not available on video or DVD.

. . .

On September 11, 2001, the world was shocked by the deaths of more than three thousand people in terrorist attacks in New York, Washington, D.C., and Pennsylvania. Ten days later, Julia took part in *America: A Tribute to Heroes,* a worldwide telethon—brought together in just six days—to raise money for the victims and their families. She had already donated $1 million to the telethon fund and another $1 million to the American Red Cross Disaster Relief Fund. She said that having been a New Yorker since 1985, and living not far from Ground Zero, she felt the horror of the attacks even more vividly. "How do you begin to imagine something so incomprehensible?" she asked Mitchell Fink of the New York *Daily News.* "It's hard to find the right words—because there aren't any. The greatest gift, the most powerful weapon we have right now, is to love one another."

Julia joined Jack Nicholson, Al Pacino, Brad Pitt, George Clooney, Whoopi Goldberg, Robert De Niro, Tom Cruise and Penélope Cruz, Jim Carrey, Halle Berry, Willie Nelson, and others on the telecast. Bruce Springsteen sang a new song, "My City of Ruins," and said, "I had no idea when I first recorded it that it would be so timely, sadly, so fitting." Billy Joel sang his "New York State of Mind." Many of the stars present did not appear on-screen but manned the telephones to take pledges.

Julia said that before she went on, she watched the proceedings for an hour and a half and was deeply touched by the many tributes to the brave policemen, firemen, airline passengers, and office workers who lost their lives. When she went on, she said, "It was a privileged and emotional place to stand there for my minute." She became so emotional that she had to brace herself before her appearance. A CBS source said, "She was determined not to break down in front of [hundreds of millions of worldwide] viewers. She knew she had to appear strong to show the world that America may be bloodied but we are not beaten." During her segment, Julia recounted tales of heroism at the Pentagon and said, "Life is so precious. Please, please, let's love one another. Reach out to one another. Be kind to each other. Peace to you." Then she reclaimed a phrase that many terrorists use to justify their acts: "God is great."

The CBS source said that "Julia bravely held back her emotions until the spotlight was off her, then, like millions of Americans in the days since the terror attacks, she broke down, letting tears of pride and patriotism flow. This was no acting job. This was the real Julia Roberts. She was overwhelmed by the tales of heroism she had described and heard."

CHAPTER THIRTY-NINE

Eyebrows shot up around Hollywood when the trade papers announced that Steven Soderbergh would direct a remake of the Frank Sinatra Rat Pack heist caper *Ocean's 11*. That film, only a modest success in 1960, wouldn't have been on many lists of top remake prospects, but with Soderbergh directing and a cast that included George Clooney as Danny Ocean; Brad Pitt, Matt Damon, Don Cheadle, Carl Reiner, and Elliott Gould as members of Ocean's theft squad; and Julia Roberts in a small role as the former Mrs. Ocean, this project (now spelled out *Ocean's Eleven*) seemed blockbuster material. (Besides, the "ring-a-ding" cool the Rat Pack personified was enjoying a new vogue in late 2000.)

The script pared down the heist targets from six Las Vegas casinos to three, and made it clear that Ocean's motive for the theft was based as much on anger at his ex-wife's relationship with the casinos' owner (Andy Garcia) as it was the sheer fun of pulling off such a complex and dangerous stunt.

As filming commenced in January 2001, the main question on the minds of Hollywood watchers was whether history would repeat itself: Would the new stars succumb—as did the original cast of Frank Sinatra, Dean Martin, Sammy Davis, Jr., Peter Lawford, and Joey Bishop—to the siren lure of Vegas's fabled bacchanalian debaucheries and negatively affect the filming?

To the disappointment of the gossips, Clooney's pack didn't emulate Sinatra's. This is, after all, a new era, in which drinking and gambling and staying up all night during a film shoot is frowned upon instead of admired. Still, the cast had fun. As Julia put it, "George and Brad are my buddies. It's always great to work with your buddies. Steven Soderbergh knows how to put a good group together. But I was in Vegas for two weeks and didn't gamble once."

When Julia heard that Soderbergh, whom she adores, was making the film, she asked whether there was a part for her. The director said no, thinking she wouldn't be interested in a role that gives her maybe fifteen minutes on-screen. But he sent her the script anyway, and she said she'd be happy to play Tess Ocean. Anthony Lane, for one, found Julia perfect for the role. "Roberts is playing someone called Mrs. Ocean: ideal casting for a woman who has overwhelmed two-thirds of the planet."

"My part in *Ocean's Eleven* is quite small," she said, "but it's a fun part." She told a reporter before the film opened, "You won't believe the costumes! I'm all glammed out—covered in Tiffany diamonds from head to toe, with all this upswept hair and really fancy dresses!"

The film's budget groaned at $85 million, and even at that, the stars had to take large cuts in their normal salaries. (Clooney, Roberts, Pitt, and Damon alone would have busted the budget with their usual fees. But they all got a cut of the profits, which—considering how well the film did at the box office—served each very well.)

The only juicy gossip to come out of the shoot were the tales that George and Julia were getting along *very well*. There was their bump-and-grind dancing at a party shortly after the filming commenced, and reports of "smooching" near the set. Some observers noticed a special spark between them; Julia explained it by calling herself "the girl version of George," but others saw a romantic and/or sexual attraction.

Julia and George added to the speculation with a playful exchange in *Esquire* magazine's December 2002 issue, for which they "interviewed" each other over lunch. Readers can decide for themselves whether the exchange is only a joke or evidence that the two superstars indeed had an affair:

Julia: How's Waldo, by the way?
George: He's really good.
Julia: Is he on the trip?
George: [*speaking into the tape recorder*] Waldo is our pet name for—
Julia: Oh *God,* George!
George: He's fine, thanks. He sure misses *you!*
[*a few minutes later*]
George: Are you an organ donor?
Julia: Absolutely.
George: It seems like a no-brainer to me.
Julia: What organs are you going to donate, George?
George: I don't really have anything I'm allowed to give away.
Julia: Don't give away Waldo!
George: Now, *that's* a major organ!

Julia and Clooney both denied that theirs was more than a close friendship. Clooney said he didn't have time to romance Julia—because, he joked, "I was too busy breaking up Tom and Nicole." While a crew member said, "She's a huge flirt. . . . There was a twinkle in their eyes when they worked together—a chemistry," he added that their relationship was "all business." Probably. But Clooney spending $1,000 for a hug and a kiss from Julia at a crew auction did little to quell the rumors.

Ocean's Eleven opened on December 27, 2001, to largely positive reviews. Owen Gleiberman of *Entertainment Weekly* was representative of the majority when he said the film was "made with so much wit and brains and dazzle and virtuosity that the sheer speed and cleverness of the caper hits you like a shot of pure oxygen." Jeffrey Chen, on the website windowtothemovies.com, was less impressed: "If you've seen other heist/con movies, you won't find new twists or surprises here, and you'll have little other reason to see *Ocean's Eleven* than to go star-gazing. To their credit, the actors look like they're having fun. George Clooney and Brad Pitt have the best chemistry as two old buds who know what they're doing. . . . The only two less-than-stellar turns are from Matt Damon and Julia Roberts. Damon plays a brash junior con; it's not a challenge for him to play a brash junior anything. Roberts just looks miserable. She plays a small, thankless role, often while wearing a frown or looking just plain tired when she should be looking desirable and gorgeous."

Any negative reviews aside, it became clear after three days that Soderbergh's big-stars-in-a-frothy-caper formula had worked beautifully. The opening-weekend box office of $38.1 million was Julia's highest ever; the film's worldwide gross of $446.8 million bested every one of her movies with the exception of *Pretty Woman*. Since Julia, Clooney, Pitt, and Damon each got 5 percent of the film's gross, they wound up making as much or more in profit participation than they usually do in salary. Not bad for what Julia has called her "little quickie diddly."

As Julia left a recording studio in the fall of 1999 after dubbing additional dialogue for *Erin Brockovich*, Soderbergh handed her an envelope. Inside, she found a $20 bill and a note: "We hear you're [at] 20 a picture now. Thank you for your time." Julia hooted as only she can. But in retrospect, one suspects Soderbergh might have been preparing her for the salary he would offer her on *Full Frontal*, a slice-of-life drama he planned to make with a handheld camera and a budget of $2 million (just over 2 percent of what it cost to make *Ocean's Eleven*). The film had been retitled twice, from the awful *How to Survive a Hotel Room Fire* (changed because of the events of September 11) to the even worse *How to Negotiate a Turn*.

Julia was in an indie mood again; she agreed to accept scale (Screen Actors Guild minimum salary, $25,000) plus a percentage of the film's profits—as did her costars. Since Soderbergh's last three films had grossed an average of $304 million internationally, it seemed like a good bet. Still, Julia said, "My agent hates it when I say this, but if someone was making a really good movie and they had a nickel they could spare to get me to do the job, I'd do it."

Full Frontal began as a stage work written by performance artist Coleman Hough, who then turned it into a screenplay. The story concerns one day in the lives of six people: Lee (Catherine Keener), who wants to leave her screenwriter/celebrity journalist husband, Carl (David Hyde Pierce) and is close to a corporate nervous breakdown. Lee's sister, Linda (Mary McCormick) is planning to go to Tucson to meet Arty (Enrico Colantoni), a hack playwright she met online. Arty and Carl have written a film called *Rendezvous* in which a reporter (Julia, in a shag wig that calls to mind Jane Fonda in *Klute*) interviews Nicholas, a handsome black movie star (Blair Underwood). They discuss the difficulty of romantically pairing actors of different races, and naturally, Julia's *Pelican Brief* kissing dilemma is mentioned. Julia did kiss Underwood, and he enjoyed it. "She has soft lips," he said. "She's terrific. We had a great time working together. . . . Julia's very professional. Obviously, she's a great actress and just nice. She's grateful for what she's been able to accomplish. She worked her butt off every day on the set, knew her lines, was on time and just a very giving actress."

Production commenced on November 6, 2001, and Soderbergh shot most of the film with a digital video camera, utilizing existing light and locations. The movie-within-the-movie, however, was filmed in thirty-five millimeter. (Soderbergh said he considered this film the unofficial sequel to *sex, lies, and videotape,* which established both his career and those of several of the film's actors.) The video footage was sometimes underexposed, sometimes overexposed. The sound was whatever the recorder captured; no postproduction sound editing was done. "A lot of it was just a reaction to coming off *Ocean's Eleven* and wanting to have a very different experience," Soderbergh said. "Because that was such a physically large undertaking, I just wanted to go out and do something small."

Just how small was made clear to the actors when Soderbergh included a ten-point memo along with the script he sent to prospective cast members. Under the heading "Important," Soderbergh advised that any actors hired for his film would have to drive themselves to the set, provide their own wardrobe and meals, "create and maintain" their own hair and makeup, and do without personal trailers. The memo concluded, "You will have fun whether you want to or not," and added that anyone unhappy with these guidelines should send the script back.

If anyone did, Soderbergh never revealed it. "Even Julia drove herself," he said. "I didn't want entourages. I was trying to send a message that you have to show up ready to work because you could be photographed getting out of your car. I had cameras going all the time, everywhere, including cameras [the actors] didn't know about. Spy cams." There was, it turned out, craft food service. "That was a psychological fake-out," Soderbergh said. "But I had prepared them for C rations, so when we actually got a caterer, everybody was slaphappy."

Soderbergh conducted—and filmed—interviews with his actors, asking them questions about themselves and their characters. "Just me and [the actors] and a camera in a room. . . . The questions could be anything. *Do you believe in UFOs? What kind of smell do you hate? What kind of TV shows did you watch growing up?* [It sounds like an episode of *Inside the Actors Studio.*] I used the material as narration throughout the film. It was part of the experiment, but part that really paid off."

Julia's interview completely flummoxed her. She played dual roles in the film—the character Francesca in *Rendezvous,* and the actress playing her, who is also named Francesca. At one point the director asked Julia, "Since winning the Oscar, do you find that other actors behave differently around you?"

According to Soderbergh, Julia stopped and "looked like [her] head was going to split open."

"I don't know who I am right now," Julia said to him. Later, she added, "I felt as though I was playing an actor who, though a kind woman, perhaps was not terribly talented, and when he said that, I thought, *It's impossible that Francesca won an Oscar.* I just remember saying what seemed like an awful lot of times, 'Who am I?' Because I'm playing two different women in this movie, and I'm about five different people at dinner with Steven on a regular basis. Shameful or not, I had just won an Oscar. So I was like, *Wow, what's going on?* It was one of the more terrifying moments in my career."

Without her own trailer, Julia was forced to take a nap in one that was being used as a set. When she woke up, she got an unpleasant surprise. "I open the door, the streets were clean, everybody was gone." The crew had moved on to the next location, and they hadn't had time to look for the biggest movie star in the world—Soderbergh was determined to complete this production in a breathtaking *eighteen days*. He did.

During filming in Los Angeles, Danny Moder visited Julia on location. Their picnic lunch was photographed by paparazzi and published in *People* and the *Globe* tabloid. Julia, wearing a fleece-lined denim jacket, looked positively scary in the tight hairnet she had to wear under her wig. As she and Danny ate artichoke salad while they sat on a patch of grass, Julia rolled a cigarette the two then shared. The paper intimated that it was a "funny" cigarette, but it wasn't. "I smoked marijuana a couple of times in my teens," Julia has said, "but I didn't like it. They made me sleepy. I spend my life trying to be as awake as possible, so why would I do something that made me want to go to sleep?"

Star magazine used the photographs, in which Julia looked gaunt and faintly extraterrestrial, to suggest that the actress was "haunted by guilt" over her affair with Moder and was showing "the tragic toll she's suffered over her forbidden love affair."

Part Six

MRS. MODER

"All my friends call me Mrs. Moder. I love that."

—Julia, 2002

CHAPTER FORTY

Julia was mad as hell, and she wasn't going to take it anymore. Vera Moder was dragging her heels over the divorce that Danny had filed for in October 2001, and worse—from Julia's point of view—she had gone public with her displeasure, telling the press that "America's Sweetheart" had "stolen my husband." Devastated when Danny left their San Fernando Valley home, Vera had tried to reason with her husband: "Look at Julia's dating life. Are you going to give up four years of marriage for a fling?"

But Vera soon realized that both Danny and Julia considered their affair anything but a fling. "He's obsessed," Vera told a reporter. "He really believes he's going to succeed where all these famous actors failed, and get Julia down the aisle. I warned him, 'She'll chew you up and spit you out.' But he wouldn't listen. She's a megastar and I'm a nobody— but I loved and cherished Danny and wanted to spend the rest of my life with him. Which I'm sure is more than Julia can say. I don't think Danny has woken up yet. But when he does, he'll realize I'm gone."

Danny told friends that his marriage to Vera was already on the path to divorce when he met Julia. But shortly before that time, he had sent Vera a dozen long-stemmed roses along with a teddy-bear card that read: "I will love you forever." *Forever* lasted five weeks, Vera said bitterly. "He wants out now, so he can marry Julia."

For her part, Julia had to have been caught in an emotional vice grip—overjoyed by this new love she had found, but deeply upset by all the ill will, not only with Danny and Vera's families but also with the public. For the first time, Julia Roberts was being seen not just as something of a romantic flibbertigibbet but as a scarlet woman. Newspapers began to refer to her as the Liz Taylor of her generation.*

*In 1962, Taylor was condemned from pulpits for her flamboyant affair with the married Richard Burton. Taylor, too, was married—to Eddie Fisher, whose marriage to Debbie Reynolds she had broken up.

Julia had done everything she could to rally the Moder family to her side. On September 4, 2001—not long after the death of Danny's mother—Danny invited her to spend time with him and his father at the elder Moder's lakeside vacation home in the scenic Big Bear area of the San Bernardino Mountains, about a hundred miles east of Los Angeles.

When she got off the small plane that had flown her to the nearby Ontario airport, Danny met her on the tarmac in his four-wheel-drive truck. Their embrace and kisses were caught by a paparazzo before Danny drove Julia up the winding highway to the bucolic, pine-tree-laden resort area seven thousand feet above sea level. In the Moder cabin that night, according to a family friend, "Julia totally charmed [Danny's father] Mike Moder. He was putty in her hands. She apologized for any misunderstandings that may have existed about her relationship with Danny and assured Mike she loved his son and hadn't wanted to hurt anyone." The next day Mike took Danny and Julia on a boat trip on the lake, which a paparazzo captured as well. The pictures show Danny and Julia cuddling while Mike skippers; Danny snapping pictures of Julia; Julia and Danny clambering back into the boat after a swim; and the couple toweling themselves dry. Just over a week earlier, the ashes of Danny's mother had been scattered in that very water.

Danny and Julia were delighted to have his father's blessing. "Family figures very heavily for Danny," a friend of his said. "They both want the blessings of their kin for this relationship. And they want their families to know how serious they are about each other."

Julia's mood fouled when she heard that Vera planned to contest Danny's divorce petition and charge him and Julia with adultery. She would accuse Julia of "turning Danny's head with sex, and throwing in offers of work in upcoming movies as a bonus," said a source. That was when Julia decided to fight back. She may bemoan the constant presence of reporters and photographers in her life, but—as do many public figures—when she needs them, she uses them. In this case, Julia went out to West Hollywood's King's Road Café. She sat at a sidewalk table, for all the world (and at least one photographer) to see, wearing a white T-shirt emblazoned with the stitched words A LOW VERA. The pun on the plant was clearly intended to send a message that Julia did not consider her rival's words and actions acceptable. Photographs of Julia's catty fashion statement were published around the world.

The gambit backfired. Many saw it as a cruel, immature gesture, one that rubbed salt in a wronged wife's wounds. Raoul Felder, a celebrity divorce lawyer, called Julia's action "a very tacky thing to do. Here she is, the most powerful woman in Hollywood, beating up on the jilted wife." Mike Moder took Julia and his son to task. "Vera is a wonderful woman," he said. "I made it clear to both [Julia and Danny] that I wasn't pleased."

Vera didn't take this lying down. She donned a T-shirt with PRETTY UGLY WOMAN written across the back. "One low blow deserves another," she said. "Julia stole my husband, but that's not enough for her. I can't believe that someone like her would stoop so low. She's not a Pretty Woman at all. She's mean in spirit. My only crime is to love my husband."

Finally, Danny told Julia that Vera might keep the divorce process stalled for a year or two, and a financial settlement might help put the matter to rest. Julia reportedly offered Vera $200,000, which she turned down, still holding out hope that she and Danny would reconcile. "Vera told Danny they could still go back to Argentina and have a life there," her cousin Juan Sebastian said, "but his mind is made up. He told her his decision was final. Vera says Julia told her to move on." Offered no hope of salvaging her marriage, and with Julia's financial offer upped to $400,000, Vera relented.

"The time has come to bite the bullet, I guess," she said. "I never wanted Julia's money, but after the nightmare this past year, I have to move on. I need to start afresh. If it had gone to court, it could have been more heartache." When the divorce became final on May 6, Julia and Danny threw a celebratory party in Cabo San Lucas, Mexico, where she had taken Jason Patric for his birthday in 1992. Members of the Moder family did not attend.

Toward the end of spring 2002, reports popped up in the press about the possibility of a second Julia Roberts marriage. Much sport was made of Julia's earlier professions of undying love for Liam, Dylan, Kiefer, Jason, Daniel, Lyle, Ross, Pat, and Benjamin. "I'm never going to talk about another man for the rest of my life," she told George Clooney during their luncheon chat for *Esquire*. (Of course, she did: "I was born to love this man [Moder]," she later gushed.)

The bulk of the published reports wondered "Will she or won't she?" In May, *Us* magazine quoted gossip columnist Marilyn Beck: "I don't think she'll ever get married or that she even wants to get married. She loves her freedom." A friend of Julia's agreed: "She loves men, but I don't think she wants to marry one." Others felt that marital bliss was inevitable. "Danny hasn't let any of this go to his head," his father said. "I've told him to be true to himself, not be Mr. Danny Roberts, and he has." A friend of Danny's added, "He doesn't care about any of the distractions—he would go down this road with Julia again. He's with her, and he's honestly and genuinely happier than I've ever seen him."

But Julia's publicists firmly denied that a marriage was imminent. On July 3, they said Julia wasn't, as rumored, throwing an Independence Day bash at which she and Danny would get hitched; rather, the couple would spend the holiday in the Hamptons on Long Island, New York. Sixty of Julia and Danny's friends, family, and associates knew otherwise.

A few weeks before, Julia and Danny had sent out invitations to a barbecue at the ranch in Taos. The cover of the card reproduced a colorful one-sheet advertisement for the 1947 Mexican film *Fantasía Ranchera*, starring Ricardo Montalban. They must have been shocked when most of his family said they wouldn't attend. The Moders suspected that throwing an "Independence Day" party was another slap at Vera. When Danny's brother, John, tried to demur, Danny had to 'fess up. "John, you've *got* to come," he pleaded. "It's our wedding party!"

John was stunned. "Danny, why didn't you tell us in the first place?"

"I wanted it to be a surprise," Danny replied. John agreed to come two days early for his brother's bachelor party.

For all except the Moders and Julia's immediate family, the surprise went unrevealed until the very last minute. Beginning on July 2, Julia flew many of the guests to Taos on the private plane she charters. Among them were her mother and sisters; Kelly Cunningham (but not Emma—or, of course, Eric); Bruce Willis; and Steven Soderbergh. Brad Pitt and Jennifer Aniston had to send their regrets. So did George Clooney, who couldn't attend because he was in Kentucky for the funeral of his aunt, Rosemary Clooney. Many of the invitees stayed in the guest cottages on Julia's property; others were ensconced in the Adobe and Stars, a bed-and-breakfast in neighboring Arroyo Seco.

The party began in the midafternoon of Thursday, July 4, under a forty-foot-by-sixty-foot white tent, with hors d'oeuvres: fried risotto balls with pesto, shrimp dumplings, vegetable spring rolls, and salmon with goat cheese. Burgers, hot dogs, and lemon-garlic chicken followed, along with sirloin shish kebabs, potato salad, corn on the cob, coleslaw, dishes of green chili and tamales, turkey cooked by Julia, beer, wine, and oceans of Julia's favorite potable, margaritas. Guests swam and lounged around the pool area, played football and basketball.

As nightfall approached, and the multicolored Christmas lights festooning the compound's billowy cottonwood trees lit up, some guests professed weariness and mentioned to Julia that they wanted to go to sleep. "Hang around," she told them. At midnight, as the desert sky sparkled with stars and a gentle breeze blew, the guests were asked to sit in white plastic lawn chairs arranged in a semicircle outside the nineteenth-century-style religious meeting house Julia had built on the property in 2000. Most thought perhaps there would be a final good-night toast with champagne, but others, noting the candles and hanging Chinese lanterns, thought, *Something must be up.*

A few minutes before midnight, Danny and Julia appeared. They had changed clothes. He wore tan pants and a deep-red shirt with ruffles down the front and at the cuffs, created by Judith Beylerian, a Los Angeles designer. Beylerian also designed Julia's long faded-pink halter-top, empire-waist dress, embroidered with pearls and antique beads and hand-painted with flowers. In her upswept hair Julia wore a small flower tiara. This time she wasn't barefoot—she wore flat-heeled pumps by Manolo Blahnik.

By now the guests got the picture. When Julia and Danny moved under a canopy made of pink-and-white silk sheaths and stood in the middle of a circle made of scattered red, white, and pink rose petals, cheers broke out—cheers that, one guest said, seemed to echo against the majestic moonlit thirteen-thousand-foot Sangre de Cristo Mountains nearby.

Danny got down on one knee and asked Julia if she would marry him. When she said yes, their guests let out new cheers. The couple then exchanged handwritten vows in a twenty-minute ceremony officiated by Julia's attorney, Barry Hirsch, who is also a minister and, reports said, a "therapist to the stars." A Navajo Indian shaman gave the couple a blessing after the nuptials.

Julia was given away by Mike Devine, the driver she had befriended in Ireland during her 1991 stay with Jason Patric. "The wedding was very spiritual and romantic," a guest said. "Danny and Julia faced each other throughout the ceremony. They had tears in their eyes as they said their vows." There was no best man, maid of honor, flower girl, or ring bearer. "It was beautiful," said Danny's father. (Only hours before the ceremony, the Taos county clerk, Jeanette Rael, had overseen the signing of marriage license number 7631. "They seemed very happy," Rael said. "They walked in holding hands, smiling and joking. Julia looked beautiful.")

At the reception, tired but happy guests who had been eating and drinking all day needed a second wind to face a new round of goodies: smoked salmon, caviar, five smallish wedding cakes, each with a Hindu theme, and champagne. They danced to country oldies and the music of Sting, Elvis, and Fatboy Slim. Most guests had brought only a plant as the invitation had requested, but one gave the couple an original Navajo totem pole.

Julia gave Danny a $2,000 pair of handmade cowboy boots; he gave her two D. H. Lawrence first editions, one of them *Lady Chatterley's Lover*, which in 1960 had forced Lawrence to undergo an obscenity trial.

"All Julia and Danny seemed to do all night was smooch," a guest said. When a fierce downpour began around one A.M., many of the partyers moved into the main house, where they continued to celebrate until dawn. The next day, Friday, many guests remained, playing basketball and baseball and dipping into the above-ground hot tub. Because the following day was Saturday, some guests stayed through the weekend.

Reports appeared that Julia and Danny had honeymooned on a trip to London, Paris, and Santorini, Greece, but that wasn't true. A few days after the wedding, they drove the nine hundred miles from Taos to Los Angeles in her Toyota Land Cruiser. In L.A., Julia did some interviews to publicize *Full Frontal*, and Danny did camera duty for a Burger King commercial. After those commitments were fulfilled, the couple drove up the coast for a two-day stay in a cottage at the bucolic San Ysidro Ranch.

Despite her vow never to talk about a man again, Julia couldn't keep herself from waxing romantic to reporters about her new hubby. "Danny is astounding. He's formidable. He's a man among men, unselfish and all-encompassing, and he stands by the choices that he's made. He'll never blame it on somebody else. And I've never seen anyone else ever do that."

She obliquely compared Danny to Ben Bratt in another interview. "We're all so quick to whine and say, 'Oh, we're trapped in a box, and oh, everybody's looking.' Danny not only has an understanding but a way to rise above and prevail [over] that kind of ridiculous moment." Julia went on, "All my friends call me Mrs. Moder, and I love that. It wasn't until one day, when we were all playing softball, and I got up to bat, that my friend Mike Oscher went, 'All right, Moder, come on!' and I thought, *Wow!* That's when it really hit me."

Julia was asked if the timing of her marriage was in reaction to Ben Bratt's wedding to Talisa Soto nine weeks earlier, or mere coincidence. "I don't know if it's a coincidence," she replied, "but how great for everybody, I think. Everybody seems like they are where they should be, and that, to me, is either coincidence or miracle."

Everybody but the first Mrs. Moder. Vera continued to speak out against the woman she blames for destroying her marriage. "I'll never be able to forgive Julia. She's a husband stealer! She's been desperate to get him down the aisle. And she's finally gotten her wish." Vera also reportedly told friends that the marriage wouldn't last a year. "Danny cheated on me and he'll cheat on her," she said.

Vera's state of mind wasn't helped when she saw Julia and Danny on the front page of most newspapers and magazines in the week after the wedding. Once again *People* got a photo exclusive, but this time it was just a single black-and-white picture by Sante D'Orazio of the newly-weds nose to nose, staring into each other's eyes. The magazine used it on its cover and again on a full page inside. D'Orazio, who had shot Julia a number of times and become a friend, was the only guest allowed to bring a camera to the gathering; but, he said, "I didn't know it was going to be a wedding or that it was going to be at night. So I didn't have any flash equipment. I had to shoot the whole thing in Instamatic."

On the metal railing of a bridge 670 feet above the Rio Grande River, near Julia's property, along with thousands of others carved by young lovers, is the inscription J LOVES D. Julia had asked Danny to marry her on that very bridge.

Full Frontal, released on August 2, became the worst financial failure in Julia's career since *Blood Red.* Shown in just over two hundred theaters, its opening-weekend box-office gross was an appalling $739,834. Its total gross in the United States: $2.5 million. (Yes, a film budgeted at $2 million and starring Julia Roberts *lost* money.) As one writer quipped, "That isn't even enough to pay Julia's annual hairstyling bill."

The reviews hardly helped. Although Richard Corliss in *Time* felt that "there's a taut grandeur in *Full Frontal*, in part because Julia the box-office queen is encased in an ensemble cast of attractive, accomplished actors," most of the critical reaction was scathing. Lawrence Toppman wrote in *The Charlotte Observer*, "When you've directed three straight movies that grossed more than $100 million and won an Oscar for one of them, you can do whatever you want on your next turn at bat. What Steven Soderbergh wanted to do was a vanity project: an artsy, somewhat improvised, faux-documentary look at six interacting but self-obsessed characters. You could look on *Full Frontal* as an examination of the film world, which makes voyeurs of us all and renders us insensible to real emotions by dramatizing phony ones onscreen. Or you could dismiss it, as I do, as an impenetrable and insufferable ball of pseudo-philosophic twaddle."

Rolling Stone's Peter Travers thought the movie "has its fun moments, and the dialogue, some of which was surely improvised, has a natural flow. But Soderbergh suffocates everything with stylistics. The jump cuts and the grainy digital-video imagery only add to the ongoing befuddlement about who's who and what's what. . . . Godard and Truffaut needed new expressive techniques because they were exploring new emotional territory. Soderbergh is exploring his navel."

One person who liked the finished product was its screenwriter, Coleman Hough. "When I heard that Steven Soderbergh wanted to take my stage show and make it into a movie, I was thrilled. Then when I heard that Julia Roberts and David Duchovny and the others were going to be in it, I was flabbergasted. I think they all did a terrific job. Steven kept things true to the spirit of my original play, and I'm grateful to him for that."

CHAPTER FORTY-ONE

When George Clooney asked Julia to play another small role in an "interesting" film that would mark Clooney's directorial debut, she agreed without hesitation, even though she would again be paid scale and would not be seen on-screen in a major role until her next film, *Mona Lisa Smile,* due for release at the end of 2003—another two-year absence from starring roles.

The project, though, *was* interesting: The film version of Chuck Barris's memoir *Confessions of a Dangerous Mind: An Unauthorized Autobiography,* in which the compact, high-energy former television producer, *Dating Game* creator, and *Gong Show* host revealed that while he was doing all that, he was also a CIA operative who had killed thirty-three people. Much skepticism arose over this claim; many felt the CIA story was fantasy intended to bolster the book's sales. (Its subtitle seemed to provide a clue that the book was written with tongue in cheek.) Clooney was asked if he thought it important whether or not Barris's tale was true. "It was important for me not to ask him the question when I met him. . . . I wanted to be able to tell the story, true or not. I wanted to be able to say I think it's a really fascinating story—if it's not true—that someone as successful as Chuck Barris felt the need to write that story."

Once Clooney had made the decision to direct, he found the script adapted by the wildly imaginative Charlie Kaufman (*Being John Malkovich, Adaptation*), brilliant but unwieldly. He cut a number of scenes that would have pushed the budget over $40 million. (By paying most of his stars scale, he was able to keep the budget under $30 million.) Earlier in the film's gestation—when other directors were attached to it—actors as different from one another as Johnny Depp, Mike Myers, Sean Penn, and Kevin Spacey had expressed interest, but Clooney did not want a famous actor playing a famous person. He persuaded Miramax boss Harvey Weinstein to take a big risk and cast the relatively unknown Sam Rockwell in the lead. In return, Weinstein made Clooney agree to do another Miramax project sometime in the future.

With Rockwell cast as Barris, Julia as a mysterious fellow CIA agent with whom he has an affair (and who tries to poison him), Drew Barrymore as Barris's hippie girlfriend, and Matt Damon and Brad Pitt as *Dating Game* contestants, Clooney had some big names in his movie—including George Clooney. The director would play the CIA man who lures Barris into the agency.

Asked about the casting process, Clooney replied, "First of all, I don't really care for any of them. They're just a tool to be used. . . . They're cattle. Actors are cattle. Who said that, Hitchcock? He meant it." Rockwell provided a more serious glimpse, saying he had to undergo a screen test to get the part. "An old-fashioned screen test, like a real Scarlett O'Hara–type screen test," Rockwell said, "which, you know, they don't really do anymore. I've done a few, and they just do it on video now. This one was tracks, dollies, [and] we had Tommy Sigel, the actual [director of photography]. We had costumes. They curled my hair and put on makeup, everything. They reenacted the *Gong Show* stuff with full costumes, tuxedos, everything."

Rockwell thought the elaborate test was a way for Clooney to "get his feet wet" as a director. "It was a day of really making a movie, in a sense . . . then about two weeks later, I got a call. They said I got it, but I didn't really have it officially. Then what happened is it got postponed, and [then] Drew Barrymore and Julia Roberts came on board. That's when they could sort of green-light me—because of them. That's basically what happened."

Filming took place over two months in Montreal, California, Nogales, Mexico, and Tucson, beginning in January 2002. Rockwell found working with Julia a revelation: "She comes in, she's like a laser, man, she just comes in and does it. She's really good. She's had a little experience, yeah. She's carried a few films. She comes in there and just knocks it out of the park, you know? Julia and Drew are different, but they're both great in their own ways."

Miramax made the strange decision to open *Confessions* at only four screens on New Year's Eve 2002, a Tuesday. Many of the reviews were excellent. Roger Ebert said, "[The fact] that this would be the first project to attract George Clooney as a director is not so surprising if you know that his father directed game shows, and he was often a backstage observer. That Clooney would direct it so well is a little surprising, and is part of that re-education by which we stop thinking of Clooney as a TV hunk and realize he is smart and curious. His first movie is not only intriguing as a story but great to look at, a marriage of bright pop images from the 1960s and 1970s and dark, cold spy capes that seem to have wandered in from John le Carré. Julia Roberts [plays] the CIA's Marlene Dietrich, her face sexily shadowed at a rendezvous. She gives him a quote from Nietzsche that could serve as his motto: "The man who despises himself still respects himself as he who despises."

Lloyd Dobler of dobleronfilm.com felt that "Clooney and Roberts are the kind of actors that when you see them on the screen you have to worry that their star personae might overshadow their performances, but this isn't the case for them in *Confessions of a Dangerous Mind.* . . . The coolness that Clooney creates for his character Jim Byrd is what is so fascinating about him. He is cool on the outside, but you can tell by his eyes that something else is going on within him. As for Roberts, she not only seduces Barris, but she also seduces the entire audience every moment that she is on the screen."

Others disagreed about Julia's value to the film. Some critics found her cameo distracting; others thought it unconvincing. Elvis Mitchell said in *The New York Times,* "When Julia Roberts shows up as a slinky double agent in hats that Diana Vreeland might have chosen, *Confessions* slides dangerously close to *Rocky and Bullwinkle.*" And Ty Burr of *The Boston Globe* felt "sometimes the in-joke casting misfires—Roberts disastrously treats her extended cameo like a lah-di-dah lark."

At first Miramax's plan to open *Confessions* on a minute scale seemed to pay off. The per-screen box-office average its opening weekend was $21,800, a good indication of strong public interest. On January 24 the film expanded to 1,769 screens and netted $5.8 million to place eighth for the weekend. In the second week of national release, however, receipts fell 26 percent, and the third week, 68 percent from that. By the seventh weekend, the number of theaters showing the movie fell to twenty-nine, and it added just $24,425 for a total of $15.9 million.

Miramax then pulled *Confessions* from release, apparently deeming it a noble failure. But on April 4, 2003, *Variety* reported that the studio, in another unusual marketing move, would re-release the film on August 15, 2003, and give it a brand-new marketing campaign. Miramax hoped to secure at least a thousand theaters for the reissue and would utilize an action-laced trailer originally cut for use overseas. "We're making the campaign more fun, more thriller-ish," chief operating officer Rick Sands told *Variety*. "When audiences saw the film, they liked it, but it went out at a very competitive time. So we think there's a lot of audience left to find the film. George made a wonderful film that got good reviews, but unfortunately, there was so much going on in the marketplace that it wasn't first choice among moviegoers."

By early summer 2003, Miramax had markedly scaled back its plans for the *Confessions* re-release. On August 15, it opened in just a few theaters in Los Angeles and New York. The DVD release in September won the film another round of positive reviews. As of this writing, if the picture is to find a cult audience, it will have to be on television screens instead of cineplexes.

Julia spent December 2002 to February 2003, one of the coldest, snowiest northeastern winters in years, in Wellesley, Massachusetts, filming *Mona Lisa Smile*. Directed by Mike Newell (*Four Weddings and a Funeral*) with a script by Lawrence Konner and Mark Rosenthal (*Mighty Joe Young, Planet of the Apes*), the story concerns primates of a higher order: Katherine Watson (Julia), a UCLA graduate and now an art history teacher at the staid Wellesley College in the early 1950s, and the female students whose lives she deeply influences by opening their minds to more than narrow, old-fashioned views.

The premise might call to mind *Dead Poets Society, Mr. Holland's Opus,* or *Dangerous Minds,* but the resemblance is only superficial. The script sets itself apart by focusing on a time and place when women struggled far more with their roles in the world than they do now. While interacting with her students, Katherine realizes that she has much to learn from them as well.

Julia was kept warm by the presence of her husband, who worked as a second-unit cameraman on the film, and by her long fifties-style dresses, which will remind viewers of Julianne Moore's in *Far from Heaven*. To prepare for the role, Julia attended an etiquette "boot camp" along with costars Kirsten Dunst and Julia Stiles to learn the cha-cha, swing dancing, and the "art of flirting." (Some would say Julia could have *taught* that class.)

A number of Wellesley students were hired as extras and for small roles, but many of them were upset that no people of color were given on-screen participation. Far fewer black and Latino students were enrolled in the 1950s, the school's president, Diana Chapman Walsh, wrote in *The Boston Globe.* "Seeing ourselves reflected in a mirror half a century old was jarring, despite our conscious efforts not to replicate destructive patterns of the past. . . . We asked the studio to open the off-camera opportunities to students who would not have an equal opportunity to play extras in the film, which they did. Our students were philosophical and gracious about the historical constraints on the casting decisions."

Early in October, Julia appeared at a press conference on campus. Designed to promote the film by charming the local press, the event had the opposite effect. *Globe* columnist Geoff Edgers, who writes about the Web, said in a column entitled "Snitty Woman" that Julia had turned the conference into "a confrontation. Publicists warned reporters not to ask about the rumors that Julia's pregnant. But they didn't warn them away from [asking Julia] questions about Boston. 'I have quite enjoyed Wellesley,' she snickered, doing her best impression of a frozen margarita. Since we know Julia better than that and recognize how fleeting movie stardom can be—can you say Demi?—we suggest 'America's Sweetjerk' take stock before it's too late." (Other reports had Julia responding to the question "How do you like Boston?" with "We're not in Boston, I'm afraid.")

Edgers then went on to list websites for Julia haters, including one that featured "alternating photos of '60s TV icon Mr. Ed and Julia, and the comparison is not flattering." Another site offered advice for pregnant women, but, Edgers asked, "What about the big C, crankiness? A movie star needs more than a few lousy Wheat Thins when dealing with those smart-alecky media hounds."

Who's calling whom cranky?

The rumors that Julia was pregnant started when Danny discussed with crew members the ways—from camera angles to costume alterations— that a pregnancy can be hidden in a movie. In early December, Julia was spotted leaving the fertility clinic of New York Presbyterian Hospital. While her publicist, Marci Engelman, said she was there to support a friend, speculation that Julia might have a problem conceiving had surfaced years earlier when, despite her oft-expressed desire to be a mother, she'd never had a baby, either in or out of wedlock. Moder's interest in how to deal with a star's pregnancy in a film may have been purely theoretical, because as of this writing, there is no indication that Julia was or is with child.

Rumors of an entirely different sort also emerged from the filming. According to on-set sources, Julia "blew up into a rage" when she heard about Danny's "flirting ways" with Kirsten Dunst (who was and remains romantically involved with Jake Gyllenhaal, brother of Maggie, another of the film's stars). One source said, "A rumor circulated around the set that Julia barged in on Danny and Kirsten when they were in her trailer. Kirsten later apologized to Julia, saying, 'Nothing really happened,' but Julia wasn't buying it." Julia and Danny patched up the rift.

Columbia Pictures executives originally set the release of *Mona Lisa Smile* for July 11, 2003. After seeing Newell's final cut, however, they decided the film and its stars had Oscar potential and rescheduled it for December 19. All concerned would be thrilled if *Mona Lisa Smile* made Julia Roberts a member of that rare breed: a two-time Oscar winner.

CHAPTER FORTY-TWO

Julia's marriage to Danny Moder, like every one of her relationships since her engagement to Kiefer Sutherland, has provided copious grist for the Hollywood rumor mill. Ben Bratt once joked that he and Julia had decided to live their lives according to what the tabloids said about them, but if Julia and Danny did the same thing, their lives would spin into a maelstrom.

There were those pregnancy/fertility-clinic stories, all denied. (One claimed that Julia wasn't the infertile partner, Danny was. Another rebutted that claim and said Vera had suffered a miscarriage with Danny's baby shortly before their breakup.) There was the blazing front-page exposé in *Star* that Julia suffered from a rare blood disease, immune thrombocytopenic purpura (ITP). Marci Engelman said the dire report was "absolutely untrue. She's in perfect health." Another story reported that Julia and Danny, unable to conceive, planned to adopt a child by Christmas 2002. The holiday came and went without news of a tyke joining the Moder household.

And, of course, there were numerous stories about marital strife: public brawls, Danny's jealousy over Julia's closeness to George Clooney, Julia "storming out" on her husband. There were several articles that said Danny had spent an evening in the L.A. strip club Fourplay. One claimed he made "unwanted advances" on one of the girls, was admonished by the management, and left in a huff; another said Danny had in fact rebuffed the woman's advances, that she had made up the story out of pique, and he had stayed there until the wee hours stuffing twenty-dollar bills into G-strings.

There was the *Star* exclusive, I SLEPT WITH JULIA'S HUBBY, in which Rosalie Rung described a night of "sizzling" sex: "We were up all night. It was very passionate. He was a good lover—we had fun. He had lots of stamina and was a very conscientious lover. He definitely wasn't selfish." The implication was clear: Danny Boy had cheated on Julia. But Rosalie told this author, "I knew him briefly in college. He was a very nice guy, fun to hang out with, affable. That was over ten years ago, and I haven't seen him since then. It was a casual fling, regardless of what the tabloids made it out to be."

Then there were the pictures of Julia smooching a "mystery man" outside her Manhattan building. And finally, the *Enquirer's* chilling front-page declaration in the spring of 2003: JULIA ROBERTS' MARRIAGE: IT'S OVER!

Rumors can usually be proved or disproved only by the passage of time, but the mystery-man brouhaha was quickly debunked. Australia's *New Idea* ran pictures of Julia hugging an attractive man in a blue shirt and "looking around to make sure no one had seen them." The article strongly implied that the seemingly romantic good-bye followed a tryst.

Star had it both ways. Their headline asked, IS NEWLYWED JULIA ROBERTS CHEATING? They published a picture of the twosome kissing, which *New Idea* didn't have. The story quoted an eyewitness in the story's second paragraph: "Julia may be a new bride, but that didn't stop her from putting on a very public display, hugging and kissing a tall, handsome man who definitely wasn't her husband. . . . I couldn't believe what I was seeing. The guy came out of the apartment building where Julia keeps a place and looked around. Then Julia followed him out. She was looking all around before she went over to him, wrapped her arms around his neck and hugged him very, very tightly."

The implication was unmistakable, but then the tabloid said it could "reveal" the innocent explanation in paragraph six. The man in the photographs was Julia's old friend Barry Tubb. The article quoted a source: "Barry has an apartment in the same building as Julia. They've been close for years."

So, Barry wasn't coming from Julia's apartment but from his own. And the hugs and kisses were a friendly farewell rather than an indication of a steamy romance. (Julia is known to be very touchy-feely with people close to her.) The fact that both Barry and Julia "looked around" would seem to indicate they wanted to avoid being photographed, which prompts the question: Why on earth didn't they say their good-byes inside the building? One wonders why Julia, after fifteen years of dealing with the paparazzi, would put herself in a position to be photographed kissing Tubb. As *Star* quoted its source, "I can just imagine Danny's reaction when he sees these photos. Would you want to see your new bride passionately embracing another man—especially in public?"

By numerous accounts, both Julia and Danny are insecure in their relationship's staying power—Danny because of Julia's history with men, and Julia because of Danny's proven appeal to the opposite sex. A story surfaced that two days before the wedding, Julia went into a rage when Danny's cell phone rang at two in the morning and it was a model he'd met at a photo shoot—to whom he'd obviously given his number. "Every once in a while a girl from Danny's past will call him at their Los Angeles apartment," said a friend. "He'll try to have a polite but stilted conversation. But as soon as he puts down the phone, he gets the third degree. That kind of confrontation sets Julia off into a rage that lasts for days. Danny's sworn to [Julia] that she's the one and only for him. But she fears that the very things that attracted her to him in the first place will continue to attract other women to him, too. It never seemed to occur to her [before the wedding] that she was falling in love with a man who cheated on his wife and could now do the same to her."

On July 4, 2003, cynics who predicted the marriage of Julia Roberts and Danny Moder wouldn't last a year were proved wrong. To celebrate their first anniversary, the couple took a romantic vacation to Italy. On June 29, they attended the wedding of one of Danny's friends, Avi Haliman, in the picturesque town of Ovada, seventy miles from Milan. They spent a few days in Tuscany (at a twenty-room medieval castle) en route to Giorgio Armani's villa atop a cliff overlooking the Mediterranean Sea on the island of Pantelleria, between Sicily and Malta. There, they celebrated the anniversary with more than a dozen friends and relatives.

The couple sunbathed and swam together; Danny went scuba diving while Julia snorkled; Julia rode a scooter to a local shop to pick up tomatoes, paté and wine. They spent other periods apart—Danny and seven others toured the waters around the island in a rubber boat while Julia slept late—but when they were together, it was clear to everyone how they felt about each other. "Always she kissed him and he kissed her," said Fausto Parodi, the owner of a café at which the Moders dined. "They looked like a couple in love."

As of this writing, months after the *Enquirer* declaimed that "There's nothing left in the marriage to save," Danny and Julia are still together. Julia's fans hope that this relationship will last, that she won't wind up as so many other female superstars before her have—alone in her old age.

After she completed filming *Mona Lisa Smile* in the spring of 2003, Julia planned to take the rest of the year off. As usual with a major star, rumors of impending projects have abounded. One of the films mentioned as being on Julia's agenda is *A Time to Be,* directed by Angelica Huston and set during World War II, about wealthy New Yorkers who use one another selfishly.

Julia and Brad Pitt were said to be "in negotiations" for the screen version of *Replay,* Ken Grimwood's well-reviewed 1990 novel about a forty-three-year-old man who dies of a heart attack, then wakes up as himself in college to correct his youthful mistakes. Another bit of wishful casting would have had Russell Crowe and Julia play Spencer Tracy and Katharine Hepburn in a biopic of their twenty-five-year relationship. While Crowe would make a terrific Tracy, it's hard to imagine Julia as Hepburn. A better choice would be Kate Mulgrew (Captain Janeway on *Star Trek: Voyager*), who played Hepburn in *Tea at Five,* a one-woman show by Matthew Lombardo, at the Promenade Theater in New York. Another title mentioned in connection with Julia is a Gore Verbinski project said to be "in the vein" of George Cukor's 1944 classic *Gaslight,* which starred Ingrid Bergman and Charles Boyer, about a man who tries to convince his wife that she's going insane.

Many of these speculations about films of interest to Julia are put out by prospective producers to heighten interest in their projects. Others are films Julia has seriously considered but either decided to pass on or was unable to do. The only film she has committed to is *Ocean's Twelve,* which will reunite the entire cast of *Ocean's Eleven* with director Steven Soderbergh. Despite the enormous success of the first film, Soderbergh has vowed to keep the budget the same. His stars will again take little up-front payment but will have profit participation, an arrangement that worked pretty well the first time around. The sequel will be filmed entirely in Europe, providing new settings and, presumably, less expensive production costs. "I had an idea a year ago that I started kicking around," said Soderbergh. "I spoke to everyone who was involved, and they all seemed willing to come back. So we're hoping a year from right now [early 2004] we'll start shooting."

Ocean's Twelve will be both George Clooney's and Julia's fourth collaboration with Soderbergh. "He's just, like, one of the best directors in the business," Clooney said. "You want to work with the good guys, and he's a really good guy."

On April 28, 2003, Julia again raised eyebrows across Hollywood when she left International Creative Management, the agency that had represented her for over ten years. Although every agency in the business attempted to court her, initial reports said that she would attempt to manage her career without representation. But two weeks later, she moved to Creative Artists Agency, which had also just signed Hilary Swank and Tobey Maguire. Julia joining CAA (where she would have a "team" of agents, she said) gives that agency a lock on most of the industry's biggest female stars: Swank, Nicole Kidman, Halle Berry, Gwyneth Paltrow, Helen Hunt, Renee Zellweger, Sandra Bullock, and Cameron Diaz, among others.

Neither Julia nor ICM would comment on the reason for her defection, but it likely had to do with Elaine Goldsmith-Thomas's departure from the agency to oversee Julia's new production company, Red Om ("Moder" spelled backward), in addition to serving as a partner at Revolution Studios, overseeing its Gotham operations. Red Om recently produced the Jennifer Lopez–Ralph Fiennes romantic comedy *Maid in Manhattan* for Revolution/Columbia Pictures.

In November, 2002, *Forbes* named Julia number 26 on its annual list of the forty richest people in America under forty years old. The magazine estimated her net worth at $145 million. What, one can't help but wonder, would Walter Roberts think of that?

Marilyn Monroe once said, "I don't care about money. I just want to be wonderful." Monroe was one of the last of the contract stars, and she was woefully underpaid in light of the millions her films brought into the coffers of 20th Century–Fox. Today many actresses can both care about money *and* be wonderful. Julia is in the enviable position of not having to worry about money while making a lot of it. This leaves her free to experiment in a film like *Full Frontal,* play dress-up in *Ocean's Eleven,* or send up Mata Hari in *Confessions of a Dangerous Mind.*

Most of her experiments—going all the way back to *Hook* and *Mary Reilly*—have failed, commercially, artistically, or both. Sometimes the fault is largely her own, other times not. After the high point of *Erin Brockovich,* the expectation bar for Julia Roberts films rose considerably; for her to have little more than cameos in three of her next five films, and for the other two to be relative trifles, disappointed many.

At this writing, *Mona Lisa Smile* promises to raise the bar once again. In September 2003, reports appeared that preview audiences had rated the picture more favorably than any Julia Roberts film ever, and *The New York Times* described it as an "audience pleaser." If general audiences feel the same way, *Mona Lisa Smile* may well emulate the commercial and artistic success of *Erin Brockovich* and reaffirm Julia's preeminent position among her female contemporaries.

Julia Roberts has more than proved herself as a personality, as a favorite with the public, and as a moneymaker. What she has yet to do is place herself among the pantheon of Hollywood's great actresses. Few doubt that she could do it, if she would only make films more like *The Hours* or *Far from Heaven* and less like *America's Sweethearts*. Perhaps *Mona Lisa Smile* will continue her on the path set by *Erin Brockovich*.

But Julia's stardom may continue to be mediocre-movie-proof. She is one of those rare women who are held in such affection by moviegoers worldwide that the pleasure of her company on-screen surmounts lesser scripts or unfunny comedies. Movie stars can usually be characterized as either actors or personalities. Meryl Streep is an actor, able to immerse herself so deeply within a character that audiences feel they are watching the person rather than a performer. Marilyn Monroe, for the first four years of her stardom, was a personality, a performer who often delighted but rarely surprised. Her development into an actress, in films like *Bus Stop* and *The Misfit*, was cut short by her untimely death. Bette Davis managed to combine the two; she was unquestionably a great actress, and her personality was never far afield of her characterizations. What set her stardom apart was her willingness to play villainesses (*The Little Foxes*) and grotesques (*Whatever Happened to Baby Jane?*).

At this point in her career, Julia has not played a villainess, a grotesque, a drunkard, or a murderess. If she attempts to, audiences might stay away as resolutely as they did from *Mary Reilly*. Because, truth be told, for better or worse, filmgoers the world over plunk down their money only to see the Julia Roberts they have come to know and love.

Anthony Lane, in his *New Yorker* profile of Julia, wrote, "She palpitates with worry and need; the famous upper lip . . . spends more time in tremble mode than in any other, and she tends to throw herself hungrily at kisses, as if she hadn't had a square meal in weeks. . . . The essence of Roberts's appeal—notably old-fashioned, if you think about it—is that she is more lovable than desirable, and that, even when love is off the menu, she cannot *not* be liked. There is no more flattering illusion in movies, none that we prefer to hear over and over again: here is a goddess, and she wants to be your friend."

For the past fifteen years, Julia Roberts's audiences have returned the favor.

ACKNOWLEDGMENTS

I would like to express heartfelt thanks to the family, friends, colleagues, and acquaintances of Julia Roberts and her family who graciously agreed to be interviewed for this book: Glenda Beard, Keith Bohannan, David Boyd, Joan Dismer Childs, Nancy Collier, Norma Daniels, Lyn Deadmore, C. Tad Devlin, Blaise Dismer, Scott DePoy, Pat Dozier, Melissa York Finkenbinder, June Mathias Finn, Bettianne Fishman, Theresa Gernazian, Keith Gossett, Jamie Hiatt, Paul Hirsch, Coleman Hough, Rance Howard, Gloria Jones, Steve Kagan, J. F. Lawton, Evan Lee, Tom Lyle, Angelina Maceas, Lexi Masterson, Peter Masterson, Don McAlpine, Ernestine McElhaney, Paula Monteith, Sandy Morse, Will Nazarowski, Peter Onorati, Greg Patin, Barbara Gaddis Patrick, Shelli Pearce, George Pefanis, Richard Pollard, Charles Purpura, Lucille Roberts, Tom Rolf, Bruno Rubeo, Rosalie Rung, Mary Summerhill, Paul Sylbert, Dorothy Whitmire, Daniece Williams, and Eugenio Zannetti.

I'd also like to thank Eric Roberts and Eliza Simon Roberts for answering many of my questions by e-mail, and for explaining to me Eric's current feelings about his father.

Several of the people interviewed for this book preferred to remain anonymous, and they are identified as such in the text. I thank them for speaking to me as well.

I owe a large debt of gratitude to a number of people who helped me in the preparation and research for this book. My fellow author and friend J. Randy Taraborrelli very generously shared with me research he had done for a book on Julia, and offered helpful advice and opinions. My dear friend and fellow author Christopher Nickens was a huge help with research and fact-checking, as usual. Cathy Griffin, a writer and private investigator in Hollywood, graciously provided me information that proved very helpful.

My partner, Terry Brown, was indispensable, not only with love and moral support but with his computer expertise, which saved me from many a PC disaster. My good friends Christopher Mossey and Jamie Smarr offered assistance and hospitality in New York. Those who also provided help were my cousin Sonny Ruberto and my friend Mike Szymanski.

Glenda Beard, Gloria Jones, Mary Summerhill, and Barbara Gaddis Patrick provided me with photographs of Julia's family. Blaise Dismer (author of *Persevering Past Panic*), Evan Lee, and Lyn Deadmore kindly sent me newspaper articles, programs, and other materials on the Actors and Writers Workshop.

The staffs of the Atlanta-Fulton Public Library, the Atlanta Public Records Office, the Margaret Herrick Library at the Academy of Motion Picture Arts and Sciences, the British Film Institute, and the Lincoln Center Library of the Performing Arts were extremely helpful with my research.

Eric Retif and Robert Sherer of Tulane University provided me with enrollment information for Walter and Betty Roberts. Tom Gunn of Emory University confirmed Walter's Emory enrollment dates. Melodie A. Wardell of the National Personnel Records Center of the National Archives provided releasable information about Walter and Betty's air force service records. The Fulton County court clerk's office provided copies of the papers in the *Roberts vs. Roberts* divorce action; the Cobb County, Georgia, superior clerk's office released to me the court papers in the divorce action of *Betty Motes vs. Michael Motes*.

Elizabeth Beier is the kind of editor every author hopes for: enthusiastic and smart. She inherited this book from another editor but never treated it as an orphan, and for that I'm very grateful. I'd also like to thank Michael Denneny, Sally Richardson, and John Murphy of St. Martin's Press for their interest in this project when I first suggested it.

Todd Schuster, my agent, was high on this book from the moment I mentioned it, and never lost an ounce of his enthusiasm. He is not only a fine representative but a valued friend.

Other people in my life whom I treasure are Richard Branson and Ned Keefe, Glen Sookiazian, Dan Conlon, Margaret Lowe, Simone Rene, Laura Van Wormer, Janet Smith, Michael Koegel, Tim and Virginia Lilly, my father, Joe, my brothers, Richard and Lewis, and my cousin Anna Zaniewski.

BIBLIOGRAPHY

BOOKS

Altman, Robert, Barbara Shulgasser, and Brian D. Leitch. *Robert Altman's Prêt-à-Porter*. New York: Miramax Books/Hyperion, 1994.

Blackwell, Richard, with Vernon Patterson. *From Rags to Bitches*. Santa Monica, Calif.: General Publishing Group, 1995.

Jenkins, Garry. *Daniel Day-Lewis: The Fire Within*. New York: St. Martin's Press, 1995.

Jordan, Neil. *Michael Collins*. New York: Plume, 1996.

Joyce, Aileen. *Julia: The Story of America's Pretty Woman*. New York: Windsor Publishing Group, 1993.

Kaufman, Anthony, ed. *Steven Soderbergh Interviews*. Jackson, Miss.: University Press of Mississippi, 2002.

Landowski, Ellen. *Julia Roberts*. New York: Time-Life Inc., 1999.

Lane, Anthony. *Nobody's Perfect*. New York: Alfred A. Knopf, 2002.

Leimbach, Marty. *Dying Young*. New York: Doubleday, 1990.

MacLaine, Shirley. *My Lucky Stars*. New York: Bantam, 1995.

Marshall, Garry. *Wake Me When It's Funny*. New York: Newmarket Press, 1995.

Martin, Valerie. *Mary Reilly*. New York: Vintage Books, 2001.

Meade, Marion. *The Unruly Life of Woody Allen*. New York: Scribner, 2000.

Millar, Ingrid. *Liam Neeson.* New York: St. Martin's Press, 1996.

O'Connor, Áine. *Hollywood Irish.* Boulder, Colo.: Roberts, Rinehart, 1997.

Parton, Dolly. *Dolly.* New York: HarperCollins, 1994.

Price, Nancy. *Sleeping with the Enemy.* New York: Simon & Schuster, 1987.

Sanello, Frank. *Julia Roberts.* Edinburgh, Scotland: Mainstream Publishing Company, 1999.

Whitburn, Joel. *The "Billboard" Book of Top 40 Hits.* New York: Billboard Books, 2000.

PRINCIPAL MAGAZINES AND NEWSPAPERS

Allis, Tom. "The Joy of Julia." *In Style,* December 1998.

Baker, James N. "Star '83." *The Movies,* November 1983.

Blair, Iain. "The Reserved Mr. Roberts." *The Hollywood Reporter,* March 1989.

Brennan, Judy. "Trouble on 'Trouble' Set?" *Los Angeles Times,* July 3, 1994.

Brown, Corie. "What's Wrong with 'Mary Reilly'?" *Premiere,* December 1995.

Burr, Ty. "America's Most Wanted." *Entertainment Weekly,* July 20, 2001.

———. "Searching for the Real Soderbergh." *The Boston Globe,* November 29, 2002.

Cagle, Jess. "Why Isn't Jason Patric a Star Yet?" *Entertainment Weekly,* December 24, 1993.

———. "Julia Roberts: Best Movie Star." *Time,* July 9, 2001.

Calio, Jim. "Pretty Happy Woman." *Redbook,* April 2000.

Chun, Rene. "When Julia Roberts Came to Dinner." *Marie Claire,* July 1999.

Connelly, Christopher. "Nobody's Fool." *Premiere,* December 1993.

Coppola, Vincent. "Eric the Angry." *Atlanta,* November 1992.

Coyne, Cate, and Beth Landman. "What Julia Knows." *Good Housekeeping,* September 2000.

Crystal, Billy. "Sitting on Top of the World." *Harper's Bazaar,* July 2001.

Curtis, Richard. "A Conversation Between Friends." *Us,* March 27, 2000.

Darling, Lynn. "How Julia Does It." *Us,* April 2, 2001.

Davis, Sally Ogle. "Julia Roberts: Shooting Star." *Ladies' Home Journal,* July 1991.

Dollar, Steve. "Julia Roberts Arrives." *The Atlanta Journal Weekend,* October 29, 1988.

Egan, Timothy. "Julia Roberts, After the Layoff and with Lyle." *The New York Times,* December 12, 1993.

Eimer, David. "Julia in the Crown." *Time Out,* August 27, 1997.

———. "Who Rattled Her Cage?" *London Sunday Times,* March 26, 2000.

Essex, Andrew. "Mothering Heights." *Entertainment Weekly,* November 27, 1998.

Fierman, Daniel. "The Rules of the Game." *Entertainment Weekly,* March 1, 2002.

Forsberg, Myra. "Julia Roberts Faces a Test of Character." *The New York Times,* March 19, 1990.

Galligan, David. "Jason Patric." *Drama-Logue,* November 26–December 2, 1987.

Gannon, Sean. "Julia Roberts: Her Turning Point." *Redbook,* October 1997.

Garey, Julianne. "The Real Julia." *Redbook,* April 2001.

Gerosa, Melina. "Fascinating Talk with Fascinating Women." *Ladies' Home Journal,* January 1999.

Goldstein, Patrick. "Producing Films, by Way of Jersey." *Los Angeles Times,* March 20, 2001.

Goodman, Joan. "A Leading Man with Character." *Marquee,* May 1984.

Gordoner, Jeff. "Living the Life of Reilly." *Entertainment Weekly,* February 23, 1996.

Graham, Caroline. "Eric Roberts: 'I'll Never Forgive Julia.'" *Night & Day* (*The Mail on Sunday*), October 8, 2000.

Green, Ray. "Julia Roberts." *Boxoffice,* June 1997.

Hackett, Pat. "Eric Roberts." *Interview,* October 1986.

Harling, Robert. "Local Boy Makes Good." *Life,* October 1989.

Haskell, Molly. "How a Small-town Girl Made Good." *Ladies' Home Journal,* April 2002.

Heath, Chris. "Portrait of a Trash-Talking Lady." *Rolling Stone,* April 13, 2000.

Hedegaard, Eric. "Eric Roberts." *Details,* April 1996.

Heyman, J. D. "Too Good to Be True." *Us,* July 16, 2001.

———. "Julia & Danny: 'This Could Go All the Way.'" *Us,* May 13, 2002.

Honeycutt, Kirk. "There's No Business Like Joe Business." *The Hollywood Reporter Joe Roth Tribute Issue,* October 1994.

Hruska, Bronwen. "Too True." *Los Angeles Times,* August 6, 1995.

Jones, Oliver. "The Lost Boy." *Details,* December 2002.

Kaplan, James. "A Starlet Is Born." *Rolling Stone,* January 12, 1989.

Kasindorf, Martin. "A Summer of Sutherlandia." New York *Newsday,* August 2, 1990.

Kelly, Kevin. "Eric Roberts Has 'Mass Appeal.'" *The Boston Globe,* October 4, 1981.

Knapp, Michael. "Will Julia Ever Settle Down?" *Redbook,* April 1996.

Kroll, Gerry. "Resurrection." *The Advocate,* January 6, 1996.

Lague, Louise, et al. "Miss Roberts Regrets." *People,* July 1, 1991.

Lane, Anthony. "Smiley Face." *The New Yorker,* March 26, 2001.

Levitt, Shelley, et al. "Hidden Star." *People,* February 8, 1993.

———. "Lovett First Sight." *People,* July 12, 1993.

———. "State of Their Union." *People,* August 8, 1994.

Lew, Julie. " 'Dying Young' Survives a Case of Serious Rumors." *The New York Times,* June 16, 1991.

Lyman, Rick. "Oscar Holds Suspense with Races Too Close to Call." *The New York Times,* March 21, 2001.

Marshall, Leslie. "Don't Fence Her In." *In Style,* January 2000.

———. "Ain't Life Grand?" *In Style,* March 2001.

McInerney, Jay. "Julia Roberts Talks with Jay McInerney." *Harper's Bazaar,* June 1994.

Morgan, Gary. "The Fight to Win Julia's Dress Oscar." *London Sunday Express,* March 25, 2001.

Murphy, Mary. "The Trials of Dylan McDermott." *TV Guide,* February 26, 2000.

Nashawaty, Chris. "The Three Amigos." *Entertainment Weekly,* March 9, 2002.

Norman, Neil. "Has Julia Cooked Her Golden Goose?" London *Evening Standard,* November 21, 1993.

O'Neill, Anne-Marie, et al. "Going for the Gold." *People,* March 19, 2001.

———. "Their Separate Ways." *People,* July 16, 2001.

Park, Jeannie, et al. "Ahoy! Neverland!" *People,* December 23, 1991.

Patterson, M. C. "What's Really Going on with Julia." *McCall's,* November 1993.

Peretz, Evgenia. "The Bratt Pact." *Vanity Fair,* August 2001.

Pond, Steve. "Shot by Shot: 'Sleeping with the Enemy.' " *Premiere,* March 1991.

———. "Kiefer Sutherland." *Us,* June 1994.

Price, Susan. "Julia: Her Lessons in Love." *Ladies' Home Journal,* June 1994.

Rebello, Stephen. "The Man with the Tarnished Halo." *Movieline,* July 1993.

———. "But What He Really Wants to Do Is Direct." *Movieline,* July 2001.

Rensin, David. "Julia Makes Trouble." *Rolling Stone,* July 14–28, 1994.

Richman, Alan. "Answered Prayers." *GQ,* December 1989.

Rush, George. "Julia Goes Hog Wild." *New York Post,* September 9, 1996.

Sager, Mike. "What Julia Said to George." *Esquire,* December 2001.

Schneider, Karen S., et al. "His Marriage Is Unusual, Lovett Says—but Solid." *People,* May 15, 1994.

———. "One Last Sad Song." *People,* April 10, 1995.

———. "Romeo & Julia." *People,* January 11, 1999.

———. "Then and Wow!" *People,* March 20, 2000.

———. "As She Likes It." *People,* March 11, 2001.

———. "What Money Can't Buy." *People,* August 27, 2001.

———. "Julia's Secret Wedding." *People,* July 22, 2002.

Schneller, Johanna. "Barefoot Girl with Cheek." *GQ,* February 1991.

Schruers, Fred. "The Howl of the Alpha Wolf." *Premiere,* May 1996.

Sella, Marshall. "Julia Tells a Lie." *Harper's Bazaar,* March 2000.

Sessums, Kevin. "The Crown Julia." *Vanity Fair,* October 1993.

Skinner, Michael. "Second Stage." *Atlanta,* November 1990.

Smith, Liz. "The Joys of Julia." *Good Housekeeping,* August 1999.

———. "Julia: 'I Want to Be Better.' " *Good Housekeeping,* August 2001.

Stevenson, Peter. "Don't Look Back." *Details,* October 1991.

Street, Linda. "Youth Acts On and Off Stage." *The Atlanta Journal,* December 14, 1965.

Svetkey, Benjamin. "The Big Night." *Entertainment Weekly,* April 6, 2001.

Taraborrelli, J. Randy. "Julia Roberts: Runaway Bride." *The Australian Women's Weekly,* December 2002.

Tauber, Michelle, et al. "Mrs. Moder's First Year." *People,* July 28, 2003.

Thompson, David. "In Defense of Julia Roberts." *Movieline,* April 1997.

———. "Is She All Mouth?" *Independent on Sunday,* August 10, 1997.

Travers, Peter. "She Will Survive." *Us,* August 1997.

Trebbe, Ann. "Julia Roberts: Still Sitting Pretty?" *McCall's,* September 1992.

Wagener, Leon. " 'Our Abusive Stepfather.' " *New Idea,* May 10, 1997.

Zemen, Ned. "Canoodling with Julia." *Vanity Fair,* June 1999.

INDEX